Prophets of Protest

Prophets of Protest

Reconsidering the History of American Abolitionism

EDITED BY
TIMOTHY PATRICK McCARTHY AND
JOHN STAUFFER

THE NEW PRESS

NEW YORK
LONDON

Requests for permission to reproduce selections from this book should be mailed
to: Permissions Department, The New Press, 38 Greene Street, New York, NY
10013

Published in the United States by The New Press, New York, 2006
Distributed by W. W. Norton & Company, Inc., New York

LIBRARY OF CONGRESS CATALOGING-IN-PUBLICATION DATA
Prophets of protest : reconsidering the history of American abolitionism /
Timothy Patrick McCarthy and John Stauffer, eds.
p.   cm.
Includes bibliographical references and index.
ISBN-13 978-1-56584-992-1 (hc)—978-1-56584-880-1 (pbk)
ISBN-10 1-56584-992-2 (hc)—ISBN 1-56584-880-2 (pbk)
1. Antislavery movements—United States—History.   2. Abolitionists—United
States—History.   3. United States—Politics and government—1783–1865.
I. McCarthy, Timothy Patrick.   II. Stauffer, John.
E441.P96 2006
973.7'114—dc22   2005057661

The New Press was established in 1990 as a not-for-profit alternative
to the large, commercial publishing houses currently dominating
the book publishing industry. The New Press operates in
the public interest rather than for private gain, and is committed
to publishing, in innovative ways, works of educational, cultural,
and community value that are often deemed insufficiently profitable.

www.thenewpress.com

Composition by dix!

Printed in Canada

2   4   6   8   10   9   7   5   3   1

In memory of Herbert Aptheker and Benjamin Quarles

Contents

PART FOUR: REPRESENTATIONS

Foreword

Michael Fellman

Writing in 1979, in the introduction to *Antislavery Reconsidered*, a collection of essays on American abolitionism, my colleague Lewis Perry and I suggested that, "as an issue fraught with public implications, abolitionism disturbs the tidy balances between narrative and analysis, between moral judgment and dispassionate research." I am glad to report that *Prophets of Protest*, which appears, now, a full generation after our earlier book, continues to press the same unease on historians and their readers.

In antebellum America, slavery—the most highly exploitative form of labor extraction ever devised—was deeply embedded into the fabric of the American capitalist economy. As a result, systemic racism was ingrained within an American "caste system" that has not gone away, emancipation notwithstanding. During the years between the American Revolution and the Civil War, most Americans either supported that system or looked the other way while profiting from it. Fueled by idealism and anger, however, the abolitionists, a small and despised minority, threw sand in the powerful machinery of public opinion. They refused to countenance the continuation of an institutional arrangement that gave lie to American pretenses that their nation represented the best hope of humankind for attaining republican liberty and true Christian fellow feeling.

Many historians writing in the first half of the twentieth century viewed the abolitionists as irrational extremists who refused to adjust to the American genius for gradual social change. Most of these scholars averted their gaze, whether they acknowledged it or not, from the apartheid system called segregation that had stripped African Americans of fundamental civil liberties and kept them in the social cellar through the continuous use of bigotry and discrimination, much of it by violent means. Even scholars with a more generous view of the abolitionists stressed the divisiveness between those who favored political action and those who insisted that moral separation from evil was the only way to destroy slavery. Much of the historical debate concerned which group of white male agitators followed the more effective path.

Starting in the late 1950s and continuing through the next decade, in tandem with the rise of the civil rights movement, many progressive historians reevaluated the abolitionists, even referring to the contemporary

movement for change in America's perception of race as the "new abolitionism." Searching for a "relevant" past, historians reconsidered abolitionism as a nineteenth-century test case of the limits and possibilities of
radicalism in America. Cast as progressive precursors, the abolitionists inspired many historians on the New Left to stress the continuity and passion
of the American party of change. To do so required overlooking the long,
fallow periods during which reform waned and a discriminatory status quo
rode roughshod over people at the bottom of society, and glossing over
abolitionist contradictions on race and economic change. But it was ener-
gizing all the same.

By the late 1970s, second thoughts had begun to complicate the "generations of freedom fighters" sensibility. Although there was certainly no
return in the historiography to viewing the abolitionists as marginal extremists, many of us began to question the racial, social, and economic attitudes of the abolitionists themselves. In addition, we began to explore the
connection and disconnection between abolitionism and the more
morally ambiguous form of antislavery that shaped the Republican party as
it worked to energize a majority among Northern white male voters in the
late 1850s. Still, the core arguments among historians about abolitionism
continued to stress the political engagement of a small but determined
cadre of white male reformers.

The broader ground for contextualizing abolitionism was beginning to
shift. Women's history, already flourishing, had broadened consideration
of the abolitionist movement to include a (somewhat elitist) focus on the
roles of leading white women abolitionists and their connection to feminism. On the whole, however, despite the pioneering efforts of such historians as Benjamin Quarles and Herbert Aptheker, the absence of scholarly
work on black abolitionism continued to represent the most glaring gap in
American history concerning abolitionism. Limitations notwithstanding,
many of the contributors to *Antislavery Reconsidered* were starting to move
toward what Perry and I then characterized as a reinvigorated study of the
abolitionist movement whose importance "derives not from its resemblance . . . to modern movements, but what it indicates about fundamental
social conflict in a different historical era."

Although twenty-five years ago no one could fully anticipate where this
call to reconsider the abolitionists within their own contexts might lead,
Prophets of Protest provides just such a rich and probing unraveling of many
of the interconnected strands of abolitionist culture. These essays illuminate much of the contested ideological ground the abolitionists tilled and
describe many of the techniques the abolitionists used to energize themselves and to press for change in the midst of a reluctant and often hostile
society.

Prophets of Protest strikingly repositions abolitionism as an African American and interracial movement, rather than merely a white one. Stemming from much recent work, and predicting where the field will continue to develop, these essays show many of the ways in which black leadership developed within the movement, and how the black rank and file became engaged in radical protest and reform. Concomitantly, some essays depict white women not just as leaders but as foot soldiers in a stirring social engagement. Popular forms of action—festivals and picnics, autobiographical and political writings by black writers, photographic representations of black reformers, and abolitionist poetry—are imaginatively explored in order to open up a richer understanding of abolitionist culture than earlier generations of historians had thought to explore.

Prophets of Protest also stretches the temporal boundaries of the movement. No longer is the immediatist outburst of William Lloyd Garrison in 1831 considered the birth date of "real" abolitionism. Rather, many of these essays look back as far as the American Revolution, and as far afield as British abolitionism, to explore long continuities in abolitionist thought and action in the Atlantic world. Here we see blacks building their own cultural institutions and resisting white racist efforts to define or constrain. And we also see whites who supported their struggle for freedom in the early days, when antislavery activism was as unpopular as it was rare.

Rather than a stopping place, *Prophets of Protest* is a sparkling progress report. These gifted scholars open up potential avenues for exploring in greater depth the relationships of abolitionists with the great political issues that confronted them. As these essays demonstrate, there was an interracial quality in the aspirations of many abolitionists, but this genuine desire for biracial democracy was often undercut by the profound racism that tinctured the imagination of many white abolitionists. For their part, some black abolitionists began to build their own institutions, leaving whites on the periphery of what they hoped would prove to become a nascent black nationalism. *Prophets of Protest* suggests that more work will strengthen the connections between black and white leaders, between women and men, and between mainstream culture and the abolitionist fringe. To be sure, these men and women built a powerful counterculture—what the editors of this collection call a "culture of dissent"—but they never abandoned agitation to upset the mainstream of American political power and social and economic privilege.

Prophets of Protest shows us many of the ways abolitionists collected and expressed their moral outrage against a nation gone off its putative libertarian and Christian footings. Here we learn much about how they built a collective movement as they prepared for political action. This is a considerable achievement, and one that remains fully engaged with the great issues of race, class, and gender that have always divided Americans against each other.

Although, as this collection demonstrates, abolitionists were not without anxiety and times of despair, the hope for positive moral change activated them, helping them to overcome the deep and pervasive fear that the system of slavery spread where ever it touched. *Prophets of Protest* bears witness to the abolitionist faith not just in political change, but, even more deeply, in personal and interpersonal liberation, and in fundamental national moral reform of their City on a Hill—a sprawling new polity that was characterized by great democratic profession and equally profound anti-democratic oppression.

Introduction

Timothy Patrick McCarthy and John Stauffer

Freedom is and has always been America's root concern, a concern that found dramatic expression in the abolitionist movement. The most important and revolutionary reform in our country's past, it forced the American people to come to grips with an anomaly that would not down—the existence of slavery in a land of the free.

—Benjamin Quarles, *Black Abolitionists* (1969)

Abolitionists expected those who joined their movement to accept and advance the principle of racial equality, regardless of the walk of life, social stratum, and religious background from which they came. . . . never before had so many white Americans labored with black Americans to lessen the distance between the races and to reconstruct a republic based on the Scriptural command "That God hath made of one blood all the nations of men for to dwell on the face of the earth."

—Paul Goodman, *Of One Blood* (1997)

Few groups in American history have experienced as complete a reassessment of their life and legacy as the abolitionists. Reviled by their contemporaries, and so often maligned or misunderstood by historians, the abolitionists have only in the last generation or so begun to receive a fair hearing among scholars of nineteenth-century America. Theirs is the typical fate of American radicals: People with the courage to fight the abuses of power and privilege around them are rarely celebrated in their own time. On the contrary, they are seen for what they are—disturbers of the status quo. The roster of American dissidents who fit this description is as distinguished as it is long: Thomas Paine, David Walker, Elizabeth Cady Stanton, Frederick Douglass, Susan B. Anthony, Sojourner Truth, John Brown, Eugene Debs, James Baldwin, Fannie Lou Hamer, Martin Luther King Jr., Malcolm X, the list goes on. In the case of the abolitionists, who engaged in a decades-long campaign against human bondage, rejection was particularly fierce. Indeed, as the socialist labor leader Eugene Debs once reminded his countrymen, the "leaders of the abolition movement. . . . were regarded as public enemies and treated accordingly." Still, Debs continued, "[y]ou are now teaching your children to revere their memories, while all of their detractors are in oblivion."[1] Addressing the jury that would ultimately convict and imprison him for espionage during World War I, Debs no doubt had his own legacy in mind. But his point remains. Despite the fact that radicals have fought and died for many of the things we now take for granted—from universal suffrage and eight-hour workdays to free speech and equal rights—Americans have generally been quite slow to give them their due.

The abolitionists are no exception. Zealous and unrelenting, they were unusually devoted to William Lloyd Garrison's famous promise to be "as harsh as truth, and as uncompromising as justice."[2] Armed with a revolutionary vision of human freedom and equality, they worked tirelessly to transform their society on the basis of Judeo-Christian teachings and democratic principles. In turn, they posed a considerable threat to an American system deeply rooted in slavery. As a result, the abolitionists were sharply criticized in the press, denounced from the pulpit, punished in the courtroom, and effectively marginalized in politics. Many of their would-be sympathizers—people who opposed slavery on moral grounds but who were nonetheless uncomfortable with abolitionist appeals to racial equality—were wary of their heated rhetoric and aggressive tactics. With few willing to defend or assist them, the abolitionists were routinely subjected to violence, capture, and imprisonment; some lost their lives in the process. Perhaps more than any other social movement in American history, abolitionism illustrates the fact that democracy is a difficult, dirty, and often bloody business.

Say what you want about their imperfect means and methods and personalities, the abolitionists were men and women of deep conviction and action. Even Abraham Lincoln—himself no fan of the abolitionists—acknowledged their persistence and impact.[3] Having once stated that "the promulgation of abolition doctrines tends rather to increase rather than abate [slavery's] evils," Lincoln later credited the abolitionists with helping to turn the moral tide of the nation against slavery.[4] Indeed, despite his longstanding misgivings about their radicalism, Lincoln understood that if "[a]ll knew that this interest [slavery] was, somehow, the cause of the war," the abolitionists had played a large role in making that so.[5] Not surprisingly, the abolitionists' stock rose dramatically, if briefly, after the Civil War, when the prospects for biracial democracy seemed bright. But as the terror of Jim Crow eclipsed the promise of Reconstruction, the abolitionists were soon condemned to America's historical dustbin, where they would remain for some time.

Ever since the Civil War, the reputation of the abolitionists has depended to a large extent on the state of the nation's commitment to civil rights and racial equality at any given moment. As Robert Forbes notes in

the lead essay of this book: "If the very project of modernity is itself implicated in the establishment of race as a fundamental category of experience, it is not surprising that the study of slavery and abolition should
prove impervious to 'objective' interpretation, since the analytical and descriptive tools of the social sciences were developed in tandem with the
codification of racial principles—indeed, they were one of the chief vehicles for the transmission of such principles." It is no coincidence, then,
that just as the abolitionists were warmly embraced in the years immediately following emancipation and during the civil rights movement of the
1960s, they were also widely disgraced between the fall of Reconstruction
and the Great Depression, when white supremacy ruled the South, and
again during the 1950s, when a new wave of conservatism led quite a number of historians to see the abolitionists as either deranged fanatics or misguided meddlers. Only recently have historians settled on the more
favorable consensus, acknowledging the mistakes and limitations of the
movement but also giving the abolitionists a lion's share of the credit for
helping to abolish slavery and insisting that equality take its place alongside freedom as an indispensable core value of American democracy.

This relatively new "consensus"—if indeed we can even call it that—is
the result of several generations of scholarly work. Two books, in particular, have played a central role in reinvigorating and also complicating our
understanding of the abolitionist movement in the United States: Martin
Duberman's *The Antislavery Vanguard* (1965) and Lewis Perry and Michael
Fellman's *Antislavery Reconsidered* (1979). Filled with original, provocative,
and often brilliant essays by many of the last generation's leading historians, these two volumes continue to be indispensable resources for scholars
working in the field of abolitionist studies. Although none of the editors
would take credit for producing a new "synthesis" or arriving at a new "consensus," it is now quite clear that these books, taken together, inspired a far
more sympathetic assessment of the abolitionists by illuminating the deep
impact the abolitionist movement has had on American history. Writing
forty years ago, in the midst of the civil rights revolution, Duberman explained the charge of his book: "In conceiving this volume, I had two objectives in mind: first, to excavate and encourage the recent tendency
toward a more sympathetic appraisal of the movement, but second, to include all scholarly points of view, so that disagreements in interpretation
might be further clarified, even if not resolved."[6] Fourteen years later,
Perry and Fellman broadened the scope of Duberman's revisionist project:
"Linked to racial oppression, sectional conflict, and other subjects central
to the historical consciousness of Americans, abolitionism has long captured the interests of the general reading public. . . . Antislavery scholarship instructs us on the experience of some Americans a century ago; it

also betokens periodic changes in the modern community of professional historians; and it provides signals of the moral ties between the profession and the community as a whole."[7] As these two earlier volumes make clear, any attempt to understand the abolitionists necessarily involves intellectual, political, and moral questions that call upon us to forge stronger linkages between the past, present, and future.

It is time once again to reconsider American abolitionism—and this book is our attempt to do just that. A generation removed from the triumphs and tragedies of the 1960s and 1970s, *Prophets of Protest* represents the new scholarship and new social contexts that have quite literally transformed the way we understand the political, cultural, and social history of the United States. In addition to the fifteen original essays included here—written by several seasoned veterans as well as some of the most promising young scholars in the field of abolitionist studies—we have asked Michael Fellman and Martin Duberman to contribute short pieces to the beginning and end of this volume as a way to both acknowledge the debt we owe them for their work and to strengthen the continuity and community that we believe should exist between generations of scholars. In that spirit, we hope that *Prophets of Protest* will earn its place at the table as another important effort to examine one of the great social movements in American history.

Few scholars of nineteenth-century American culture have managed to avoid the abolitionists and their crusade to end slavery. They show up almost everywhere—in studies of antebellum political parties and civic institutions, of religion and reform, and of ideology and its many forms of expression. From an extensive archive of primary sources, historians have explored the contested "origins" of antislavery agitation as well as how the abolitionist legacy has influenced modern struggles for civil rights and other forms of social justice. Some scholars have traced the "inner history" of the movement—the interplay of people, ideas, tactics, and goals—while others have looked outward to examine how abolitionism related to broader social forces such as law, political party formation, economics, and religion. Some of the most creative and compelling scholarship in recent years has traced the connections between abolitionism and other antebellum social and intellectual movements like woman's rights and transcendentalism, and there is also, predictably, a rich body of work on the relationship between abolitionism and African American culture. As Ronald G. Walters, one of the more sophisticated chroniclers of abolitionism, has observed: "The more that is written about antislavery the more trouble we have finding its boundaries."[8]

In attempting to find those boundaries, each generation of abolitionist scholars has addressed three central concerns: When and why did abolitionism begin? Who were the abolitionists? How, and to what end, did they go about the work of abolition? Each of these, in turn, has inspired its own debate, which, for the sake of simplicity, we will characterize as the "origins" debate, the "character" debate, and the "means and ends" debate.

Most scholars agree that the origins debate began in earnest with the publication of Gilbert Barnes's pathbreaking study, *The Antislavery Impulse*, in 1933.[9] Following his discovery of the extant correspondence between early abolitionists James G. Birney, Theodore Dwight Weld, and Sarah and Angelina Grimké, Barnes used evidence of strong evangelical impulses in their writings to argue that abolitionists in the Midwest were profoundly influenced by the religious revivals that characterized the Second Great Awakening, especially the teachings of Charles Grandison Finney. Before then, William Lloyd Garrison's eastern antislavery establishment had dominated the histories of the abolitionist movement. It didn't matter whether Garrison was viewed as a positive or negative force, he was still considered the principal inspiration—the so-called "dean"—of American abolitionism. Barnes's work helped to downplay the influence of eastern radicals like Garrison, significantly broadening the geographic scope of the investigation of the abolitionist movement, and inspiring other historians to more fully examine its diverse religious origins and character. As a result, subsequent studies have identified a host of other influences— Quakerism in Pennsylvania, New England Hopkinsianism, Methodism in the mid-Atlantic region, and evangelical Baptism in Garrison's Boston— that proliferated in the eighteenth and nineteenth centuries, locating the origins of antislavery sentiment in new understandings and practices of Christianity.

These religious awakenings coincided with the emergence of a broad reform impulse that historian Walter Hugins has characterized as "a humanitarian belief that society could be improved by human effort and that the individual was capable of moral redemption and ultimate perfection."[10] Associated with a range of reforms—temperance, sabbatarianism, worker's and woman's rights, prison and education reform, utopianism and socialism, to name just a few—these humanitarian efforts were designed to improve society by improving the lives and conditions of individuals and groups. Some of these were secular movements designed to uproot structural inequalities so that more people could enjoy the full promise of the political and market revolutions that were in the process of transforming the West. Other reforms, like temperance and sabbatarianism, were more directly related to the evangelical visions that were percolating in antebellum America. By successfully integrating the sacred and the secular, abolitionism marked a profound cultural shift in attitudes about the capacity of men and women, acting in accordance with God's will, to change and redeem—to "perfect"—their society.[11]

Seeking to explain if and how these humanitarian impulses led to the emergence of abolitionism, several historians have identified yet another aspect of the origins debate: the relationship between antislavery sentiment and capitalism. Building on the scholarship of Eric Williams—who argued that the decline of plantation slavery in the West Indies was due to economic interests linked to the rise of capitalism rather than the moral opposition of British abolitionists—scholars like David Brion Davis, Thomas L. Haskell, and John Ashworth have examined the rise of antislavery militancy by viewing it in relation to the developing market economy and its shifting class interests.[12] Davis, in particular, extended his earlier comparative studies of the various legal, philosophical, and religious dimensions of Western antislavery thought to argue that in England strong critiques of slavery, emerging for the first time during the "Age of Revolution," helped to reinforce and legitimize the interests of the developing economic elite, with its concomitant embrace of free labor principles. A rejection of slavery, Davis argued, at times involved implicit support for the rise of market capitalism—and vice versa.[13]

From all of this scholarship, we now know that a variety of forces—religion, humanitarian reform, and the market revolution, as well as Enlightenment philosophy, improvements in literacy, and democratic political revolution—hastened the emergence of abolitionism. But there was another factor as well, one that has, until recently, been almost completely ignored by historians: black protest. The American Revolution helped set in motion a paradoxical development that was among the most important features of the early republic: the gradual abolition of slavery in the North and the rapid extension of slavery in the South.[14] Moreover, just as Northern blacks were enjoying their first taste of freedom, their white compatriots—among them many of the "Founding Fathers"—were developing plans for a *"herrenvolk* republic," a white supremacist national ideal enacted through the removal of emancipated blacks from the United States. When the American Colonization Society was founded in December 1816 to do just that, most African Americans from Baltimore to Boston were quick to publicly denounce the "colonizing scheme," instead asserting their rightful claim to American citizenship.[15] In the generation before Garrison first published *The Liberator,* the abolitionist movement's flagship newspaper that debuted on January 1, 1831, Northern free blacks created a range of institutions and media—including African American churches, annual freedom celebrations, political pamphlets, and serial newspapers—to assert their opposition to both slavery and colonization as part of the broader struggle for freedom and racial equality. It was during this time that a number of prominent white reformers, including Garrison himself, abandoned the colonization argument and joined the abolitionist cause, many of them citing the influence of black protest as the principal catalyst for their "conversion." As several essays in this book demonstrate, black protest within the United States was one of the most important factors in terms of recruiting whites to abolitionism, and investing the movement with its dual commitment to ending slavery and achieving racial equality. In short, African Americans were the first abolitionists.[16]

Once we acknowledge the influence of black protest on the origins of American abolitionism, we can begin to view the character and means and ends debates in a new light. The question of who actually constituted the rank and file of the abolitionist movement has been extremely difficult to answer. The frustration has many sources. First, the abolitionists never compiled a comprehensive "membership" list, and even when records of meeting attendance and financial donations were kept, they were incomplete. Indeed, despite the vast amount of primary source material available to antislavery historians, archival limitations and biases are perhaps the strongest impediments for scholars of the abolitionist movement. There is simply more information available about certain institutions, organizations, and individuals than others, making it all but impossible to achieve a complete or balanced portrait of the movement as a whole.

Another problem has to do with the many regional, ideological, and religious differences that characterized the movement from its inception. In an effort to simplify them, scholars have tended to divide the abolitionists into two major camps that were often at odds with, and increasingly independent of, one another: the "radical" abolitionists, who orbited around Garrison and who rejected the U.S. Constitution, mainstream political parties, and churches as "proslavery" institutions; and the "political" abolitionists, regarded as a more pragmatic group, who embraced formal politics—the Liberty, Free Soil, and Republican parties—as the best channel for achieving their antislavery goals.[17] Given the fierce political debates that raged among abolitionists, there is certainly strong merit to these designations. As is often the case with social movements, the question of "authenticity"—who was or was not most effectively committed to the cause—was as important to the abolitionists as it has been to historians who write about them. But broad categories like these are sometimes more limiting than illuminating. Indeed, the rivalries and tensions that developed within the movement were as much religious and regional and racial as they were political or ideological. And certainly none of these operated discretely or in a vacuum.

Perhaps the greatest source of frustration has been the longstanding presumption, still alive and well in some quarters, that the abolitionist movement was a white man's struggle to end slavery. Until recently, the standard narratives of abolitionism—both celebratory and critical—have emphasized the evangelical impulses of white middle-class and elite male reformers. The effect of this has been to underestimate or ignore the cultural and political contributions of other groups of people: African Americans, women, immigrants, the native-born poor, the working class, illiterate people, and the like. To its credit, much of the scholarship of the last generation has worked to correct this earlier neglect. Scholars of African American and women's history have been especially important in this regard, opening up new avenues to explore the central role that blacks and women played in the abolitionist movement. It would not be too much to say that their work has almost entirely transformed our understanding of nineteenth-century American culture, generally, and of the abolitionist movement, in particular. Still, there is a "separate but equal" quality to some of this corrective work. With few exceptions, historians are left with three relatively discrete narratives: an older story dominated by white, mostly well-to-do men, and two newer ones told from the perspective of African Americans and women. Despite the fact that we now know that the abolitionist movement was one of the most diverse social movements in American history—made up of men and women from every class, color, circumstance, and creed—we do not yet have a new synthesis, a new standard narrative, that incorporates all of the findings of this recent scholarship. We may never be able to fully resolve the character debate regarding abolitionism, but we should continue to push harder to examine the coalitions and tensions—and not just the political ones—between the various groups involved in abolition. Doing so will help to emphasize the extent to which interaction and collaboration—particularly between blacks and whites, and between women and men—were essential aspects of both the abolitionist movement and the effort to build a more inclusive, multicultural, and egalitarian democracy in the United States.

Broadening our understanding of the origins and character of abolitionism helps us, finally, to reconsider the means and ends debate as well. Although the abolitionists were hardly the most self-indulgent people in nineteenth-century America, they were, at times, the most self-critical. They understood that doing battle against slavery required them to be certain about the tactics they used and the goals they sought. In small groups and large gatherings, on the page and in person, in private letters and public lyceums, they debated virtually everything: colonization and emigration; immediatism and gradualism; the use of violence; the viability of mainstream politics; the trustworthiness of churches; the integrity of the Constitution; the role of women and blacks in the movement; the paternalism of white male leaders; the legality of slavery and slave resistance; the protection of fugitives; the efficacy of petitions; the benefits and limitations of "free labor"; the language, rhetoric, and images they used to plead their cause—you name it, they dealt with it. Because of their many differences, the abolitionists never resolved all of these tactical debates, and so a variety of means were used to achieve the one end they could all agree on: the abolition of slavery in the United States. Writing of Garrison, historian Aileen Kraditor remarked that "[his] real choice was not between democratic and undemocratic, or fanatical and reasonable, agitation; it was between antislavery agitation and silence."[18] On this matter, certainly, the abolitionists were in full accord.

Like the abolitionists, historians have also spent quite a bit of time debating the various tactics of the antislavery movement, as well as its extensive organizational culture—the antislavery societies, vigilance committees, newspaper presses, petition campaigns, lecture tours, etc., that the abolitionists developed to advance their cause. But while scholars have ably described the structure of abolitionist culture, they have been somewhat less successful in examining its meaning and function. For the abolitionists, the art of persuasion—the use of language and image to help "convert" people to their cause—was central to their work. Indeed, one thing that historians have generally overlooked in their assessment of American abolitionism is that it emerged within what Michael Warner has characterized as a "republic of letters," and coincided with what Cathy Davidson has called "a reading revolution."[19] In other words, the abolitionists waged their campaign against slavery at the same time that a culture of print and literary publication was experiencing an unprecedented expansion and influence, and when literacy was also on the rise. That historians have somehow missed this connection is largely due to the fact that they have generally been slow to adopt the insights of other disciplines—in this case, literary and cultural studies—that would allow them to examine the culture of abolitionism in a fresher, more interdisciplinary light.

Visual images and print culture were among the most effective weapons in the fight against slavery. In addition to their use of etchings, illustrations, and daguerreotypes, the abolitionists wrote, edited, published, and distributed tens of thousands of pamphlets and broadsides, thousands of poems and petitions, hundreds of songs and newspapers, and dozens of novels and autobiographical narratives. Given the rapid development of print and photographic technologies as well as the expansion of common education, literacy, and publishing markets during the antebellum era, the abolitionists seized a critical moment in the expansion of markets for print culture to intervene in the debate over slavery. In their use of small printing presses, established publishing houses, and an abundance of printing and distribution resources made available to them through the

various national, regional, and local reform organizations, the abolitionists disseminated their social critique by employing a tactical approach—
not unlike the radical pamphleteers of the American Revolution—that
reached well beyond the margins of antislavery radicalism into the private
and public spheres of American life. Over time, many of the most prominent writers of the antebellum era—Lydia Maria Child, Ralph Waldo
Emerson, Margaret Fuller, Henry David Thoreau, Walt Whitman, Herman
Melville, Frederick Douglass, William Wells Brown, Henry Wadsworth
Longfellow, Harriet Beecher Stowe, and others—added their considerable
literary talents to the growing chorus of opposition to slavery, thus afford-
ing the abolitionist movement a certain degree of respectability heretofore
denied to them in elite cultural circles. In effect, the abolitionists created
what we might call a broad *culture of dissent,* wherein they made liberal use
of print and image—language and representation—to shape political discourse and alter public opinion in an effort to liberate the nation from the
bonds of slavery and place it on the road to greater democratic equality. It
is high time we paid closer attention to these matters.[20]

We have organized *Prophets of Protest* in four parts. Part One, "Revisions,"
summarizes the state of the field. It shows how histories of abolition have
evolved over the last two hundred years and suggests approaches for future
research. The remaining three parts address the debates over origins,
character, and means and ends that continue to shape our understanding
of the movement. The essays in Part Two, "Origins," reexamine the origins
of American abolitionism, highlighting its interracial features and emphasizing continuity between the early "gradualist" phase and the later "immediatist" phase. Part Three, "Revolutions," centers on John Brown, whose
proclivity for violence has made him the most controversial abolitionist—
in his time as well as our own. Part Four, "Representations," focuses on the
"art" of abolitionism: the rhetorical and aesthetic strategies used by abolitionists to convert people to their cause.

    From the beginning, histories of the abolitionist movement have been
greatly influenced by ideology. As Robert Forbes's essay emphasizes, the
quest for objectivity in history is especially problematic in the study of abolitionism. The rise of social science, which (among other things) treated
history as a science, coincided with the rise of "scientific" evidence claiming that Africans and their offspring were innately inferior to other "races."
This twin rise of scientific history and pseudo-scientific racism obviously
had enormous consequences for histories of abolitionism: for almost a
century, historians assumed that history was becoming more scientific—
more accurate and knowable—and they never questioned the racist beliefs
embedded in science.

Treating history as a science also meant downplaying its rhetorical aspects: the ways in which the form and structure of the historical narrative, and the presentations of evidence, were used to convince readers of the integrity of the work. As Louis Menand has noted: "The test for a successful history is the same as the test for any successful narrative: integrity in motion. It's not the facts, snapshots of the past, that make history; it's the story, the facts run by the eye at the correct speed." "Integrity in motion" is another name for rhetoric.[21]

The abolitionists understood the importance of rhetoric. Their primary goal was to convince their audience that slavery was a horrible sin that needed to be abolished. At times they stacked the deck to bolster their case: they ignored some facts and altered others so that their argument would fit their preexisting beliefs. Slaveowners were much more reckless with evidence; they dismissed or silenced abolitionists' histories and created their own version of the past, at the center of which was the view that slavery was a good thing for slaves and society. To a large extent slaveowners won this ideological battle over slavery. Well into the twentieth century, in their efforts to "redeem" the South, professional historians continued to dismiss or ignore evidence from abolitionists and slaves on the grounds that it was unreliable, or "unscientific." The pattern continues today. Although the study of slavery and abolition has changed dramatically in the last forty years, the general public often does not like the "speed" and "integrity" of these new stories.[22]

Forbes shows how these debates over slavery, abolition, and civil rights coincided with changing attitudes toward history. The first stage in the history of abolition was written by the movement's principal actors. They wrote "providential" history, and viewed abolition, as well as history and progress, as part of God's providence. In the second, "racialist progressive" stage, writers replaced their belief in God's providence for a belief in science, empiricism, and natural rights, and embraced a simultaneously racist and progressive understanding of the past, based on their assertion of "white and English superiority." In the third, "modernist revisionist" stage, writers beginning with W.E.B. Du Bois reacted against the racist progressives. Deeply influenced by Marxist theory, they focused on material forces to understand the past, and revised the progressive paradigm. Yet revisionists, while tending to endorse the historical determinism of the progressives, failed to distinguish between the religious and scientific bases of the first two generations of historians. As a result, they mistakenly thought that both providentialists and progressives accepted racist doctrines. The crucial turning point in the transition from providential to progressive ideologies occurred in the 1840s and 1850s, a period when racist beliefs increased dramatically. Darwin's theory of natural selection was a product of racialist progressive thought; its scientific method depended as much on racial theory as it did on empirical evidence.

The debates between providential and progressive views of history continue to affect historians today. As Forbes concludes: "If contemporary scholars have abandoned the naïve optimism and triumphalism of the progressive view, we have retained its debilitating core: the conviction that we know more, and understand more clearly, than our ancestors." He urges historians to take seriously the providential views of the pioneer abolitionists, who, unlike the progressives, acted on the principle that equality of condition was God's design. And he refers to the example of Dr. Martin Luther King Jr., who accepted the providential view of history. In the civil rights battle against racism, King imagined that "power came only from God, who has no race." In a providential world, therefore, "race had no power." Understanding the danger of progressive thinking will enable historians to see the effects of slavery on "all of our institutions," including history.

Manisha Sinha focuses on the evolution of black abolitionist history. Her stages of history differ from Forbes's. Instead of looking primarily at intellectual and ideological currents, she focuses on the work of individuals and generations. The first blacks to write the history of abolition were, like their white counterparts, principals in the movement—men such as William Cooper Nell, William Wells Brown, and Martin Delany. These early black historians focused on the interracial character of the movement and on its quest for racial equality. They used biography as a method and emphasized the role of individuals in shaping history. The next generation of histories came from the ranks of professional historians—W.E.B. Du Bois, George Washington Williams, Carter G. Woodson, Charles Wesley, and Dorothy Porter. Like their predecessors, they documented the role of blacks in the movement and emphasized the interracial aspect of abolitionism, largely in response to white historians who totally ignored the presence of blacks in the movement. The third generation began with Benjamin Quarles, whose now classic *Black Abolitionists* bridged the older documentary tradition with newer analytical history. Quarles was the first historian to fully emphasize the centrality of blacks in America's revolutionary tradition. The focus of the present generation has been primarily to deepen our understanding of community-building efforts, the uses of black nationalism, and the effects of political activism and social protest.

Read together, Forbes's and Sinha's essays highlight the need for an interracial historiography: an understanding of how blacks and whites influenced each other's views of history and progress, as well as the social meaning of "race" and modern political ideals. Was there a transformation from a providential to progressive understanding of the past among black writers? If so, what forms did it take and how did it influence white writers? In what ways did Enlightenment thought and progressivism, generally seen as the province of white elites, shape black thought? And how, in turn, did blacks refashion or revise Enlightenment thought?

Part Two, "Origins," addresses some of these questions. The five essays in this section all argue for greater continuity than scholars have generally acknowledged between Revolutionary-era abolitionists and antebellum-era abolitionists. To understand the importance of this continuity, we need to briefly sketch out what the differences between these two groups were.

The American Revolutionary era revolved in part around Enlightenment beliefs in rational order, hierarchy, and social deference. Enlightenment thought was torn between "the ideal of the autonomous individual," which was antithetical to slavery, and the "ideal of a rational and efficient social order," which feared the social chaos which would result from ending slavery too quickly. As a result, there were comparatively few recorded instances of interracial equality and pleas for immediate and universal emancipation in the late eighteenth century. The first abolition societies, for instance, refused to accept African Americans as members; and the Quakers, the first white abolitionists, generally did not welcome free blacks into their churches and homes. White abolitionists sought gradual means for ending slavery, primarily through colonization, which reflected their belief that blacks, "the victims of the great sin of slavery," were also "the embodiment of sin."[23]

The first generation of black abolitionists was also influenced by Enlightenment thought (though the degree to which they shaped it has not been fully explored).[24] In general, they accepted patient and gradual abolition, and emigration to Africa—though not through the American Colonization Society—as a potentially pragmatic solution to racism and the lack of freedom. In this context, black leaders tended to act deferentially toward white antislavery advocates. In other words, they were willing to compromise and delay their desire for immediate emancipation and equality in exchange for some semblance of safety and the prevention of bloodshed. For example, Phillis Wheatley, in her 1775 poem, "To His Excellency General Washington," reveres Washington as a champion of freedom. Yet, unlike the later generation of black abolitionists, she makes no mention of him owning slaves or failing to advocate abolition throughout his life (he did, as we know, free his slaves upon his death). The very structure of Wheatley's poem—formal closed couplets—highlights her emphasis on order and deference to authority, both political and literary. Absalom Jones and Richard Allen protested against white racism in similarly deferential language in 1794. "We do not wish to make you [whites] angry," they wrote, "but excite your attention to consider how hateful slavery is in the sight of God, who hath destroyed kings and princes for their oppression of the poor slaves." Their protest rhetoric emphasized control rather than defiance. Three years later, Prince Hall urged "patience" to his black brethren in attacking slavery. And James Forten referred to "white men" as "our protectors" in his pleas for "rational liberty."[25]

These examples of deference reflect the newness of antislavery thought and the desire for an orderly transition from slavery to freedom. Throughout history, few people have accepted their condition as slaves without rebelling in some way. Until the Age of Revolution, however, rebels sought to invert the master-slave hierarchy instead of advocating universal freedom.[26] The St. Domingue (Haitian) rebellion of 1791, which was influenced by Enlightenment beliefs in the rights of man, marked a major shift in the rise of antislavery thought and the strategy of rebellion. It was the first known instance in which slave rebels also advocated universal freedom, and can thus be seen as the first real expression of immediatism in the modern world.[27]

Immediatism represented both a shift in strategy and a change in outlook. While white gradualists embraced colonization and boycotts as a means to end slavery, black gradualists accepted voluntary emigration and deferred to white authorities as a pragmatic attempt to retain their tenuous freedom and prevent a race war. Immediatists advocated a total and swift transformation of society, and they initially emphasized moral suasion and nonviolence. But immediatism also reflected a shift from Enlightenment to Romantic worldviews, from a "detached, rationalistic perspective on history and progress, to a personal commitment to make no compromise with sin," as David Brion Davis has written. Immediatism was an expression of inner freedom and triumph over wordly conventions; it reflected a sharp break from linear notions of progress and history, and assumed that a new age was dawning. As such, it was an appropriate doctrine for a new Romantic age.[28] As a result, immediatism brought blacks and whites together as allies and friends in a way that had not occurred before.[29] They advocated racial equality and worked to achieve it, and there was a moral certainty to their immediatist outlook, which was absent among the earlier generation of gradual abolitionists. While gradualists were willing to compromise with sin, immediatist believed that the nation would soon become all one thing or all the other—to paraphrase Lincoln's 1858 "House Divided" speech—and so one needed to do the right thing *immediately*. With such moral certainty came an acceptance of social chaos and eventually violence; indeed, moral certainty of any kind can more easily lead to chaos and bloodshed than order.[30]

Intervening in this fluid and volatile landscape, T.K. Hunter poses the important question, "Where is the law?" and concludes that laws regulating slavery depended on time and place. She compares two legal cases—the *Somerset* case (1771–72) in England and the *Commonwealth v. Aves* case (1836) in Massachusetts—and reveals striking connections between geography and legal definitions of freedom in the early Atlantic world. Geographies are more than lines drawn on a map; they are also ideological constructions. The central question in both cases was not whether slavery contradicted the concept of natural rights, but whether it was contrary to the laws of a specific geographic setting that was deemed "free." The power of place—its beliefs and customs as well as bricks and mortar—was crucial to the laws of slavery. England in the 1770s and Massachusetts in the 1830s were places where the idea of liberty "was particularly favored"; but such liberty was exclusionary, bounded by specific geographic settings. In this sense, these legal cases reflected a gradualist worldview in 1770s England and 1830s Massachusetts. And after the passage of the Fugitive Slave Law of 1850, and then the Kansas-Nebraska Act of 1854, which repealed the Missouri Compromise, slavery became legal in places that had earlier prohibited it. In other words, Hunter argues, freedom was neither inevitable nor transcendent in the century that spanned the American Revolution and the Civil War.[31]

Richard S. Newman looks at the revolutionary generation of black abolitionists and its significance to the later generation of more famous activists like Frederick Douglass, Sojourner Truth, Harriet Tubman, William Wells Brown, and others. These "Black Founders"—men and women who came of age with the nation's white "Founding Fathers"—have been, until the last few years, largely overlooked by historians. But they left an important legacy: by living as free men in the Age of Revolution, building communities and institutions, and expressing their rights as citizens (even when laws denied them citizenship), they defined America as an interracial republic from the very beginning. While Black Founders differed from antebellum blacks in the specific means they advocated for achieving citizenship, both groups shared the same goals: to be accepted as free citizens, to co-exist peacefully with whites, and to "share equal privileges," as the Reverend Peter Williams Jr., phrased it. Through their pamphlets of protest, the Black Founders established the foundations for future antislavery dissent. They understood that protest movements need an organ to spread the word.

Julie Winch elaborates on the importance of the Black Founders by focusing on James Forten and linking him to black abolitionists in the 1840s and 1850s. Forten came of age in the midst of the American, French, and

Haitian Revolutions, was particularly inspired by the American Revolution, and "welcomed revolutions" as long as they upheld the ideal of freedom from tyranny. *Freedom from tyranny* was a revolutionary concept in the 1770s, Winch notes, and this belief served as the bridge connecting Forten's revolutionary ethos with those of Frederick Douglass, James McCune Smith, and William Wells Brown, who demanded an immediate end to slavery and racial oppression. Their differences were in how to achieve these goals. As slavery spread and racial oppression increased from the 1770s to the 1840s, the new generation of black abolitionists accepted extra-legal violence as a viable tactic in pursuit of their ideals. Since Forten came of age in an era in which society seemed to be gradually abolishing tyranny, he believed in peaceful revolution. Like other Black Founders, Forten never abandoned his emphasis on patient, prudent, and pragmatic solutions, and avoided the temptations of vengeance and blood atonement for the sins of whites.

Like Forten, John Brown Russwurm was a practical abolitionist, but his ideas did not sit well with blacks of his generation. He embraced colonization, which Black Founders from Forten and Richard Allen to Paul Cuffe and Prince Hall had also accepted. But Russwurm lived in the wrong time and place; he would have been more comfortable, and certainly his legacy would have endured, had he been a member of the generation of Black Founders. He co-edited *Freedom's Journal* in 1827–28, the nation's first black newspaper, which embraced immediatism and attacked the American Colonization Society and its gradualist measures for ending slavery. The ACS, which was founded by elite whites, sought to ship free blacks to its colony of Liberia; many members assumed that colonizing free blacks would—somehow and at some distant time—lead to the abolition of slavery.[32] But most blacks denounced the ACS, arguing that the organization was a tool for white slaveowners who felt threatened by the growing presence of free blacks in the United States. Beginning in the late 1820s, attacking colonization became something of a rite of passage for the vast majority of white and black immediatists. Thus, when Russwurm—an elite free black who was one of the few formally educated black men of his day—endorsed colonization in the pages of *Freedom's Journal,* and then emigrated to Liberia under the auspices of the ACS, he was not only dismissed by the black community, but also written out of black history altogether. Sandra Sandiford Young recovers the life and times of this fascinating figure.

As Timothy Patrick McCarthy notes, *Freedom's Journal* was "the first antislavery periodical to advocate both immediate abolition and racial equality as interrelated goals." McCarthy shows how black writing and protest "helped to create the context" for a united interracial front within the abolitionist movement, in which blacks and whites worked together to end slavery and usher in a new age of equality. African American print culture, especially *Freedom's Journal* and David Walker's *Appeal to the Coloured Citizens of the World* (1829), helped to convert white activists from a gradualist embrace of colonization to an immediatist belief in racial equality. While William Lloyd Garrison, usually regarded as the "founder" of immediatism, considered Walker's *Appeal* to be "injudicious," and even "deprecated" its militant "spirit and tendency," he was also deeply influenced by it.[33] As McCarthy documents, the differences between Revolutionary-era and antebellum-era antislavery thought got telescoped into a few years in the late 1820s, resulting in a cauldron of interracial tension and transformation that had its origins in black abolitionist print culture.

John Brown represents the endpoint of the antebellum quest for interracial equality. More than any other white person on historical record, he forged close friendships with blacks, lived with them, established an interracial army and "Provisional Constitution" to fulfill, in his words, "those eternal and self-evident truths set forth in our Declaration of Independence," which the nation had "utterly disregarded and violated," and sacrificed his life in the cause of black freedom and equality.

Yet Brown has always been an enigma for historians; to understand him, one must view him in perpetual context. By focusing on his racial egalitarianism, it is easy to overlook the numerous deaths he caused, of both blacks and whites. His attempt to incite a slave insurrection was, like most slave revolts in modern slave societies, suicidal.[34] On the other hand, by focusing on violent resistance, it is easy to ignore the violence that was inherent in the institution of slavery itself: slavery could never exist without the use of force or threat of it. Brown understood the violent nature of slavery, as did slaves and most free blacks. And he felt increasingly alienated in a "slave republic." After going bankrupt and losing his home and almost all of his worldly possessions, he entered a world of American desperation best understood by slaves. He identified closely with free blacks and slaves, defined slavery as a state of war, and concluded that America was engaged in civil war.[35] Throughout the South, masters and overseers were maiming and killing slaves. Brown sought to end this war and preserve the peace. He saw himself as a peacemaker.

Brown's violent ways and his closeness to blacks went hand in hand. You couldn't have one without the other. In many ways, the 1850s were the ideal context for Brown, as this was a decade in which blacks and whites came together as friends and equals as never before. It was also a very bloody decade, wherein the conflicts between antislavery and proslavery forces reached a violent crescendo. By focusing on Brown, Karl Gridley and Hannah Geffert highlight these tensions and conflicts during the 1850s. They examine Brown's relationship to black and white comrades in war zones where he committed his bloodiest deeds: "Bleeding Kansas" is the context for Gridley; Harpers Ferry for Geffert. Their essays show how Brown was an inextricable part of a community of other activists—black and white abolitionists, as well as slaves. And they reveal how radical inter-racialism had become inseparable from bloodshed during the turbulent decade before the Civil War. Indeed, these were the essential ingredients for achieving the abolitionist revolution.

Until very recently, historians of abolitionism rarely read poetry or fiction from the nineteenth century, and few concerned themselves with the advent of photography. Likewise, most critics of abolitionist literature read very little history from the period. Historians were not concerned with rhetoric and aesthetics, and literary scholars were not concerned with historiography. But as our final section, "Representations," makes clear, this gap has begun to narrow among abolitionist scholars. This is partly due to scholars' increasing awareness of the fact that the abolitionists themselves were deeply interested in history, literature, and visual arts. They paid particularly close attention to history and to how they represented themselves, both in form and content. They believed that art, history, and rhetoric were important tools for ending slavery and breaking down social barriers. Indeed, these were essential to the art of persuasion.[36]

Patrick Rael examines how blacks combated racial science from the Revolution to the Civil War and explores the effectiveness of their rhetorical strategies. He summarizes five different strategies: concession, in which black protest accepted some aspects of black inferiority as a way to appeal to humanitarian sentiment and empathy; living proof refutations, where blacks used autobiography to refute scientific claims; uses of the past, where writers looked to literature and libraries rather than skulls and other biological sources to refute ethnologists; the genius of races, in which black historians parodied, satirized, and condemned Anglo-Saxon history; and negative environmentalism, which conceded black degradation but ascribed it to environment rather than genes and blamed whites for it. While these rhetorical strategies did not prevent whites from internalizing racist discourse (especially discourse that targeted Native Americans and Chinese), they were effective, for they undermined the very principle of racial hierarchy. As Rael notes: "Black thinkers set forth a notion of blackness that largely avoided succumbing to the racial essentialism of their day, yet remained deeply engaged with the discourses of the American public sphere." Such rhetoric offered "tremendous benefits," for it gave blacks a potent set of tools for changing white minds.

Julie Roy Jeffrey examines how American abolitionists used history, politics, rhetoric, and art in their British emancipation day celebrations. England initiated the process of peaceful emancipation in the West Indies on August 1, 1834. Thereafter, black and white activists in America began celebrating August 1 as an important symbol of freedom that was grounded in recent history and pointed to the possibility of freedom and citizenship for blacks in the United States. Their celebrations united politics with performance art, and incorporated speeches, music, banners, and eventually parades to participate in the larger public debate over slavery, freedom, and civic equality. The nature of August 1 celebrations changed over time: white participation increased dramatically by the 1850s; the rhetoric became more militant and the celebrations themselves became more public. These changes reflected the broader evolution of the abolitionist movement.

From its very inception, Dickson Bruce argues, the abolitionist movement made ample use of poetry to advance its cause. Anyone reading abolitionist newspapers could not help but notice the abundance of poetry in them. Yet until a few years ago, there were no collections of abolitionist poetry, and very few scholars analyzed it.[37] Bruce explores the nature and function of antebellum poetry. He argues, as Garrison did in 1831, that "by presenting it as a poem, the story is made more public." Poetry enabled a message to enter the public sphere; it was one of the most public of mediums, and Americans widely believed that poetry had the power to convert people to a specific cause. But poetry had other uses as well: it helped abolitionists define their sense of place; it "had a special power to carry its reader to the truths that only intuition could supply"; it kept readers active in the abolitionist community (sometimes as amateur poets themselves); and it created an imagined community of racial equality—a community that abolitionists believed would spread throughout the nation. As Bruce concludes, poetry helped abolitionists realize a vision of a better America while also making themselves an example for others.

Broadening the analysis of antislavery literature, Augusta Rohrbach compares two abolitionist writers, Louisa May Alcott and Sojourner Truth, to understand how abolitionist women negotiated the antebellum literary marketplace. Both women adapted themselves to the conventions of the market, and became famous in the process. They relied on their publications to support themselves and provide for their families; but while Alcott was "an efficient writing machine," Truth remained illiterate her entire life, dictating her stories to an amanuensis. Rohrbach explores how these two women used the market, showing how the racial and gender identities of these authors were manifested in print and in public.

As effectively as the abolitionists used print culture, they also used pictures and other visual images as important tools for ending slavery and racial oppression. John Stauffer examines how black abolitionists were invested in the power of pictures as a way to acquire a public voice, to enter into the public sphere, and to revise public opinion. Black abolitionists believed that "true" art was a social leveler. They considered photographs, and accurate engravings cut from them, to be truthful, authentic images. Their portraits, they believed, depicted them as fully human and equal to whites. As a result, their pictorial art was a potent weapon against the degrading representation of blacks, and exposed the inhumanity of both slavery and white supremacy. For black abolitionists, being the subject of a work of art (a photograph or image) was far more empowering than being an image-maker or photographer.

Moving forward, Casey King focuses on abolitionist images in the twentieth century, and in doing so, returns us to questions about the uses of the past that Robert Forbes addresses at the opening of our book. King explores how abolitionists have been represented in film. Film became in the twentieth century the primary medium by which most Americans understand their history. But abolitionists have not fared well in these popular histories. In fact, filmmakers have virtually written abolitionists out of history. There are only a few instances in which they are portrayed sympathetically as major characters in film. Even during the civil rights struggles of the 1960s, abolitionists and their movement remained "conspicuously absent," despite renewed interest in and sympathy for them among scholars. And in the 1990s, when Hollywood finally discovered black abolitionists, "a profound mistrust of religiously inspired reform has served to further denigrate the historical role of abolitionists, and the historical reality of the religious basis on all profound American reform." By analyzing the few instances in which abolitionists are featured in film, King reveals the causes for these popular attitudes toward history and abolitionism. His essay, together with *Prophets of Protest* as a whole, should help to revise our popular conceptions of abolitionism.

Every generation of historians must assess for itself the meaning of the past. As the preeminent scholar Eric Hobsbawm once noted, historians are the "professional remembrancers of what their fellow citizens wish to forget."[38] As such, we have a dual professional charge: first, to take the facts and artifacts we've inherited and create new modes of understanding and interpretation; and second, to do so in a way that illuminates the past for the broadest possible public. This requires a certain distance and diligence, certainly, but it also means that we have to wrestle with all the passions and prejudices that come with any honest attempt to balance our duty as scholars with our calling as citizens. Indeed, at our best, we, as scholars, are also citizens, using the past to understand the present and in-fluence the future. We act as workers—observers, narrators, reformers—in what W.E.B. Du Bois once called "the kingdom of culture." In doing so, we must acknowledge that the study of the past is a dynamic, evolving, subjec-tive, and incomplete enterprise that constantly beckons new research and fresh interpretations. With this in mind, we hope that the following recon-siderations of American abolitionism will help to inspire a new under-standing of our precious yet still precarious experiment in democracy.

PART ONE

Revisions

"Truth Systematised": The Changing Debate Over Slavery and Abolition, 1761–1916

Robert P. Forbes

The study of historiography serves to remind us to accept our predecessors only after due criticism. We must ask, "Why was that problem investigated? Why was that method chosen?" before we decide if the results are correct or incorrect, stimulating or barren. Similarly, the study of historiography reminds us (as historians) that we are part of the subject we profess, just as our predecessors have always been.

    —F.G. Levy, Foreword to *The Theory and Practice of History*
                     by Leopold von Ranke

It is obvious to every unprejudiced observer—and even to many prejudiced ones—that the legacy of racial slavery persists on many levels.[1] A growing movement in the United States and elsewhere is calling for reparations to compensate the descendants of slaves for the economic and other damages inflicted upon them by slavery. A wide range of studies has linked the continuing disparity in levels of health, economic well-being, and educational attainments between Americans of African ancestry and other Americans to factors originating in slavery, though whether the factor of enslavement is itself the cause of the problem or of secondary importance—i.e., the result of persisting stigmatization—is unclear.

As difficult as it may be to measure the empirical impact of slavery on contemporary descendants of slaves, the *ideological* legacy of the slavery controversy is far harder to assess. There is reason to believe, however, that its effects have been pervasive—perhaps more far-reaching than the effects of slavery itself.

The era of the struggle over slavery coincided with the emergence of Enlightenment thought, the advent of nationalism, the overthrow of aristocracy, and the rise of democratization—those aspects of historical development regarded collectively as "modernity." Yet, as Scott Malcomson has noted, the concepts of an inherited racial basis of identity and of fixed racial bases of slavery and "savagery" are also products of modernity. "Whether modernity can exist as such without these blood notions remains an open question," Malcomson observes. "But we can be certain that, for most of its life, it has not."[2]

For a variety of reasons, the English society that colonized the eastern seaboard of North America regarded slavery in the abstract as a serious evil, antithetical to English (and later British) values. Few involved in the colonial enterprise permitted abstract scruples about slavery to interfere with the practical matter of profits. The growth of slavery in the English colonies provoked some concern, even consternation, and substantial disappointment—as when James Oglethorpe's colony of Georgia relented to the demands of its colonists and dispensed with its free-labor policy—but little in the way of outrage or soul-searching.

Before the rise of the antislavery movement, then, African slavery in the Americas neither needed nor received a formal defense. The patriots of the American Revolution, with their sweeping appropriation of the metaphor of slavery, unintentionally put the real thing on center stage. "Would anyone believe that I am master of Slave[s] of my own purchase," Patrick Henry wrote after the war. "I am drawn along by the general inconveniency of living without them, I will not, I cannot justify it."[3] West Indian planters, unconstrained by the equalitarian assumptions of the Revolution, had no such compunctions, and quickly turned their hands to fashioning justifications for slavery. Although government ministers and trade officials found the West Indian lobby's bribes and payoffs more influential, sensitive contemporaries regarded the attempt to defend slavery within a British context to be fundamentally alarming.

"It is impossible for the considerate and unprejudiced mind to think of slavery without horror," asserted the Scottish philosopher James Beattie in 1793, adding: "If this be equitable, or excusable, or pardonable, it is vain to talk any longer of the eternal distinctions of right and wrong, truth and falsehood, good and evil." The English abolitionist Granville Sharp amplified upon this view in 1797. "The terms *Slave Trade* and *Slavery* . . . comprehend systems of *oppression* and *injustice,* which are utterly *inconsistent with the fundamental principles of English Law,*" and for Parliament to tolerate them was to "act as if there was no distinction to be observed between *good* and *evil, right* or *wrong*"—a condition that, he asserted on biblical authority, threatened "the *natural foundations of the earth.*"[4]

In his *Appeal to the Coloured Citizens of the World,* the African American pamphleteer David Walker sounded a furious alarm to his people of the threat to their existence posed not merely by slavery, but by the marriage of

Enlightenment principles of the rights of man to the nascent scientific racism of the era, which carried with it the imprimatur of Thomas Jefferson. It was precisely because of the greatness of Jefferson's "writings for the world, and public labours for the United States of America," the value of which Walker fully acknowledged, that he regarded Jefferson's tentative strictures on black inferiority as so dangerous. "Do you believe that the assertions of such a man, will pass away into oblivion unobserved by this people and the world?" he asked. "If you do you are much mistaken."[5] Like Sharp, Walker believed that the perversion of justice involved in the sanctioning of slavery by enlightened Anglo-Saxon Christians—of all the world's people the best equipped to understand the true meaning of liberty—called into question the very nature of physical reality: If God failed to raise up a deliverer to punish the "Christians of America" for their gross impiety, "it is because the world in which we live does not exist, and we are deceived with regard to its existence." The possibility that injustice might be allowed to go unrequited does not provoke in Walker the typically modern doubt in the existence of God; rather, the entire ontological structure of the world is called into question.[6]

If the very project of modernity is itself implicated in the establishment of race as a fundamental category of experience, it is not surprising that the study of slavery and abolition should prove impervious to "objective" interpretation, since the analytical and descriptive tools of the social sciences were developed in tandem with the codification of racial principles—indeed, they were one of the chief vehicles for the transmission of such principles. At the same time, the subject has inevitably served as a signifier for larger questions about human nature and purpose. As Stanley Elkins observed in 1959, "How a person thinks about Negro slavery historically makes a great deal of difference here and now; it tends to locate him morally in relation to a whole range of very immediate political, social, and philosophical issues which in some way refer back to slavery."[7]

Few fields of history have experienced greater advances in understanding, sophistication, methodology, or sheer knowledge over the course of the last half century than slavery and abolition. There is thus a certain irony, and for many scholars much frustration, in the fact that the general public not only remains unreceptive to this new scholarship and holds adamantly to many long-disproved myths about slavery, it adopts new ones without any foundation in fact. Thus, for example, the still widely held view that slavery was not a cause of the Civil War has been supplemented by the increasingly accepted fiction that thousands of slaves bore arms for the Confederacy. Other debates over slavery, equally untethered to empirical evidence (though routinely garbed in the language and apparatus of academic scholarship) have raged over such issues as the number of Africans transported in the middle passage and the role of Jews in the transatlantic slave trade.[8]

"There is a coerciveness to the debate over slavery," complains Elkins: "it continues to be the same debate."[9] The problem is, it is *not* the same. While the combatants in the "race question" have employed the same vocabulary for generations, the meanings and contexts of the language have shifted. Unless we are attentive to these shifts, we will indeed be forced to cover the same ground over and over again, with little to show for it.

There is no easy way out of this dilemma. Since, as F.J. Levy reminds us, as historians "we are part of the subject we profess," we must approach the past with the awareness that we are the inheritors of biases of which we have no conscious knowledge; that our tools of analysis and investigation have a suspect heritage; that some of our most prized ideas may well be built on obsolete foundations of self-deception.

It will not do, moreover, to argue that the distorted viewpoint of modernity can be rectified by the salutary tonic of postmodernity. This facile approach merely adds another layer of obscurity, one that itself stands on the same foundation of accreted ideas as the flawed intellectual structure it seeks to dismantle. Instead, we must attempt to understand earlier interpretations on their own terms, and to be attentive to the meaning of changes in perspective in the context of their own times.

It is with these ideas in view that I have sought to reexamine the extraordinary transformation which took place in the debate over slavery, abolition, and race in British and American historical writing over the course of the late eighteenth and nineteenth centuries. By no means is this essay intended to be a comprehensive overview of the available material. Rather, it attempts to recover a set of basic assumptions about human nature and destiny at the beginning of this period, and to chart the outline of a change in these assumptions by the end of it. This exercise is necessarily tentative, speculative, and incomplete. I hope, however, that it will prove suggestive and stimulating to more thorough researches.

The debate over slavery and its abolition has undergone a profound and significant series of revisions since the first major work in the field, Thomas Clarkson's *History of the Rise, Progress and Accomplishment of the Abolition of the African Slave-Trade by the British Parliament,* appeared in 1808. Very broadly, the first three of these stages can be delineated as follows:[10]

1. Members of the first generation to write about abolition—Clarkson, Granville Sharp, Zachary Macaulay, James Stephen—were themselves principals in the movement. Almost without exception, they were devout evangelical Christians. They viewed abolition primarily if not exclusively as a religious question, fought and won on religious

grounds, and as a manifestation of God's Providence, in the strictest sense of the term. Thus I will refer to this group of writers as "Providentials," and the phase of historiography as "Providential."

2. The next stage witnessed a gradual shift from regarding abolition as the active intervention of divine providence—an evangelical or "enthusiastic" interpretation that was by no means universally shared by contemporaries—to seeing it as a step in the inexorable and impersonal march of Progress, as defined and driven by the Anglo-Saxon peoples.[11] By the latter part of the nineteenth century all subtlety about this view had evaporated: the dominant writers on abolition had adopted a thoroughgoing assertion of white and English superiority, based in large part on the fact of abolition itself, and employed it as an explicit rationale for colonialism and imperialism. The champions of this interpretation of slavery and emancipation can perhaps best be characterized as the "Racialist Progress" school of historiography.

3. The third shift, hinted at in W.E.B. Du Bois's pathbreaking study, *Black Reconstruction in America,* and carried to fruition by the Trinidadian historian and statesman Eric Williams in his seminal *Capitalism and Slavery,* represented a strong reaction against the hypocrisy and self-righteousness of the second-stage Anglo-Saxonists. First published in 1944, *Capitalism and Slavery* did not gain recognition until the early 1960s, when decolonization and the independence struggles of the Third World lent an extraordinary relevance to its themes of imperialist colonial policy and economic change. To a great degree, however, exponents of this viewpoint failed to distinguish between the attitudes of the "Providentials" of the first generation and the "Racialist Progressives" of the later period—and indeed, they seem unconsciously to have absorbed much of the frame of reference of the latter, in particular, their historical determinism. While most of this third group of interpreters are materialists, Marxist or otherwise, certainly not all are, and for the purposes of this essay they will be more broadly described as "Modernist Revisionists."

Two important considerations should be kept in mind concerning the three stages of the abolition debate outlined above. First, these are intellectual categories, not chronological ones. Conflicting attitudes are regularly found in the same period—indeed, they often occur in the same individual. This is entirely to be expected. Just as Marc Bloch found the outlines of medieval fields still plainly distinguishable in the modern contours of French farms, so the imprints of earlier intellectual concepts may be traced in the thoughts of later writers.

Second, the categories outlined above are not to be viewed as anything more than general constructs, designed only to illuminate in very broad strokes certain major intellectual trends. They are in no way intended to be definitive, merely suggestive. Indeed, once the reader has grasped the argument they are intended to illustrate, they may properly be discarded as conscious, if perhaps useful, oversimplifications.

I am primarily concerned with the transition from the providential viewpoint on abolition and emancipation to the racialist progressive. The basic approach used here, of illustrating the chief points of conflict between the earlier and later phase and addressing the reasons for that conflict, can just as appropriately be applied to the later stages.

If it is now generally accepted that the origins of abolitionism were fundamentally religious, it is important to recognize that in the eighteenth century, religion was not viewed as conflicting with "science" in any important sense. The ideas of Newton and Locke (themselves practicing Christians and serious biblical scholars) were common intellectual property for Britons and Americans, explicitly including those who were strongly religiously inclined. The later-perceived conflict between "enlightened" ideas and religion, which was born on the continent, did not become especially relevant to British and American thought until later.

Indeed, far from creating a gulf between faith and reason, it appears that these Newtonian and Lockean concepts were closely tied to the religious explosion of the First Great Awakening. John Wesley, for example, felt that "a deep fear of God, and reverence for his word" was "discernable throughout the whole" of Locke's *Essay on Human Understanding*.[12] Perry Miller traced the even more remarkable effect of Locke's psychology and Newton's physics in shaping the religious views of Jonathan Edwards. Miller called Edward's discovery of Locke, at the age of fourteen, "the central and decisive event in his intellectual life," and showed how Locke's doctrine that the mind depends upon direct experience for its ideas was at the heart of Edwards's insistence upon the direct experience of Christ's light.[13] Likewise, Miller argued, Edwards relied upon Newton's elucidation of the principle of cause and effect for his own analysis of the relation between faith and salvation. The explicitly religious element in American revolutionary ideology is now generally recognized.[14] Certainly in the mind of an American patriot there was unlikely to be the slightest conflict between religious and political thought.

We need to be aware of this context when we consider that "the attack on slavery was formulated in religious terms and, from first to last, practicing Christians provided leadership for the cause."[15] This fact provided an enormous stumbling block to later historians, particularly those of the "revisionist" tendency briefly sketched above. As Bernard Semmel noted, "most liberal, secular-minded historians have judged Methodism to be a reactionary movement, a protest against the Enlightenment and reason";[16] they have tended to consider evangelicalism as worse than Methodism. Inevitably, the outcome of such an assessment was to regard the abolitionists as deluded do-gooders, at best; as self-satisfied hypocrites, at worst.

Much of the reason for this attitude toward the abolitionists can be found in twentieth-century revisionists' marked ignorance of the theological consistency of the evangelical position—an ignorance stemming from a general antipathy toward religious concerns.[17] Even historians sympathetic to the abolitionists often lack a clear understanding of the relevant issues.

If the religious revival of the eighteenth century was indeed an organic product of the age, one must acknowledge that it was not necessarily the century's dominant attitude. As Winthrop Jordan reminds us:

> It is from the final quarter of the eighteenth century that we may date the widespread interest in elucidating & characterizing [human] differences with scalpels and calipers. At the same time, men devoted to the ancient Christian ideal of human unity began to scent danger, partly because there was good reason to fear the effects of probing into physiological differences among men and partly because they rightly felt that the cause of revealed religion was otherwise undergoing challenge. In this age it was still possible for them to defend religion with the principles of science, a procedure which was to become in the nineteenth century rather more difficult.[18]

Significantly, John Wesley's fiery *Thoughts on Slavery,* published in 1774, employed language and arguments reminiscent of *Two Treatises of Government* and contained not a single explicit biblical reference. "Liberty is the right of every human creature as soon as he breathes the vital air," Wesley wrote. "And no human law can deprive him of that right which he derived from a *law of nature*"[19] (emphasis added).

Many religious figures could, and did, see a conflict between an appeal to "natural law" and the moral imperatives of revealed religion; indeed, Wesley's colleague George Whitefield, who preached passionately to blacks in the West Indies and America, rejected the argument against slavery altogether as a temporal distraction from eternal concerns. Many of the abolitionists themselves, including their leader William Wilberforce, felt that the invocation of newfangled "rights of man" in the antislavery cause was both religiously and intellectually unsound, and likely to cause a dangerous blurring of the issues; likewise with the slippery call of "progress," especially as it overlapped with the sense of Christian mission.

An insight into Wilberforce's attitude can be gleaned from an argument which he had with Boswell, who supported slavery and claimed that the Negroes were far happier at work on West Indian plantations than they were in Africa. "Be it so," Wilberforce shot back; "but we have no right to make people happy against their will."[20]

On the other hand, not surprisingly, many abolitionists were full adherents of the new gospel of natural rights, including many who were themselves very religious—as for example Wesley, as suggested above. Others, such as Granville Sharp, the ordnance department clerk who taught himself Hebrew and Greek in order to argue the Bible and the law and combat slavery in the English courts, combined a fervent Christianity, an uncompromising republicanism, and a strong belief in human progress with no evident sense of contradiction. Thomas Clarkson (whose sophisticated racial attitudes Eric Williams praised as "only . . . equalled by the best of modern sociology"[!][21]) was a friend of Lafayette and a longtime correspondent of Toussaint L'Ouverture and Robespierre—as well as the founder of the "providential" historiographical tradition.

If the empirical, mechanistic world view of Newton and Locke was not at odds with religion, as the modernist revisionists would have it, the union of the two systems was not as unproblematic as contemporaries believed. The principle of cause and effect imported into mainstream Christian thought a mechanistic understanding of natural phenomena that, combined with the Enlightenment search for order, endowed the traditional religious concept of rewards and punishments with the certitude of natural law.

In America, this view received encouragement from revolutionary leaders who viewed it as conducive to civic virtue. Even skeptical and freethinking patriots such as Benjamin Franklin tended to believe that the new American republic, constructed out of the volatile material of revolution, required the powerful moral reinforcement of a strong sense of eternal rewards and punishments to bolster the fragile prop of human reason, which neither experience nor the "approved authorities" regarded as sufficient in itself. "[T]here is no truth more thoroughly established," George Washington asserted, "than that there exists in the economy and course of nature an indissoluble union between virtue and happiness; between duty and advantage; between . . . an honest and magnanimous policy and the solid rewards of public prosperity and felicity." Washington intended his words as an inducement to virtuous conduct, rather than as a vindication of present and future American prosperity.[22] Ominously, however, they could be interpreted in precisely that way.

On its face, there was nothing new about this American concept of moral economy. After all, Alexander Pope had claimed a kind of divine right for the status quo in his celebrated *Essay on Man:* "[I]n erring

Reason's spite, One truth is clear, 'Whatever IS, is RIGHT.' "[23] This was a doctrine, however, better adapted to a static social order than to the kaleidoscopically changing, economically unfettered American experience.

But if many abolitionists held Enlightenment opinions, by no means were all followers of the Enlightenment abolitionists. The link between the thought of the *philosophes* and the eighteenth-century struggles for freedom is more ambiguous than is generally recognized. The Enlightenment, in the view of its most fervent champion, Voltaire, "was never intended for cobblers or servants."[24] Voltaire "regularly made chilling value judgements, above all a Manichean distinction between whites and blacks," notes Leon Poliakov. "He was a polygynist *avant la lettre*, a fervent one and for reasons that were totally unscientific . . . driven on by an anticlerical passion."[25] For Voltaire, as for many of the *philosophes*, the Church was the foremost enemy of human progress; attacking one of its key doctrines, the common descent of all people from Adam and Eve, was principally a tactic to undermine its authority. The injury done to Africans and other non-Europeans was basically collateral damage.

The early French economists, or "physiocrats," placed an equally low priority on the concerns of others, apart from the European elites, but couched their prejudices in the quasi-objective terminology of the nascent social sciences, which they helped to coin. Starting from the assumption that the goal of society is to provide the greatest possible happiness for its members, the physiocrat Mercier de la Rivière went on to define "happiness" in strict materialist terms: "The greatest happiness possible . . . consists in the greatest possible abundance of objects suitable to our enjoyment and in the greatest liberty to profit by them."[26] "The practical inference" of the economists' doctrines, writes J.B. Bury, "was that the chief function of government was to protect property and that complete freedom should be left to private enterprise to exploit the resources of the earth . . . They held that inequality of condition was one of [society's] immutable features, immutable because it is a consequence of the inequality of physical powers."[27]

The "progressive" view, which began to crystallize in the mid-nineteenth century, saw in history the inevitable triumph of liberty, science, and reason over barbarism, superstition, and obscurantism, with the Enlightenment representing the crucial turning point. Of course, once the paradigm of Progress working through History began to replace the narrative of Providence working through individuals touched by grace, the abolitionists' contribution was largely eclipsed, and the extinction of slavery came to be seen as an economic and historical inevitability, the men of the Enlightenment its prophets.

The sharpest difficulty with this schema was precisely the case of America, the avatar of progress, where the rhetoric of freedom clashed with the reality of slavery. Everyone is familiar with Dr. Johnson's ironic query, "How is it that we hear the loudest *yelps* for liberty among the drivers of Negroes?" The challenge to the progressives was to formulate an answer to this question, and to live by it. Thomas Jefferson bequeathed to history the classic testament in defense of liberty; by his elaborate rationalization of his own slaveholding, he also stands as the prototype of the racialist progressive in the abolitionist debate. Moreover, just as David Walker had feared, Jefferson's imprimatur on racialist ideas helped to further their acceptance by later advocates of progress—including the future architects of British imperialism.

It is instructive, if painful, to contrast John Wesley's statements on blacks with Jefferson's. "The African," said Wesley in 1774, "is in no respect inferior to the European." Any appearance to the contrary is the "natural effect" of slavery: "You kept them stupid and wicked, by cutting them off from all opportunities of improving either in knowledge or virtue: And now you assign their want of wisdom and goodness as the reason for using them worse than brute beasts!"[28]

Jefferson also pursued the question of environment: "It will be right to make great allowances for the difference of condition, of education, of conversation, of the sphere in which [blacks] move," he conceded. Nevertheless, he was able to conclude that while "in memory [blacks] are equal to the whites," they are "much inferior" in reason, "as I think one could scarcely be found capable of tracing and comprehending the investigations of Euclid"; furthermore, "in imagination they are dull, tasteless, and anomalous."[29] But Jefferson went further—veering into quasi-metaphysical speculations on the Negroes' blackness, groundless assertions of their sexual preference for whites, and fabulous, obscene digressions concerning the "Oran-ootan."[30] According to Winthrop D. Jordan, in his masterful study of American racial attitudes, "Until well into the nineteenth century Jefferson's judgment on [African intellectual ability] stood as the strongest suggestion of inferiority expressed by any native American."[31]

The events of the Age of Revolutions—American, French, and Haitian—determined once and for all that the struggle against slavery would have to be fought on the battleground of natural rights, rather than on purely ethical or religious grounds. One effect of this development, in the short term, was to tar abolition with the brush of the French Revolution and the Terror, and to set the cause back several years. In particular, the wars with France made antislavery seem somehow unpatriotic: planters and conservatives frequently charged abolitionists with treasonous relations with French antislavery groups (themselves later suppressed by Napoleon on the same pretext).

In addition, the natural rights position was not merely "highly controversial and inflammatory," it was distinctly double-edged. Caribbean and Virginian *philosophes* were quick to adopt the arguments (and the language) of the Declaration of Independence in defense of their right to hold slaves, pointedly reinserting the Lockean "inalienable right" of property in place of Jefferson's less tangible "pursuit of happiness."[32] Invoking the Revolutionary theme of "tyranny" and styling their provincial assemblies as Caribbean counterparts to the Continental Congress, West Indian planters loudly proclaimed their willingness—and their right—to renounce their allegiance to the Crown.[33] Naturally, however, no West Indian politicians were so rash as to permit their sense of principle to induce them to relinquish their seats in Parliament.

Because of their strong inclination to regard religious activity as intrinsically conservative, Modernist Revisionist historians misjudged the character of the abolitionist movement and downplayed its social radicalism (though not its fanaticism). The campaign against slavery launched a public involvement in politics not seen before in British history. Lecture tours and mass meetings reached millions of citizens. Church pulpits across the nation echoed with calls to political action. Religious organizations, antislavery associations, and private individuals engaged in what James Walvin calls "tract warfare" with the West Indian interests, the Anti-Slavery Society alone printing 2,802,773 tracts between 1823 and 1831.[34] Activists forcefully pressured political candidates into signing abolitionist pledges, and the accusation of "gradualism" (support for anything less than immediate and total emancipation) was, by 1830, a damaging political indictment. One of the most visible elements of the struggle was the great outpouring of abolitionist petitions to Parliament from every part of the British Isles. A careful historian has estimated that "more than one British male in five over the age of fifteen probably signed the anti-slavery petitions of 1814 and 1833."[35] Perhaps most importantly, the abolition crusade was the first political movement in Britain in which women, the lower classes, and the young were all vitally engaged.[36]

The parallel antislavery movement in the United States during the period from the closing of the slave trade to the publication of Garrison's *Liberator* has been drastically understudied and overlooked (as the title of what is still the major work on the subject, Alice Dana Adams's nearly century-old *The Neglected Period of Anti-Slavery in America: 1808–1831*, makes clear).[37] This neglect derives in part from the coercive power of the Garrisonian narrative, and also from the widespread related perception that the colonization movement, with which most early antislavery activity was linked, constituted a stalking horse for proslavery. In reality, however, the pre-Garrisonian antislavery movement in the United States paralleled, in many aspects, both the elite and popular dimensions of the British movement of the same period. The major difference, of course, stemmed from the enormous political, economic, and social constraints that resulted from the presence of more than a million slaves.

All of this unprecedented political activism over abolition and emancipation was bound to create a backlash. A number of factors guaranteed that the reaction, when it came, would be particularly ugly. First, it would be naïve not to recognize that a political movement as broad as abolitionism was unlikely to be particularly deep. In Britain, abolition "had become the one harmless reform cause," C. Duncan Rice observed, "an anodyne commitment which carried no ideological risk."[38] The hard core of supporters had weathered setbacks and fought disillusionment for years, but by the late 1820s many people had joined the movement simply because it was no longer socially or politically acceptable not to. Similarly, many opponents of slavery in the northern United States espoused the cause in large measure out of a knee-jerk reflex of following English cultural trends, in this as in most other fashions. These "fair-weather abolitionists" were likely to desert at the first sign of trouble.

Second, as suggested above, defenders of abolition had negligently permitted "providential" and "rights of man" arguments against slavery to become illogically intertwined, hence vulnerable to effective rhetorical attack on grounds of hypocrisy and inconsistency. "Humanity is in fashion—it's Popular . . . the Subject is sublime," wrote one disgusted observer, and a later historian of the Progressive school seemed to document an early manifestation of the "liberal guilt syndrome": "It was said that in London the fashionable way to quiet one's conscience was by subscription to a missionary society or signing a petition against slavery."[39]

Third, the religious revolution of the late eighteenth and early nineteenth centuries had a genuinely transformative effect on society in both Britain and the United States—one by no means pleasing to all of its members. British conservatives who had long charged dissenters and evangelicals with promoting "disorder" and "fanaticism" felt themselves vindicated by the great wave of political activity culminating in abolition and emancipation, chartism, religious toleration legislation, and the Reform Bill. American conservatives, some of whom had welcomed the revival and chided the British for their hostility to "heart religion," now looked on aghast as women, children, and even slaves preached to "promiscuous" congregations in fervid camp meetings. The Reverend Calvin Colton, a New England Presbyterian, traveled to England in 1831 as a correspondent for the *New York Observer* and wrote a defense of American revivals a year later; when he returned to the United States in 1835, the emotional, political, and racial upheaval of the evangelical movement so shocked him that he repudiated both the revival and reformed Protestantism, converting to the Episcopal church and becoming a full-time crusader against the excesses of democracy.[40] On a national scale, what had once appeared to be a genteel, elite effort to fine-tune the social order now assumed the aspect of an uncontrolled radical movement whose eventual outcome no one could begin to guess.

In the Caribbean, the slaves' heightened political awareness had even more fundamental effects upon society, as well as even more explicitly religious origins. A major slave revolt in Jamaica in 1831, abetted if not inspired by white Baptist missionaries, underlined the deadly seriousness of the struggle and of the blacks' determination to be free—and showed the potential for cataclysmic, Haitian-scale violence.

Finally, the conviction of liberal economic theorists that free labor would prove more efficient than slave labor adopted enthusiastically by pragmatic abolitionists—turned out to be dead wrong. When in the years after emancipation the promised economic renewal of the islands under a system of "free" labor failed to materialize and the British sugar colonies plunged into stagnation, opponents of emancipation gained powerful new ammunition.[41]

If it is true that in religion, as A. D. Nock used to say, "nothing fails like success," then perhaps the same can be said of movements for social change. Simply put, after emancipation became a reality, it was no longer necessary to fight for it. When the apprenticeship period came to an end in 1838, British public interest in the fate of the blacks fell off precipitously. The English generation which had fought the battle for slaves' freedom, which had been willing to risk life and honor to confront the powerful plantocracy, had given way to a younger generation that took all of these victories for granted.

Indeed, now that the battle had been won, its supporters set about attempting to minimize its radicalism and back off from its extremism. In their laudatory 1838 biography, William Wilberforce's sons provided a distinctly watered-down version of their famous father. Missing, for example, from a letter Wilberforce wrote at the height of the French Terror was the following sentence: "If I thought the immediate Abolition of the Slave Trade would cause an insurrection in our islands, I should not for an instant remit my most strenuous endeavours."[42] Sadly, the saintly, tepid portraits painted by the second generation stuck to the abolitionists for over a century.

Although the British navy continued to enforce the interdictions on the

slave trade after public interest in the task declined, it seemed to perform
the function only because the bureaucracy set up to do so had become fully
entrenched.[43] "The British humanitarian impulse, its immediate objectives
accomplished, had apparently ossified into complacent sentimentality and
a sanctimonious belief in England's civilizing mission."[44]

In effect, Britain decided that it had a kind of moral "manifest destiny."
As David Brion Davis summarized:

> For two centuries the British had enslaved countless Africans but had
> now resolved . . . to force, cajole, persuade and prevent other people
> from slavery. Having imposed their slaving systems on vast tracts of
> Africa and the New World, the British with an almost evangelical zeal
> hawked their abolitionist conscience around the world and, in a no
> less imperious manner, obliged others to accept their revulsion and
> reject slavery.[45]

What made this attitude particularly obnoxious was that a movement
which had been founded on an appeal to conscience was now grounded
upon an assertion of superiority. Sir Robert Peel, a particularly belated
convert to the gospel of antislavery, called in 1840 for the colonization of
Africa in order to convince the Africans of the moral superiority of their
European fellow men, to "rescue Africa from debasing superstitions, and
to put an end to her miseries by the introduction of the arts of civilization
and peace."[46]

After almost a century of rocky relations, Christianity and the "liberal
spirit" were largely reconciled to one another. The English clergy ranked
themselves just as completely on the side of "progress" as any secular-
minded Utilitarian. Furthermore, the churches felt an evangelical imperative to bring this "progress," along with salvation, to every part of the
human race. Wilberforce's assertion that "we have no right to make people
happy against their will," would have been incomprehensible to a Victorian missionary.

Parallel developments in the United States had even more portentous
implications, marking the rise of race as an analytical category and as a
basis for exemption—for those encompassed within the embrace of
"whiteness"—from norms of morality and justice. It is highly significant
that the "mulatto" co-editor of *Freedom's Journal,* John Brown Russwurm,
after a career spent defending African Americans' equal rights to citizenship, decided within days of Andrew Jackson's accession to the presidency
in 1829 to leave the country for Liberia. In short order thereafter, officials
of Georgia moved to evict the Cherokee from their tribal lands within the

state, in defiance of the U.S. Supreme Court but with full confidence of their vindication by the "higher law" of Jacksonian providence.

The following year, in his annual address, Jackson rejoiced that the "benevolent" policy of Indian removal was nearing "a happy consummation." "Humanity has often wept over the fate of the aborigines of this country," the president mused, "and Philanthropy has been long busily employed in devising means to avert it, but its progress has never for a moment been arrested, and one by one have many powerful tribes disappeared from the earth. To follow to the tomb the last of his race and to tread on the graves of extinct nations excite melancholy reflections." Jackson rhetorically transmuted the illegal dispossession of the Indians—and by extension, crimes against other "savage" races—from the category of present-day injustices to that of an inexorable historic process. While the process of destruction might be tragic to those races falling victim to it, "true philanthropy reconciles the mind to these vicissitudes as it does to the extinction of one generation to make room for another." Viewed from the broad perspective "of the general interests of the human race," white Americans, the victors in this struggle of races, had nothing to apologize for—they were merely the beneficiaries of a just but impersonal cosmic process of rewards and punishments.

Within a few years, driven by the escalating imperatives of national politics, Jacksonian racialism arrived at its logical conclusion. In 1838, during a debate over the conduct of the Seminole war, Democratic Congressman Jonathan Cilley of Maine chided Whigs for their "false philanthropy" and endorsed prosecuting the war "with vigor, on the old New England plan, where the Indians had been wholly exterminated."[47] This extreme position remained a minority view, even among Democrats, but a rhetoric of white supremacism and Anglo-Saxon preeminence permeated Jacksonian political thought, finding its most typical and lasting expression in John O'Sullivan's "Young America" movement and its invocation of Manifest Destiny.[48]

Once the idea of racial progress had become thoroughly disseminated throughout the society, an attack on African institutions and culture became inevitable. A true conservative of the older generation, such as Edmund Burke, could condemn non-Europeans for their barbarism, yet admire them for fidelity to their traditions, even approve of the strength of their "prejudices"; a modern conservative wedded to progress, such as Sir Robert Peel, would display no such restraint, and his attack on Africans would be utterly without compunction.

The 1840s and 1850s mark the crucial point for the transition between the providential and progressive ideologies in the slavery debate. The period's true significance is difficult to grasp without paying rather close attention to theological nuances, because it is at this time that social conservatives begin to employ the form and language of religion for strictly secular purposes of control. Our modern categories of the religious versus the secular, Right versus Left, or conservative versus liberal can only be sources of confusion when applied to the nineteenth century. The events surrounding the European revolutions of 1848 and their aftermath provide a case in point: It would be difficult to find a single appropriate ism to characterize a Richard Wagner, a Pius IX, or a Louis Napoleon.

Thomas Carlyle is an exceptionally interesting representative of the period. More clearly than most of his contemporaries, Carlyle recognized how drastically the world had changed since the French Revolution, which he characterized as a "huge explosion, bursting through all formulas and customs; confounding into wreck and chaos the ordered arrangements of earthly life; blotting-out, one may say, the very firmament and skyey loadstars . . ."[49] A close reading of Carlyle shows that for him, as certainly as for Nietzsche, the Christian God was one of the casualties of the explosion. Indeed, Carlyle's choice of a replacement for God is the same as Nietzsche's: a hero, an "Ableman."

Carlyle's religious vision has no place in it for mercy; his definition of justice turns the Biblical concept on its head. "What is injustice?" asks Carlyle. "Another name for disorder. . . . As disorder, insane by the nature of it, is the hatefulest of things to man . . . so injustice is the worst evil, some call it the only evil, in this world." For a moment he sounds like a conventional Christian preacher of salvation: "All men submit to toil, to disappointment, to unhappiness; it is their lot here; but in all hearts, inextinguishable by sceptic logic, by sorrow, perversion or despair itself, there is a small still voice intimating that it is not the final lot; that wild, waste, incoherent as it looks, a God presides over it." So far, so good, but now this: "That it is not an injustice, but a justice."[50] Hope, it seems, lies not in the contemplation of the world to come beyond this vale of tears, but in the apotheosis of worldly oppression.

If professed conservatives such as Carlyle had no trouble impugning the humanity of blacks, those who had adopted "advanced," progressive, heterodox beliefs were now encouraged in their racism by scholarly opinion, particularly scientific. The "comparative study of the races of mankind," so fervently desired by Jefferson, was, alas, no longer "in its infancy." Coming on the heels of Mobile physician Josiah Nott's self-described "Nigger hallucinations" and his English colleague George Gliddon's researches into the "Antiquity of Niggers,"[51] Count Gobineau's influential work, *The Inequality of Human Races,* had set the tone for future investigations.

Of far greater significance was the work of Charles Darwin. Darwin's concepts of "natural selection" and "the struggle for existence" undoubtedly owed as much to social theorists as to earlier scientists such as Saint-Hilaire, Lamarck, and his own grandfather, Erasmus Darwin; indeed, Darwin himself says of it, "This is the doctrine of Malthus, applied throughout the whole animal and vegetable kingdoms." Darwin returned from his voyages laden with suggestive data on plants and animals which social scientists eagerly applied to the conditions of industrial Britain, clearly with his acquiescence if not encouragement. "In the future I see open fields for far more important researchers," he predicted. "Psychology will be securely based on the foundation already well laid by Mr. Herbert Spencer."[52] Like Carlyle, who saw life as "wild, waste, incoherent," and concluded that "a God presides over it . . . it is not an injustice, but a justice," so Darwin helped to create a new vision of the divine through his evolutionary theory:

> Thus, from the war of nature, from famine and death, the most exalted object which we are capable of conceiving, namely the production of the higher animals, directly follows. *There is grandeur in this view of life,* with its several powers, having been originally breathed by the Creator into a few forms or into one; and that, whilst this planet has gone cycling on according to the fixed law of gravity, from so simple a beginning endless forms most beautiful and most wonderful have been, and are being evolved.[53] (Emphasis added)

Grandeur, perhaps, if one has the good fortune to be one of the "exalted" individuals rather than one of the "unfit" casualties of natural selection's tangled bank. Truly, the one-time candidate for the ministry turned evangelist of evolution had produced a theology that turned predation into a sacrament.

The role which the ideals of social Darwinism played in justifying colonization is well known. It was an easy matter to exhume all of the myths of black inferiority created over the centuries to justify slavery, and, with only minimal modification, to graft them to the new justification of colonial exploitation. Researchers such as Francis Galton, who tied heredity to intelligence, and Cesare Lombroso, who did the same for criminality, received widespread intellectual acceptance and were considered among the most advanced minds of their day; work such as theirs has been termed "pseudoscience" only in retrospect. Two important parallel developments of modern western history—the "liberation" of science from religious influences and the exaltation of man as the master of nature—permitted, justified, and even decreed enormous crimes against non-Europeans. First, the elimination of an operative belief in a transcendent, absolute reality—

God—suggested that the progress of the human race was in human hands. Second, it ensured that people's values would ultimately be self-referencing; no principle existed to offset the common tendency to regard one's own kind as superior.[54] Drawing support from Darwin's theory of evolution, nineteenth-century neo-Malthusian activist doctrines took the debate one step further: subjugation of the "inferior" races was no longer viewed as just a matter of self-interest, or even as a noble step toward progress; it was now an inexorable process of "natural law."

This high-blown theorizing fit neatly with less theoretical, more impressionistic popular attitudes. Kenneth Little notes:

> Convincing as natural and evolutionary theories of race may have been to certain intellectuals and *litterateurs* of the day, it is doubtful if they moved the common man very much. The general public never had much patience with abstract notions of race and racial superiority. It is likely that the general belief in "Civilization" and the whole philosophy of "Progress" was far more conclusive in justifying . . . what the racialists claimed in less understandable language.[55]

This analysis points to an important conclusion: that racism in its most highly developed form was the creation of intellectuals. Whether it welled up from the masses, or was imposed on them from above, is a more difficult question; but in no way can it be considered strictly as a popular or populist response fundamentally alien to the intelligentsia, as much postwar scholarship has implied.

This essay is not the place to discuss in any detail such matters as phrenology, "germ plasm," or early I.Q. testing.[56] The scientific bankruptcy of these movements is here taken for granted. In their day, however, these theories were accepted as scientific fact and therefore placed beyond the range of discussion or dispute, since, as an influential racialist author asserted, "science is only truth systematised."[57] This outlook—in effect willed ignorance masquerading as insight—played havoc with much of the world's non-European population. One of the most significant characteristics of the nineteenth-century scientific attitude was its almost willful abandonment of earlier knowledge. Basil Davidson has followed this transformation in the history of European relations with the Congo:

> The connection undoubtedly began with something of a golden age of peace and friendship. It just as surely degenerated into violence, hatred and distrust. So complete was this decay that when the nineteenth century finally brought colonial conquest, the conquerors

seemed to have utterly forgotten the experience and accumulated knowledge of earlier Europeans.[58]

For whites as well as blacks, the process of recovering the past has been beset with interpretive obstacles, the more imposing in that they have been largely invisible. We are burdened in our attempt to see the past clearly with presuppositions and assumptions whose origins, if we recognized them, would repel us. Most daunting of all, we are hobbled by our understandable need to cling to the belief, in spite of our postmodern sophistication, that knowledge and conditions advance—that "progress" always marches forward. If contemporary scholars have abandoned the naïve optimism and triumphalism of the progressive view, we have retained its debilitating core: the conviction that we know more, and understand more clearly, than our ancestors. "The modern world tends to be skeptical about everything that makes demands on man's higher faculties," wrote E.F. Schumacher. "But it is not at all skeptical about skepticism, which demands hardly anything."[59] There is evidence that historians of the abolition debate are beginning to heed this criticism. David Brion Davis has warned against holding on to assumptions that "lead easily into a crude reductionism in which 'sin,' for example, means something other than sin and in which religious motivation is explained in terms of various secular interests."[60] The late Roger Anstey, from an avowed position of Christian faith, had no difficulty in avoiding this pitfall; more recent scholars, including Robert Fogel, Seymour Drescher, and Christopher Brown, are pursuing the more challenging road of doing so as secular academics.

A character in Tom Stoppard's play *Jumpers* writes of preparing a speech which he hopes will "set British moral philosophy back forty years, which is roughly when it went off the rails."[61] If the secular intellectual culture to which we are heir does indeed have the deadly antinomy of race embedded in its basic fabric, perhaps we need to take seriously the thought of those pioneers of antislavery, all of them wedded to assumptions we have long since rejected, who acted on principles formulated before Western civilization "went off the rails." To do so will not be easy. Americans of all races have been "reluctant to yield their privileges and their protections against each other, however strangely conceived those privileges and protections may have been," Scott Malcomson observed. Discussing the civil rights demonstrations of 1963, in which fire hoses and police dogs were turned upon children, Malcomson argued that its truly disturbing effect was to reveal

[t]hat race really was an arbitrary matter of skin tone and that the nation had been living upside down. The adult mind sped to register

this notion, so . . . deeply disturbing to a grown-up for whom the past was meant to be something other than an accumulation of shame and error. Adults tend to understand social relations in terms of justified power. In the fight against the power category of race, [the Reverend Martin Luther] King had imagined that power came only from God, who has no race—therefore race had no power. To understand this would be like suddenly awakening after the sleep of one's life, to be like a child again.[62]

It is a pattern of American life to suppress or rewrite the past when it is ugly, inconvenient, or disgraceful. On some level, many Americans seem willing, at last, to accept the reality of the profound role that slavery has played in our history. Unless we are willing to work our way back, and to look at the effects of slavery on all of our institutions, and to be changed by what we find, we are unlikely to find an exit any time soon from our continuing dilemma of race. If we are willing to do this, however, and to truly listen to the past, we may find that change—if not "progress"—is indeed possible.

2

Coming of Age:
The Historiography of Black Abolitionism

Manisha Sinha

Most historians are well aware of the long and checkered historiography of the abolitionist movement, from vilification to vindication and then, in the post-revisionist, post-1960s phase, to an almost excessive scrutiny with its failures and shortcomings as a reform movement.[1] Indeed, the sympathetic portrayal of abolition as a radical, even revolutionary movement for social change during the civil rights era has enjoyed a relatively brief afterlife among American historians.[2] Despite some prominent exceptions, the dominant picture of abolitionists in American history is that of bourgeois reformers burdened by racial paternalism and economic conservatism.[3] This view does little justice to the burgeoning scholarly literature on African American and women abolitionists that challenge conventional notions of the movement. A reappraisal of the abolition movement in light of these historiographical developments is long overdue.

I will examine the historiography of a topic that is perhaps the most vital subfield in abolitionist studies today, black abolitionism, but one that has yet to be the subject of a full-length essay. With increased interest in African American history, the historiography of black abolitionism has come into its own. It has its own issues and concerns but it also leads us to appreciate anew the interracial and radical nature of the antebellum movement to abolish slavery. I hope then not only to chart the origins and progress of the study of black abolitionism but also to speak to the central issues in abolitionist historiography and current interpretations of abolition.

As the dean of black abolitionist historiography, Benjamin Quarles, noted a long time ago, the writing of the history of black abolitionism has its roots in the antebellum era.[4] Some of the pioneers in writing the history of black abolitionism were African American abolitionists themselves, such as William Cooper Nell, William Wells Brown, and Martin Delany. While their work may have been mainly "contributionist" in tone—the dominant characteristic of early African American history—they are invaluable sources and a necessary starting point in studying black abolitionists. Like the more famous slave narratives, they serve a dual function, of political advocacy and of firsthand historical accounts recorded by participants. If the slave narratives are at their most basic level individual histories, autobiographies of fugitive slaves, these books serve as histories of the race and the movement. While such narratives remain an indispensable source in reconstructing the black historical experience under slavery and in the rise of African American literature, early historical writings by black abolitionists serve as foundational texts for the field of African American history.

In a series of snapshot portraits of black leaders from the Revolutionary to the antebellum period in his *The Colored Patriots of the Revolution* (1855), William Cooper Nell anticipated some of the modern interpretations of black abolitionism. He not only left behind a comprehensive list of African American abolitionists but also revealed the continuity in the black abolitionist tradition, which predated the start of the formal movement. Nell's reproduction of Revolutionary-era black petitions for the abolition of slavery and the slave trade and his discussion of black communities state by state amply demonstrated the grassroots nature of African American activism too easily dismissed by some historians as being mired in the strictures of middle-class reform and elitism. For him, the revolutionary nature of black abolitionism was self-evident and he included within its ranks slave rebels like Nat Turner, Madison Washington, and "Denmark Veazie." In developing a history of the black tradition of protest in this country, Nell demonstrated the interplay between slave resistance and the tradition of free black activism in the north, a point that was developed by historians such as Vincent Harding and, more recently, Peter Hinks.

Nell, a staunch Garrisonian, insisted that abolition was primarily an interracial movement, an insight whose implications we have only started to appreciate. In his telling, blacks were not simply part of a white-dominated movement. In fact, white abolitionists had become "colored all over," or as John Stauffer, following black abolitionist James McCune Smith, has argued, acquired black hearts. In contrast to some scholars' emphasis on the stifling presence of racism even within the abolition movement, Nell shows the ability of abolition to displace and question the rigid lines of race in antebellum America and the "colorophobia" of most white Americans. At the same time, the plight of African Americans in a relentlessly racist society and a vindication of the race of black people remained the lodestar of his understanding of abolitionism. Black Garrisonians as well as more self-conscious "race leaders" shared this essential perspective. Nell thus pointedly quotes at length Frederick Douglass's address to the National Colored Convention at Rochester in 1853 to make his argument:

> As a people, we feel ourselves to be not only deeply injured, but grossly misunderstood. Our white fellow-countrymen do not know us. They are strangers to our character, ignorant of our capacity, oblivious of our history and progress, and are misinformed as to the principles and ideas that control and guide us, as a people. The great mass of American citizens estimate us, as being a characterless and purposeless people; and hence we hold up our heads, if at all, against the withering influence of a nation's scorn and contempt.[5]

Like Nell's book, William Wells Brown's *The Black Man: His Antecedents, His Genius, and His Achievements* (1863) is essentially a collective biography of prominent black leaders and abolitionists. Unlike Nell, Brown includes in his pantheon of heroes not just slave rebels and black military heroes of the Civil War but also African American women abolitionists such as Charlotte Forten and Francis Ellen Watkins Harper. After Wells Brown—and only in the last few decades, with the rise of black women's history—have historians done justice to the role of black women in the abolition movement. Brown's work also preceded the contemporary interest in the transatlantic nature of black activism by including leaders of the Haitian revolution, Toussaint L'Ouverture, Jean Jacques Dessalines, and Henri Christophe in his prosopography, revealing the enormous ideological inspiration that the Haitian revolution exercised on the political imagination of black abolitionists. Brown's sense of black abolitionism is more expansive in nature than Nell's and his book signals the shift in black abolitionist leadership from free black men like Prince Hall, Paul Cuffe, James Forten, William Watkins, and Nell (a son of South Carolina slaves) to fugitive slaves such as Brown, Henry Highland Garnet, and Frederick Douglass in the 1840s and 1850s. Brown attaches his memoir to the book and recounts the story of "a man without name," loosely based on his own narrative and representative of the majority of African Americans who labored under slavery before the Civil War. Even more than Nell, Brown pioneered in writing a collective biography of black abolitionists, a genre that has been deftly revived by historians such as Richard J.M. Blackett.[6]

In contrast to Nell's and Brown's books, Martin Delany's *The Condition, Elevation, Emigration, and Destiny of the Colored People of the United States* (1852) is not known as a history of black abolitionism but for its advocacy of black emigration outside the United States. In fact, two thirds of Delany's book, fifteen of the twenty-three chapters, is a history of African American activism and Northern free blacks in the tradition of black abolitionist writing. Only the last few chapters of the book are exclusively devoted to the idea of emigration and finding a suitable place for black emigrants. Black Garrisonians such as Nell and Brown and emigrationists such as Delany shared a common understanding of the history of black abolitionism but Delany went beyond both Nell and Brown in arguing for the pioneering role of African Americans in the rise of the abolition movement.

Contending that African Americans in the United States were the most oppressed of all the classes and groups that had been denied citizenship and rights in world history, Delany began his history of black abolitionism tellingly with the meeting of the first black National Convention in 1830 that had advocated emigration to Canada in the wake of the Cincinnati race riot. It was black men, Delany wrote, who changed William Lloyd Garrison's views on colonization and gradual emancipation, a claim that was substantiated by Quarles and other historians including Paul Goodman, Donald Jacobs, and Richard Newman. African Americans, as Garrison openly acknowledged, heavily influenced the abolitionist program of immediatism, anticolonization, and racial equality. According to Delany, "Anti-slavery took its rise among *colored men,* just at the time they were introducing their greatest projects for their own elevation, and that our Anti-Slavery brethren were converts of the colored men, in behalf of their elevation." Delany spent considerable time detailing black protests against the American Colonization Society in the 1820s and the role of pioneering black abolitionists such as James Forten, Abraham D. Shadd, and James Barbadoes, among others. At the same time, he pointed to the importance of the publication of *The Liberator* and Garrison's seminal 1832 anticolonization pamphlet in the growth of an interracial abolitionism. For a book that is suffused with the spirit of black nationalism and pride, Delany never fails to appreciate the significance of Garrison and his philosophical radicalism to the interracial struggle for black equality.

From a discussion of early black abolitionism, Delany quickly moved to the history of the "colored citizens" of the United States. He detailed the contributions of African Americans in clearing and settling the land in colonial America, and during the Revolutionary War and the War of 1812. Like Nell and Brown, he developed a collective portrait of famous black figures of the Revolutionary era, Phillis Wheatley and Paul Cuffee, to black abolitionists like James McCune Smith, Samuel Ringgold Ward, J.W.C. Pennington, Charles Lenox Remond, Mary Ann Shadd Cary, and George Vashon. The glaring absence of Frederick Douglass from this list of black luminaries was probably due to the author's well-known falling out and rivalry with Douglass and his attempt to argue for a much larger group of black achievers than the one representative black abolitionist known to most white Americans. He does grudgingly mention Douglass and his paper in a long footnote containing a glossary of antebellum black newspapers and their editors. Delany's subsequent chapters read like a veritable who's who of antebellum blacks, listing many other less famous African Americans from every walk of life.[7] In the context of black abolitionist historiography, Delany's book represents a continuation of the antebellum African American political and intellectual tradition rather than a break from it.

African American abolitionists not only attempted to leave behind a historical record of black abolitionism, they also spent considerable time deconstructing racial thought and pseudoscientific racism in early America. In this sense, too, their work anticipated the current scholarship on the construction of race and racism in American history. Black abolitionist Hosea Easton, whose family was well represented in the ranks of New England abolitionism, offered the most searing and comprehensive rebuttal of popular racism in the early republic. Easton's work, *A Treatise on the Intellectual Character and Civil and Political Condition of the Colored people of the United States; and the Prejudice Exercised Towards Them* (1837), predated the rise of the pseudoscience of race but his recognition of the all-encompassing oppression and crime of racism prefigured the work of those African American thinkers who sought to systematically refute its premises and conclusions. As he wrote feelingly:

> O Prejudice, thou art slavery in disguise! . . . If there are degrees of intensity to the misery of the damned, that being must feel it in eternity, in whose heart prejudice reigned in this world. O Prejudice, I cannot let thee pass without telling thee and thy possessors, that thou art a compound of all evil—of all corrupt passions of the heart. Yea, thou art a participant in all the purposes of the wicked one—thou art the very essence of hell.

Historians Mia Bay, Bruce Dain, and Patrick Rael have highlighted the importance and political implications of the African American response to pseudoscientific racism. Most black abolitionists disputed its pernicious conclusions that started to dominate the academy and popular culture in mid-nineteenth-century America. The pseudoscience of race was in fact an important handmaiden of the proslavery argument. It was American and Southern in origin and closely tied to the question of slavery, as Stephen Jay Gould showed in his classic *The Mismeasure of Man*.[8]

Two black abolitionists, the Reverend James W.C. Pennington and Henry Highland Garnet, sought to critique notions of race and racism from outside the intellectual hegemony of the fashionable "racial science" of the day. They refused to develop their critiques of the concept of race and racism by deploying the dominant categories and ideas used by scientific racists. In his *Text Book of the Origin and History of the Colored People* (1841), Pennington challenged popular, biblical, and pseudoscientific notions of race. A clergyman and a scholar who had received an honorary doctorate from the University of Heidelberg, Pennington disputed the notion that the enslavement of Africans was justified by Noah's curse on Ham's descendants. Like earlier black abolitionists David Walker and William Hamilton, he did not hesitate to take on Thomas Jefferson's "suspicions" of black inferiority. Sarcastically remarking on the "adverse influence of slavery on his great mind," Pennington gives Jefferson the benefit of the doubt that the latter had denied black slaves of his own era by comparing them unfavorably to the slaves of antiquity. In fact, Pennington grounds his entire argument on equality of "intellect," a God-given gift. Dismissing the scientific racists, he trenchantly writes, "He who in discussing the nature of man, can stoop to talk about monkeys, apes, and ourangoutans, offers insult to the majesty of his own nature, for which he ought to be ashamed." Pennington's highly religious frame of reference would have probably led him to dismiss evolution as well as the pseudoscientific discourse on race.

However, in attempting to define racism and its ill effects, he ventures beyond the strictures of the Bible and develops one of the best indictments of racism in antebellum America. According to Pennington, "American prejudice" was "supreme selfishness." "It is emphatically ill will." It reflects a "blindness of mind." It is not the victim who is intellectually inferior but the racist. It engenders "dishonesty," "injustice," "hypocrisy," and "brutish and uncivil manners," and owes its origin to "slavery . . . the fountain of this bitter stream." For Pennington, racism was "absurd," intellectually bankrupt, immoral and irreligious and socially harmful. It is his practical and ethical condemnation of racism that is far more effective than any attempt to engage racists on their own terms.[9]

Garnet, who like Pennington was a clergyman, rejects the notion of the existence of different "races." In his speech published as an influential pamphlet, *The Past and Present Condition and the Destiny of the Colored Race* (1848), Garnet apologizes: "In order to pursue my subject I must, for the sake of distinction, use some of the improper terms of our times. I shall, therefore, speak of *races*, when in fact there is but one race, as there was but one Adam." Garnet repeatedly argues that it is the "condition" of the "colored race" rather than its color, physical attributes, or nature that shapes racism. His pamphlet is for the most part a refutation of racism by recalling the biblical and secular history of Africans rather than dignifying the pseudoscience of race with a response. An antiemigrationist at this point, Garnet predicts that "This western world is destined to be filled with a mixed race" and racism would cease to matter. Calling for unity of political action among black abolitionists, he argued that only African American activism and abolitionism could end the injustices of slavery and racism in this country.[10]

Other black abolitionists such as Douglass and Delany chose to refute the "science" of "races" on the terrain of contemporary scholarship. Delany reverted to advocating black emigration and a separation of the "races" after the failure of Reconstruction. Nevertheless, he continued to "discard" the pseudoscientific premise of polygenesis and, anticipating the findings of modern science, insisted that Africans were the first humans in his *Principia of Ethnology* (1879). In his famous speech, "The Claims of the Negro Ethnologically Considered" (1854), Douglass argued, anticipating W.E.B. Du Bois, that "the relation subsisting between the white and black people of this country is the vital question of the age." No amount of "scientific moonshine" or the "southern pretenders to science" could place black men on a "sliding scale of humanity" or see them as less than human. Complaining that pseudoscientific racists compared the most "degraded" black men with "those of the highest cultivation," Douglass memorably wrote that the "very crimes of slavery become slavery's best defense." While he argued that environmental influences can explain diversity among mankind, Douglass insisted on the unity of man and the universal application of human rights. Noting how different peoples and areas of the world had become connected for the first time, he chided:

> I say it is remarkable—nay, it is strange that there should arise a phalanx of learned men—speaking in the name of *science*—to forbid the magnificent reunion of mankind in one brotherhood. A mortifying proof is here given, that the moral growth of a nation, or an age, does not always keep pace with the increase of knowledge, and suggests the necessity to increase human love with human learning.

Douglass's answer to the pseudoscience of race or "ethnology" in nineteenth-century parlance, did not just invoke environmentalism but was also more broadly philosophical and ethical in the tradition of secular Enlightenment thought.[11]

The roots of black abolitionist historiography that dealt with the growth of the black radical tradition and African Americans' intellectual engagement with the problems of slavery and racism lay firmly among black abolitionists themselves. Not only did their sensibility carry over to the first generation of historians who wrote about black abolitionism, many of their insights on black participation in the abolitionist movement, the interracial nature of the movement, its connection to broader traditions of black resistance have been developed in contemporary historical scholarship on African American abolitionists. In this sense, African American abolitionists act not just as subjects of black abolitionist historiography but also its founders.

The first generation of black historians, most of whom worked outside of the academy, and were generally unrecognized by it, continued to write the history of abolitionism in the tradition of black abolitionists. Even as prominent American historians and revisionist historians of the Civil War and Reconstruction sought to discredit the abolition movement and demonize its leaders as irresponsible fanatics, their legacy lay safe in the hands of African American historians and intellectuals. Archibald Grimke, the son of South Carolina slaves and an intrepid advocate of black rights, wrote some of the first biographies of Garrison, Wendell Phillips, and Charles Sumner. In his massive two-volume *History of the Negro Race*, George Washington Williams, arguably the first professional black historian, devoted two celebratory chapters to the abolition movement, one of which detailed the efforts of African Americans in the movement against slavery. W.E.B. Du Bois wrote a sympathetic biography of John Brown. In his magnum opus, *Black Reconstruction* (1935), Du Bois defended the political activism of the Southern black masses and Radical Republicans like Sumner and Thaddeus Stevens, heirs of the antebellum interracial struggle for black equality.[12]

Early African American historians such as Carter G. Woodson, the father of black history, Charles H. Wesley, and Dorothy Porter Wesley served essentially as the archivists of black abolitionism, reproducing and reprinting long-forgotten speeches, pamphlets, letters, narratives, and the proceedings and addresses of meetings, associations, and conventions. They also produced some of the earliest scholarly biographies of prominent black abolitionists.[13] In the era of Jim Crow, disfranchisement, and lynching, an implicit political function underlay their "objective" histories of the race. The dual purpose of education and protest, though somewhat muted, lived on in their works. And just as an alternative view of slavery can be found in their writings when the plantation myth held sway among American historians, they produced an alternative history of abolition, especially black abolition. Without the painstaking works of Woodson, the Wesleys, and later, Herbert Aptheker, Phillip S. Foner, Howard Bell, and Dorothy Sterling the historiography of black abolitionism would have been stillborn. It was due to their work that some historical surveys of the abolition movement by Louis Filler and especially Dwight Dumond mentioned African American abolitionists.[14]

The efforts of early historians of black abolitionists to document their

history and develop a published and easily accessible archive of black abolitionism also lives on in contemporary collections of black abolitionist papers and pamphlets edited by C. Peter Ripley and John Blassingame,
among others. This prominent genre in black abolitionist historiography,
the publication of primary sources, testifies to the repeated efforts of generations of historians to make a case for the saliency of black abolitionism.[15]

More than any other historian, Benjamin Quarles must be viewed as the
progenitor of modern black abolitionist historiography. Trained at the
University of Wisconsin, Madison, Quarles's dissertation became the first
authoritative, published modern biography of Frederick Douglass. His
most important work, *Black Abolitionists* (1969), was the first comprehensive text on the subject at a time when most historians of abolitionism still
viewed the movement as a predominantly white, middle-class movement.
In fact, the biggest debate in the field, when Quarles started writing, revolved around whether abolitionism must be viewed as primarily Western
and evangelical in inspiration, as Gilbert Barnes and Dumond argued, or
as a Garrisonian, New England–based movement. In the post–World War
II era, some of the most influential essays on abolition uncritically borrowed methods and theories from the social sciences to produce modern
updates of the revisionists' "irresponsible-fanatics" thesis. Stanley Elkins
saw abolitionists as essentially anti-institutional and destructive in orientation and David Donald portrayed them as suffering from status anxiety, as
social misfits and psychological basket cases. Donald's influential two-
volume "psychobiography" of Charles Sumner and John Thomas's unsym-
pathetic biography of William Lloyd Garrison drew far more attention
than Quarles's book on Douglass. Even Aileen Kraditor's masterful *Means
and Ends in American Abolitionism* (1967), which effectively challenged
these historians and produced the most sophisticated understanding of
Garrisonian abolitionism and the issues involved in the abolitionist split of
1839–40 that we have, virtually ignored black abolitionists including Douglass, whose purchase appeared in the book as a matter of controversy
among white abolitionists. Quarles's detailed 1938 essay on the breach between Douglass and Garrison, which he characterized as marked by ideological and political differences rather than simply as personal or racial,
escaped her attention.[16]

Given the state of abolitionist studies in the postwar period, it is no wonder that Quarles felt compelled to simply document the presence of
African Americans in the abolition movement. He explained that his approach sought "to reduce any credibility gap" and hoped that it did not de-
scend to "mere cataloguing." In this sense, Quarles's scholarship, as August
Meier has noted, harks back to an older black historiography. In an earlier

essay, he had reproduced letters written by black abolitionists to Gerrit Smith, the abolitionist "sage of Peterboro." Quarles was not only continuing the tradition of archival work but also showing the strength and numbers of black abolitionists in the north. "With a few exceptions," he wrote, "Smith received at least one letter from every literate Negro who was prominent in the North during the twenty years preceding the Civil War." Quarles clearly highlighted the political partnership that Smith forged with African Americans that led him to set aside land grants for free blacks from his substantial estate in New York and to support John Brown's raid at Harpers Ferry.[17]

Quarles's *Black Abolitionists,* unlike his previous work, goes beyond contributionism and acts as a bridge to the new history of black abolitionism. Here Quarles, by drawing attention to African Americans' foundational contribution to the rise of Garrisonian immediatism and to the distinct ideological debates among black abolitionists, illustrated the centrality of African Americans to the movement. In his reading, black Americans were not just passive victims but architects of their own liberation, a premise that undergirds much of black history today. As he concludes, "To the extent that America had a revolutionary tradition, he [the black man] was its protagonist no less than its symbol." Indeed, the influence of the republican tradition on black thought lay at the heart of Quarles's numerous works on black history, which include *The Negro in the American Revolution* (1961), *The Negro in the Making of America* (1964), and *The Negro in the Civil War* (1953). Using Douglass's brilliant Fourth of July address as a starting point, Quarles argued how the "spirit of '76" influenced a host of black abolitionists. The American Revolution was, as he put it, a "black Declaration of Independence," too. The wide-ranging influence of Quarles's original emphasis on the importance of Revolutionary thought for early black protest is evident by the way in which this idea is taken for granted by most contemporary scholars writing on black abolitionism. But as his later books on John Brown and African Americans, *Allies for Freedom* (1974) and *Blacks on John Brown* (1972), demonstrate, Quarles's appreciation of black abolitionists' appropriation of Revolutionary republicanism was never simply a matter of celebrating ideas divorced from the necessity of radical action.[18]

With the onset of the civil rights movement and the rise of the new black history, several historians joined Quarles in fostering a new appreciation of the "radicalness" of the abolition movement.[19] As works on abolition proliferated after the 1960s, the field of abolitionist studies broke along racial lines, with few scholars willing to bridge the gap. In a departure from the scholarship of Quarles and his predecessors, works by Jane and William Pease and Leon Litwack tended to stress racism within the movement. But while the Peases argued for the ineffectiveness of African Americans, Litwack more usefully traced the growth of an autonomous black radical tradition, the "emancipation," as he called it, of the black abolitionist from a white-dominated movement.[20] On the other hand, none of the broader studies on abolition, which explored various aspects of abolitionist thought and expanded our understanding of the political, ideological, and religious inspirations for the movement, paid much attention to black abolitionists. Instead, in most cases, they castigated pro forma the racialist or racist thought of white abolitionists.[21] In his classic book on racism in American history published at this time, George Fredrickson memorably dubbed white northerners' and abolitionists' racial attitudes as "romantic racialism." A recent scholar has gone so far as to hold African Americans, who allegedly internalized Northern racial discourses, also complicit in "the construction of race" in the antebellum north.[22] Ironically, the emphasis on "race" and racial difference leaves us with little appreciation of the black protest tradition and its influence on the ideology and tactics of the abolition movement as a whole. It presents us with a victimization model of free blacks and abolitionists, a Northern counterpart, one might say, of Stanley Elkins's long-discredited Sambo thesis for Southern slaves.

The dominant nationalist sensibility of the new black history, which came into being during the black power or nationalist phase of the civil rights movement, further segregated the history of African American abolitionists though it considerably enriched our comprehension of the long tradition of black protest in this country. Vincent Harding's eloquent *There Is a River* (1981) squarely placed black abolitionists in the broader historical trajectory of black resistance to slavery. But he was critical of Douglass and other black abolitionists for relying on the goodwill of white Americans and their ability to change. According to Harding, the African identity and ethos of black people as victims of racist oppression rather than the interracial movement for abolition and racial equality was the proper setting for an authentic black radicalism.

Recent studies of black nationalism have exploded the dualism of separatism versus integration by revealing how these categories simplify rather than describe the thought of prominent pre–Civil War black leaders. Nor can black nationalism be viewed simply as a project devoted to black emigration outside the United States divorced from the numerous efforts at institution building that characterized free black communities throughout the country since the American Revolution. And though black nationalism has commonly been portrayed as the most radical tendency in African American political thought, historians such as Wilson Moses and, more extremely, Tunde Adeleke have pointed to the Western, Christian, and "civilizational" orientation of nineteenth-century black nationalists. According to Adeleke, it made them surrogates of European imperialism in Africa. While it is probably unfair to hold African American leaders responsible for the crimes of imperialism, such work helps us reevaluate the easy use of the terms "conservative" and "radical" to characterize different variants of black abolitionism.[23] African American abolitionists, like their white counterparts, subscribed to a variety of political projects and beliefs in their struggle against slavery and racism and it would be simplistic to tar them all with one brush or place them in ideological boxes of our own making.

Some historians have even viewed Southern slaves as proponents of a truly radical black nationalism as opposed to the more integrationist and supposedly bourgeois mindset of most Northern black abolitionists. They have of course missed out on Du Bois's and Harding's attempts to argue for a unified black protest tradition that included slave rebels as well as black abolitionists and that arguably came together during the heady days of Reconstruction in an attempt to inaugurate an interracial democracy in this country. It would be ahistorical to differentiate too deeply between traditions of slave resistance and northern black activism, which influenced each other and grew in tandem. There was no chasm between Southern slavery and black abolitionism nor was identification with slaves merely a political ploy on the part of African American abolitionists. Some Northern blacks were sold South to circumvent emancipation laws, and throughout the antebellum period free African Americans were fair game for kidnappers who sold them into Southern slavery. Fugitive slaves, in fact, were disproportionately represented among black abolitionists in the late antebellum period and the fugitive slave issue or, one might say, slave resistance fostered a radical response from Northern black communities and abolitionists. Historian Ira Berlin has gone so far as to call Northern blacks "maroon" communities of runaway slaves, with even the freeborn living under the perpetual shadow of racial slavery.[24]

Despite the long and painful demise of slavery and continued legal discrimination in the free states, Northern blacks no doubt could develop a more vocal tradition of protest and autonomous institutions than Southern slaves or free black people. Litwack's pathbreaking book on the Northern free black population powerfully evoked the pervasive racism faced by them, their political disfranchisement and precarious position in the northern economy. However, studies by Shane White, Gary Nash, James and Lois Horton, Leonard Curry, Craig Wilder, Christopher Phillips, among others, have rekindled an appreciation of the immense community-building efforts of a largely impoverished people and the grassroots nature of black political and social activism. The founding of black churches, literary societies, schools, and the black press is testimony to the practical, institutional side of black nationalism and ideas of racial autonomy. The Hortons have been most successful in combining the history of Northern free black people with that of black abolitionism. Their synthesis of the history of Northern blacks, in contrast to Litwack's emphasis on white racism, stresses both community building and political activism. More recently, Leslie Harris has sought to combine both approaches with an analysis of growing class differentiation within New York city's black community.[25]

If the social histories of Northern black communities have added depth to our picture of the growth of black abolitionism, the proliferation of biographies of prominent African American abolitionist men and women has revived the field. The persistence of biography as a way to recover the history of black abolitionism is a testimony to how much the writings of black abolitionists continue to shape the field. As Blackett, who has astutely defended this genre, writes, a "touch of filiopietism" is "essential to good biography." Biographies of not just prominent black abolitionists like Douglass, Delany, and Garnet, but also of lesser-known figures such as Richard Allen, Paul Cuffee, James Forten, John Mercer Langston, Jermain Loguen, and J.W.C. Pennington have finally given us a collective portrait of black abolitionism.[26] In fact, the theoretical sophistication of the intellectual biographies of Douglass by David Blight and Waldo Martin, of Delany and Douglass by Robert S. Levine, of Sojourner Truth by Nell Painter, of David Walker by Peter Hinks, and recently, of the Revolutionary-era black clergyman Lemuel Haynes by John Saillant have marked the coming of age of black abolitionist biography.

The "new black intellectual history," as Patrick Rael has dubbed it, has finally put to rest the conclusions of Frederick Cooper's influential yet glib view of black abolitionism as narrowly characterized by the ideas of moral uplift and self-improvement and as a reflection of dominant white middle-class or Victorian and bourgeois values. Cooper's politically defanged and intellectually bankrupt black abolitionist leaders appeared as self-serving individuals divorced from the plight of Southern slaves and Northern black masses. In his article on the Glasgow-trained physician and abolitionist, James McCune Smith, Blight instead revealed the complexity of black abolitionist ideology. McCune Smith meditated extensively on ideas of uplift along with the issues of identity, class, education, community, protest, violence, emigration, and racism. And as a radical black intellectual, he struggled to connect with the anonymous, toiling black workers he wrote about. Similarly, Martin's and Blight's works on Douglass reveal him to be an original and astute thinker, whose understanding and use of American political traditions of millennial nationalism, Revolutionary republicanism, and democracy was matched by few of his contemporaries. Levine's subtle study of Delany and Douglass further illustrates that they did not represent two ideological poles in black abolitionism. Rather, the two men played their ideas against, and influenced, each other. Saillant's biography not only recovers the integrity of Haynes's orthodox Calvinism and revolutionary thought but also provides us with the first intellectually coherent rendition of eighteenth-century black abolitionism.[27] The picture we have of black abolitionism is far richer and more complex thanks to the work of these historians.

Three important books on antebellum black abolitionism have also overturned Cooper's unfavorable assessment of black abolitionist ideology and the Peases' dismal conclusion that African American abolitionism was a grand failure. In his *Building an Antislavery Wall* (1983), Blackett insisted on the startling and unique success of black abolitionist speakers in the propaganda war over slavery in Britain. African American abolitionists, he argued, helped construct a cordon sanitaire against racial slavery in the Atlantic world. Patrick Rael's detailed work on antebellum black protest also makes a strong case for its impact in the public sphere. His study of African American ideas on uplift, nation building, race, and identity has produced the most comprehensive look at black abolitionist ideology to date. Eddie Glaude's work on antebellum black nationalism builds on and deepens Harding's insight of African Americans' sense of their own history as part of a providential design dominated by the religious motif of Exodus, and their identification with the enslavement and suffering of the children of Israel. His analysis, a product of the current sophistication in conceptualizing black nationalism that does not simply equate it with racial separatism and emigrationism, argues for the redemptive power in black nationalism to save the soul of American democracy, what he calls "soul-craft politics."[28]

With the exception of Blackett, who includes Sarah Parker Remond in his discussion of abolition's unofficial black ambassadors, much of the new scholarship on black abolitionism chooses not to deal with the issue of gender or African American women. Ironically, in this respect, some of the older "contributionist" historians were more broad ranging and inclusive than their considerably more sophisticated descendants. This unfortunate fact also reflects the emergence of women's history as a distinct field of inquiry and the gendered division of labor among historians, a characteristic that marks recent studies of both white and black abolitionists. A further subdivision in the study of female abolitionists has most studies of white women abolitionists ignoring the thought and efforts of African American women.[29]

However, in the last decade or so the study of black women abolitionists has also come of age and matches the theoretical complexity of the new black intellectual history. The groundbreaking work done by Nell Painter, Carla Peterson, Melba Boyd, Jane Rhodes, Jennifer Fleischner, Brenda

Stevenson, Jean Fagan Yellin, Francis Smith Foster, Gayle Tate, and Shirley Yee has challenged the invisibility of black women in abolitionist studies. In her deeply researched biography of Truth, Painter reveals how much Truth herself, as the white feminist abolitionists who wrote about and for her, was responsible for the construction of her public persona. She deftly traces the triumph of the symbolic Truth while detailing the life story of the historical Truth. Biographies of Francis Ellen Watkins Harper and Mary Ann Shadd Cary by Boyd and Rhodes present us for the first time with a full-bodied and complete picture of these women's lives, writings, and activism. Their work belongs as much to the broader genre of biography in black abolitionist historiography as they do to black women's history and literature. But if biographies of prominent African American women abolitionists present them often as loners, Peterson's study of black women speakers and writers in the North resurrects a community of activist "race women," who shared a distinct position on questions of racial and gender oppression.[30] This growing and diverse body of scholarship on black women abolitionists has undoubtedly contributed to the contemporary renaissance in black abolitionist historiography.

As the above survey of black abolitionist historiography reveals, we have at present an embarrassment of riches. However, even as the field explodes with new books, fresh insights, and the historical recovery of long-forgotten figures, little attempt has been made to connect this work with the history of the abolition movement as a whole or reevaluate it in light of its findings. Discussions of the influence of black abolitionism on Garrisonian immediatism usually stop short in the 1830s. A new synthesis of the abolition movement, which would explore the place and the extent of influence of African Americans in the movement, is overdue. One can argue for the importance of black abolitionism without ignoring some of the most influential theorists of the movement: Garrison, Wendell Phillips, Lydia Maria Child, Theodore Weld, the Grimke sisters, James Birney, Thomas Wentworth Higginson, Gerrit Smith, and many other lesser-known white abolitionists. And the range and significance of the black presence in abolition should hardly be confined to a mere muckraking of the racialism of their white allies.

The curse of specialization has fallen hard on abolitionist studies, which are now much richer than in previous years but also considerably more fragmented. Some of the most exciting new research in abolition is being done on women and African Americans. Ironically, while the study of abolition has expanded beyond the disciplinary boundaries of history into literature and cultural studies, the new historiography of black abolitionism has yet to make a decisive impact on that of the abolition movement.

We still await a broad new historical synthesis of abolition that would reflect the dramatic expansion in the study of African American and female abolitionists. Black abolitionist historiography has come of age and is poised to revive the relatively dormant state of abolitionist studies. To borrow terminology from post-colonial theory, the periphery will redefine the center.

PART TWO

Origins

3

Geographies of Liberty:
A Brief Look at Two Cases

T.K. Hunter

In late November 1771, on the river Thames in London, a ship rode at anchor bobbing in the swells. Smoke and damp hung in the air; river rats—lured by rubbish and the plenty it provided—foraged undeterred by the chill. In the dimness of a ship's hold—well-secured out of sight and sound of anyone above deck or on shore—James Somerset did the only thing he could do: he waited. Somerset was a member of the African diaspora and, by bill of sale in one of Britain's North American colonies, an enslaved person. Two years earlier, Somerset had been on board a similar ship but under less confining circumstances as he traveled with Charles Stuart, his master, from colonial Boston to Britain's metropole. While in London he ran away and, once found, had been delivered at the behest of his master into the hands of John Knowles, captain of the *Ann and Mary*.

In theory, the change in Somerset's whereabouts, from one place in the empire to another, would not effect a change in his status: in either place, he was still a slave. In practice, however, Somerset's particular geographic relocation carried with it the potential to challenge the legal effectiveness of the designation of "slave." Unbeknownst to him, Stuart's decision to bring Somerset with him from America to Britain forced a revision of certain legal precedents regarding slavery and freedom in the Atlantic world. Whereas previous cases rested on the question "*What* is the law?" Somerset's future hinged in a new, more consequential question: "*Where* is the law?"

More than fifty years after Britain lost her North American colonies, a little girl traveled from New Orleans to Boston on a journey similar to Somerset's transatlantic voyage. In the spring of 1836, Mary Slater, the wife of a slaveowner, prepared to depart from the South around the first of May for a visit of some length to her father in Boston. With her was an enslaved child about six years of age, a little girl called Med. Together Med and her mistress traveled north. They participated in a time-honored seasonal flight from the fatigue of intense heat, sailing away from the humidity and

the enervating summer climate of New Orleans to the comparative coolness of Boston.

Like Somerset, Med's journey required her to traverse the geographies
of slavery and freedom. However, instead of crossing an ocean and being
brought to London from the colonial periphery, Med journeyed within the
United States. As a result, Somerset and Med found themselves at the center of important court cases whose purpose it was to determine publicly
their relationship to liberty. However, neither case could have been
heard—that is, with the hope of a favorable decision—if their respective
relocations had not been embedded in the ideological debates then current in the Atlantic world. At the core of both excursions was this: James
Somerset and Med were taken by their masters from one legal jurisdiction
to another—with differing legal attitudes toward slavery. How regretful
their masters would be.[1]

The 1771–1772 *Somerset* case was a landmark in the annals of law in the
English-speaking Atlantic. Largely misinterpreted as having single-
handedly ended English slavery, the case in fact did no such thing. Its importance lies, rather, in the centrality of the ideology of a "geography of
liberty"—that is, the concept of designating a locale "free" and the potential application of such a designation. From this, certain questions arise,
namely, how could the eighteenth-century English insist that their soil—as
well as their air—was a haven for liberty while simultaneously participating
in a practice based upon the full and complete denial of liberty to African
people? Furthermore, how was Britain's geography of liberty challenged in
a legal forum when Africans entered its ideological and physical jurisdiction? Indeed, James Somerset did not run away to England; he was brought
there by his master. The *Somerset* case wrestled with this: Can the law allow
the presence of bondage within a geographic space designated by its inhabitants to be a haven—both ideologically and practically—of liberty?[2]

Commonwealth v. Aves, an American case tried in Massachusetts in 1836,
looked directly to the English *Somerset* case for its legal precedent, not only
because American law was based on English common law but because the
circumstances involved were ideologically equivalent. The case was heard
in the Massachusetts courts years after the putative end of slavery in the
state; Med's presence in Boston forced the testing of Massachusetts as a
designated locale of liberty. The child, Med, did not run away to Massachusetts in search of her liberty; like Somerset, she was brought there by her
owner. The *Commonwealth* case once again brought to the fore the same
question as *Somerset: Where* was the law applicable?

In short, the *Somerset* and *Commonwealth* cases are trenchant examples of
the deep ideological problems that arose when slaves and those who acted
on their behalf tested the limits of slavery in the context of new legal geog-

raphies. It was not physical distance that enabled each case to go forward; in a time when New World slavery thrived and "Africanness" equaled slavery, one could not necessarily count on a measure of miles to change one's status from slave to free man or woman. Rather, it was how this distance was traversed, and the nature of the geographic area on the other end of the journey, that made it possible for Somerset's and Med's advocates to advance a case to secure their liberty. The suggestion here is not that Somerset and Med were the only two slaves involved in cases that would decide their liberty, nor is it that Somerset and Med were the first and last slaves to have their liberty granted as a result of a court decision. Rather, it is to suggest that the *Somerset* and *Commonwealth* cases were emblematic of an important consideration that had until then gone strangely unexamined: the location of the law as essential to the operation of the law. Liberty, in other words, was determined by geography.

The exploration of law, liberty, and geography involves an examination of three areas that are not typically associated with one another. The convergence of liberty and law are perhaps the easiest to recognize because the former was frequently contested in courts throughout the eighteenth-century Atlantic and beyond. The articulation and subsequent flourishing of ideologies of liberty (whether those ideologies were embodied by the elite, middle, or lower classes) served to fuel the contestation of liberty in relation to politics and the law. An expanding British empire encouraged the assessment of institutional relationships that had been unfamiliar: When the political, physical, and intellectual center of government was an ocean away, what were its subjects to do regarding the arbitration of issues that surely affected the metropole, but that were—in practical terms— more immediately relevant to the colonies? Should the rigors and rhythms—the preferences and pecuniary interests—of the colony take precedence? If so, when, and under what circumstances?[3]

These were questions that deserved serious attention. Their consideration became more urgent in the context of a lucrative system of labor that filled both the purses of private citizens and the coffers of government. A thriving slave trade and all that it entailed created difficult challenges regarding the individual slave—and, by implication, the institution of slavery, in terms of his or her relation to legal and spatial ideologies of liberty. Indeed, while slaves were shipped en masse from Africa to Britain's New World colonies in the Caribbean and in North America, many were brought to Britain *individually* by their masters—a simple act of transportation that was fraught with unforeseen complications and consequences.[4]

But the geography under discussion isn't simply "here" versus "there" as indicated on a map. After all, there are no lines drawn in the dirt, no color-coding in the soil to designate separate areas of sovereignty—whether those areas are colonies, states, or nations. Geographies are separated by something even more powerful than physical borders; they are separated by ideologies. Ideological constructions lie at the heart of geographic demarcations. What, then, would happen to slaves as they moved from one legally discrete locale to another, where protean but nonetheless widely circulating ideologies of liberty were themselves contested? What would happen if changes were made to the physical, ideological, and legal ground on which they were based? Such questions illustrate the potential implications of geography by underscoring the role geography plays in the consideration of the law.

Enslaved Africans were treated as commercial items—both vendible and movable. As chattel property, the enslaved were subject to a host of municipal laws, all of which varied according to time and space. Indeed, despite the fact that the British empire encompassed a vast territory, defined politically as one entity, its laws were far from consistent. Courts were frequently surprised by cases that highlighted the lack of legal uniformity across the empire. Many a case concerning liberty and the status of Africans in relation to the law thus involved the careful determination of the question of primacy of municipal laws.

The intersection of law and geography bears crucially upon how certain questions were addressed and resolved within the context of movable chattel property, shifting locations, and the ways in which political and social ideologies were upheld and applied. Geographies—areas that are circumscribed and delimited in order to physically include or exclude—help to define law, and law, in turn, helps to define geographies. As such, at its simplest and most straightforward, English law held sway within the geographic borders that defined England; French law held sway within the geographic borders that defined France, and so forth. However, when a country had colonies that were at once independent and co-dependent, the importance of geography in relation to the law, and law in relation to geography, quickly becomes more complex. When colonies devised procedures and laws based on those of the home country, what was the extent to which those laws bolstered or extended, superceded, or even contravened certain procedures and laws back home? Consistency would certainly ease the physical transition from colony to metropole. But as Africans were moved around—or moved themselves around—from one locale to another, their movement soon begged the persistent and uncomfortable question: What was the status of Africans in relation to the law and to ideologies that were supported or circumvented by the law within a particular locale?[5]

In the case of England, it was not the mere presence of Africans that posed a problem; they were there as early as the sixteenth century. Neither were inhabitants of Massachusetts unfamiliar with people of African descent. Rather, it was the ideological questions that their presence as slaves raised that precipitated certain difficulties—difficulties that were brought to the courts for resolution. In England, a country described by its inhabitants as fundamentally free—as a place whose very soil and air was free—the presence of enslaved Africans challenged the ideology of liberty. In 1830s Massachusetts, where slavery had been abolished according to many and where liberty and natural rights were ostensibly guaranteed to all people within its boundaries, the enslaved posed similar challenges. Would the presence of transplanted slaves on free soil influence their status in relation to the law? In other words, by being relocated, could slaves become free?[6]

Within the context of the British tradition, it is important to understand that common law is best defined in relation to what it is not—that is, statute law. Common law consists of "those principles and rules of action relating to the government and security of persons and of property which derive their authority solely from usages and customs of immemorial antiquity." It is the expression and operation of customs and actions whose existence is frequently described as "ancient and immemorial." Eighteenth-century England operated under common law. Like all law, common law was a balancing act: preeminence was given neither to ancient practices nor to what was called "the sudden changes of a present arbitrary power." Statute law, by contrast, is legislative: "that body of law created by acts of the legislature." While the purpose here is not to discuss the merits of legal systems, suffice it to say that as a legal system, common law is thorny, messy, and frustrating for those who prefer the clarity of statutes; nonetheless, it is extraordinary. In its basis upon "ancient usages" and customs, one can more clearly see the formation and persistence of various ideologies in common law as they were outlined.[7]

The 1772 *Somerset* case was a signal event in the annals of British common law. Although it was not the first case that decided in favor of the liberty of an enslaved man, it was a landmark because of the grounds on which it was argued, its extensive coverage in English newspapers, its apparently uncategorical statements about the heinous character of slavery (in light of natural rights), and finally, its seeming refusal to guarantee to slaveholders protection of the property they held dear when they brought their slaves to England. Many aspects of the arguments were compelling, but the most powerful—and certainly the most enduring—was the insistence upon the longstanding and unique character of English soil—it was free and would not support the abject bondage that was by definition African slavery. Only positive law (law specifically enacted), declared Lord Mansfield (the chief justice who heard the case), might allow the presence of that species of bondage, but then whether or not such law superceded the enduring free character of English soil remained questionable.[8]

England had a longstanding practice whereby a foreigner or slave who set foot upon its soil became *eo instanti* free. In his *Commentaries on the Laws of England,* William Blackstone noted that both the idea and practice of civil liberty flourished and had nearly perfect expression in England. Furthermore, he asserted that not only was the spirit of liberty firmly embedded in the English constitution, it was "rooted even in our very soil." The power of that soil, therefore, freed all who set foot upon it—whatever his state. As Blackstone insisted, "a slave or a negro, the moment he lands in England, falls under the protection of the laws, and with regard to all natural rights becomes *eo instanti* a freeman." But Blackstone was not the author of the idea of instantaneous freedom upon setting foot on English soil. The sentiment was expressed by Edward Chamberlayne in his *Angliae Notitia or The Present State of England* (1669) and prior to that in Raphael Holinshed's *Chronicles of England* (1580), which stated that "[s]laves in England are none since Christianity prevailed. A slave brought into England, is upon landing *ipso facto* free from slavery, but not from ordinary service" and "[a]s for slaves and bondsmen, we have none; nay, such is the privilege of our country by the especial Grace of God and bounty of our princes, that if any come hither from other realms, so soon as they set foot on the land they become so free of condition as their masters, whereby all note of servile bondage is utterly removed from them." The liberty inherent in England's very soil and its character effectively transformed slaves and bondsmen into free men.[9]

English slaves were not in abundance in England, and English law appeared ill-prepared to address the question of enslaved Africans. As Africans increasingly came before the English courts, various counsel for individual masters or plantation merchants devised arguments against the liberty of Africans and favorable to their clients—arguments that turned on such points as the vendibility of Africans and their status as heathens. Africans might be bought and sold in all locales because it was customary to buy and sell them throughout the continent of Africa, not to mention Britain's New World plantation colonies. In a handy bit of circular reasoning, Africans' status as non-Christians gave license to good Christian men to buy or sell them: Africans were vendible heathens because they were bought and sold, and they were bought and sold precisely because they were vendible heathens. However, as Africans made the potentially transformative passage from heathen to Christian, their journey brought them closer to being considered in the light of liberty.

As Africans were brought to England—either singly or in small groups—they were brought to both a political center where their presence shattered the silence of the metropole, and to a locale with a long tradition of being characterized as free. Their presence as they came before the courts destabilized the meaning of "slave" and transformed the arena in which the status quo of enslaved Africans—quite literally, their relationship to the law—would be discussed.[10]

The first known reported instance that addressed the status of Africans in Britain in relation to the law was the 1677 *Butts v. Penny* case—a handful of printed lines that emphasized the extra-Christian status of Africans, offered no final judgment, and, strictly speaking, established no legal precedent. While there *might* have been property in Africans "sufficient to maintain trover," the indecision also suggested that there *might not* have been property in Africans sufficient to maintain trover. In short, Africans, neither by virtue of their "Africanness" nor by virtue of the fact that they had been enslaved, were not always considered de facto goods or chattel. The initial legal uncertainty concerning their status in relation to the law would later be an advantage when confronting questions of liberty.

The court cases in the years between *Butts v. Penny* (1677) and *Somerset* (1771–72) are too numerous to be summarized here. Suffice it to say that only twenty years after *Butts*, in the case of *Chamberlain v. Harvey* (1697), arguments used by counsel for the defense assisted in skewing the meaning of slave while highlighting the importance of geography. The enslaved man in question was unnamed at the time and remains so today. Nevertheless, his passage from Barbados to England at the hands of his master (who later turned him out of his service), his baptism into the Church of England, and his subsequent service to several masters, forced the consideration of the efficacy of colonial Barbadian law on the legal condition of the unnamed man once he was brought to England. Chamberlain was denied his so-called slave inheritance, the denial of which questioned the durability of forced associations forged in other locales when those relationships entered a new geography considered to be conducive to liberty.[11]

Seventy-five years later, Chief Justice William Murray, Lord Mansfield agonized over a decision concerning questions that pertained to the nature of English soil, the law's *in favorem libertatis* tendency, and the potential limits of slavery in England. He encountered the task of ruling on the status of James Somerset, who, having run away several years after living in London with his master, was captured and prepared for forcible removal to and resale in the Caribbean plantation colonies.[12]

A writ of habeas corpus directed the ship's captain, John Knowles, to present Somerset before Mansfield at the beginning of the legal proceedings. And in the course of describing his relationship to Somerset's master, Charles Stuart, Knowles included an interesting set of statements about Somerset's status. Somerset had been brought from Africa where there

had been and still were great numbers of "negro slaves." Moreover, there
was still a trade

> carried on by his majesty's subjects, from Africa to his majesty's
> colonies or plantations of Virginia and Jamaica in America, and
> other colonies and plantations belonging to his majesty in America,
> for the necessary supplying of the aforesaid colonies and plantations
> with negro slaves; and that negro slaves brought in the course of the
> said trade . . . have been, and are saleable and sold as goods and chat-
> tels, and upon the sale thereof have become and been, and are the
> slaves and property of the purchases thereof.

The attempt to establish Somerset's past sanctioned vendibility throughout the geographies encompassed by Britain's New World colonies, and his
continued chattel condition when brought to England recalled a combination of arguments employed in previous cases.[13]

In the ensuing years, however, the terms of discussion surrounding the
question of the enslaved in England and their status in relation to the law
had in some measure changed. Increasingly, arguments had been formed
against the sanctioning of slavery in England—arguments founded upon
the unique concept of "free British soil," as well as the unique character of
English law. James Somerset's counsel, Francis Hargrave, insisted that not
only did "negroes become free on being brought into this country, but that
the law of England confers the gift of liberty entire and unincumbered
[sic]; not in name only, but really and substantially." Anything less was contrary to "the genius of English law."[14]

Part of Hargrave's goal was to stake out an intellectual and legal area in
which slavery could be argued and proved a liability—particularly to the
master, but in part to the society that depended upon slavery. Though
moral arguments could be useful, what proved to be more compelling was
the rehearsal of the presence and subsequent eradication of villeinage in
England, the eradication of which was seen as a triumph of the English Enlightenment. Villeinage had sprung up under ancient "barbarous" circumstances which had been subsequently nullified; surely the country would
not willingly admit to still being "barbarous" in what was considered the
modern times of the late eighteenth century. (The eradication of a barbarous villeinage and an insistence upon English soil being free effectively
reinforced each other.) Slavery could not be considered a form of
villeinage because villeinage implied the ability to swear, to bind oneself, to
make a contract. Slavery had no contract and, furthermore, its very nature
as it was currently practiced meant that slavery was heritable and perpetual. And should the villeinage-as-anti-modern argument fail to sway, the
protection of the integrity of the genius of English law would prevail.[15]

Protecting the integrity and ascendancy of English law was exactly what Lord Mansfield adhered to as he made comments in the course of the trial, and in rendering his decision at the end of the trial. Counsel for Somerset's master contended that the relation between a Negro and his owner might well be maintained on the grounds of a contract between master and servant. Lord Mansfield, however, was on record as finding the idea of contract between master and slave "utterly repugnant and destructive of every idea of a contract between parties." It was an important articulation of Mansfield's somewhat literalist view of the law.[16]

After five months of hearing the case, Mansfield offered a closely rendered decision. He stripped away the contingent questions about whether slaves were bought and sold, whether slavery arose legitimately out of captivity in war, and whether slavery could be equated with villeinage or servanthood. These questions masked another single, awkwardly persistent one: Was slavery legitimate within the geographic limits of England? The answer to that would determine whether or not Stuart had a right to Somerset's person as a slave on free English soil, and thus a right to forcibly detain him with the express intent of willfully disposing of him in the plantation colonies.

Preferring not to directly or conclusively answer the question of slavery's legitimacy within the England's borders, Lord Mansfield offered no such decision. He insisted that the only issue to be decided in the case was whether or not the cause in the return to the writ was sufficient. In other words, was the reason for James Somerset's forcible detention in chains, at the behest of Charles Stuart, on board the *Ann and Mary* adequate? If the reason for his detention was sufficient, Somerset would be remanded, that is, returned to the rightful custody of his detainers; if insufficient, he would be released.

"The return [to the writ of habeas corpus] states," Mansfield began, "that the slave departed and refused to serve; whereupon he was kept, to be sold abroad. So high an act of dominion must be recognized by the law of the country where it is used." Never seeming to fully accord to Somerset the status of slave (despite Somerset's opposition to referring to him as such), Mansfield further implied that the legality of detaining him under such assumptions was deeply questionable. In a careful, neutral acknowledgment of the existence of the species of bondage called slavery, and the master/slave relationship in other geographic locales, Mansfield continued, noting that the "power of a master over his slave has been extremely different, in different countries." Shifting, then, to the quality of the state of slavery in relation to the law, the chief justice noted that the "state of slavery is of such a nature, that it is incapable of being introduced on any reasons, moral or political, but only by positive law, which preserves its force

long after the reasons, occasions, and time itself from whence it was created, is erased from memory. It is so odious, that nothing can be suffered to
support it, but positive law." In short, in order for slavery to be supported,
there must be a specific law established to that effect.[17]

Declaring the need for positive law to bring about the institution of slavery was not the same as saying that English soil was free, despite the fact
that the free character of English soil had been duly argued and accepted.
But it did suggest that as a locale, England encouraged liberty by requiring
the specific decree of positive law in order to legitimately introduce slavery
or its recognition on English soil.[18]

Mansfield decided that regardless of the inconveniences that might follow from his decision he could not "say this case is allowed or approved by
the law of England; and therefore the black must be discharged." The "inconveniences" to which he referred were the legitimate financial losses
sustained in the short run by Stuart, but more important, in the long run
by West Indian planters who had supported Stuart's case. Potential financial losses or not, the nurturing of liberty in a geographic locale deemed
"free" meant that even exclusionary liberty—that is, liberty not expressly
defined with enslaved Africans and their descendants in mind—when skillfully pressed, could be expanded to include African slaves. Mansfield's decision, however narrow and reluctantly rendered, in its adherence to the
letter of the law, managed to preserve the spirit and genius of English law
in the end. Because of this, because of his ruling's insistence that liberty
was contingent upon geography, James Somerset went free.[19]

In the summer of 1836, when members of the Boston Female Anti-Slavery
Society discovered the presence of the young enslaved girl named Med in the
home of a Boston resident, they insisted that no one had the right to detain
her as a slave in Massachusetts. As women and mothers, they were especially
sensitized to the perils that plagued enslaved girls; much of their work was directed by that sensitivity. They applied to an attorney—the husband of one
of their members—for his legal assistance in order for them to "claim for her
[Med] the protection of the laws of Massachusetts." Their action was predicated on the belief that Massachusetts constituted a particular geographic locale, both physically and ideologically distinct from Louisiana, where Med's
master and mistress resided. In other words, they believed it was a place singularly conducive to liberty. As in the instance of James Somerset, what appeared to be incontestable in one locale, proved to be contestable (and
favorably so) in another place. Little Med's status in relation to the law in
Louisiana (a status regarded by her master as fixed) was destabilized within
the borders of Massachusetts. Within that limited compass, the law, deeply in-
flected by the tendency towards liberty, operated differently.[20]

That Med's case was connected to *Somerset* was more than incidental. When Chief Justice Lemuel Shaw considered the case, he looked to England and *Somerset*—and to fellow jurist Lord Mansfield's reasoning. Once again, both the counsel for the enslaved and the chief justice availed themselves of the powerful arguments used in 1772: that of the character of the soil contained within the geographic boundaries of Massachusetts, and the recognition that the odious nature of slavery demanded positive law to legitimize it. Shaw noted that lawyers believed that "if a slave is brought voluntarily and unnecessarily within the limits of this State [of Massachusetts], he becomes free." In trying to ascertain the possibility of admitting the presence of slavery in Massachusetts (which he believed had been abolished by that state's constitution), Shaw determined that it was necessary to inquire how far that rule of law might be modified in its operation "by the law of other nations and states, as admitted by the comity of nations to have a limited operation within a particular state," or by U.S. laws and the nation's constitution. He decided that in considering the parameters of the law, "we may assume that the law of this State is analogous to the law of England in this respect." Shaw's statements clearly demonstrated the ideological and legal connections between the *Somerset* and *Commonwealth* cases.[21]

Med's case, heard in Massachusetts, was a legal action best understood in the larger context of an expanding United States and the growing tensions that accompanied it. As territories gained entry into the Union, the essential relationship between geography and liberty became increasingly apparent. The problem of slavery bedeviled the Union as more territories were acquired and became states. And these tensions both derived from and fueled the nation's increasing sectionalism. The question of admitting Missouri into the Union was complicated by the interplay between liberty and geography, and the 1820 Missouri Compromise contributed to its own complexities in its failure to directly address the problem of slavery. According to the Missouri Compromise, the latitudinal location at 36°30' constituted a boundary—both measurable and ideological—beyond which, to the North, slavery was prohibited; it was a legal boundary that marked places of potential liberty. The question of borders was thus integral to political debates in antebellum America: Which places would be constituted as free, and where would slavery be allowed to exist?[22]

The legal action on Med's behalf began on August 16, 1836, five days after confirming her presence at the home of Thomas Aves, Mary Slater's father. Unlike James Somerset's case, it was the state—the Commonwealth of Massachusetts—that advanced the suit. A writ of habeas corpus was served to Thomas Aves summoning him to present Med in court in a timely fashion; it was he, not his daughter, who was charged. Thomas Aves's compliance—in the form of a Return to the Writ—was witnessed by Benjamin R. Curtis who would become Aves's main counsel in the case.[23]

Once again, the court was faced with considering the effect that movement from one legal geography to another might have upon slavery and liberty. Mary Slater did not have to cross an ocean with Med in tow to experience the power of being within a new geography that was conducive to liberty. But what was the meaning of such relocation? It was a question that Benjamin Curtis, counsel for Aves and Slater, had to address. He limited his arguments to two basic questions:

1. Since by Louisiana law Med was a slave, regardless of Massachusetts law, would she be so emancipated by her visit that upon her return to Louisiana that she'd be free?
2. What is the effect of Louisiana law in Massachusetts?

The questions were straightforward. What was remarkable, however, was the tacit recognition of a concept embedded in both: the understanding that Massachusetts constituted a legal geography different from Louisiana. While the geography of antebellum America (particularly regarding slavery) was generally divided into North and South, this runs the risk of oversimplification. Indeed, the "good" (anti-slavery) North versus the "bad" (pro-slavery) South assumes a monolithic reality that was not, in fact, the case. The law in each place was not only different but shaped by particular political and legal ideologies that prevailed within specific boundaries or geographies. Put another way, neither geography nor law was black-and-white.

Courts throughout the United States had not uniformly agreed upon a legal precedent as concerned slaves who were removed to a free state. In addition, legislative acts such as the Missouri Compromise, though it declared a geographic boundary between slavery and freedom, did not address the future of slavery with any degree of finality. For example, what would occur when the provisions of the Fugitive Slave Act of 1793 encountered the boundary of the Missouri Compromise? Admittedly, there were different laws governing slaves who were brought to free states and those who escaped to them. Nevertheless, the patchwork of laws and lack of uniformity challenged the letter and the spirit of the law. A few cases in the 1820s and 1830s had been decided in favor of the slave's freedom—or, more strongly, decided that the slave, once free by residing in a geographic locale deemed free, could not be forcibly removed to a slave state. Although Med's case appeared similar on the surface, the operative word in the earlier court decisions was "residence." The slave in question had to have acquired residence in a free territory (while being held by a master) in order to effect a change in status. Med's mistress, Mrs. Slater, clearly intended to carry her back out of Massachusetts to Louisiana and she had not acquired resident status on the strength of a visit to her father. The core question, then, to be decided was: When a temporary situation obtained, what was the status of a slave brought into a free locale?[24]

Benjamin Curtis's strategy was to maintain the ascendancy of Louisiana law—the law that defined the condition of both master and slave—over the local Massachusetts law, or in legal terms: Louisiana *lex domicilli* over Massachusetts *lex loci*. The preeminence of Louisiana *lex domicilli*—that is, the law that governed the Slaters, whose home, or residence, was Louisiana—stood at the core of Curtis's question: Would Med's mere visit to the putatively liberty-loving locale of Massachusetts emancipate her in such a way that upon her return to Louisiana she would be considered free? The legal answer, he maintained, was "no," and he drew the attention of all assembled to a number of cases in which the dispute over the status of a slave who had lived on free soil was central. But residency notwithstanding, Curtis was essentially acknowledging that Med's movement to Massachusetts brought her within a different legal geography.[25]

For Curtis, *lex domicilli* must prove the more effective: little Med's status as an enslaved child derived from the locale where she had been declared a slave initially, and where her master was legally a resident. Though he did not utilize the language of English villeinage (which, in America, was not applicable), Curtis hoped to demonstrate that the child's status was equivalent to that of a *villein regardant*—in essence, attached to Slater's correlative "manor" in Louisiana. Such an attachment would not prevent her physical transportation nor would it compromise her enduring relationship to the "manor." Med's passage across geographies should not affect her, according to those who defended slavery and its continuance in locales beyond where it had been initially legislated. Pro-slavery proponents insisted upon the immutability of status. However, it should be remembered that a similar argument had been used in England to no avail. The idea of free English soil exerted an influence upon the operation of the law there. So, too, would the idea of Massachusetts's free soil be conducive to favoring liberty.[26]

Curtis suggested that comity—the legal principle by which the laws of another nation are recognized as far as practicable—should be observed in the situation, thus construing the Slaters to be legally "foreigners" in Massachusetts, and considering Louisiana the equivalent of a sovereign legal sphere with different laws. Therefore, the doctrine of comity should obtain and Massachusetts courts should be obliged to acknowledge the continued legal relationship (according to Louisiana law) between Med and her master.[27]

Ellis Gray Loring, counsel for Med, insisted by contrast that observing comity was entirely unsatisfactory on a variety of grounds, challenging it with five points. By dispensing with the treatment of Louisiana as a foreign country worthy of the courtesy of comity, Loring was able to turn to the question of *lex loci* and its admissibility (as it related to the doctrine of comity) in the case. Therefore, if one *did not* embrace Loring's statements against the applicability of the doctrine of comity of nations, were there accepted legal instances in which comity of nations did *not* take precedence over the *lex loci* of the Commonwealth of Massachusetts?[28]

There were in fact such instances—and Loring needed only to prove that slavery, though acceptable in Louisiana, fit at least one of those exceptions. Four possible situations provided the exceptions to comity of nations superseding *lex loci:* if the law offended the local morals, if it contravened the state's policy, if it violated public law, or if it offered a "pernicious example." Although Ellis Gray Loring needed only to prove one of those exceptions, he proved all four—primarily arguing the immorality of slavery. The basic question was this: Was slavery contrary to the laws of Massachusetts, or was slavery contrary to natural rights; which was determinative?[29]

This, of course, was an echo of the issue before Lord Mansfield in 1772, and Loring invoked the *Somerset* case in his arguments. He insisted, though somewhat erroneously, that the case had been largely argued and decided on the basis of slavery's immoral and corrupt character. (Francis Hargrave had in fact used morality only to punctuate his arguments about the eradication of villeinage in England.) What Loring quoted was a passage that recognized England as a place of liberty. "The air of England was declared to be too pure for slaves to breathe in," he noted, asserting the principle of a geographic locale consciously constituted as a place of liberty. It was a principle that was equally true for 1836 Massachusetts. Loring proceeded to liken Massachusetts air to English air, using the association to introduce the resonances that the Med case had with free English soil and free English air. By doing so, Loring's recognition of Massachusetts as constituting a geography of liberty becomes evident: its very soil was free. Loring also referred to another more recent English case, *Forbes v. Cochrane,* to reinforce the continued invocation of free English soil up to the present day. The *Somerset* case's reliance on the concept of free English soil, then, was not an aberration locked in time some sixty-four years in the past. Indeed, more than deploying the case of *Somerset* and the crucial reminder it provided of free English soil, *Forbes v. Cochrane* underscored the persistent power of geographies of liberty and how the law acted in concert with such geographies.[30]

Massachusetts, Loring argued, had already passed laws against slavery and it had done so with a swift decisiveness, early in the Commonwealth's history. The timing of Massachusetts laws established the long-term nature of the Commonwealth's ideological commitment to liberty. Ellis Gray Loring insisted that the "law of this Commonwealth, on slavery, from the adoption of the Constitution of Massachusetts to the ratification of the Federal Constitution, was, to all intents and purposes, the same with the law of England." It was a powerful statement, declaring as it did legal equivalency with England. But if that was not enough, Loring further asserted that "Somersett's [sic] case, in 1772, [settled] that the common law abhors, and will not endure the existence of slavery on English soil." Massachusetts law was the equivalent of English law and the soil within the geographic boundaries of Massachusetts, like England's soil, was free. Still, as with all ideologies, inconsistencies abounded and Massachusetts, like England profited from the fruits of enslaved labor even as it championed liberty.[31]

Inconsistencies notwithstanding, the prospect of allowing the master-slave relationship to continue within locales that tended toward liberty often meant admitting slavery in all of its various consequences. Even the slightest allowance for slavery in Massachusetts or anywhere else brought with it the attendant evils of the institution; it was impossible to admit slavery by partial measures. Similarly, it is ideologically impossible to speak of liberty in partial terms. Both, of course, can be rationalized, and were rationalized. But the conditions are fundamental, constitutive: one is enslaved or not, one has liberty or not.

In the end, Chief Justice Lemuel Shaw gave his opinion on the Med case. The question to be answered with great care can be broken down into its several parts:

- Can a citizen of a state where slavery is recognized and established leave that state for a limited amount of time, for either vacation or business purposes?
- Can he stay in a state (for a period of time, but without acquiring residence there) where slavery is not recognized, carrying a slave with him as a personal attendant?
- Can he restrict the slave's liberty for the duration of the trip, and finally convey the slave out of the state without the slave's consent?

These were complex questions which, as with the *Somerset* case, had the potential for causing startling shifts in the way liberty and slavery were understood. And again, as in *Somerset*, the chief justice's opinion was rendered on a comparatively narrow point: Shaw was careful to note that the general rights of a master over his slave were not at issue, just as Lord Mansfield asserted that contracts for the sale of slaves were legitimate in England and thus were not in dispute in the case.

Shaw included in his lengthy opinion a review of the history of the Commonwealth's laws—both before and after the adoption of the Constitution of the United States—as they related to the institution of slavery. This opinion went as far back as the Massachusetts Body of Liberties (1641), which stated that there should be "no bond slavery, villanage [sic], or captivity amongst us."[32] Much like Edward Chamberlayne's *Angliae Notitia* (1669), a written declaration of the ideological character of England and the soil within its geographic boundaries, Shaw's invocation of the Body of Liberties demonstrated a similar ideological pedigree. Although the seventeenth-century document did not declare Massachusetts soil free in so many words, it did serve to underscore the longstanding tendency toward liberty within its borders. In addition, the chief justice pronounced that at the very least, the 1780 Massachusetts Declaration of Rights abolished slavery in that state—should anyone be so foolish as to argue that the earlier codified examples of the intolerance of slavery in Massachusetts were invalid. Furthermore, the state's jurisprudential history was consistent with the Declaration of Rights. On the one hand, Justice Shaw observed that both slavery and the slave trade were considered contrary to natural rights, but that judicial decisions of England and America admitted that slavery was not contrary to the law of nations. (That is, clearly nations did not outlaw slavery, but an adherence to the belief in natural rights did.) On the other hand, slavery was by its nature odious, but it *could* exist by positive law, as Mansfield's Somerset decision indicated. Such twistings and turnings proved crucial to Shaw's ability to establish that while the thought of slavery was invidious to some, it was entirely possible, under the proper legal circumstances, for it to be admissible.

Acknowledging that slavery was a relationship founded in force, not in right, and thus under the protection of local law (in that case, the law of Louisiana) beyond the bounds of which it ceases to be recognized, Shaw concluded that it could not exist within the Commonwealth of Massachusetts because "it is contrary to natural right, and repugnant to numerous provisions of the constitution and laws, designed to secure the liberty and personal rights of all persons within its limits." Within the geography described by Massachusetts resided provisions designed not just to favor the liberty of those who came within its borders, but to actively secure that liberty.[33]

Finally, Shaw pronounced that in the opinion of the court a slave owner from a slavery-sanctioning state who voluntarily brought a slave with him to the state of Massachusetts had no authority to detain the slave against his will or to carry him back out of the state in order to return him to slavery. Here is the operative phrase: "to the state of Massachusetts." It was a phrase that recognized and endorsed a geography of liberty described by actual borders and whose effect was limited to the space within those borders. Like Somerset, Med could neither be summarily detained nor removed from that particular place against her wishes. Thus it was that Med—James Somerset's ideological heir—went free.

The geographies of liberty of 1772 England and 1836 Massachusetts, though varied, had been constructed long before the cases of either James Somerset or Little Med came before the courts. And in the process of being constructed, the inhabitants of those locales gave little thought to Africans and their descendants. Such lack of thought regarding enslaved Africans had the potential to cut both ways legally. As Lord Mansfield noted, concurring with a fellow jurist, "the law takes no notice of Negroes"; it was a statement that potentially provided hope while simultaneously propagating further confusion. Though it was meant to be an assurance of blind justice (that is, Negroes were not of themselves a particular, disdained category to which the law attended), it could also mean that Negroes were not a category which the law had seen fit to consider. James Somerset benefited from the law's lack of notice of Negroes. The obliviousness of the law supported the idea of England as a location in whose very soil and air the essence of liberty resided.

When Med came to the attention of the courts in Massachusetts, she, too, benefited from being brought to a specific location where liberty had (according to its inhabitants) long resided. From the advent of the Massachusetts Body of Liberties to its Constitution, which included a statement of seemingly universal natural rights, the people of Massachusetts understood themselves to reside in a place that was liberty-loving. The language of liberty that we associate with revolutionary Massachusetts—promulgated by the Sons of Liberty and spread by colonists—invoked liberty as it stood in contrast to political slavery. The liberty they espoused in large part did not extend to the actual enslaved in their midst. Nevertheless, Med owed her freedom to such espousals.

The circumstances surrounding both Somerset and Med were, of course, quite different from those who escaped slavery in pursuit of freedom. Clearly, runaways understood how geography and law were interconnected when it came to the question of liberty. However, over the course of the early republic and antebellum years, the law conspired to curtail geographic avenues to liberty. Article IV, Section 2 of the U.S. Constitution amounted to a fugitive slave clause, although its wording did not specifically name "slaves" and "indentured servants" as included within the category of persons held to service or labor. In 1793, however, Congress outlined the methods for returning such runaways, making it possible for masters and agents acting on their behalf to recapture slaves, returning them to the state where they "owed service." Moreover, as mentioned previously, the Missouri Compromise failed to address directly and perma-

nently the question of slavery. While the measurable boundary offered as a
compromise to pro-slavery proponents delineated a possible locale conducive to liberty, time and growing sectional tensions gradually eroded the
meaning of the boundary where fugitives were concerned. The Compromise of 1850, with its harsh Fugitive Slave Law, and the Kansas-Nebraska
Act of 1854 combined to introduce slavery to locales where it had been
previously prohibited, thus eradicating the notion of a safe haven on free
soil. In 1857, the infamous *Dred Scott* decision confirmed that the relationship between geography and liberty was under assault. In short, as the nation moved closer to violent sectional conflict, the legal geographies where
ideologies of liberty once flourished, however imperfectly, could no longer
be taken for granted.[34]

That there were places where the operation of the law tended toward
liberty, and that England and Massachusetts constituted two such important examples of geographies favorable to liberty, is crucial to our understanding of the ability of legal actions to be advanced in certain venues. An
examination of the *Somerset* and *Commonwealth* cases provides an important
opportunity to consider the very tangible ways in which law, ideology, and
geography interacted to salutary effect. The power of a locale characterized as liberty-loving cannot be overstated. Those places—because of the
ideology that was an integral part of their development—had the ability to
confer liberty upon those who came within their delineated boundaries.
There, ideological language, often considered theoretical, combined with
the law to produce a practical application of liberty to a group of people
whose natural rights had been violated by slavery.

To argue that England and Massachusetts were geographies more favorable to liberty is not to argue that they were without limitation or contradiction. It is important to understand that while 1770s England and 1830s
Massachusetts were places where the idea of liberty was particularly favored, it was nonetheless still defined in an exclusionary way; although neither place would necessarily admit to such exclusion. The enslaved and
their advocates understood that such geographical locales had not been
constituted with them in mind. Nevertheless, it was the awareness of the
ideologies of those places and the ways in which the law reinforced those
ideologies that gave hope to slaves when they entered these jurisdictions.
By their enduring presence, slaves forced a reexamination of those geographies and the potential application of liberty to all who come within certain geographic borders. The enslaved were keenly aware of the change of
fortunes that certain relocations could engender. Those new locations
were places where natural rights had the potential to flourish and where
the fullest expression of liberty might, at last, be applied to all who were
fortunate enough to come within those emerging geographies of liberty.

4

"A Chosen Generation": Black Founders and Early America

Richard S. Newman

In January 1794, Richard Allen and Absalom Jones, former slaves who became two of Philadelphia's leading free black figures, marched into the federal government's copyright office and deposited their recently completed pamphlet, "A Narrative of the Proceedings of the Black People During the Late Awful Calamity in Philadelphia, in the year 1793; and a Refutation of Some Censures Thrown Upon Them in Some Late Publications." The work became a hallmark of black protest. The pamphlet criticized the racist stereotypes perpetrated by printer Matthew Carey, whose own best-selling pamphlet about Philadelphia's yellow fever epidemic castigated blacks for allegedly pillaging and plundering white homes. Not so, Allen and Jones corrected Carey; blacks saved Philadelphia through their virtuous volunteer work. The pamphlet also contained an important addendum: Richard Allen's antislavery appeal. In one of his most stunning passages, Allen almost appeared to be talking directly with Thomas Jefferson, the American founder who most palpably feared that mass emancipation would lead to mass destruction. Allen denied Jefferson's logic. "If you love your children," he pleaded, "if you love your country, if you love the God of Love, clear your hands from slaves, burden not your children or country with them." Because the federal government met in Allen's hometown of Philadelphia during the 1790s, and because Southern officials had a temporary pass on Pennsylvania's gradual abolition act, Allen decided to confront them in the best and probably only way he knew how: in print.[1]

Allen and Jones's document was a milestone. Quite simply, it was the first black-written pamphlet to earn copyright status by the federal government. Section One, Article Eight of the Constitution guaranteed that Congress would fully protect inventors' intellectual property rights—and Allen and Jones clearly believed that they had an idea worthy of such copyright protection. In a period when black votes were either denied or diluted, this was an important moment, for Allen and Jones as well as for their generation of black founders. Not only would African Americans protest publicly in the new nation but, they could now rightfully claim that black protest had an official seal and formal sanction. Looking back nearly a century and a half later, African American writer Charles Wesley declared that Allen and Jones were "pioneer publicists," true founders of black protest.[2]

In our time, there has been much talk of "great generations" and key American eras. Journalist Tom Brokaw got the ball rolling by dubbing World War II–era folks "the greatest generation" of all time. David Mc-Cullough, Richard Brookhiser, John Firling, and dozens of other popular historians have countered this claim by calling American revolutionaries the number-one generation in American history. It was, Firling wrote, the group that "set the world on fire." Even American history's original losers—the antifederalists—have found new champions in the battle of founding generations: Saul Cornell has labeled them our "other founders."[3]

For many years, even while historians rummaged through history to discover key generational moments and heroes, black founders like Allen and Jones lived in relative obscurity. True, they often were cited as exemplars of early black uplift. But rarely were Allen, Jones, James Forten, or others studied in depth as significant abolitionists. To study abolition meant to study the antebellum era—and for a long period of time even antebellum abolitionism meant white reformers like Garrison, the Tappan brothers, and Wendell Phillips. The first revolution in the study of abolition found scholars in the 1960s studying reformers coming well after Allen and Jones. John Bracey, August Meier, and Elliott Rudwick's seminal book *Blacks in the Abolition Movement,* for example, contained only one essay (out of thirteen) on a black founder: James Forten.[4] This trend continued as the second wave of abolitionist scholarship took flight in the 1990s. Despite an avalanche of new work on abolitionism, as James Stewart put it, early black leaders faded from prominence. There were new biographies of Douglass and Sojourner Truth, as well as of unheralded figures such as John Mercer Langston, slave rebels Denmark Vesey, Nat Turner, and many others.[5] But no one had written a modern biography of Richard Allen since the 1930s; no one had written a biography of James Forten since the nineteenth century; and no one had ever written one of Absalom Jones.

The tide has finally turned for black founders. There now exist in-depth biographies of James Forten and Lemuel Haynes and other studies are due shortly on Richard Allen and John Marrant. There is also a host of new literature on race and slavery in the early republic which includes commentary on black founders. Perhaps best of all, two of the editors of the *Black Abolitionist Papers* have recently begun a project to catalogue all of the writings of African American activists in the period preceding 1830.[6] In short, the time is ripe for a reappraisal of the black founding generation. Just who were black founders and why must we recall their activism?

"Black founders" is a fancy term to describe the charter generation of free blacks in early national America. Born in the eighteenth century, some free (like James Forten of Philadelphia) but many enslaved (like Richard Allen, Prince Hall, and Venture Smith, all of whom struggled mightily for their freedom), black founders came of age just as the American nation took shape. With only a few exceptions, these men and women would pass on by the early 1830s, leaving to the next generation battles which they had started. But start them they did. The charter generation of free blacks bequeathed a powerful legacy to their heirs—that more famous set of African American leaders of pre–Civil War years: Frederick Douglass, William Wells Brown, Sojourner Truth. Black founders were hailed by antebellum African Americans as true innovators, mentors in the arts of protest and community activism. Frederick Douglass made sure to honor his forebears in black protest. In 1849, he gave one of his most moving speeches in saluting James Forten, a name, Douglass cried out, that "makes my bosom swell with pride." "They were giants back then," a black magazine commented in 1859 of black founders.[7] If the names of Forten, Allen, Jones, or Prince Hall were less familiar by 1860, they were no less important, the *Anglo-African Magazine* declared. For they were of the generation that first battled bondage in an organized fashion, the generation that created vibrant free black institutions throughout the nation, and that innovated protest tactics—from establishing print as a key form of black activism to aiding fugitive slaves and distressed free blacks to forming the first national conventions dedicated to racial justice and independence— which still held sway on the eve of the Civil War. And long before W.E.B. Du Bois ever formulated his famous concept of "double consciousness" to characterize the essential paradox of black life, the charter generation of black leaders struggled to reconcile multiple identities: American, African, former slaves, would-be citizens.

Except perhaps among academic specialists, it is all too easy to forget that black founders lived through a tumultuous era of American race relations. Not only was the American Revolution a fresh event in the minds of the charter generation—one that heralded a black as well as white rallying cry, "liberty and justice for all"—so too was the nation's first experiment with emancipation: the ending of slavery by Northern states between 1780 (when Pennsylvania passed the first gradual abolition act) and 1804 (when New Jersey passed the last such bill).[8] Black founders also witnessed two of the most stunning demographic developments during the early republic: on the one hand, the massive growth of slavery in the South and Southwest;

on the other hand, the incredible growth and maturation of free black communities, mostly in Northern and Midwestern locales. While scholars have long examined the former trend (the doubling of slaves between 1790 and 1830, from 700,000 to nearly 2 million), they have only recently begun to focus on the significance of the latter (the quadrupling of the free black population during the same years, from 70,000 persons to a quarter million).[9]

Stark numbers like these indicate that the world black founders inhabited was filled with high hopes and dashing disappointments. This generation of African Americans saw not only emancipation acts passed in every Northern state but also the first wave of discriminatory codes and practices, from segregated seating at Northern churches (inequality in the House of the Lord, Richard Allen would exclaim!) to voting rights rescinded by many Northern states (New York restricted black voting rights in the 1820s). Black founders also witnessed the ending of the overseas slave trade in 1808, only to see it followed by a surge in the domestic slave trade—a trend that threatened free blacks in Philadelphia, Baltimore, New York, and elsewhere. This generation saw the colonization movement rear up and threaten to export free blacks overseas as an enticement to Southern emancipation. This generation also established deep economic roots inside the American nation, building black businesses and cultural institutions as never before, thereby deepening the legitimacy of blacks' claim to American citizenship.

Just who belonged to this charter generation of free blacks? In the broadest sense, the pantheon of black founders included men and women who fought against racial oppression in some way, shape, or form, and thereby established models of protest for later activists. They included rabble-rousers and revolutionaries like Virginia slave rebel Gabriel Prosser, born in 1776 and put to death in 1800 after his slave rebellion failed before even getting started.[10] If nothing else, Prosser's spirit animated generations of blacks to continue the struggle against racial oppression, even if they did not embrace such radical means as he did. Black founders also encompassed brash but bookish figures like Phillis Wheatley. Unheralded names could be added to the list of black founders, too: the four Massachusetts slaves who in 1773 petitioned the colonial assembly for liberty before America had declared its independence; the band of South Carolina slaves who marched through Charleston's streets in 1776 verbally demanding their freedom; and countless other black men and women who ran away from their masters during the War of Independence—or fought for American liberty only to be denied their own freedom. Their stories are lost to history but, all the same, the story of black freedom rests on their efforts. A poem written by an anonymous black man in the 1790s, and transcribed by a Pennsylvania abolitionist (it was never published), indicated the existence of some of these lost voices: "I cannot read nor use the pen / but yet can think with other men / I have a wish that you should see / the effect of aristocracy."[11] In America, the black poet claimed, aristocracy had taken the form of racial domination, not simply economic status. Black Americans would never let such assumptions go unchallenged.

But the charter generation of black leaders was not only the most visible group of black activists in the early republic, on the one hand, or the nameless and faceless masses, on the other, but race leaders who sought to create a nonviolent movement capable of challenging slavery and racial discrimination over the long haul. Black founders created the social and economic infrastructure that defined free black life through much of the late eighteenth and all of the nineteenth century, developing autonomous black churches, insurance and self-help organizations, and early abolitionist strategies.

One key example is illustrative. In Philadelphia, Richard Allen and his sometime ally James Forten amassed two of the most substantial property holdings of any citizen, white or black. They each belonged to the city's leading black churches (Allen to his beloved Bethel African Methodist Episcopal Church, Forten to St. Thomas's African Episcopal Church), and each employed apprentices in his own businesses (Allen as a master chimney sweep and nail producer; Forten as a sailmaker). More generally, as recent scholars have shown, they were the tip of a new iceberg: free black property holders in the new republic. In Philadelphia, black property holders included not just Allen and Forten but dozens of other people. In one abolitionist survey at the beginning of the 1790s, black Philadelphians owned nearly 100 homes. While most of the city's free population was comprised of laborers, black homeowners impressed white reformers as equal, if not superior, to whites of the same station and means.[12] Throughout early national America, African Americans began accumulating property, starting businesses (barbershops, smithing operations, chimney-sweeping concerns), and funding charity and religious groups.

In this sense, before they conceived of a national protest movement, black founders laid down roots in local communities following American independence. Like Richard Allen, founder of the Bethel AME Church in 1794, they sought to build autonomous black institutions in locales that were undergoing the transition from slavery to freedom. Like Allen, too, they moved from local to global politics by establishing baselines of nonviolent political protest for people of color. Blacks *were* Americans, as Allen and his compatriots James Forten and Absalom Jones consistently claimed in speeches, pamphlets, and petitions. So important were Allen, Forten, and Jones that historian Julie Winch has termed the trio Philadelphia's "black elite." For decades, they gave shape to black leadership locally and nationally. In other cities, too, black elites emerged in this fashion. In New York, the charter generation of black leaders coalesced around longtime activists Peter Williams and William Hamilton, who chartered black churches, schools, and political protest movements in a city long known as the colonial North's leading slave center, a place where roughly one of every five New York families owned slaves. In New England, a talented quartet of black leaders burst forth in the last years of the eighteenth century—Prince Hall, Paul Cuffe, Lemuel Haynes, and Hosea Easton. Hall started the first Masonic Lodge in black America in 1777, and used his home and meetinghouse over the next three decades as a base for black political activity, until his death in 1807. Based in New Bedford, Cuffe became a model black businessman. Although an advocate of African resettlement, he also supported black institution-building efforts in Massachusetts, Rhode Island, and Pennsylvania. Haynes and Easton were prominent black preachers in New Hampshire and Connecticut, respectively, as well as authors of pamphlets that challenged Americans to live up to their noble notions of equality. In the South, too, there were black founders, men like the Maryland preacher Daniel Coker and the Baltimore essayist William Watkins.

Together, these men helped build early free black society from the ground up. Quoting one of his favorite passages from the Bible, Coker wondered aloud at the miracles accomplished by black founders—those who built black churches, schools, and modes of protest where none previously had existed—in just a few short years: "Ye are a chosen generation, a royal priesthood, and a holy nation, a peculiar people" (I Peter II:9–10). Before the Revolution, Coker knew, the overwhelming majority of blacks in colonial America were slaves; now, in the early part of the nineteenth century, free black communities thrived along the Atlantic coast and blacks were claiming the new nation as their own. They were indeed a "chosen generation."

That generation's struggle was never easy, to say the least. Sometimes it lasted generations within the same family. The father-son combination within the Easton family remains one of the great examples. The father of antebellum black pamphleteer Hosea Easton, James Easton grew up free in Massachusetts before the American Revolution. After serving as an engineer in the fledgling continental forces during the Revolutionary war, Easton settled outside of Boston. He built his blacksmith's operation into one of the leading enterprises of its kind in the already clubby city; as Bruce Dain notes, he built the city's famed Tremont Theater and was happily known around town as "the black lawyer." Equally important, the elder Easton was an activist force, "inveigh[ing] against segregation in Boston's churches and in the community in general." He imparted this activist spirit to his son, who became a preacher and one of the earliest black lecturers in the immediate abolition movement of the 1830s. Easton the younger channeled Easton the elder's anger in his own two pamphlets, railing against early national America's continued racial exclusiveness. The more famous of these addresses, his 1837 treatise, expressed dismay at white power, and pushed harder than ever for immediate action to redress black grievances. The lesser-known essay, his Thanksgiving Day address to blacks in Providence in 1830, echoed these concerns but was still optimistic that nonviolent change could occur. That same year, Easton believed that African Americans must strive to achieve better education even while oppressed or enslaved. Still, in both essays, Easton echoed his father's concerns, wondering aloud at white discrimination and violence.[13]

The Paul family of Boston offers another example of what James Oliver Horton has referred to as "generations of protest." The story begins in 1789 when Thomas Paul, a young freeman, began preaching and worshipping with an assortment of free blacks in New England. In the early 1800s, Paul joined a man named Scipio Dalton in Boston to form the African Baptist Church. "Largely through his church ministry," Horton writes, "Thomas Paul became an important leader. He was instrumental in the establishment of separate black religious and educational institutions, not only in Boston but also other cities." One of those cities was New York, where Paul helped create the Abyssinian Baptist Church in 1808. As important, Thomas Paul passed on lessons in community activism to his son, Nathaniel, and to his daughter, Susan Paul. Nathaniel became a leading New York preacher and abolitionist in the 1820s and 1830s while Susan became "one of the most distinguished female reformers in Boston in the ante-bellum period . . . deeply involved in the anti-slavery movement." Horton concludes that the Paul clan was not unique: "This pattern of family involvement in community affairs over generations may be seen in other black Boston families." He might have added that it was not unique in other black communities either. One of the leading families of Philadelphia, the Fortens, served in black and white reform movements from patriarch James Forten's day in the 1790s through his son-in-law Robert Purvis's day in the antebellum period. And the roots of all of this activism were formed in James Forten's youth.[14]

Community building and early black activism required more than figureheads who provided direction and leadership; they required community interaction on what that direction should be. In Richard Allen's Philadelphia, for example, community building included the views of struggling former slaves, day laborers, and the indentured blacks who were soon to be skilled artisans or mechanics—in other words, the bulk of

Philadelphia's roughly two thousand free blacks in 1793 (when Allen founded his church), unheralded men and women who, unlike Allen, did not own their own homes or businesses. Nevertheless, they sent their children to Allen's Sunday school (or to abolitionist-run schools), they learned a decent trade, and, wherever possible, they sought to gain literacy skills to compete in early national society. In short, they generally ratified Allen's vision that a free black community must coalesce around values of uplift, education, and communal support. This vision of a thriving free black community capable of sustaining itself economically would naturally, in Allen's view, contradict stereotypes which were still used to justify black bondage. To Allen, racial uplift translated into a powerful means to strike at slavery. And yet, while some scholars have criticized Allen for foisting such concerns on the black masses, one often found "amens" among men and women in Allen's own community.[15]

One key example of a person who ratified Allen's vision was black schoolteacher Eleanor Harris, who by 1796 instructed fifty young black children in Philadelphia's abolitionist free school. She earned $25 per year for this work, a fine sum for a black woman at the time but certainly not what Allen brought home. But her job—and vision of that job—was equally critical to the black community at that time, as her abolitionist employers noted gleefully in a report from her schoolroom: Harris was responsible for black pupils' striking "degree of proficiency in reading . . . [and] improvement in general in spelling and reading." So successful was this experiment—and so much did black parents want their children to gain basic schooling of this sort—that abolitionists planned a second school, this one, as they excitedly reported, run by "Anthony Fowles, a black man . . . [and] tutor."[16]

Examining indentures of both slaves and free blacks in the 1790s, the persistence with which "average" black persons in Philadelphia insisted on gaining practical skills and education of some sort remains striking. James Nixon, a young black man, signed an indenture agreement in February 1794 with Absalom Jones (and by extension, with Jones's business partner at the time, Richard Allen) to learn the trade of nailor. His mother, Rachel, showed up at the indenture meeting with a local alderman, white abolitionists, and Absalom Jones, to make sure that her son not only had "sufficient meat, drink, and wearing apparel," but "two quarters night schooling" as well. In another case that same year, an African American woman emphasized to white abolitionists her overwhelming desire to see that her son "may have a trade" that would prove successful in early national Philadelphia. In a third indenture case for 1794, a young man named Charles freed himself from slavery in New Jersey in exchange for serving nearly twenty years as a Philadelphia merchant's waiter. At the end

of this indenture, Charles hoped to gain not only "freedom dues," or a
fancy new suit (as was the custom for many indentures, white as well as
black), but assurances that he would "be taught to read and write in a legi-
ble hand, arithmetic," and other basic literacy skills that would allow
Charles to prosper on his own.

For these reasons and more, Philadelphia became a free black capital by
the 1790s as well as a destination for slaves and former slaves. Maryland
masters became increasingly alarmed at the attractions Pennsylvania held
to their slaves. They petitioned their assembly to warn Pennsylvania to stop
enticing, as it were, slaves to flee.[17] But how? Much of this enticement came
from the very creation and steady rise of that free black community in
Philadelphia, one with a black founder like Richard Allen keeping a steady
eye on who was in his community, and why and what they needed. For
Allen, community building was tantamount to a political argument against
slavery and racial oppression. Stephen Hahn gives a similar meaning to
black community building among Southern slaves and freed people later
in the nineteenth century. According to Hahn, community was not something that Southern blacks could *ever* take for granted. But it also had more
than mere filial meaning—extended relationships and such. Community
had a political edge. The black community as a whole stood up—as much
as was possible in the midst of slavery   to masters' incessant desire to control blacks' every movement. Put another way, black community revolved
around notions of power—building a power base in a time and place that
stripped blacks of every vestige of power.[18]

In this sense, just as Richard Allen had always predicted, black community building and black abolitionism became inseparable before the 1830s.

Founders build things—nations, constitutions, institutions of governance
and learning, belief systems that open up worlds others scarcely know exist.
"There was no American nation, no army at the start," David McCulloch
has written of America's founding generation, men like McCulloch's favorite biographical subject of that era, John Adams. Like his famous compatriots, McCulloch observes, Adams built the American nation from the
ground up, ideologically as well as materially. White founders like Adams
drafted the Declaration of Independence and Constitution, refined its
governing ideology, and upheld America's intellectual relevance to the
world. "We can never know enough about him," or that which he built,
McCulloch wistfully comments of Adams and his generation.

The same might be said of black founders, who built both material and
ideological foundations in African American communities: materially,
they constructed the physical edifices (churches, schools, self-help groups)
that molded together early black communities; ideologically, black

founders created mental maps for their brethren, ideas about abolitionism, black civic participation, and equal rights that helped guide early
black activism through an American culture profoundly skeptical of them.
Black founders also focused on the means of communicating these ideas to
both black and white audiences via pamphlets, petitions, and the like.
Here, too, they envisioned a black presence and place in publications (so
important in the civic-minded American republic) where one simply did
not exist before. One of the best, if little-known, examples of this comes
from New York City in 1790. A man referring to himself as "Rusticus" authored an antiblack screed, asserting that blacks were inferior in mind, but
superior in body. As such, he argued, emancipation was foolish. Beyond
Rusticus's ideas, his very tone suggested that the debate over slavery and
race excluded African Americans themselves. If they were inferior, how
could they even respond? And so blacks, he concluded flatly, must be the
missing link between apes and man.

A few days later, however, a black writer calling himself "Africanus" published a bold challenge to the white writer's assumption that blacks played
no role in public discussions over slavery. "I am a sheep hairy Negro," he
proclaimed, "the son of an African man and woman, who by a train of fortunate events . . . was let free when very young . . . received a common English school education, and was instructed in the Christian religion." An
independent tradesman and friend to many "generous Americans who are
pleased to praise me for employing my time so much more rationally (as
they say) than most white men in the same station of life," Africanus
claimed an unqualified right to respond in print to the antiblack slanders
of Rusticus and his ilk. "The American and the African are one species," he
summed up, "and I, the son of a sheep hairy African Negro, being free and
in some degree enlightened, feel myself equal to the duties of any spirited,
and noble, and generous American Freeman."[19] According to Africanus,
emancipation was not only righteous but blacks must be consulted about
its political and social efficacy.

Here one sees the three great elements of black abolitionism unfolding
in Africanus's reply: antislavery, equality, and printed protest. William
McFeeley has argued that the bedrock of Frederick Douglass's creed revolved around the belief that blacks *had* constitutional rights. Douglass
himself believed that one way to strive for rights was through print and
public mediation. There is no "Negro problem," he liked to say, only a
problem of whether or not white American will live up to their noble words
and ideas. His corpus of printed works—the autobiographies, his work at
the *North Star,* his pamphlets and reprinted addresses—cited various authorities as a source for this notion but Douglass also made clear that his
protest (both its ideas and forms) stemmed from black founders. One such

man was James Forten; Douglass also may have used Peter Williams's and Richard Allen's words as a basis for his own reformist ideals. Each of these black founders wrote in language eerily familiar to one another, and certainly in words which can be found in Douglass's great speeches.[20] In Richard Allen's famous anticolonization letter of 1827 (published in the black newspaper *Freedom's Journal*), the preacher called America a black homeland.[21] "This land," Allen asserted, "which we have watered with our tears and our blood, is now our mother country and we are well satisfied to stay where wisdom abounds and the gospel is free." In 1830, Peter Williams said almost the exact same thing:

> We are natives of this country, we ask only to be treated as well as foreigners. Not a few of our fathers suffered and bled to purchase its independence; we ask only to be treated as well as those who fought against it. We have toiled to cultivate it, and to raise it to its present prosperous condition; we ask only to share equal privileges with those who come from distant lands to enjoy the fruits of our labour.[22]

No less than their white counterparts, black founders circulated ideas and texts (Allen and Jones read Prince Hall, who in turn read Allen and Jones), and so these echoes may be evidence of shared texts. On the other hand, the ideas were so much a part of black founders' very being ("We *are* Americans," they claimed over and over) that the common language of Williams and Allen (and later Douglass) merely suggests a black abolitionist wellspring.

In any event, these ideas—this mental map which outlined a vision of antislavery activism and black equality within the American nation—first took root (and then flourished) in free black churches: Allen's Mother Bethel and Jones's St. Thomas's in Philadelphia; Thomas Paul's African Baptist Church in Boston; William Hamilton's African Methodist Episcopal (AME) Zion Church in New York City. As Albert Raboteau has argued, these early black churches were not merely islands of autonomy for distressed blacks—although they most certainly served that function—but antislavery centers. "Black churches defended the antislavery position that most white churches had abandoned or never held in the first place."[23] In Philadelphia, Allen's Bethel Church became the center for black meetings on the ending of the slave trade, protests against colonization, and speeches about black abolitionism itself. In one of the most famous examples, Allen eulogized George Washington from his Bethel pulpit, telling his parishioners that Washington (who had provided for his slaves' liberation at his wife's death) practiced what America preached: liberty and justice for all. Americans, he said, must now live up to Washington's emancipatory "zeal." Allen's Bethel speech soon morphed into a national antislavery message as (white) newspaper editors in Baltimore, New York, and Philadelphia reprinted the address as an example of blacks' potential civic virtue. While editors focused on Allen's apparent sadness at Washington's death (an event, he stated, in which African Americans "participate in common" with the country at large), Allen used the national spotlight to issue a challenge to all Americans. "May a double portion of his spirit," he called out, "rest on all the officers of the Government of the United States and . . . the whole of the American people." If you remember anything about Washington, Allen told white as well as black citizens, remember not his heroic military deeds or sturdy occupation of the president's office. No, recall his final deed of deliverance—ending slavery. The entire episode began in Allen's church.[24]

Baltimore's Daniel Coker linked early black abolitionism to the formation of black churches in his 1810 pamphlet, "A Dialogue Between an African minister and a Virginian." In this Socratic dialogue with a racial twist—a conversation between a black man and a white master—Coker called for general but gradual (and uncompensated) emancipation of slaves. Significantly, Coker cast his African American character as a minister—a black man who not only knew the Word of God but could apply its abolitionist lessons to whites with particular agility. At the document's end, Coker skillfully attached a survey of "African churches" throughout the United States. These institutions existed, he made clear, in New York, New Jersey, Massachusetts, and Pennsylvania, as well as in such "slave states" as Delaware and even South Carolina. Readers made the connection: these churches contained the types of black abolitionists Coker depicted in his pamphlet. Coker went a step further in his text, making sure that readers understood his abolitionist appeal: "But there is one thing more," the African minister says to the slaveholder, "that I would request of you, and that is, before you die, make it in your will, that at your death, those slaves who may wish to continue with you shall be free; for your children, or heirs, A, B, or C, may not be of your humane disposition."[25] The end of religion, Coker declared, was justice; hence, abolition was not radical but just. Unfettered in their own churches now, black founders could, and did, make this point.

Beyond churches, black founders pressed for equality in workplaces, courts of law, and schools. In both Philadelphia and New York, for example, African Americans sought legal aid from white abolitionists, forcing them to deploy more lawyers and more funds to defending black freedom suits. In early national New York, blacks challenged white supremacy by filing an increasing number of lawsuits in local courts during the early 1800s. "African New Yorkers saw a little point in gaining freedom if they continued to be treated as if they were slaves," Shane White has recently written. He relates the story of one Henry Lawson, who went to work as a servant for a white merchant in 1811. After a dispute, Lawson quit, but he refused to accept anything less than a month's pay for his work. According to White's wonderful detective work, Lawson sued the white merchant. While he failed to gain extra wages via the courts, Lawson did succeed in pressing charges against his former employer for assault and battery. As White concludes, Lawson did not want to be treated like a slave any longer, a man who existed merely to please white men and women.[26] Lawson's act stands out as much more than a specific example of a black man defending himself publicly; it represented a broader ideology circulating through early national free black life: African Americans must demand their rights as citizens. That message was made early and often in free black communities, and passed down through the generations of black reformers.

For some early black leaders, there was no real distinction between the style of secular protest envisioned by a man like Lawson and the beliefs of autonomous black churches. David Walker, perhaps the most important of all black pamphleteers, imbibed much of his militant protest sensibility from his travels among mid-Atlantic black churches and communities during the early years of nineteenth century. Walker remains an icon for the publication of his electrifying *Appeal to the Coloured Citizens of the World* (1829), a document which called for continent-wide black solidarity, and put a bounty on his own head by various Southern officials. Peter Hinks, the preeminent authority on Walker, argues that he had been "nurtured in the rich black Methodism of Wilmington [Delaware]" and even Charleston, South Carolina, where he attended Methodist gatherings. In local revival meetings he saw versions of a liberation theology (a belief that God was on the side of the oppressed) that contained the possibilities of national black organization and action. Walker also became a disciple of black founder Richard Allen; Hinks actually refers to Walker's "adulation of Richard Allen, whom he believed was among the 'greatest divines who have lived since the apostolic Age.' " According to Hinks, Walker might very well have journeyed to Philadelphia to commune with the great man, before continuing on to his final destination of Boston and his eventual publication of the *Appeal* a few years later. Whether or not they actually met, "Walker was convinced that Allen would be the savior of African-America." In Walker's eyes, Allen's twin examples of black autonomy (organizing black freemen in an independent church) and activism (calling for slavery's end publicly and in print) "filled my soul with all those emotions which would take the pen of Addison to portray."[27]

Walker's celebration of Allen, in which he referred specifically to Allen's anticolonizationist writings, brings us back to the importance of print. One of the key reasons that black founders became a source of inspiration to subsequent generations of activists (Douglass in particular) was that they left a paper trial. It is important to emphasize that early black leaders—and not their antebellum counterparts—innovated print as a daily protest tool. From the moment many blacks gained freedom in the post–Revolutionary era and early republic, they focused on the one political tool available to them: printed protest. Virtually every major early black leader printed what Dorothy Porter once called "protest pamphlets." "Long before the Civil War," Porter argued in 1969, "black men who were denied redress of their grievances in courts or state legislatures frequently had recourse to literary means [for] . . . stating their protests." Patrick Rael has updated Porter's claim, noting that post–Revolutionary era black leaders recognized that they were "in a different time and place": a republic which had an aggressive public sphere. Black leaders quickly set out to utilize print for public protest purposes.[28]

This public sphere, black leaders understood, was their only conduit to the American public. And it was through this public sphere that black leaders envisioned confronting whites with the most pressing racial issues of the day—issues which many white founders (Jefferson, Madison) scrupulously hoped to avoid. In his award-winning book *Founding Brothers,* historian Joseph Ellis writes of slavery that the nation's best and brightest men "managed to take the most threatening and divisive issue off the political agenda." Ellis calls this "the silence," a conscious strategy of avoiding open discussion of a problem with "the deepest social and economic roots in the American nation."[29] The new nation's African American leaders provided what can only be called "The Reply"—a collective attempt to discuss openly and often the issues of ending slavery and instituting racial justice. Black founders echoed and amplified Allen's abolitionism and keen sense of racial equality. In perhaps the most fully articulated expression of early African American claims to liberty, "Series of Letters of a Man of Color" (1813), James Forten asked whether Americans would live up to their hallowed beliefs. Although a more elaborate constitutional and legal treatise than anything Allen ever wrote, Forten's pamphlet remained grounded in the preacher's principles: America was a black homeland, constitutionally no less than spiritually. "We hold this truth to be self-evident," Forten began, "that God created all men equal." This principle, Forten explained, was the American nation's founding creed. Anything—or anyone—violating it should be condemned as a tyrant and traitor to America, particularly those laws and leaders embracing calls for racial domination.[30]

Lemuel Haynes utilized print to convey his belief that slavery was wrong and that blacks must be viewed as would-be citizens in the new republic. Although he reiterated versions of this creed in various pamphlets, Haynes

first penned them in a remarkable 1776 abolitionist essay. As John Saillant
has written in his fine biography of the man, Haynes "wrestled with the
question of whether revolutionary republicanism implied slavery or freedom, oppression or equality, exclusion or inclusion, for African-Americans
in a time when major white theoreticians of republicanism such as Thomas
Jefferson and James Madison carried their political philosophy to antiblack extremes." And Haynes, in Saillant's eyes, made a clear final statement on this matter: he "regarded himself as a citizen."[31]

Similar examples pervade black protest. In Philadelphia, not only did
Allen and Absalom Jones together publish the first pamphlet but they each
continued to publish protest documents on their own. Between 1799 and
1807, for example, Allen published three important documents aimed at
the public: a eulogy of George Washington celebrating his emancipation
will, a eulogy of Quaker activist Warner Mifflin, and a moral reform pamphlet that defended blacks from further degrading stereotypes. Jones published two documents: a famous sermon on the ending of the slave trade
and a shorter pamphlet heralding the formation of a reform group at St.
Thomas's Church. Similarly, in both Boston and New York, black leaders
took to print early and often. In 1809, for example, New York's William
Hamilton told a group of black congregants that he was honored to speak
before them on the theme of African freedom in the American republic,
but the group's request to publish the speech as a pamphlet was an even
greater honor, for it would allow him to combat "opinions of learned men
that Africans are inferior in mind."[32]

In this manner, print became a metaphor for black autonomy in the
early republic.[33] As a strategy, pamphleteering offered blacks control over
their message and its distribution. Pamphlets were smaller, cheaper to produce, and were thought to be more ephemeral documents than expensive
leatherbound books. Thus, unlike the antebellum slave narratives, which
reached a wider white audience but involved the potentially intrusive hand
of white editors and philanthropists, early black pamphleteers retained
command of their documents. Moreover, the very process of getting a
pamphlet published was evidence of a new black politics of public engagement. Beginning in the 1790s, black writers in Philadelphia, New York,
Boston, and elsewhere began searching for white printers who might publish their work. Most printers were simply hired guns: if an author had
enough money, a printer would produce his or her product. But certain
printers refused to publish African American works. Others published
black pamphlets but refrained from inserting their names on the title page
(forgoing what was essentially free advertising of a printer's work). Neither
of Prince Hall's pamphlets carried his publishers' names, although both
printing houses had longstanding liberal reputations in Massachusetts

(both had printed documents for insurgent colonial and then independent state legislatures during the 1770s). When white ruffians attempted to intimidate free blacks like Prince Hall from stepping out into the civic arena, Hall stood firm. When white printers shied away from distributing his works, Hall sold copies from his masonic lodge.[34] In this manner, African American writers' very act of putting their words into print in the early republic was a political statement: it announced black independence and control, and, through efforts to secure printers, told white audiences that blacks were determined to enter the public sphere.

Of course, print culture had a twofold purpose: it allowed blacks a vehicle to protest racial oppression and, at the same time, displayed black humanity through mastery of the literary arts. Jefferson famously sneered that blacks had never proven their worth in writings or the literary arts. Black pamphlets proved otherwise. Print was equally important tactically: it allowed black leaders to envision a continent-wide protest movement. With no national movement, with no central governing body—black conventions of the 1830s or 1840s, say—printed protest functioned as a sort of web: black leaders in one community could pipe into what was occurring in another community, adopt that form, and tweak it for local purposes. Philadelphia blacks corresponded with African American reformers in Rhode Island and Massachusetts, and all black pamphleteers aimed to have their productions preserved in personal libraries or donated to "colored reading societies."

If print conveyed the message, the message itself went beyond mere calls for whites to live up to the letter of the law. Indeed, beyond calls for racial equality and the abolition of slavery, early African American leaders claimed that they shared a cause and country with white leaders. Here the idea of a mental map took on somewhat different dimensions. Instead of the jeremiad—the *crie de coeur*—some black founders emphasized a shared history of struggle with Revolutionary-era whites. That first generation of African Americans, like their white counterparts, had put life and limb on the line for independence. Peter Williams, a New Yorker by birth but an American by choice, would tell the story of his father's dedication to American liberty writ large. As Williams told citizens in the 1830s and subsequently in a printed address, his father was almost killed by the British in the 1780s for protecting a wanted white preacher and known patriot from the English gallows. The man, a family friend from New Jersey, was on the run from the British when Williams's father, a slave at the time, picked him up on his horse and made a mad dash through the Jersey meadows before delivering him to a safe haven. Then the elder Williams ran into real trouble: a British officer who insisted on knowing the preacher's whereabouts. "Where is Parson Chapman?" the officer demanded, his saber raised. "I cannot tell," Williams's father coolly replied. "Tell me where he is," the British man repeated, "or I'll instantly cut you down!" The elder Williams refused to move. The officer raced off in disgust.

Williams told the story in 1834 amid racial riots in his New York City parish. As colonizationists and abolitionists battled over the future of African Americans in the United States, Williams was forced to leave his Episcopal church because he reputedly presided over the marriage of an interracial couple. Although he resigned his position to save the parish, Williams refused to resign his claims to the American republic. With a father who put his life literally on the line for American freedom, Williams proudly claimed American citizenship, come what may. Indeed, his attachment to America flowed from his own father's "attachment to the country of his birth": America. Soon after the elder Williams saved the Jersey patriot, whites in his neighborhood secured money for his own freedom. (And to think that Williams's son would later be told that he was not allowed to embrace the principles of the American Revolution!) Williams later recalled that to hear his father talk of the Revolution when he was a young boy "filled my soul with an ardent love for the American government and made me feel . . . that it was my greatest glory to be an American."[35]

Like Williams, Richard Allen attempted to define himself as part of American civic culture. While he did not pretend to be a constitutional creator or a general—a Madison or Washington—he made clear that African American leaders had a moral compass desperately needed during the Revolutionary era and in the early republic. In other words, Allen believed that "liberty and justice for all" was a binding agent, a ligament connecting black and white Americans. The job for early African American leaders was to represent black interests before white founders; white founders had to represent black interests in courts of law, state legislatures, and Congress. Allen's very first pamphlet in 1794 attempted not just to critique white stereotypes of blacks but to establish a bridge to white founders. "We do not wish to make you angry," he wrote in one section, "but excite your attention to consider how hateful slavery is in the eyes of God." What did this mean? Free your slaves, Allen pleaded, educate them, "cultivate their minds with the same care [as white children] . . . [and] you will find then upon the trial, they were *not* inferior in mental endowments" to whites. In sum, Allen claimed that slaves could be useful citizens of the future; the problem was *not* black nature but whites' failure to nurture blacks as equals.

As if to make sure that white founders like Jefferson understood black founders' intellectual abilities, Allen included sly references to the Declaration of Independence and Jefferson's own concerns about slavery, evidence surely that Allen was more widely read than a mere commoner and capable of witty repartee. For example, his antislavery appeal followed Jefferson's very model of fighting oppression à la the Declaration by telling American leaders that blacks "have [now] shown the cause of our incapacity" and that this peaceable protest document should not be deemed by the ruling class as mere "insolence." He even invoked Enlightenment sensibilities, arguing that as contended as slaves appear "in your sight," their own "insurrections" should be enough "to convince any reasonable man" that they too desire liberty. But the point was surely that slavery must end and that white leaders had it in their power to make abolition a reality. Now that black leaders had spoken, white founders had no excuse *not* to strike a blow for black freedom.

It is important to note that prior to the 1820s many black leaders called for the gradual, not immediate abolition of slavery. For black founders, this gradualist call might very well prove African Americans' civic virtue— they realized how sensitive the issue of emancipation was among whites. The Reverend Coker issued one of the most famous such calls in his 1810 pamphlet, the dialogue between a black and white man in the South. Coker called for general but gradual emancipation of slaves. Perhaps knowing that Chesapeake masters were particularly wary of even this policy in the wake of two planned slave rebellions in the early 1800s, Coker cast his African minister in a deferential manner. Indeed, to make the case for even gradual emancipation, Coker's African minister concedes that "the immediate liberation of all the slaves may be attended with some difficulty." But, he goes on, this should not be used as a reason against gradual abolition.[36]

Coker, like many black founders, called for gradual abolition because he believed it would prove that blacks were both sensitive and moral citizens: far from avenging brutes (as Jefferson and Madison feared), blacks would peacefully co-exist with former masters and slowly meld into the nation's civic culture. Both Richard Allen and Lemuel Haynes used religious appeals to make this same point. As Allen put it, many black Americans were converting to evangelical religion, and they therefore prayed to the same God as whites. This, Allen argued, would bind white and blacks into a covenant with a higher power. In short, blacks would not violate God's laws to get back at whites. Correspondingly, whites must not violate God's law by keeping slaves. The larger message? Whites and blacks could co-exist in the here and now—once slavery was abolished. Abolition, therefore, was central to the full realization of the nation's founding principles.

Far from an assimilationist ethic, in which blacks simply dissolved racial identity altogether, this gradualist ideology assumed that once free from slavery blacks would become valued citizens while also maintaining an au-

tonomous social and cultural identity. In one of the most forceful medita-
tions on this subject, William Hamilton told members of the Free African
Church in 1809 to maintain their independent society as a means of preserving black cultural space but also to keep their eyes on the prize of
American citizenship. "Our advancement in every point of view depends
much on our being united in social bodies," he called out. But (perhaps
addressing white readers) he also hoped that the future would bring blacks
into the nation's political realm as equal citizens, for America was *their*
country, too. After all, did blacks not identify with the country's ideal of
freedom and justice for all? "The sources of slavery are drying up," he went
on, noting that African American literary production had already staked a
claim to civic integration. "If we continue to produce specimens like
these," he told his audience while holding up examples of black writing,
"we shall soon put our enemies to the blush; abashed and confounded,
they shall quit the field and no longer urge their superiority of their souls."
With slavery routed and the sons of Africa rising, white Americans would
soon see blacks as their political brethren.[37]

As for any potential rift between people who gained their freedom and
those who remained enslaved, black founders emphasized that it must not
happen—that free black and enslaved people shared variations of a racial
condition in America. At the first chance Richard Allen and Absalom Jones
had to address the broader reading public in 1794, they took the time to
craft a special message "To the People of Color." "Feeling an engagement
of mind for your welfare," they observed, "we address you with an affec-
tionate sympathy, having been ourselves slaves and as desirous of freedom
as any of you." Allen and Jones did not just commiserate; they reminded
their enslaved brethren that God and a new generation of reformers acted
in their behalf. A few years later, in December 1799, Jones made good on
this word by circulating a petition against slave trading—and even slavery
itself—in Philadelphia's free black community. The petition was presented
to Congress, then meeting in Philadelphia for the last time. Although the
petition was returned by a vote of 84 to 1, James Forten told the sole white
congressman who supported blacks' cause that this was not the whimsy of
free black leaders; "700,000 of our race were interested in the petition."[38]

This connection between free blacks and enslaved people eventually became a bedrock position of black anticolonization protest and even the interracial immediatist movements of the 1830s. But it started in the very
early years of the republic as free blacks meditated on the meaning of their
condition in states where slavery still existed. It is important to remember
that when black founders like Allen, Jones, and Forten in Philadelphia (or
Prince Hall in Massachusetts, or William Hamilton in New York) spoke of
their claims to American rights and liberties, Northern states were in the

process of gradually ending slavery. Free persons of color already knew and mingled with enslaved people in Pennsylvania, New York, or New Jersey. When slavery became essentially a Southern institution in the 1820s, black leaders did not skip a beat in directing their cause of racial justice to enslaved Southerners. In short, they had already created a mental map linking black struggles across lines of status. The most famous declaration of this sentiment, of course, came in the famous 1817 anticolonizationist meeting at Allen's Bethel church. "We pledge never to separate from our enslaved brethren," Philadelphia blacks proclaimed on that occasion. By the 1830s, this sentiment was an article of faith among black activists. But the tone was set down during Allen's day.[39]

The activism of black founders was not at all haphazard. It was organized around specific institutions, had distinctive tactics and objectives, and it emphasized certain overarching themes: slavery must be ended by America's civic leaders, and black Americans could aid in destroying bondage; black justice must occur *in* America, the problem could not be exported or colonized; African Americans were (or should be conceived as) American citizens. To be sure, black founders themselves grew pessimistic during the 1810s and 1820s about Americans' unwillingness to abolish slavery and embrace African American equality—their reluctance to really treat blacks as American citizens. By the second decade of the nineteenth century, Richard Allen grew so doubtful about achieving justice on American soil that he even began embracing the idea of Haitian emigration. He served as president of the Haitian Emigration Society of Philadelphia and helped dozens of blacks to Haiti in 1825. Overall, perhaps as many as seven to twelve thousand blacks departed America in the 1820s.

But Allen himself never left. Nor did Forten or William Hamilton. By the late 1820s, black leaders in every major city redoubled their efforts to protest racism and slavery in America, inaugurating the first black conventions, independently run black newspapers, and other cultural and political institutions. When a new generation of abolitionists emerged in the 1830s to wage war on bondage, black founders were there to teach them the art of protest. And even after black founders passed on—Allen in 1831, Hamilton in 1834, Williams in 1838, Forten in 1842—their legacy loomed large. Antebellum black Pennsylvanians certainly used Allen's and Forten's memory to inform their own activism and identity. Prosecuting the cause of voting rights in Pennsylvania in 1848, about a decade after white officials had rescinded them, a state convention of black leaders wrapped themselves in black founders' coattails. "[We] rest our cause," the group announced, "on the republican standard of the revolutionary Fathers, while we knock at the doors of the Constitution and demand an entrance."

And just who were these revolutionary fathers? They included illustrious and well-known names—Benjamin Rush, Benjamin Franklin—as well as black founders, men like Allen and Forten. "Their tales should resonate in the mind of every Pennsylvanian—and American!"[40]

As *Frederick Douglass's Paper* put it in 1855, one could do no better in learning about the foundations of black protest than by traveling to Philadelphia to visit "a church called Bethel." This spot, the paper's correspondent argued, "is the sight of a revolution or reform, which happened 70 years ago, a reform which, in grasp of free thought, determined energy, spiritual majesty, holy zeal, and gospel of truthfulness, equaled, if it did not excel any kindred event in the history of humankind." That revolution was the establishment of Allen's Bethel AME Church, a church which stood itself as a monument not just to religious liberty but to the aspirations and achievements of black activism and abolitionism. Beneath that church "lies the remains of Richard Allen," the most prominent of America's black founders.[41]

5

"Onward, Onward, Is Indeed the Watchword": James Forten's Reflections on Revolutions and Liberty

Julie Winch

One afternoon in January 1825, Mr. S.H. Cowles, a zealous young reformer fresh out of college, called on Philadelphia businessman James Forten. An ardent promoter of the American Colonization Society, Cowles had high hopes of persuading Forten, whom he knew to be one of the nation's most influential free men of color, to emigrate to Liberia. He came armed with letters of introduction and arguments he was sure would convince Forten of the wisdom of free black people leaving the United States for their "true" homeland in Africa, but he was to find that Forten would not be moved, literally or figuratively. Moreover, Forten had some home truths to tell Cowles that the young man found most unsettling to hear.

The white college graduate and the self-made black entrepreneur almost four decades his senior must have made a striking contrast as they sat facing each other in the tastefully decorated parlor of the Forten family home on Lombard Street, one of Philadelphia's main thoroughfares. The home and everything in it spoke eloquently to Forten's success in business. Profits from his thriving sail business along the Delaware had been plowed into real estate, money lending, the purchase of stock in banks, and a host of other enterprises, and back into his sail-making operation.[1] A man of Forten's wealth and commercial know-how would be an invaluable recruit to the colonization project. Alas, Cowles's bid to win James Forten over was doomed to failure.

As he later confessed, Cowles found the interview most distressing. To begin with, he did not take to Forten. White visitors were usually charmed by the black businessman, for he was a witty and well-informed conversationalist.[2] Cowles was not charmed. He described Forten as "a boisterous talker . . . proud of his money and vain of his abilities which . . . enabled him to get it." To make matters worse, Forten rebutted every one of

Cowles's carefully rehearsed arguments. Worst of all, it soon became evident that Forten's world-view differed radically from that of his guest. Cowles was obliged to report that Forten.

> seems to have a stern satisfaction in being w[h]ere he is and as he is. For he said repeatedly, that reasoning from the righteousness of God and the manifest tendency of events he was brought to the conclusion that the time was fast approaching and to judge from his manner was already at the door when the 250,000,000 who had for centuries been the oppressors of the remaining 600,000,000 of the human race would find the tables turned upon them and would expiate by their own sufferings the sufferings . . . [what] they had inflicted on others.[3]

Cowles left the Forten home sadder and, one suspects, none the wiser. What had Forten meant? Was he another Toussaint L'Ouverture or Henri Christophe, looking forward to a general blood-letting when "the last shall be first, and the first last"? He had actually told Cowles he applauded the Haitian revolution and admired its leaders. Did he perhaps want radical social and political change, a restructuring of the American republic? Or did he anticipate a revolution "not of this world"? What Cowles could not or would not see was that Forten's character had been shaped by forces totally different from those that had shaped his own. For Forten, race and condition were inextricably intertwined with a sense of what was and what could be. He was no revolutionary lusting after blood and crying out for vengeance on the white race, as Cowles feared—but he *was* a revolutionary. James Forten had grown up in the midst of revolutions. He positively welcomed revolutions, provided their achievements were not betrayed. For him, revolution and reform were part of the greater picture, with freedom from tyranny of all kinds—slavery, the prejudice of caste, the oppression of the majority by a self-appointed and self-perpetuating minority—as the goal. How fast freedom came, and how steadfast the heirs of one revolution were to their revolutionary heritage, would determine the nature and extent of the next upheaval. In short, Forten was a revolutionary in a sense that entirely eluded his young visitor, and he would remain one until the day he died.

James Forten had had an early introduction to revolutions. Born of free parents in Philadelphia in 1766, like the other inhabitants of Britain's North American colonies, he knew no earthly ruler except the king of England.[4] But much happened in a short period of time to erode his loyalty to a king in a distant land. He was four when the Boston massacre took place, seven when a gang of "Mohawks" threw hundreds of chests of tea into Boston Harbor and incurred the wrath of king and Parliament. His family lived just yards from Carpenters' Hall, where delegates to the First Continental Congress assembled in the fall of 1774.[5] At nine years of age he stood in the yard of Philadelphia's state house and heard the Declaration of Independence—"that glorious fabrick of collected wisdom," as he later described it—read to the public for the first time.[6] He saw slaves converting the rebellion against Britain into a personal war for liberation. With the benefit of two years of formal education at the Quakers' African School, he had no trouble reading the text of Pennsylvania's Gradual Abolition Act of 1780. The joy that white legislators expressed that it was in "our power to extend a portion of that freedom to others, which hath been extended to us" was heartening indeed.[7] As for freeborn people of African descent like himself, they could surely expect to gain in a revolution that preached the overthrow of tyranny and the triumph of liberty. The conviction that the American Revolution was not and never had been exclusively a white man's war remained with Forten all his life.

He soon had the opportunity to support the patriots' war effort and fight for "liberty," although he did so at the risk of his own freedom. In 1781, in a move prompted as much by his family's financial plight as it was by commitment to the cause of independence, he joined the crew of a Philadelphia privateer, the *Royal Louis* (named, ironically enough, for a foreign ruler who was anything but a champion of liberty). The first cruise was very successful, with plenty of prize money to be shared around, but on her second cruise the *Royal Louis* was captured.[8] Held on board a British warship, the *Amphion*, with his shipmates, Forten feared he would be sold into slavery in the West Indies, a fate he heard had befallen other black prisoners, but a chance event spared him. John Bazely, the *Amphion*'s captain, selected the fifteen-year-old Forten to act as companion to his son, Henry, who was making his first voyage in preparation for a career in the Royal Navy. The two young sailors from such very different backgrounds struck up a friendship, and as the *Amphion* neared the British-held port of New York, Captain Bazely made Forten a remarkable offer. He could be sent with the other American captives to a prison hulk, or he could go to England with Henry, be educated with him, and enjoy the patronage of the influential Bazely family. Forten chose imprisonment over a life of privilege in England, insisting, as he later told the story: "I have been taken prisoner for the liberties of my country, and never will prove a traitor to her interest."[9] Bazely had no option but to send him to one of the prison ships, although he took steps to ensure that the young Philadelphian would not be treated any differently from the white prisoners.

Forten endured seven months of imprisonment before being released in the summer of 1782 in a general exchange. During those months he had one opportunity to escape, but he gave up that chance of freedom to a white prisoner, Daniel Brewton, "his companion . . . in suffering." For Forten it was not a question of race. He and Brewton were brothers in arms, warriors in a shared conflict. Brewton's lifelong gratitude and friendship only confirmed Forten in that belief.[10]

These are the bare bones of Forten's Revolutionary War service. In later years, as one of the most articulate leaders of the Northern free black community, he would construct from them, and from the contributions of other black patriots, a validation of his rights and the rights of all African Americans—the right to physical freedom, the right to participate in the political process, the right to remain in the country of their birth—in short, the right to live as other Americans lived.

Forten was distressed to find that memories faded fast. Promises of freedom and equality for "all men" were soon broken. He was determined to keep those promises at the forefront of political discourse. Again and again, in pamphlets, petitions, and personal encounters, he showed white Americans the ironies inherent in their Revolutionary heritage and their treatment of those who had shared in the struggle for independence. In his 1813 pamphlet, *Letters from a Man of Colour,* a work he prefaced with lines from the great British Whig writer Joseph Addison on the blessings of liberty, he addressed Pennsylvania's lawmakers and sought to awaken them to a new sense of the nation's founding principles.[11] He wrote in an attempt to defeat hostile legislation pending before the state senate that would reduce free black citizens to little more than slaves. He spoke of his sense of certainty that the men of the Revolutionary generation had meant what they said about freedom. "Those patriotick citizens . . . after resting from the toils of an arduous war, which achieved our Independence and laid the foundation of the only reasonable Republick upon earth," had truly believed that "All men are born equally free and independent, and have certain inherent and indefeasible rights, among which are those of enjoying life and liberty."[12] Their descendants were now implying that those early legislators had not known what they were about, or worse, had lied. Forten refused to accept that, writing:

> It cannot be that the authors of our Constitution intended to exclude us from its benefits, for just emerging from cruel and unjust emancipation, their souls were too much affected with their own deprivations to commence the reign of terrour [sic] over others. They knew we were deeper skinned than they were, but they acknowledged us as

men, and found that many an honest heart beat beneath a dusky bosom. They felt that they had no more authority to enslave us, than England had to tyrannize over them.[13]

Forten demanded to know what had happened to the ideals of the Revolution in a generation. Why were some Americans now to be excluded not only from the enjoyment of basic rights, but, ironically, from even joining in the celebration of independence? He wrote feelingly about the degeneration of Philadelphia's Fourth of July observances. African American veterans such as himself must stay home on the Fourth or risk the threats and insults of drunken whites. "Is it not wonderful, that the day set apart for the festival of Liberty, should be abused by the advocates of Freedom, in endeavouring to sully what they profess to adore."[14] Americans of African descent, it seemed, had no share in the "liberty" they had helped win for the nation.

Forten began to fear that the American republic was headed for a reign of terror. What he knew of the aftermath of the French Revolution appalled him. Like so many of his contemporaries, he had rejoiced at the news of the fall of the Bastille. He would speak with admiration of one of the men who had led the assault. The Marquis de Lafayette had "flown to the aid of an oppressed people" in America, and then returned home to spearhead a revolution in France. He was a true revolutionary in that he found human bondage morally repugnant, and publicly committed himself to the fight to abolish slavery throughout France's empire.[15] Sadly, through no fault of his own, the Revolution soon gave way to the Terror, with its "heroes," in Forten's words, crying " 'Vive la Republick,' while the decapitated Nun was precipitated into the general reservoir of death, and the palpitating embryo decorated the point of the bayonet."[16]

James Forten was growing increasingly apprehensive that the American Revolution was going the same way as the French Revolution. Indeed, were the barbarous acts in France during the Terror—and Forten was an avid reader of Philadelphia's Federalist press, which carried innumerable reports of French atrocities, real or imagined—any worse than what went on in those regions of the United States where the power of slavery reigned supreme?

Forten had started to have his doubts about America's commitment to liberty long before he penned *Letters from a Man of Colour.* Back in 1799, some eighty free black Philadelphians had joined in petitioning Congress to end the transatlantic slave trade and pass a law to prevent the kidnapping of free people of color in the United States, a practice they knew to be all too common.[17] Congress refused even to consider the petition, most legislators maintaining that black men had no right to seek redress of wrongs from the federal government, as they were not citizens. A shocked Forten wrote to the one man who had argued that the petition should be heard, Federalist congressman George Thacher of Massachusetts. Speaking for "Africans and descendants of that unhappy race," Forten observed that "Seven hundred thousand of the human race were concerned in our petition"—the total number of black people, free and enslaved, living in the United States. Those held in bondage obviously could not approach Congress. Their more fortunate brethren who enjoyed the blessings of freedom had done so on their behalf. Yet even the free could not feel complacent about their own situation. Given the waning of egalitarian fervor that Forten insisted was only too evident, "we knew not but ere long we might be reduced to Slavery."[18] As for charges made by some in Congress that black people were too simpleminded to know what was in their best interests, Forten responded:

> Though our faces are black, yet we are men, and though many among us cannot write because our rulers have thought proper to keep us in ignorant [sic], yet we all have the feelings and the passions of men, are as anxious to enjoy the birthright of the human race, as those who, from our ignorance, draw an argument aganest [sic] our petition.

Forten applauded Thacher's readiness to concede that "by principles of natural law our thraldom is unjust."[19]

Forten told Thacher that he and other people of color believed it was "only" by the actions of the "general government" that "we can expect to be relieved from our deplorable state." He intended that to be a reassuring phrase, for he and Thacher knew that black people elsewhere had given up waiting for those in authority to redress their wrongs.[20] The rebellion of the slaves on the island of Saint Domingue fascinated and heartened Forten. He might deplore the suffering it brought, but he would point out that that was the inevitable consequence of liberty denied. He read press accounts of the revolution. He talked with people like Antoine Servance, an African-born neighbor in Philadelphia who had gained his liberty as a result of the slave uprising.[21] The establishment of the Haitian republic was proof to Forten that black people in America "would become a great nation" and that they "could not always be detained in their present bondage." As he told S.H. Cowles in their 1825 meeting, he saw "in the great men of Hayti the deliverers and the avengers of his race."[22]

Although Forten rejected Liberia as a place of settlement for African Americans, Haiti was another matter. As an officer of the Haytien Emigration Society in the mid-1820s, he urged women and men of color to leave the United States for Haiti if they felt they must emigrate. The Haitian government was offering very attractive terms to would-be settlers. They could do well for themselves *and* assist the cause of black liberation by demonstrating to cynics in America and Europe that an independent black republic could indeed flourish. Dismissing rumors that the French were making plans to retake their lost colony by force, Forten and his fellow officers of the Emigration Society insisted: "[W]ere it so, it should not deter our going, but be a motive to urge our departure. . . . [I]s not Hayti the only spot where the coloured man has gained his rights? And could it be overthrown, would it not be putting out the very sun of our hopes?"[23] Forten's brother-in-law eventually emigrated, as did two of his apprentices and a number of his friends. He himself remained in close contact with events in Haiti throughout his life. In fact, one of the last gifts he received was a copy of English author Harriet Martineau's *The Hour and the Man,* a novel based on the life of Toussaint L'Ouverture. Martineau had called upon Forten during her American tour some years earlier and presumably knew how welcome her gift would be to a man who revered the Haitian revolution and its great hero.[24]

But what of events closer to home? As the years passed, Forten continued to hope for the best, but he began to fear the worst. According to his son-in-law, Robert Purvis, he often spoke of his conviction that his country's sin in betraying its founding principles "would bring down the vengeance of heaven," and he would quote Jefferson's dire warning: "I tremble for my country, when I reflect that God is just, and that his justice will not sleep for ever."[25] Forten imparted his views to his children. His daughter, Sarah Louisa, challenged slaveholders:

> [C]an you think He . . . who created all men free and equal—He, who made the sun to shine on the black man as well as the white, will always allow you to rest tranquil on your downy couches?—No,—He is just, and his anger will not always slumber. He will wipe the tear from Ethiopia's eye; He will shake the tree of liberty, and its blossoms shall spread over the earth.

Turning from prose to verse, she was equally scathing:

> Speak not of "my country," unless she shall be,
> In truth, the bright home of the "brave and the free!"[26]

Her brother, James Forten Jr., expressed his own fears for a country that rejoiced over "the downfall of tyranny in foreign nations" while sanctioning human bondage at home. "The time cannot be far distant," he predicted, "when Justice, armed more powerful than human aid can afford, will break the bonds of oppression, and wield the sceptre of liberty and independence throughout the nation."[27]

What, their father demanded to know, had happened to America's Revolution? How and why had it been stolen? He wanted to remain optimistic, especially in light of what he read and heard about events in Europe. As he wrote William Lloyd Garrison, his ally in another "revolution," in December 1830, libertarian movements were erupting everywhere. The United States would find it impossible "to go in opposition to the spirit of the times." Forten continued: "Whilst so much is doing in the world, to ameliorate the condition of mankind, and the spirit of Freedom is marching with rapid Strides, and causing Tyrants to tremble; may America awake from the apathy in which she has long slumbered. She must sooner or later, fall in with the irresistible current."[28]

A few weeks later he observed: "The year 1831 seems to be big with great events. Mankind are becoming more enlightened, and all tyrants, and the tyrants of this country, must tremble."[29] But frustration was never far away. "That we are not treated as freemen, in any part of the United States, is certain," Forten wrote. "This usage . . . is in direct opposition to the Constitution; which positively declares, that all men are born equal, and endowed with certain inalienable rights."[30] Why did it seem to be only "foreign oppression" that "call[ed] forth the sympathy of the Americans"? Why did they continue to ignore the plight of "the oppressed of their own country"?[31] Things must change, and Forten insisted that he and those who thought as he did must *make* them change. "[S]o long as we can learn wisdom from the fate of nations . . . so long as we can view all nations every where contending for their long lost rights; we cannot be silent nor satisfied, until we are in possession of that boon of heaven—*the inalienable rights of man.*"[32]

There were those who insisted that what Forten, Garrison, and others in the radical antislavery ranks had in mind was servile insurrection. A letter of Forten's that Garrison printed in the *Liberator* in August 1831 under the title "Men Must Be Free" appeared less than two days before Nat Turner and his rebel band began their murderous rampage in Virginia. Forten's criticism of the hypocrisy practiced "in this boasted land of liberty" was hardly intended as a call for a bloodbath, but that was how the defenders of slavery and the racial status quo saw it. Forten wrote:

When we . . . hear of almost every nation fighting for its liberty, is it to be expected that the African race will continue always in the degraded state they are now? No. The time is fast approaching when the words 'Fight for liberty, or die in the attempt,' will he sounded in

every African ear . . . and when he will throw off his fetters, and flock
to the banner . . . with the following words inscribed upon it—'Liberty or Death.'[33]

In the racially charged atmosphere of the early 1830s, that was incitement
enough to condemn Forten and his fellow abolitionists as the aiders and
abettors of Nat Turner.

Despite harsh criticism and the occasional death threat, Forten refused
to back down. Why did it seem that the United States, the nation whose
people, according to him, had struck the first blow for liberty, was betraying its libertarian heritage? That this was the case was abundantly clear, he
felt, and he recognized his personal obligation to speak out. In 1832, for
instance, in a memorial to the Pennsylvania legislature regarding the passage of a more stringent statewide fugitive slave law, Forten, Robert Purvis,
and William Whipper, their ally in a number of such initiatives, observed
that they "cannot but lament, that at a moment when all mankind seems to
be struggling for freedom, and endeavoring to throw off the shackles of
political oppression, the constituted authorities of this great state should
entertain a resolution, which has a tendency to abridge the liberties
heretofore accorded to a race of men confessedly oppressed." History
alone was sufficient to condemn the lawmakers and hold them up to
ridicule for their hypocrisy. The petitioners continued: "Our country asserts for itself the glory of being the freest upon the face of the globe. She
wrested that freedom . . . by force of arms, at the expense of infinite blood
and treasure, from a . . . most powerful adversary. She proclaimed freedom to all mankind—and offered her soil as a refuge to the enslaved of all
nations."

But time had wrought a profound change. "[T]he . . . nation from
which we . . . wrested our . . . liberties" had now become a bastion of freedom. Abolition in the British Empire was on the horizon, and slavery was a
dead letter in Britain itself. "Let a man of the deepest jet be brought before
[a British judge], and it is the glorious prerogative of that judge to exclaim:
'your feet are on English soil—therefore you are free!' " But "here, in this
republican land . . . the judge, the American judge, the Pennsylvania
judge, himself a freeman, is bound by our laws, tied down" and forced to
return a human being to bondage without the benefit of a jury trial.[34] To
those who argued that the petitioners were unpatriotic, Forten answered
that they were the true patriots, for they loved America too much to see it
betray its principles.

The emergence of the American Colonization Society was further proof
to Forten, assuming he needed any, that America's Revolutionary ideals
were indeed being undermined. True, he admired several of the founders

of the ACS, and he understood that some high-minded individuals had been deluded into supporting it because they believed it would speed the progress of emancipation. However, Forten insisted, the ACS had soon been taken over by Southern slaveholders and their Northern sympathizers who feared that the free people of color "have too much liberty." "We ask not their . . . aid, in assisting us to emigrate to Africa, we are contented in the land that gave us birth, and which many of us fought for, during the war which established our Independence." [35] But times had changed. The America of Forten's old age was not the America of his youth, the new nation that he and other men of color had risked their lives to create. "[A]ll this appears to be forgotten now—and the descendants of these Men . . . are intended to be removed to a distant . . . Country, while the Emigrants from every other Country, are permitted to seek an asylum here from oppression." [36]

Saddened by the abandonment of revolutionary principles, and apprehensive that the nation was risking either more bloody slave insurrections, or divine vengeance, or both, James Forten continued to pin his hopes on revolution. The only difference was that this new revolution must be peaceful and must effect profound moral and social changes. The first American revolution had brought victory on the battlefield. The second must bring a more far-reaching victory over entrenched habits of thought and behavior. Should this second revolution fail, Forten feared that the consequences would be dreadful indeed.

Advancing age did not diminish the strength of his commitment. He threw himself as wholeheartedly into this new struggle as he had into the conflict against Britain. In the 1830s, as president of the American Moral Reform Society, he advocated a sweeping agenda that included antislavery, women's rights, education, temperance, pacifism, and the relief of poverty. Critics might assail his demands for a second revolution as unrealistic and "visionary in the extreme," but he ignored them, preferring to continue to place his faith in the redemptive power of revolution, and declaring: "[W]e live in stir[r]ing times, and every day brings news of some fresh effort for liberty, either at home or abroad—onward, onward, is indeed the watchword." [37] A revolutionary to the last, James Forten never abandoned hope that America would experience in a second revolution a new birth of freedom, a rededication to the spirit and the reality of liberty for *all* its people.

6

John Brown Russwurm's Dilemma: Citizenship or Emigration?

Sandra Sandiford Young

We have always said that when convinced of our error we would hasten to ac-
knowledge it. That time has now arrived. The change which has taken place
has not been the hasty conclusion of a moment; we have pondered much on this
interesting subject, and read every article in our reach both for and against the
Society . . . we have carefully examined the different plans now in operation
for our benefit, and none, we believe, can reach half so efficiently the masses as
the plan of colonization on the West coast of Africa.
——John Brown Russwurm, *Freedom's Journal*, March 21, 1829[1]

At the age of thirty, John Brown Russwurm announced that he had decided to emigrate to Liberia under the auspices of the American Colonization Society. Given his position as the prominent editor of America's
first black newspaper, *Freedom's Journal*, Russwurm's surprise pronounce-
ment ignited a firestorm of controversy among Northern free blacks.

There are many elements that led to this confrontation between Russwurm and the black community he served, but the most important of these
was the recent emergence of a common political agenda among the fledgling free black community in the North. The evolution of a more con-
certed and communal political consciousness was spurred on in large part
by the constant pressure of whites who sought to circumscribe the rights
and freedom of African Americans, or who sought to remove free blacks
entirely from American society. The passage of repressive laws, particularly
the Fugitive Slave Act of 1793, and the increasingly harsh (and racialized)
restrictions on the rights of state and national citizenship forced free
blacks to organize to protect themselves and to strategize plans for resistance and opposition to white prejudice and authority. Any action along
these lines required leaders to articulate the concerns, goals, and actions
of the black community more broadly. It is within the context of this urgent
need for greater public and political representation that Russwurm's personal views on colonization got him into considerable trouble.

For African Americans, slavery was both a personal and communal problem. Unlike white communities, blacks understood that the abolitionist struggle required constant vigilance; everyone had a role to play in achieving freedom from slavery, both for themselves and for those still held in bondage. Blacks approached abolition with a twofold agenda: the elimination of chattel slavery and the struggle for civic equality. As long as slavery existed in the United States, no black person would ever really be free—nor would they be able to fully enjoy the rights and privileges of citizenship. Thus, the tactics that blacks employed to combat slavery included more than formal political appeals and petitions; they also included direct action such as escape, self-purchase, and resettlement or emigration. These, too, were cornerstones of black resistance.

From the mid-eighteenth century, free blacks regularly explored resettlement options in remote areas of the United States, as well as emigration to Canada, Africa, and the Caribbean. These possibilities were part of the continuous effort on the part of free blacks to improve their circumstances and forge their own freedom on their own terms. African Americans understood well that they might never be free (or equal) in the new nation. The aftermath of the American Revolution—the slow pace of emancipation in the North coupled with the rapid expansion of slavery in the South—offered little hope that abolition would be swift or complete. Even before the nation declared its own independence, people of African descent debated the relative merits of emigration, many early black leaders embracing emigration as a viable solution to (or escape from) slavery long before Russwurm articulated his own views on the subject. Which begs the question: as emigration was in the 1820s hardly a new strategy for African Americans, why the unprecedented public outcry against Russwurm? This is especially perplexing given that his personal decision to leave the country under the auspices of the American Colonization Society, dominated as it was by Southern slaveholders, posed neither a sufficient or significant threat to the larger community of free blacks living in the United States. This essay examines the complex events that led Russwurm to embrace colonization and emigrate to Liberia—decisions that ultimately made him a pariah among his people.

John Brown Russwurm was a young man at the time black emigration activities were at their peak. When he was eight years old his father, a white American merchant, sent him from his home in Port Antonio, Jamaica, to boarding school in the province of Quebec, Canada, where he remained for three years. On plantations in Jamaica, it was customary for favored mulatto children to live in their father's home, where they received both an education and a reprieve from arduous plantation chores. As a result, they came to regard themselves as different from, and better than, blacks with darker skin. There was even further exclusion if their mothers—often the "housekeeper," or slave master's mistress—lived in or near a large town such as Port Antonio, where the presence of similarly privileged mulattos provided a context for elite socialization. In some instances, these favored children and their mothers lived independently in wealth and extreme comfort, sometimes holding slaves and estates of their own.[2] By the age of eight, then, John Brown's vision of himself had been forged within this relatively rarefied world of mulatto privilege. His favored status and his fair skin placed him at the top of plantation hierarchy.

John Brown's early childhood was exceptional not only for blacks, but for West Indian whites of this period. For example, planters were expected to provide their offspring with suitable schooling. However, the planters of Portland parish, where Brown was raised, had complained to the Jamaican legislature that they could not afford to establish a suitable school, that the cost of sending their children abroad was prohibitive.[3] Soon thereafter, a school was established for the planters at Titchfield and maintained by the parish. The white settlers of Portland continued the custom of sending their children to the Titchfield Trust Free School.

When the sugar boom in Port Antonio began to fade, Russwurm Senior moved his young son to Portland, Maine, where he was enrolled in Hebron Academy. Father and son lived on a seventy-five-acre farm at Back Cove, just outside of Portland. By all accounts, they had a close relationship, which John T. Hall, an associate of John Brown's, recalled years later:

> Mr. Russwurm when he came to Portland with his son who was named John Brown, did not conceal the relationship that existed between them. He was proud of this son. He introduced him into the best society in Portland, where he was honored and respected. He attended the best schools and had all the privileges that other boys of the best families enjoyed.[4]

In 1813 Russwurm's father married Susan Goold Blanchard, a young widow with three children of her own. The following year, she gave birth to a son, Francis Edward Russwurm. Shortly thereafter, in 1815, Russwurm Senior died; John Brown was just sixteen years old. Providentially, the boy had an excellent relationship with his stepmother with whom he remained close throughout his life.[5] During this period, John Brown lived outside of any black settlements; he had no significant contact with African Americans and he did not express any awareness of the concerns of the black world. In what would later seem ironic, the future "race man" was born and bred in an almost exclusively—and certainly exclusive—white world.

Russwurm graduated from Hebron Academy in 1819. He had received a comfortable inheritance of $2,000 from his father's will, some of which he used to complete his schooling at Hebron. Early on, he had expressed a desire to go on to college and he likely used the remainder of his inheritance for that purpose. Russwurm also began to express some concern about establishing himself professionally. In a letter to his cousin John Sumner Russwurm, Russwurm wrote, "[N]othing more shall ever escape me concerning my situation in life."[6] Russwurm had also written to a classmate, John Otis, in the summer after his graduation from Hebron Academy, stating that he would attend Gorham Academy for two months to further prepare for acceptance to university.[7]

In 1821 Portland experienced a severe recession. Unable to find employment near his home, Russwurm, then twenty years old, moved to Boston to gain some work experience and make his own way.[8] He taught at the Abiel Smith and Primus Hall Schools, schools that had been established for black children.[9] It was during this period that Russwurm was first introduced to the reality of black life in early-nineteenth-century America.

Russwurm's move to Boston catapulted him into a world vastly different from his previous experiences. Portland's wide avenues, well-situated houses, and agrarian pace proved a sharp contrast to the hurly-burly, raucous pace of Boston's packed wharf district, the competitive ethos of the shopkeepers and artisans, and the large groups of day laborers who milled about on the commons, in the taverns, and on the piers. The sheer number of people living in Boston must have been breathtaking to Russwurm. By 1790 Boston's black population had grown to 800—not exactly the pre–Revolutionary War figure of 10 percent but a significant number nonetheless.[10] Between 1780 and 1820 the free black population in the North had doubled but the white population increased even faster as a result of growing immigration rates. The constant influx of white immigrants to Northern cities helped to shift the public debate over slavery's abolition to a broader concern over how to manage the growing free black population within an increasingly competitive labor market. Boston embodied all of these trends.

Massachusetts had been hit particularly hard because it was unable to use its port during the war. Blacks and whites competed for what few laboring jobs were available. Put off by this competition, whites began to insult and accost blacks on the streets in an attempt to intimidate them, hoping to prevent blacks from applying for the limited number of jobs. Given the city's increasingly tense racial climate, blacks gradually stopped attending white churches or allowing their children to attend the city's predominantly white schools. Whites generally refused to acknowledge these problems—at least publicly—and the legislature refused a number of petitions from the black community requesting separate schools for their children.

The harassment of blacks on the streets escalated to more direct action. In New York City and Boston, whites banded together on the waterfront and refused to labor alongside blacks who had traditionally worked as stevedores, caulkers, sail makers, coopers, and day laborers, thus effectively cutting off this relatively reliable means of employment for blacks. Living in the black community for the first time, Russwurm was exposed to these larger economic and racial issues, an experience that no doubt seemed foreign to him given his privileged upbringing. Over time, however, Russwurm developed a more acutely "black" sensibility about the world around him—a transformation of his political and racial consciousness that allowed him to see things in a vastly different light.

The contrast between the easy acceptance of his life in Portland and the concentrated hostility faced by the black community in Boston likely accentuated the significance of these incidents of violence and discrimination for Russwurm. His skills and education would most certainly have drawn him into discussions of the ways and means the black community could both protect itself and resist such encroachments. Among the strategies of resistance developed and debated by blacks at this time, emigration was seriously explored as a means of survival. For a short period after the American Revolution, blacks remained optimistic about the abolition of slavery, as well as the prospects for full inclusion in the life and opportunities of the new nation. Within ten years, however, it became increasingly obvious that slavery would continue more strongly than ever in the South, even as it was being gradually dismantled in the North. This reality, coupled with rising antiblack sentiment in the North, inspired some blacks to explore other options. By the time Russwurm had arrived in Boston, emigration had been a viable alternative for more than forty years.

In 1773 four slaves in Boston petitioned the state legislature "for the right to set aside one day a week during which they could earn money toward the purchase of their freedom" so that they could return to Africa.[11] Likewise, as spokesman for a group of seventy-three "African blacks," Prince Hall petitioned the General Court of Massachusetts in 1787 for financial support to resettle in Africa "due to the disagreeable and disadvantageous circumstances that attended them in the United States."[12] In November 1780, the African Union Society was established in Newport, Rhode Island, as a mutual benefit and moral improvement society. The majority of its members were African-born and the main political agenda was to emigrate to their homelands to establish independent black settlements that were not beholden to white interests or authority.[13] "For the Africans and Afro-Americans of the Newport organization, emigration was a banner to unite all black peoples—in Africa, the West Indies, and the United States."[14] While emigration was a shared interest within the black community, the keenest proponents were African-born blacks, a trend that helped guarantee the success, albeit limited, of this political strategy.

An attempt to scout and purchase land in Africa for emigration failed when the principal backer, Samuel Hopkins, decided that the Newport group's agent, James McKenzie, had conducted himself improperly. His refusal to endorse the group of hopeful settlers from Providence doomed the project.[15] Hopkins, a well-known minister of the First Congregational Church of Newport, had proposed several grandiose schemes for returning blacks to Africa in an effort to both Christianize the Africans and end the slave trade. As the chief exponent of the doctrine of benevolence, Hopkins had developed a theological concept of dynamic evangelicalism. He proposed training Negroes in Calvinism and returning them to Africa to work as missionaries to redeem the continent. "In this way," Hopkins said, "whites could compensate for [the] 'injury and injustice' of the slave trade."[16]

Although colonization and emigration certainly had its white advocates and financiers, several prominent African Americans also emerged as its chief proponents. Paul Cuffe—a wealthy Massachusetts merchant of African and Native American descent—became interested in the emigration movement after the establishment of Sierra Leone in 1809. Cuffe corresponded extensively with friends and associates to gather ideas and support for his emigration plans. Robert Finley, the founder of the American Colonization Society, was one of his most enthusiastic correspondents. Originally, Cuffe planned to return to Africa once a year with a cargo and settlers, but the War of 1812 intervened. It would be 1816 before Cuffe was able to bring thirty-eight settlers to Freetown. Cuffe had planned to sail again the following year, but he fell ill and died on September 7, 1817.

These failures to establish a viable emigration policy to Africa diminished New England's role as a leader of the emigration movement. Such failure, however, was muted by the extensive contacts that had been developed in Haiti. Slave buyers in northeastern seaboard cities had maintained a long-standing relationship with the West Indies, preferring seasoned Africans with skills suitable for urban settings. As a result, extensive contacts were established between blacks living in Saint Domingue, Barbados, and Trinidad, and their counterparts in Philadelphia and New York. A special relationship with Saint Domingue began during the Revolutionary War when a French auxiliary corps fought beside American troops at the siege of Savannah. Part of that corps was a detachment of 545 mulattos, many of whom subsequently became leaders of the Haitian revolution. When one of the detachment leaders, Henri Christophe, became the king of Haiti he began the first of several attempts to resettle black emigrants from the United States in Haiti. British abolitionists William Wilberforce and Thomas Clarkson convinced Christophe to extend asylum to American slaves. When Prince Saunders—a Vermont-born teacher from the African School of Boston and a disciple of Cuffe—visited Haiti, he convinced Christophe to extend asylum to American free blacks as well.[17] Later, during a coup d'état, Christophe committed suicide. But the emigration venture itself refused to die.

Recognizing his nation's desperate need for workers, Haiti's new ruler, Jean Pierre Boyer, contacted Philadelphia's black leaders to express his support for black emigration. James Forten had been a supporter of Cuffe's efforts and led the recruitment efforts for Haiti as well. Much of the information about Haiti Russwurm later published in *Freedom's Journal* came from Forten's Haitian contacts. Through his agent, Jonathan Granville, President Boyer declared that all settlers would enjoy the full protection of the Haitian constitution the moment their feet touched Haitian soil. He disseminated a plan detailing settlement regions, including the number of settlers, skills needed, and conditions under which settlers were to repay their relocation expenses and receive land. The plan delineated three classes of settlers: skilled agricultural labor; unskilled labor; and artisans, merchants and teachers.[18]

The issues of black emigration and Haitian independence were widely discussed during Russwurm's stay in Boston. Reverend Thomas Paul, pastor of the African Baptist Church, where some of the classes Russwurm taught were held, had spent six months in Haiti. In a letter to the *Columbian Sentinal,* a Boston newspaper, he aligned himself with the emigrationists, urging free blacks to settle in Haiti:

> Having been a resident for some months in the Island of Hayti, I am fully persuaded that it is the best and most suitable place of residence which Providence has hitherto offered to emancipated people of colour, for the enjoyment of liberty and equality with their attendant blessings. At an interview which I had with President Boyer, some months ago, he was pleased to make a verbal statement of the same offers . . . to the free people of colour in the United States.[19]

Published during Russwurm's stay in Boston, President Boyer's invitation to black Americans presented a seemingly solid alternative to life in the United States. It was at this time that Russwurm began to speak more seriously about the merits of emigration for black people living in the United States.

In 1824, Russwurm was admitted to Bowdoin College in Brunswick,

Maine. In his *Personal Recollections of Nathaniel Hawthorne,* Horatio Bridge reported that Russwurm chose to live with a carpenter outside of Brunswick rather than in dormitory housing with other students.[20] Bridge also commented that although he and Nathaniel Hawthorne visited the young scholar, the visits were not returned "due to his [Russwurm's] sensitiveness." Curiously, Russwurm displayed neither "sensitiveness" nor a need to be housed separately from his classmates during his previous schooling. In his earlier letter to Hebron Academy classmate John Otis, Russwurm had clearly identified himself as a member of the student fraternity and gleefully recounted the latest news of their old alma mater:

> Well what think you friend Otis, Hebron Academy burnt down? Astonishing, you would reply. Not at all so, I consider it as the judgement of Heaven for their treatment of the few independent souls who resided with them during this past year. True is the saying "all for the best," for we see it plainly proved in the visitations of heaven on the Hebronites.[21]

By the 1820s, the buoyancy of Russwurm's youth had been tempered by his exposure to the realities of race in the early republic. After his time in Boston, Russwurm would never be the same. Russwurm's time there exposed him to enough of the difficulties black Americans faced in earning a living that he began to entertain the idea of settling abroad, especially in Haiti. Evidence of this willingness can be found in a letter he wrote to his cousin, John Sumner Russwurm, on January 9, 1826: "If not particularly invited by the Haytien Govt then, I shall study Medicine in Boston previous to an emigration to Hayti."[22] Russwurm's precarious financial circumstance further emphasized his changed status since his father's death. In that same letter he stated that he was "just able to keep my present standing." He also noted that by "correct deportment" he had made valuable friends, both in Boston and at Bowdoin. Russwurm never pursued his stated desire to become a doctor, either because of his poor finances or because of an inability to find an apprenticeship in medicine. However, his "valuable friends" no doubt played a role in convincing the American Colonization Society to offer Russwurm a position in a letter dated December 25, 1826. He replied on February 26, 1827, writing: "All whose advice I have consulted on the subject, are of the opinion, that at present, it would not be advisable to accept the liberal offer of your Board of Managers."[23] This was Russwurm's first encounter with the ACS.

Russwurm had an exemplary career at Bowdoin and was asked to speak at his commencement. His speech received considerable attention both for its content and for the fact that a black man had delivered it. It was published in the *Eastern Argus,* in Portland, Maine, on September 12, 1826, and later reprinted in the *Boston Courier, National Philanthropist,* and *Genius of Universal Emancipation.* Russwurm's address, entitled "The Condition and Prospects of Hayti," spoke to his continuing interest in Haiti and what its successful revolution meant to him:

> . . . the Revolution in Hayti holds a conspicuous place—The former political condition of Hayti we all doubtless know. After years of san-guinary struggles for freedom and a political existence, the Haytians on the auspicious day of January first-1804 declared themselves a free and independent nation. Nothing can ever induce them to re-cede from this declaration. They know too well by their past misfor-tunes, by their wounds which are yet bleeding, that security can be expected only from within themselves. Rather would they devote themselves to death than return to their former condition.[24]

After his graduation in August 1827, a coalition of community leaders headed by Boston Crummell, an activist and businessman, invited Russ-wurm to New York to join with them and Reverend Samuel Cornish in launching *Freedom's Journal,* what Timothy Patrick McCarthy has argued was "the first antislavery periodical to advocate immediate abolition and racial equality as interrelated goals."[25] Cornish and Russwurm were to be its co-editors. The need to develop an effective voice for African Americans had become critical. Widespread propaganda decrying the rise of the free black community ascribed every manner of evil to the growing population of free blacks, and although the spread of this vilification came from every quarter, the American Colonization Society became the focal point of black anger.

Robert Finley, the son of an immigrant Scottish merchant, founded the American Colonization Society.[26] For twenty-two years Finley served as a Presbyterian minister and master of the local academy in Baskingridge, New Jersey, one of the strongest congregations in the presbytery. Some of his students went on to become senators, governors, university presidents, secretary of the navy, as well as influential politicians and military heroes. In the New Jersey presbytery Hopkins's doctrine of benevolence sparked a desire to do something about the growing free black population. Believing that the "free Negro was an anomaly in American society," Finley proposed "that systematic colonization would strengthen society and benefit the emigrating blacks."[27] Echoing this view, in Philadelphia, the General As-sembly of the Presbyterian Church expressed in 1818 their views on slave-holding and slavery:

> We do, indeed, tenderly sympathize with those portions of our church and our country, where the evil of slavery has been entailed upon them; where a *great,* and *the most virtuous part* of the *community* abhor slavery, and wish its extermination, as sincerely as any other; but where the number of slaves, their ignorance, and their vicious habits generally, render an immediate and universal emancipation inconsistent, alike, with the safety and happiness of the master and the slave.[28]

Whites believed that the emancipation of slaves only worsened their condition. As historian Early Lee Fox has described: "In general black people gain little, in many instances they are great losers, by emancipation. Law may relieve them from slavery, but laws cannot change their colour."[29] Whites constantly declared that free blacks were immoral, lazy, ignorant, and that the majority ended up in the jails and prisons of the country. Furthermore, they believed that large numbers of freedmen would be idle and thus become a burden on the community. Having frightened themselves with their own propaganda, whites became certain that the presence of a large number of freedmen would encourage dissent and rebellion among those still enslaved, and that wholesale emancipation of blacks would lead to civil insurrections as former slaves attempted to rule their former masters. With such opinions in the air, the supporters of African colonization felt there was fertile ground for their plans to export all freed slaves willing to resettle in Africa.

By every measure, the rolls of the American Colonization Society were impressive. Charter members included Francis Scott Key, the prominent Washington, D.C., attorney who authored "The Star-Spangled Banner," and Elias Cauldwell, Supreme Court clerk and the brother-in-law of ACS founder Robert Finley. These men, in turn, persuaded other men of elite stature to join the organization: Stephen B. Balch, Presbyterian clergyman at Georgetown; Bushrod Washington, nephew of George Washington, veteran Supreme Court justice, and then squire of Mount Vernon; Henry Clay, speaker of the House of Representatives; and former U.S. Senator John Randolph, of Roanoke.

For two years prior to the first organizational meeting of the American Colonization Society in December 1816, Finley wrote to supporters of colonization, lectured to groups across the country, and encouraged the formation of local societies for colonization. More than 200 chapters proliferated in the years following the ACS's inception. Finley's articles promulgated the idea that resettlement would repay the country's debt to the freed black population, bring about the eventual elimination of slavery, and at the same time, alleviate the stresses large populations of free blacks were causing society. Declaring that while Negroes were capable of improvement and self-government, Finley averred that equality was impossible as long as they remained among whites. They were sons of Africa by color, temperament, and fortune, and God had destined them to dwell in Africa. "The friends of man will strive in vain to raise them to a proper level while they remain among us," he warned. Entrenched prejudice and a sense of inferiority conspired against any real improvement. Only in Africa—the "land of their fathers"—could "Africans" (as Finley insisted on calling all Negroes) find true freedom and equality.[30] Finley was also very thorough in his research on African colonization efforts already under way. Indeed, after Paul Cuffe died he used his correspondence to infer that Cuffe had been an agent for the ACS.[31]

Recognizing the enormous expense of transporting and providing basic support to large numbers of free blacks, Finley intended to seek the support and assistance of the United States government:

> The whole nation shared national guilt for slavery, "the great violation of the laws of nature." Only the nation's representatives could make the "atoning sacrifice" and correct "injuries done to humanity by our ancestors."[32]

The involvement of so many prominent and influential men in the formation of the ACS was a deliberate strategy designed to win congressional support for financial backing. While Finley was able to gain some government funding for the ACS, he was never as successful as he had hoped.

What Finley did not understand was that unlike other emigration efforts the American Colonization Society included no blacks as members. Moreover, the advertisements and letters soliciting funds on behalf of the ACS were filled with patronizing descriptions of the so-called "degraded" conditions and habits of free blacks and the necessity of protecting America from them. With the likes of Henry Clay and Bushrod Washington on the membership rolls, the majority of blacks were suspicious and fearful of the plans and intentions of the ACS—which they frequently denounced as "schemes." White colonizationists' support for the eventual emancipation of all slaves was hard to believe given that at least half of the membership espoused the colonization of free blacks while also maintaining large plantations populated by slaves.

One month after the formation of the American Colonization Society, an estimated 3,000 African Americans, both free and slave, met in Richard Allen's African Methodist Episcopal Bethel Church in Philadelphia.[33] The meeting resoundingly concluded that colonization was an attempt to solidify slavery's grasp by removing free blacks from American soil. Those in attendance also felt that the ACS propaganda "stigmatized the free Negro population"[34] in direct violation of the espoused principles of the founding documents of the United States. "We will never separate ourselves voluntarily from the slave population of this country," stated a resolution that passed unanimously at the meeting.[35] This powerful resolution—the denunciation of colonization—was a pivotal moment in the formation of a more aggressively political African American communal identity. Those blacks who had previously supported Cuffe's plans for emigration to Africa found themselves in the precarious position of running against the tide of popular feeling. For example, James Forten—previously one of the most prominent supporters of Cuffe's plans—wrote Cuffe of his predicament:

> Indeed, the people of color here was very much frightened. At first they were afraid that all the free people would be compelled to go, particularly [those] in the southern states. We had a large meeting of males at the Rev. R. Allen's church the other evening. Three thousand at least attended, and there was not one soul that was in favor of going to Africa. They think the slaveholders wants to get rid of them so as to make their property more secure.
>
> However, it appears to me that if the Father of all Mercies is in this interesting subject (for it appeared that they all think that something must and ought to be done, but do not know where nor how to begin), the way will be made straight and clear. We, however, have agreed to remain silent, as the people, here both white and color, are decided against the measure. My opinion is that they will never become a people until they come out from amongst the white people. But as the majority is decidedly against me, I am determined to remain silent, except as to my opinion which I freely give when asked.[36]

In light of his personal opinions, Forten, who chaired this meeting, exhibited a striking public reticence regarding his political views on African emigration. Curiously, his silence enhanced his position as the free black community's most important leader. Black resistance to the ACS coincided with persistent hopes for Haitian emigration, a venture in which Forten was still deeply involved.

The American Colonization Society continued to seek support from the United States government, benevolent societies, churches, and like-minded people—all of whom were white. The ACS actively undermined the Haitian emigration venture and continuously pushed for the emigration of the black elite, thus confirming in the minds of most free blacks that its main purpose was to eliminate the free black community in order to preserve the institution of slavery. It is at this point that events began to converge.

In response to this constant pressure, the nascent free black communities began to develop a respected group of leaders to serve as their spokesmen: Prince Hall and Thomas Paul in Boston; Boston Crummell, Samuel Cornish, and Reverend Peter Williams in New York; James Forten, Robert Purvis, and Richard Allen in Philadelphia. These men corresponded with one another and joined together to support various efforts on behalf of their communities. In solicitations of support for schools, orphanages, and churches, the names of these men figured prominently. They served as officers and founding members of African Free Schools, a wide variety of benevolent societies, and women's groups such as the Dorcas organization in New York City. These men were even featured prominently in the minutes of white manumission societies and state abolition groups. While all had supported emigration efforts, none of these leaders seemed interested in emigrating themselves; instead, they explored possible trade and business opportunities. Furthermore, as emigration movements had historically been the provenance of blacks, the growing class of black elite was increasingly determined to resist what they viewed as the encroachment of the ACS on their leadership role.

Tensions between different philosophies within the communities and competition between Northern free black communities were aired in *Freedom's Journal*. As a consequence, there was intense scrutiny by whites of the newly invigorated activities and increasingly public character of the free black communities. Following the pattern established in articles by the white editor (and prominent racist) Mordecai Noah in the *National Advocate*, the white press found the idea of free blacks having parties and balls a source of great amusement. Where none had been held, it would make them up, or exaggerate an event until it bore no resemblance to reality.

The mocking exaggerations of the white press lodged in the attention given to black social and political organizations contained an implicit threat. The specter of white retaliation against free blacks who dared to hold frivolous balls, or other, more serious functions, was so powerful that Russwurm and Cornish felt compelled to investigate the smallest details and lay the true facts before the public because of the "many articles which daily appear, much to our disadvantage." In a very real sense, then, *Freedom's Journal* provided an important counterpoint to the pervasiveness of racism in the white press and the public sphere. Yet there was no complaint against the presumption of the white press setting itself up as the arbiter of acceptable black social events.

The various articles, letters, and commentary throughout the life of *Freedom's Journal* attested to the continuous scrutiny of the white press. Commentary appeared regularly on the license that newspapers were allowed in their unchecked accusations. Black communities in all Northern cities were bitterly aware that this campaign of misinformation was disastrous to their future aspirations. "The press is a most efficient engine, and when directed to the destruction of private character, few can withstand its power."[37] Russwurm himself eventually became exasperated by his own community's insistence on public balls: "In our humble opinion the mania which many have for dancing, is a sure indication, in most cases, of a mind uncultivated and unaccustomed to reflection."[38]

Russwurm felt that the black community should avoid any activities that made it an easy target of white racism. His frustrations over having to constantly refute the exaggerations of the white press culminated in this stinging, and perhaps unjustified, attack on his people:

> We confess, that we have been much tried during the past winter, upon hearing the daily accounts of balls, cotillion parties, &c. in which many of our respectable coloured friends have seen proper to indulge in this our city of New York. Were a few moments devoted to counting the cost, waste of time and injury to health, many who are now great admirers of Balls, &c. would in another winter, we believe, be convicted that all this waste of time, and health, and money, is highly impolitic, and might easily be dispensed with; and in the stead thereof, be willing and anxious to devote their leisure hours to the more important subject of self-cultivation, in the more solid branches of education.

His lectures to the community on their behavior exposed to the public Russwurm's bias that poor black people were more inclined to waste their money in this fashion. However, his personal expressions of distaste did not seem to take into account the desires of the growing black middle class, which felt entitled to enjoy the same kinds of things as the white middle class. A prominent example of the possibility for black class mobility and privilege, Russwurm was certainly aware of the education, culture, and social attainments of this group. But there is no indication in his writings that he differentiated between this group and the larger public of free blacks who were so very poor. Instead, Russwurm's responses seem to place him squarely in the camp of those who felt that black people should indulge in social activities reflecting their status and not try to emulate the customs of the wealthier, white citizenry. Russwurm never came to fully appreciate the importance—both symbolic and real—of the free black community's claim and use of public space. Instead, he appeared to be both embarrassed and frustrated by his community's insistence on public displays.

His reaction to the community's New York Emancipation Day observances exposed these biases. As Russwurm had expressed deep exasperation with "the daily accounts of balls, cotillion parties &c." held in the free
black community, neither was he a fan of parades. This position went
against the predilections of the larger African American community,
which apparently felt that a parade was an appropriate way to begin almost
any significant observance. The New York Emancipation Day celebrations
proved to be the straw that broke Russwurm's patience.

In the July 18, 1828, issue of *Freedom's Journal*, Russwurm chided "our
Brethren of Brooklyn" for having a Brooklyn Emancipation Day celebration after participating with the observances of greater New York City. The
fact that "a grand procession . . . was conducted with order and propriety,
and great credit was gained by it from all classes" only exacerbated Russwurm's anger. The Brooklyn celebration commenced with a half-mile-long
parade populated by marchers clad in secondhand uniforms to "appear as
Generals or Marshals, or Admirals." These displays, Russwurm contended,
made them "complete and appropriate laughing stocks for thousands of
our citizens, and to the more considerate of our brethren, objects of compassion and shame." He was even more annoyed when he learned that
both men and women were publicly drunk and disorderly, acknowledging
that his pleas for temperance and restraint had been ignored. After revil-
ing his community's habit of dressing ostentatiously, Russwurm appealed
to "the younger members of our Colour, from whose discretion and knowledge we expect more" to engage instead in the kind of activity "which has a
tendency to raise us in public estimation."[39]

Somehow, exposure to the complex idiosyncrasies of the black community during the publication of *Freedom's Journal* had resulted in Russwurm
assuming a position as public judge and arbiter of his race. He, however,
did not seem to find much gratification in this unenviable role. Less than
two weeks later, Russwurm introduced an article with the following lead:
"ANOTHER CELEBRATION!!!"[40] Unable to find any evidence that could
condemn the marchers of improper behavior, Russwurm was, nonetheless,
still against the march. Assuring his readers that while he supported the
work of mutual societies and the decorum of the "Daughters of Israel" procession, he opposed such outward shows. Russwurm allowed that an anniversary celebration of the society was reasonable, but he cautioned: "let
there be nothing of the Pharisee about the proceedings on such occasions—let there be no white dress and cap and ribbon to shew [sic] that we
belong to the 'Daughters of Israel,' or any other society."[41]

A part of Russwurm's distaste for such processions was the considerable
expense the participants undertook, particularly in light of the extreme
poverty of the community. On some level, he considered such occasions to

be ostentatious and gratuitous, an affront to those who were struggling to make ends meet. More importantly, most processions—no matter how orderly or decorous—tended to attract the notice of white men and boys who followed along. Seldom constrained by the authorities, these mobs would taunt, ape, and assault the marchers, sometimes even causing severe physical harm. The white press avidly reported on these parades, exaggerating the marchers' costumes and behavior, and inventing scenarios that mocked the proceedings. Newspapers invited their readers to laugh at the marchers and incited repeated violence against the black community. Acutely aware of this growing trend, Russwurm could not understand why his community would not avoid providing fodder for these crass depictions.

Unfortunately, Russwurm's personal distaste for lavish public display prevented him from appreciating the political implications of blacks forcing the larger community to acknowledge, if not accept, their presence in the public domain. He may have felt that by not drawing attention to themselves, residents of the free black community would be safer. In this instance, however, Russwurm's taste clouded his judgment. And while he would not change his opinions regarding the use of public space, his detractors within the free black community were not reluctant to challenge him.

As editor of *Freedom's Journal*, Russwurm had publicly supported anti–American Colonization Society sentiment:

> Messrs. Editors—I beg leave to draw your attention to Mr. Clay's Speech, delivered before the last Annual Meeting of the Colonization Society, at Washington. It should be matter of no small concern to the free people of colour, to perceive the rapid progress of the Colonization Society; its increase cannot be viewed in another light, than a desire to get effectually rid of the free people. Mr. Clay particularly informs us, that it is to have nothing to do with the delicate question of Slavery: it is, says he, intended to be exclusively applied to the free people. . . . The colonizing plan, as exposed by Mr. Clay is intended indirectly to force the free people to emigrate, particularly those in the Southern States. . . .
>
> Mr. Clay's proposal is to remove annually six thousand of those persons, and thus he says keep down their alarming increase; this he avows to be the grand object of the Society.[42]

Freedom's Journal regularly published letters and articles from black leaders such as James Forten, Russell Parrott, and Bishop Richard Allen. In them, they attacked the ACS's positions on slavery, free blacks, and the idea that the United States was a "white man's country." One typical letter read:

> Let me repeat the friends of this Society, three fourths of them are slave-holders: the Legislatures of Maryland, Georgia, Tennessee, Kentucky, all slave-holding states have approved it; every member of this Auxilliary Society is, either in himself or his nearest relatives interested in holding slaves. . . . Again, he says, "It is no Abolition Society; it addresses as yet no arguments to the Master, and disavows with horror the idea of offering temptations to any slave. It denies the design of any right or power to emancipate, and declares that the states have exclusively the right to regulate the whole subject of slavery."[43]

Philadelphians, particularly friends of Forten, used the newspaper to disseminate their opinions on African emigration and the American Colonization Society, pushing for a consensus on these issues. Given the style of the letters, Forten was most likely the author of regularly published letters from "A Man of Colour," whose writings addressed a wide range of subjects—opposition to the ACS, protests against oppressive legislation being passed by the Pennsylvania Legislature, and discourses on the manners and mores of Philadelphia citizens, white and black. On January 25, 1828, *Freedom's Journal* published what was to become a kind of "official" position of the black community against the ACS. It was a response to an article published in the *African Repository,* the official journal of the ACS:

> We can assure our friends of Liberia, that limited as they are pleased to consider our views, they extend not only to the improvement of our own condition, but to the ultimate emancipation of our brethren who are in bondage: and never shall we consent to emigrate from America, until their prior removal from this land of their degradation and suffering. And even then, we would not ask the aid of the American Colonization Society, to carry us to their land "flowing with milk and honey."[44]

Throughout the paper's short run (1827–1829), news items, letters, and commentary on the history, conditions, and prospects of Haiti appeared regularly. Ultimately, Russwurm was unable to pursue his desire to emigrate to Haiti because the major settlement begun in 1824 had run into serious difficulty by late 1826. Of the estimated 6,000 settlers whose passage had been paid by the Haitian government, 2,000 had already returned to America. Differences in language and class, as well as the emigrants' unwillingness to subordinate themselves to the Haitians, had contributed to the settlers' disenchantment and inspired their return. In addition, the Haitian government of President Boyer had hoped the establishment of this settlement would win recognition of his government from Washington. Given the horror with which the United States government and the broader white population had viewed the revolution, this hope for recognition was extremely unrealistic. Boyer had also expected to use American blacks primarily for labor on sugar plantations, but the majority of blacks who emigrated to Haiti came from the eastern seaboard cities and thus had negligible agricultural skills. When his expectations did not materialize, Boyer withdrew government support from the emigration venture. Even worse, by spring 1828, the reports from Haiti had become quite grim. News items revealed that most nations would not recognize the sovereignty of Haiti. Troubling reports of currency failures and major swindles by Americans, Europeans, and the Haitians themselves were exposed in articles like this one, from *Freedom's Journal:*

HAYTI – We have a letter before us from Cape Haytien, dated June 7, which gives a gloomy picture of the affairs of that island, both political and commercial. Want of wisdom in the government, the writer considers the primary cause of its embarassments. . . . There are no bills to be bought at this time at any rate. The merchants at Port-au-Prince have made a manly stand against this measure, and will be supported by those in Cape Haytien. Should this policy of the government be continued, we shall have to leave the Island.[45]

For Russwurm, both the collapse of the Haitian emigration venture and the severely limited opportunities for black economic advancement posed a serious dilemma. As knowledge of the failure of the Haitian emigration venture became widely known, the American Colonization Society redoubled its efforts to get the black elite to emigrate, to virtually no avail. James Forten, for example, declined a lucrative partnership to establish a regular packet service between Philadelphia and Monrovia, Liberia's capital. The American Colonization Society failed to understand that the black elite were attracted to the Haitian emigration venture not only because of the significance of an independent black republic, but because, as Cuffe's work demonstrated, they had been directly sought out and asked to use their influence as community leaders. They were equal partners, not supplicants. Indeed, the ACS did not understand how important this distinction—between black-initiated emigration and white-sponsored colonization—was to African Americans seeking to forge a place for themselves in free society.

Against this backdrop, Russwurm's decision to emigrate under the auspices of the American Colonization Society was not merely an unexpected blow to the free black community; it was widely viewed as a rejection of this developing black leadership. James Forten and Bishop Allen, in particular, having used *Freedom's Journal* to advance their anticolonizationist views, found Russwurm's change of heart especially difficult to accept. Russwurm made an eloquent case for his decision when he wrote in *Freedom's Journal* on March 21, 1829:

> In the bosom of the most enlightened community on the globe, we are ignorant and degraded; under the most republican government, we are denied all the rights and privileges of citizens; and what is still worse, we see no probability, that we as a community will ever make it . . . to rise from our ignorance and degradation. . . . We consider it mere waste of words to talk of ever enjoying citizenship in this country.

As this article suggests, the ugly realities of free black life in the United States provided powerful support for his position. For Russwurm, the political had become all too personal. His longstanding desire to establish himself had culminated in his bitterly frustrated denouncement of the conditions under which blacks were forced to exist. In light of this, he decided to take advantage of the best opportunity that was presented to him. Others, however, saw this as selfish and counterproductive. Had they accepted Russwurm's position, they argued, they would have forfeited control of this issue and the political capital it represented in the black community.

Still, Russwurm not only announced his decision to accept the ACS's offer to take a position as superintendent of schools in Monrovia, he reversed his public position regarding the ACS. His last editorials so enraged the black communities that they burned him in effigy in Philadelphia. He arrived in Monrovia in November 1829 and made Liberia his home until his death in 1851.

Russwurm's drive to establish himself in the absence of business opportunities and his abhorrence of the violence perpetrated against free blacks were the likely catalysts for his decision. For many free blacks, emigration had been a long-held survival strategy, and Russwurm plainly felt that his decision to go to Africa would be accepted. Unfortunately, he misjudged the timing of his actions; he accepted ACS's assistance just as a black communal identity, firmly rooted in its opposition to the ACS, was emerging in the United States. For the first time, black communities flexed their political muscle by insisting that colonization was not a viable option. In letters and articles, as well as the burning in effigy, the black community expressed its particular contempt for Russwurm's action and he was shunned for the rest of his life. Ironically, his decision to emigrate had made him unwelcome in his community at home.

Russwurm's continuous criticism of black communal activities and his tone of paternal exasperation could not have won him much favor, yet his undoubted excellence as a journalist nonetheless ensured his position as a respected leader throughout the North. It is curious that Russwurm was not able to make a personal connection with James Forten, or even with Forten's son-in-law, Robert Purvis—men who were clearly his peers in terms of education, social class, and privilege. The result of this personal isolation made Russwurm blind to the myriad nuances of black life. The subtleties of alliances and the empathy to understand when and how to navigate the ever-changing realities free blacks faced seemed to completely escape Russwurm's understanding. With few if any close associates within the black community, Russwurm was, in one sense, virtually "white." Although he had certain sympathies with the plight of African Americans— he was, after all, the editor of America's first black newspaper—he had been raised, and was most comfortable, in a world of white privilege, a peculiar reality that made his decision to emigrate to Liberia even more complex. Given his unique and elusive character, Russwurm became an acceptable target for ridicule and scorn.

Forten intuitively understood this, and his activism against the ACS was made even more effective by keeping the image of Russwurm as a traitor in the forefront of the black community's consciousness. Forten spearheaded the push to defeat the American Colonization Society and solidified his position at the forefront of black leadership. He reminded blacks of the Bethel Church meeting that culminated in the "spirit of 1817," an articulation of the first *national* black communal position: the refusal of Northern free black communities to emigrate as long as slavery existed in the United States. Whatever differences various groups might have had they coalesced around their mutual determination to promote this goal. They defiantly stated in letters, newspaper articles, and speeches that their blood had made America their homeland and that they would not leave the United States while their brothers and sisters were still in chains. This powerful stand persisted from 1829 until 1850 when the issue of emigration attracted renewed interest among blacks nationwide after the passage of the Fugitive Slave Law and other repressive, proslavery legislation.

Subsequent black visionaries, such as Alexander Crummell, endured some hostility when they emigrated to Africa, but unlike Russwurm they returned to live in the United States. Perhaps because their return was viewed as a tacit admission that the United States was their true home, they were eventually forgiven and welcomed back into the community. Russ-

wurm, however, never returned to live in the United States and never re-
canted his stated opinions on the possibilities Africa offered black Americans. And he was never forgiven. The national consensus that effectively
ostracized him provided black leadership with an important political victory. Their implacable stand on emigration prevented the American Colonization Society from ever realizing its dream of resettlement of all free
blacks in Africa and eventually forced the society to the fringes of American political life.

This important political victory obscured an equally important and un-
shakable fact: Russwurm was successful in Liberia. In spite of the admitted
difficulties of climate, hostile tribes, and an inept, patriarchal administration, the colonies there succeeded and Russwurm thrived. During his so-
journ in Monrovia, Russwurm secured land, began a reasonably successful
trading business, served as superintendent of schools, restarted the mori-
bund *Liberia Herald,* and was elected secretary of the settlers council. In
1833, four years after his resettlement, Russwurm married Sarah E. McGill,
the daughter of the most prominent family in Monrovia, with whom he
had four children. Russwurm's education and social standing, combined
with his position as colonial secretary and editor of the *Herald,* earned him
acceptance into the elite group who served as advisors for the colony.

In Liberia, Russwurm developed a friendship with Dr. James Hall who
came to serve as the colony's doctor in 1831. Hall had graduated from
Bowdoin Medical School in 1822 and put his stay in Monrovia to good use,
significantly improving the colonists' health and advancing his knowledge
of diseases in the region.[46] Hall also explored the surrounding area and
came to know many of the local tribes, learning their customs and languages.

Because of his familiarity with Monrovia and Cape Palmas, Hall was
asked to head the colony of the Maryland State Colonization Society
(MSCS) at Cape Palmas. Although he proved to be an excellent adminis-
trator, unfortunately his health deteriorated and eventually he was forced
to submit his resignation to the MSCS board. He recommended that they
appoint a colored man to the post. A disastrous interim governor forced
the MSCS board to reopen the search for a governor of the Cape Palmas
colony. When Hall arrived in Baltimore in June 1836 the board was still de-
liberating. In late September, Hall finally convinced the MSCS board to
offer Russwurm the position. He assumed office in October 1836.

Russwurm enjoyed both professional success and personal satisfaction.
Russwurm's steady character, calmness in crises, and problem-solving ca-
pabilities as governor won acclaim from the board and from John H. Latrobe, president of the Maryland State Colonization Society. His manners
and courteousness were widely praised and won the colony friends from

visiting British and American naval commanders as well as various other foreign dignitaries.

During Russwurm's service as governor, he was able to employ his diplomatic skills in maintaining cordial relations with the surrounding tribes by tirelessly visiting outlying farms, mission stations, and tribal enclaves. These visits helped to extend the boundaries of the original settlement with a minimum amount of turmoil. Through such visits Russwurm also helped to encourage trade relations between the tribes and the colony. The MSCS board maintained titular control of the colony through an annual stipend that, to some extent, served as a security blanket for the colonists. Russwurm was fully aware, however, that the MSCS board was constantly strapped for money and, further, had always viewed the stipend as temporary. As a result, he believed that the colony needed to become self-sustaining as quickly as possible. To facilitate trade Russwurm negotiated with the board of MSCS to issue new money backed by palm oil and camwood, two of the colony's biggest exports. He changed the monetary system from fractions to decimals, which helped trade and regularized duties, taxes, and fees imposed by the colony.[47]

As a result of his leadership, Russwurm established a strong foundation for the future of the Cape Palmas settlement. He extended the roads, established a judiciary, a body of laws and regulations to govern the colony, a military and police presence, treaties and alliances with surrounding tribes, schools, and medical services. Russwurm himself successfully pursued trading ventures and became one of the richest men in the Liberian colonies.[48]

For two years starting in 1846, terrible illness swept the colony. Animals died of distemper and citizens died of fever in unprecedented numbers. The Cape Palmas colony had never experienced such devastation, which was compounded the following summer when sickness once again swept the settlements. Russwurm was among those stricken by illness, and although his spirits recovered enough for him to continue his duties, his health never did. In his last letter to Latrobe, written in his usual meticulous style, he passed on information about the continuing tribal war and discussed the colonists' aspirations for independence. Latrobe responded with a detailed plan, first, for increasing the colony's security, and then with careful discussion of the options for independence proposing that a confederation would provide stability and protection for the colony and prevent the loss of their annual stipend.[49] Unfortunately, Russwurm died before Latrobe's response could reach him.

Shortly after Russwurm's death, Latrobe eloquently memorialized his colleague and friend to the board of the Maryland State Colonization Society:

None knew better or so well as the board under what daily responsibilities Governor Russwurm's life in Africa was passed, and how con-
scientiously he discharged them; how, at periods when the very
existence of the then infant colony depended upon its relations with
surrounding tribes of excited nations, his coolness and admirable
judgement obviated or averted impending perils; how, when lamen-
table controversies with civilized and angry white men, the calm
decorum of his conduct brought even his opponents over to his side;
how, when popular clamor among the colonists called upon him as a
judge to disregard the forms of law and sacrifice an offending individual in the absence of legal proof, he rebuked the angry multitude
by the stern integrity of his conduct; and how, when on his visit to Baltimore in 1848 he was thanked personally by the members of the
board, he deprecated the praise bestowed on him for the performance of his duty, and impressed all who saw him with the modest
manliness of his character and his most excellent and courteous
bearing.[50]

At their October 21, 1851, meeting, the board voted to establish a monument in Russwurm's honor. Latrobe described it as

an obelisk, on a heavy granite base, on which were engraved the following inscriptions. On the north side, "In memory of John B. Russwurm, born 1799, died 1851"; on the south side, "Able, learned and
faithful—an honor to his race"; on the east side, "The first Governor
of African descent appointed in Liberia"; on the west side, "Erected
by the Maryland State Colonization Society, as a tribute of respect for
eminent services."[51]

Russwurm's tenure was not without the usual succession of trials and
tribulations, successes and failures. The important fact, however, is that
John Brown Russwurm served as governor of Cape Palmas for fifteen years
after he emigrated from the United States. Moreover, the colony succeeded in the face of daunting odds. Such success and resilience flew
squarely in the face of white American theories of black racial inferiority
and incompetence. Unfortunately, in denouncing Russwurm so furiously,
the American free black community denied itself a powerful weapon
against these insidious lies. So completely did they turn their eyes away
from Liberia and Africa that the community as a whole came to adopt
much of white America's view of Africa as an untamed dark wilderness
filled with savages and without civilization. Increasingly, black Americans
refused to view Africa as a place that was peopled by brothers and cousins;

shrouded in myth, it no longer elicited an immediate or visceral affection among African Americans.

With this in mind, what do we make of Russwurm? His decision to emigrate surely had a profound effect on the options the black community considered when confronting white racial prejudice in the United States. Conversely, having a convenient and visible foe whom they were unafraid to fight helped the black leadership to solidify its credibility, while fostering a sense of collective identity among the free black population in the North. Having denounced Russwurm and the American Colonization Society, they could get on with the business of establishing themselves as American citizens. In other words, Russwurm's alienation provided the perfect opportunity for free black leaders to build consensus—to promote and sustain an emerging racial consciousness—across geographic, economic, educational, and social lines. Russwurm could go back to Africa if he wanted, but they were Americans now—and they were here to stay.

7

"To Plead Our Own Cause":
Black Print Culture and the Origins of
American Abolitionism

Timothy Patrick McCarthy

We wish to plead our own cause. Too long have others spoken for us. Too long has the public been deceived by misrepresentations, in things which concern us dearly.
—*Freedom's Journal*, March 16, 1827

To the extent that America had a revolutionary tradition, [the black American in the abolitionist crusade] was its protagonist no less than its symbol.
—Benjamin Quarles, *Black Abolitionists* (1969)

Just after noon on July 5, 1827, the black abolitionist minister Nathaniel Paul rose to the pulpit to address a jubilant crowd so large it nearly ruptured the walls of the largest African American church in Albany, New York. "Through the long lapse of ages," the pastor of Albany's first African Baptist Society preached to his attentive brethren, "it has been common for nations to record whatever was peculiar or interesting in the course of their history." And this day was interesting, indeed, "an occasion which required public acknowledgment . . . that deserved to be retained with gratitude of heart": the abolition of slavery—the "peculiar" institution—in New York State.[1] Throughout the state, African Americans celebrated this day "as the beginning of a new era."[2] That Reverend Paul would also use the occasion to emphasize the importance of recording history calls attention to the ways blacks in the early republic expressed, as one scholar has noted, "a will to remember and the determination to construct an African-American memory—one which often ran counter to the national memory—and a desire to accomplish a 'dream deferred' and an unfinished revolution."[3] Marking the transition from an oppressive past to a brighter, if uncertain, future, the abolition of slavery in New York, an event that hastened what Arthur Zilversmit calls "the first emancipation," initiated among blacks a more organized effort to incorporate their own struggle for equality into the project of American nationalism.[4] Beginning in the 1820s, as they rejected white plans for African colonization and made increasingly aggressive demands for equal citizenship, free blacks became the driving force behind the transformation of American abolitionism.[5]

This process gained an important voice on March 16, 1827, when the first issue of *Freedom's Journal* was published. "We wish to plead our own cause," wrote co-editors John Russwurm and Samuel Cornish in the opening editorial. "Too long have others spoken for us. Too long has the public been deceived by misrepresentations, in things which concern us dearly." With an aim to confront racial prejudice in the North, and to "vindicate our brethren, when oppressed," *Freedom's Journal* marked an important "first" in the history of African American culture: the creation of a new print medium designed to galvanize the black community by representing a more unified political voice based on black interests and opinions. "In the spirit of candor and humility," wrote the editors, "we intend by a simple representation of facts to lay our case before the public, with a view to arrest the progress of prejudice, and to shield ourselves against the consequent evils."[6]

Here, then, was the first organized attempt by black Americans to use a serial publication to "lay [their] case before the public"—a public more broadly defined to include blacks as well as whites.[7] In addition to being the first black-edited newspaper in the United States, *Freedom's Journal* was also the first antislavery periodical to advocate immediate abolition and racial equality as interrelated goals. That these two developments—the abolition of slavery in the North and the birth of black print culture—occurred at essentially the same historical moment provides a new framework for discussing the relationship between the formation of racial identity and the rise of antislavery radicalism in nineteenth-century America.

Among Northern blacks, a group John Hope Franklin has referred to as "quasi-free Negroes," the looming reality that slavery and freedom were still strange but intimate bedfellows demanded a more organized and vocal abolitionist presence.[8] To coincide with the abolition of slavery throughout the North, African Americans organized public and private events to commemorate this historic milestone.[9] But these were not merely celebrations of newfound freedom; they were also sharp challenges to enduring *inequalities,* occasions designed to criticize and expose America's failure to live up its most revolutionary ideals. On July 4, 1827, one day prior to Reverend Paul's address in Albany, his fellow black abolitionist William Hamilton delivered a provocative sermon during an Abolition Day celebration at the African Zion Church in New York City. Extolling the virtues of equality while deriding the Founding Fathers—and white Americans, generally—for their inadequate efforts to ensure it, Hamilton urged that the "names of WASHINGTON and JEFFERSON should not be pronounced *in the hearing of your children* until they learned who were the true defenders of American liberty." The "true defenders" Hamilton was referring to were Crispus Attacks and other blacks who fought and died in the American Revolution. By risking their lives in the battle for independence, these black patriots had proven their equality despite the fact that the white architects of the new republic denied African Americans the same political rights they guaranteed themselves in the nation's founding documents.[10]

In their radical challenge to the racial inequalities embedded in early American nationalism, black abolitionists made two overlapping demands: the immediate end to American slavery and the equal rights of American citizenship. These two goals constituted the core of what would soon become a full-blown abolitionist movement. Building on the protests over colonization that took place in the decade between the founding of the American Colonization Society and the publication of *Freedom's Journal*, black Americans extended their political voice and cultural influence— both within and beyond the boundaries of racial segregation—to organize a broader culture of dissent that would influence whites as well as blacks.

This essay explores the various ways African Americans shaped an emerging abolitionist print culture during the four years that preceded the Boston debut of William Lloyd Garrison's *Liberator*, which historians have long considered to be the official beginning of abolitionism. To assume, as many historians do, that white abolitionists were the principal architects of the movement from its inception ignores evidence of the significant influence African Americans had on the transformation of abolitionism in its early years. More to the point, it obscures the important role that free blacks, especially, played in making the struggle for racial equality a primary goal of abolitionism. Indeed, it was free blacks—not their white counterparts—who first rejected colonization as a viable means of dealing with the "problem" of racial co-existence in the new republic.[11] In challenging slavery and racial prejudice simultaneously, free blacks made particularly effective use of print culture to persuade and energize their readership around a range of issues important to the black community. This had the important dual effect of inspiring a heightened black political consciousness and generating a new spirit of racial egalitarianism among whites who were just starting to become comfortable with the idea of joining ranks with blacks to fight slavery and remake the nation. In the pages of *Freedom's Journal* and in black pamphlets like David Walker's *Appeal to the*

Coloured Citizens of the World (1829), we see the origins of American abolitionism.[12]

On March 16, 1827, black abolitionists John Brown Russwurm and Reverend Samuel E. Cornish hastened this "work" by announcing the debut of *Freedom's Journal*. Marking the official birth of black and abolitionist print culture in the United States, *Freedom's Journal* initiated a powerful effort to showcase black culture and political ideology—as well as the ongoing struggle for freedom and equality—by claiming a public voice aimed at garnering the solidarity of blacks and the attention of whites nationwide. As Benedict Anderson has shown in his work on the relationship between nationalism and print culture, newspapers "made it possible for rapidly growing numbers of people to think about themselves, and to relate themselves to others, in profoundly new ways."[13] Likewise, *Freedom's Journal* served to connect both free black communities and a sympathetic white readership—in effect, building bridges across lines of race, region, class, and circumstance—in the ongoing process of creating an "imagined community" of abolitionists.

The significance of blacks launching a newspaper "to plead our own cause" cannot be overestimated. Building on the work of black writers from the Revolutionary era, *Freedom's Journal* continued the trend among African Americans of moving away from explicitly oral modes of expression toward a growing reliance on print culture as a site of political discourse. In so doing, *Freedom's Journal* also situated black people within what Michael Warner calls "a republic of letters," inaugurated by the traditions of radical pamphleteering and political and literary dissent practiced by revolutionaries such as Thomas Paine, Benjamin Franklin, and Thomas Jefferson, as well as their European predecessors John Milton, Edmund Burke, and Jonathan Swift.[14] The birth of black print culture was, in essence, a successful claim to freedom of expression, a cultural mechanism through which African Americans could plead the cause of abolition and racial equality while simultaneously displaying their various literary talents, political sympathies, and social aspirations. In this sense, the launching of *Freedom's Journal* was a revolutionary achievement. Pervasive theories about the cultural and intellectual inferiority of blacks were as old as the institution of slavery itself, and whites adhered to these ideologies as justifications for racism, segregation, forced labor, colonization, and legal prohibitions on everything from suffrage to interracial marriage.[15] *Freedom's Journal* was established partially as a defense against such widespread claims to black inferiority. In an effort to "arrest the progress of prejudice, and to shield ourselves against the consequent evils," African Americans used print culture, as William Hamilton urged in one of his characteristically firebrand sermons in 1809, to "prove false, to wit, that Africans do not possess minds as ingenious as other men." [16]

Just as Anglo-American literary culture fused the oral (sermon) and the written (political essay), so too did black print culture evolve in a similar fashion. Each issue of *Freedom's Journal* showcased poetry (new work by amateur poets as well as more famous poems by Phillis Wheatley and others) and published texts from religious sermons and public speeches, as well as historical and political essays on topics ranging from the Haitian revolution and African colonization to common education and the benefits of free labor. Like black religious traditions, which relied on the basic liturgical unit fusing the spoken and written word with song and prayer, black print culture represented and relied upon a combination of literary and performative modes of expression. By developing a written cultural tradition, predicated on the power of ideas through words, the editors of *Freedom's Journal* tried, as one scholar has suggested, "to evaluate the contribution of black people in the building of the nation, to assess the progress of the race and its capacity for self-government . . . to develop race pride as well as race memory . . . setting themselves in the place of the Founding Fathers, as those who could take the dream of liberty one step further and perhaps bring it to completion." [17] It is not surprising, then, that black print culture—later responsible for sparking a national interest in such black literature as slave narratives and serialized antislavery fiction—became the primary expressive medium, along with Garrison's *Liberator* and other abolitionist newspapers, for radical political dissent, militant abolitionism, and black cultural production in antebellum America.

"We form a spoke in the human wheel," asserted Russwurm and Cornish in their opening editorial, "and it is necessary that we should understand our pendence [sic] on the different parts, and theirs on us, in order to perform our part with propriety." In essence, *Freedom's Journal* was both a "medium of intercourse between our [black] brethren" throughout the United States, and an attempt to reverse the tide of racism and discrimination by demonstrating to white readers that blacks were entitled—by their intellectual, moral, and political merits—to an equal share of freedom. Published "every Friday at No. 5 Varick-street in New York," its readership was far from local. [18] Every issue printed a listing of its "Authorized Agents" (those responsible for collecting the subscription rate of "three dollars a year") representing the paper's extensive and growing geographic influence:

Mr. Reuben Ruby, Portland, Maine
" David Walker, Boston

Rev. Thomas Paul, do. [sic]
Mr. John Raymond, Salem, Mass.
" George C. Willis, Providence, R. I.
" Isaac Rodgers, New London, Conn.
" Francis Webb, Philadelphia
" Stephen Smith, Columbus, Penn.
Messrs. R. Cooley & Chs. Hackett, Baltimore
Mr. John W. Prou, Washington, D.C.
Rev. Nathaniel Paul, Albany
Mr. Theodore Wright, Princeton, N.J.
" James Cowes, New-Brunswick, N.J.
Rev. B. F. Hughes, Newark, N.J.[19]

Anticipating its wide-ranging readership, the inaugural issue noted "the interesting fact that there are FIVE HUNDRED THOUSAND free persons of colour, one half of whom might peruse, and the whole be benefited by the publications of the Journal." Moreover, the editors argued, "no publication, as yet, has been devoted exclusively to their [black peoples'] improvement . . . that this large body of our citizens have no public channel." And yet, despite its obvious concern for advancing the cause and condition of their "injured race," in "defense of five hundred thousand free people of colour," *Freedom's Journal* readily acknowledged its kinship with black slaves in the United States and throughout the African diaspora (particularly those who fought in the Haitian revolution, which received generous and regular column space). "[W]e would not be unmindful of our brethren who are still in the iron fetters of bondage," wrote the editors. "They are our kindred by all the ties of nature." By dedicating itself both to the freedom of expression and the larger political struggles of black people to attain liberty for all "brethren when oppressed," *Freedom's Journal* employed various mechanisms to reach blacks everywhere in an effort to form a "spoke in the human wheel."[20]

Not surprisingly, the African-American response to *Freedom's Journal* was extremely positive, especially when it came to the individual efforts of Cornish, a Presbyterian minister, and Russwurm, an educator and one of the first blacks to graduate from college in the United States (Bowdoin, in 1826).[21] On the evening of February 20, 1827, "at a repectable [sic] Meeting of the People of Colour of the city of Boston," a group of black leaders gathered "at the house of David Walker" to vote to give "aid and support" to *Freedom's Journal.* "[T]here is reason to believe," wrote George B. Holmes, the newly elected secretary of the group, "that great good will result to the People of Colour by the publication . . . [t]hat we freely and voluntarily agree to give it our aid and support, and to use our utmost exertions to increase its patronage."[22] Contributions like these, often sent from places like Philadelphia and Boston, where black abolitionists were especially active, reflected just how far the newspaper's trumpet call rang.

Of course, there were expressions of white disapproval, like the following reprinted from a newspaper in New Jersey:

> The Rev. Dr. Miller of Princetown, N.J. has denounced the "Freedom's Journal," a paper printed in New-York, as exerting an unfavorable influence upon the coloured population in New-Jersey, and as unworthy the support of the wise and good among them. The frequent desertion of slaves from their masters, in that State, since the slave-emancipating laws of New-York went into operation, are ascribed in part to the circulation of that paper.[23]

On May 29, 1827, the editors of the *Georgetown Columbian and District Advertiser* went so far as to speculate that *Freedom's Journal* was written and produced by Northern white radicals obsessed with "rendering [the free coloured population] distrustful" of the motives of the "wise and philanthropic men" affiliated with the American Colonization Society, which, ironically, was denounced on the pages of *Freedom's Journal* as being both proslavery and antiblack.[24] Nonetheless, despite instances of disapproval—from whites and/or those who favored colonization—*Freedom's Journal* was celebrated within the black community, and also among a good number of whites as well, who were increasingly sympathetic to the antislavery cause as a result of reading the paper.

Aside from generous financial and volunteer support from blacks throughout the country, *Freedom's Journal* also received contributions of articles, poetry, editorial commentaries, and letters to the editor—strongly encouraged in each issue—which usually offered strong praise for the paper and its editors. In a testimonial submitted on January 17, 1827, Reverend Samuel H. Cox, Pastor of the Laight-Street Church in New York, wrote: "I am free to express my confidence in the promise of their [Russwurm's and Cornish's] enterprise, and in the relative competency with which its concerns will be conducted." Writing on the same day, Thomas Eddy considered the editors "very competent to the undertaking of the proposed work."[25] In a much lengthier exaltation, an unsigned letter from "a gentlemen of high and deserved standing in Albany" opined that not "since the Christian era" had anyone "engaged in a more important enterprise, than the one you have commenced." Week after week, letters from readers offered approval of the paper's mission of fostering black pride and uplifting black people. By enclosing "five dollars" this "gentlemen of high and deserved standing" hoped to send a strong message to blacks statewide, that "[t]he total annihilation of slavery in the Union, depends much, very much, on the conduct of the coloured population of New York."[26]

The personal conduct of black men and women was extremely important to the contributors of *Freedom's Journal*, and unlike the generous tone of most letters to the editor, much of the writing that appeared in the newspaper on the subjects of black behavior and self-improvement was at once exhortatory and critical. In the opening editorial, Russwurm and Cornish stated that one of the central missions of *Freedom's Journal* was "the dissemination of useful knowledge among our brethren, and to their moral and religious improvement." Hoping that "all men acknowledge the excellency of [Benjamin] Franklin's maxims," the editors sought to use the paper as a vehicle to promote individual virtue and moral improvement. They recognized, of course, that the "degradation and misery" they witnessed among blacks was largely the result of circumstances beyond their control. Thus, while "the publick [has] been deceived by misrepresentations" of blacks, their long history of being subjected to slavery and racial discrimination had produced a "lethargy of years" that they must work to overcome. "We are aware," admitted the editors, "that there [sic] many instances of vice among us, but we avow that it is because no one has taught its subjects to be virtuous; many instances of poverty, because no sufficient efforts accommodated to minds contradicted by slavery." By offering avenues to develop mechanisms for self-improvement and racial unity, *Freedom's Journal* was devoted to the total education of its brethren in the struggle for equality.

For African Americans in the early republic, public and private respectability was of paramount importance to attain the goal of racial uplift. "Of the many subjects, which merit our consideration as reasonable things," one writer declared, "none deserves more notice than propriety of conduct." Decrying hoarded wealth, public folly, and blind ostentation, the writer asserted that propriety of conduct, personal responsibility, and self-restraint would enable men and women to rise in standing in American society. "As bad as the world is," he continued, "if a man's outward conduct has been marked by the rules of propriety, economy, and virtue: in the hour of adversity and trouble, he will always find friends." The conduct of black men and women was, of course, even more important considering the precarious existence of blacks in a white-dominated society skeptical of their virtue. To engage in "mere trifles"—"smoking in the streets" or "dressing to the very extent of our purses"—was "foolish" given the fact that blacks lived within "a prejudiced community." "Placed as we are in society," the writer concluded, "propriety of conduct, never was more essential for any people than to us."[27] In other words, because whites were so quick "to enlarge upon the least trifle . . . and denounce our whole body for the misconduct of this guilty one," *Freedom's Journal* devoted a great deal of its space to issues of morality, behavior, and propriety.

Given the disproportionate emphasis that was placed on personal conduct, it was hardly surprising that education and intellectual improvement were also central concerns in *Freedom's Journal*. "Education being an object of the highest importance to the welfare of society," wrote Russwurm and Cornish, "we shall endeavor to present just and adequate views of it, and to urge upon our brethren the necessity and expediency of training their children, while young, to habits of industry, and thus forming them for becoming useful members of society."[28] In fact, each issue of the paper contained an advertisement that "E.F. Hughes' School," run "Under St. Philip's Church, is now ready for the admission of Pupils."[29] Designed "For Coloured Children of both Sexes," E.F. Hughes's School offered classes in "READING, WRITING, ARITHMETIC, ENGLISH, GRAMMAR, GEOGRAPHY; with the use of Maps and Globes, and HISTORY." Terms cost "from two to four dollars per quarter," and teachers included prominent black ministers from local churches, including Reverends Benjamin Paul and Cornish.

There were, of course, significant impediments to establishing viable avenues for scholastic instruction for blacks. In the 1820s, most Northern states were still in the early stages of developing public, or common, schools for whites as well as blacks. However, as one historian has noted, "As the concept of public education emerged, so also did that of segregated schools." Indeed, the forces of racial prejudice, which led to the segregation of other public spaces, also influenced the configuration of the emerging educational system. In 1823, rather than supporting the establishment of common schools for black and white children to study together, New York embraced segregation, organizing all-black African Free Schools, a practice that was copied in other states and one that would last until the Civil War.[30] For the most part, African Free Schools were supported and run by whites, although they often received the help of adults in the black community, especially ministers and others active in black churches who had never been slaves, and who, because they had achieved some degree of education, could serve as instructors.

Still, the educational opportunities provided by the African Free Schools, while a sign of progress, were grossly insufficient. As one writer lamented, "While the benevolence of the age has founded and endowed Seminaries of Learning for all other classes and nations . . . as yet, no door is open to receive the degraded children of Africa."[31] By June 1827, *Free-*

dom's Journal reported that "to the best of our knowledge" there were only twelve African Free Schools in existence in the Northeast: one in Portland Maine; three in Boston; one in Salem, Massachusetts (which "from causes unknown . . . closed . . . after six months"); two in New Haven; three in Philadelphia; and two in New York City. A dozen schools could not possibly begin to accommodate the large and eager black population in the North, particularly in cities like New York, Boston, and Philadelphia, where the largest numbers of free blacks resided. Two schools in New York City, for instance, had to serve an eligible black population of some fifteen thousand. In Philadelphia the burden was at least as great: three schools for a population of twenty thousand. Moreover, because African Free Schools were located in urban areas, African Americans who resided in rural settings had no access to formal education beyond what could be obtained at home or through individual effort. Regardless of location, the schools that did exist were severely underfunded and understaffed. Only the three schools in Boston, which provided the best school-to-student ratio of any region—1 to 670—were financially solvent, due to the "liberal donation of the late Abiel Smith Esq.," who "left by will, for the support of African children, $4,000 of three per cent stock" and several shares of property. For the most part, however, African Free Schools struggled to remain open, always searching for supplies, funds, and capable, unbiased teachers.[32]

Despite the difficulties involved in sustaining viable educational institutions, the instruction of children seemed to be a virtual obsession among black adults. "An ignorant schoolmaster is a nuisance to society," extolled a contributor to the "Varieties" section of *Freedom's Journal*, "the injury he does to the youth committed to his care, is beyond calculation."[33] "Our children must be educated in order to be useful, and it is our duty and interest to adopt the wisest and best means in our power to bring about an abject so desirable." On March 30, 1827, *Freedom's Journal* initiated a five-part series entitled "Education," in which the writer, PHILANTHROPAS, was "led to offer a few remarks on the vast importance of education" for black people, among whom "the deplorable effects of ignorance are every where visible."[34]

The discourse surrounding black schools represented a growing democratic faith in common education throughout the country that manifested itself powerfully within the African American community. Just as intellectual achievement was considered essential to racial uplift, so were schools considered the breeding ground for a virtuous citizenry. In his final editorial in the series on education, PHILANTHROPAS exhorted blacks to be "united and firm" in their collective vision for developing "an enlightened coloured population." Likewise, another writer argued, "[education] is the pillar of civilization, the foundation of good order." Yet another writer asserted that schools were most "necessary to the welfare and existence of society."[35] Writers often invoked ancient Greece and Rome (and even the Pilgrims and Puritans in early New England) as examples of great civilizations that considered the education of youth to be "a most sacred duty." In addition to supporting the African Free Schools, editorials also sought to remind white philanthropists and political leaders of the need for state-sponsored schools that would be responsible for educating white and black citizens. One writer, CIVIS, while advocating for integrated public schools, decried the existence of military academies as undermining both democracy and peace. "I consider our liberty and scrutiny," he wrote, "and consequently our happiness to depend on the courage, honesty, and patriotism of our hard yeomanry . . . our main strength should be in a high-minded free people whose spirit has not been broken by military restraint." Furthermore, CIVIS concluded, "let [America's] funds be extended throughout the land, in free schools, where all may learn, and not concentrated in a large military establishment . . . where few can come. I am the advocate of the many, and not the few."[36]

The issue of black education was perhaps the first to seriously unite the energies of white and black abolitionists, a development that no doubt prefigured radical efforts in subsequent decades. In mid-December 1827, a "meeting was held by a committee from the Manumission Society" of New York "to take into consideration the present state of the African Free Schools in this city, and to adopt some efficient measures for a more regular attendance of the pupils." Upon hearing from Mr. Andrews, a teacher at "School No. 2," that "for the last fifteen years, the school had never been so poorly attended as at present," the committee decided to district the city and appoint a committee to each district, whose "duty it should be to visit every family of colour within their limits" in order to increase and sustain attendance at the African Free Schools. An additional agent was also to be appointed whose responsibility it would be to promote education generally to all black families in New York City.

Prior to Christmas of that same year several meetings were held, again in New York, at which various members of the Manumission Society discussed the "interesting subject of establishing African Infant Schools," modeled after those already in existence in Britain. Acknowledging that "the period from two to five years was the important one of a child's life," the committee declared that such "places of instruction" should "be opened to children of colour." Here, again, those present at the meeting appointed a committee, this time to "lay the plan before our most influential men, for their cordial approbations and support." *Freedom's Journal* exhorted blacks to "pledge . . . to render every assistance in our power" to the efforts of the members of the New York Manumission Society. As the year came to a close, blacks were joining with whites to work together to improve educational opportunities for black children. "Knowing . . . that learning . . . is to be preferred to ignorance," a writer with the initial "S" wrote in his Christmas editorial, "we should impress these principles on the minds of the youthful, and persuade the ignorant to acquire useful knowledge" so that "we shall see the sons of Africa . . . being seated among the nations of the earth, enjoy in peace their natural rights, and sing under their flowing banners, the song of Liberty and Equality!"[37]

The "song of Liberty and Equality," however, was noticeably off-key, as blacks remained in a state of economic dependence. In general, and with good reason, African Americans were concerned about the effects of economic inequality in their community. As historian Phyllis Field has noted, the "absence of discriminatory laws did not necessarily imply the absence of discrimination. The social mores of the white citizens often resulted in *de facto* segregation where the law itself was silent."[38] While blacks were not legally restricted to the most menial jobs, in reality this was often the case. Most black men and women occupied the lowest paid, most unskilled positions, usually as laborers and domestic servants, where they encountered hostility at every turn. The racism of working-class whites, derived from anxiety and fear over competition with blacks for jobs, produced a hostile work environment where violence on the docks and the streets was commonplace. This is not to say that middle- and upper-class whites were innocent of economic discrimination against blacks; they were just situated differently within the economic order. Rather than competing against blacks for low-wage jobs, they were supervising or hiring them. Nonetheless, because of the mutual antipathy fueled by economic competition at the lowest levels of employment, violence between blacks and working-class whites persisted throughout the antebellum period, culminating in dramatic fashion in the 1863 draft riots in New York City.[39] Such unfortunate dynamics prompted Frederick Douglass to complain: "Every hour sees us elbowed out of some employment to make room perhaps for some newly arrived immigrants, whose hunger and color are thought to give them a title to especial favor."[40] As one black youth lamented, "No one will employ me; white boys won't work with me."[41] In the wake of Northern abolition, then, economic hardship, job discrimination, and widespread poverty quickly replaced slavery to effectively deny blacks access to decent work, wages, and property.

For blacks, new immigrants, and native-born white laborers alike, these harsh economic realities were only exacerbated by the transformations of capitalism in the nineteenth century. By the 1820s, critics were able to describe a social and economic situation similar to that of Europe, where "the two extremes of costly luxury in living, expensive establishments and improvident waste are presented in daily and hourly contrast with squalid misery and hopeless destitution." For blacks who consistently occupied the bottom rungs of the social ladder, such economic "misery" and "destitution" was as routine as it was disturbing. For example, in New York City, where a large concentration of free blacks resided, this was compounded by the fact that in 1828 the wealthiest 4 percent of white residents owned nearly 60 percent of the total wealth. This shrinking window of economic opportunity produced inadequate opportunities for the vast majority of black and white workers in New York.[42]

Overcoming poverty and economic hardship was an important goal of the black community, even if most blacks remained skeptical of great wealth. "Remember at all times," cautioned A. Steward in an Abolition Day oration, "that money, even in *your* hands, is power." However, he continued, because "idleness, poverty, and wretchedness are inseparable companions," blacks should seek to amass enough money to safeguard themselves against poverty without approaching the dangers of wealth and power, which were most often and clearly associated, in their minds, with white racism.[43] In fact, some blacks recognized the direct correlation between economics and racial discrimination. Masking racial ideology in a speech advocating for colonization, a white minister from New Jersey argued that the condition of the emancipated "free coloured population," three fourths of whom, he argued, were "idle, ignorant, and depraved," provided ample justification for their removal to Africa. The editors of *Freedom's Journal* immediately refuted the minister's claims by printing their own assessment of the "numbers of paupers," black and white. Drawing from "the annual census of our city's [New York's] alms house," they listed the following:

Number of Paupers

White Men, 468; Coloured Men, 17
White Women, 482; Coloured Women, 43
White Boys, 308; Coloured Boys, 14
White Girls, 153; Coloured Girls, 7
Total Whites, 1391; Total Coloureds, 81

The editors noted that even in terms of the percentage of "paupers" to the total population, blacks still had an advantage: "one coloured pauper to every 185, and one white pauper to every 115." According to both statistics and daily observation, poverty transcended the color line in antebellum America. However, despite small attempts to defend the honor of the black community against such racist inaccuracy, the real economic issue for blacks was the glaring inequality of access to mechanisms for economic improvement—decent paying jobs, adequate education, property ownership—not the percentage of blacks to whites annually subjected to poverty or prison.[44]

The difficulty blacks had in gaining some small degree of economic independence was compounded by the intrinsically problematic concept of "free labor" in the antebellum North. During the period of the early republic, the rise of capitalism and the simultaneous sharpening of distinctions between "free" and "slave" labor had produced two increasingly distinct economic systems in the North and South. In his study of the rise of the Republican party before the Civil War, Eric Foner has argued that Northern "free labor ideology" was "grounded in the precepts that free labor was economically and socially superior to slave labor and that the distinctive quality of northern society was the opportunity it offered wage earners to rise to property-owning independence." Moreover, in the context of distinctive transformations in the "social relations of production," Sean Wilentz has argued that members of the white working class "began to interpret their shared ideals of commonwealth, virtue, independence, citizenship, and equality," in effect, elaborating "their own democratic variant of American republican ideology, bound to their expectations about workshop production."[45]

This interrelated shift in economic relationships and political ideologies further illuminated the precarious position of Northern blacks in relation to emerging conceptions of "free labor." Generally, Northern laborers were divided into two groups: wage workers and independent proprietors. Despite sharp differences in their economic status, these two types "had in common the fact that they were not slaves, that the economic relationships into which they entered were understood as 'voluntary' rather than arising from personal dependence."[46] The implicit dependence of wage laborers on their employers, however, posed a serious challenge to those who equated "free labor" with economic "freedom."[47] The very idea of free labor, as Foner explains, was riddled with contradictions to Americans' emerging understanding of worker autonomy during this era, contradictions made even more glaring in light of the relative lack of economic freedom for the majority of African Americans.[48] In most instances, blacks occupied positions outside or on the margins of the market economy, doubly manipulated by the "invisible hands" of racism and capitalism.

Despite the disjunction between free labor ideology and their own economic reality, African Americans acknowledged the advantages of free labor, especially since slavery was the closest and most familiar alternative for them. As with the issue of education, *Freedom's Journal* published a series of passionate editorials, written by black abolitionists from New York to Ohio to Virginia, on the "Comparative Costs of Free and Slave Labor," which denounced slavery as both "impolitic" and a "pecuniary disadvantage." According to an editorial submitted by the Benevolent Society of Alexandria, the political evils of slavery were compounded by "the depreciation it occasions in the pecuniary resources of the country." Citing the relative decline in economic productivity and property values in the Southern states, the editorial argued the following:

> By the census of 1820 the valuation of the land and houses in New York and Pennsylvania, under the directions of the Marshals, amounted to more than six hundred dollars,—whilst the aggregate of the lands and houses including more than one million of slaves, of Maryland, Virginia, North-Carolina, South-Carolina, Georgia, Tennessee and Kentucky, seven of the largest and most wealthy slave states covering a much larger territory, was less than 520,000.000 of dollars, or nearly one sixth less than those slave states! What a commentary do these facts afford up upon the political tendency of slavery?[49]

The editorial also reported that the Northern states generally enjoyed a far greater degree of economic health, measured by "the great public works they have executed, the large capital they have invested in manufacturers, and the great extent of their commerce."[50] On the most practical level, free labor was simply more efficient, both in terms of cost and productivity, than slave labor. Another writer challenged the views of a well-known political economist, saying, "whatever may be the nature of the cultivation, the labour of the free cultivator is always preferred to that of the slave." Relying on his own calculations as well as popular economic theories, he concluded that slave labor was neither as productive nor as cheap as free labor. Indeed, slaveowners were responsible for so many additional burdens in maintaining a slave labor force—covering the "wear and tear" of slaves, caring for older slaves, raising slave children, paying the wages of an overseer—that, according to "a statement from one of the slave districts in the United States," the cost of slave labor was "at least 25 per cent dearer than that of the free laborer in the neighboring districts." Furthermore, the author concluded, "the slave working always for another, and never for himself, being limited to bare subsistence, and seeing no prospect of improving his condition, loses all stimulus to exertion, he becomes a machine, often very obstinate and very difficult to manage." That slave labor was both less productive and far more costly should convince any naysayers of the "absolute superiority of free to slave labor."[51]

The gross inconsistency between slave labor and America's political ideals did not escape black abolitionists concerned with their own economic freedom. Recalling the political maxim that "all power derives from the people," one writer asked: "What deep rooted attachment to the liberal government can we expect from those who in childhood are accustomed to domineer over their fellow creatures?" Furthermore, he asked, "can the liberties of a nation be thought secure when we have removed the holy basis—a conviction in the minds of the people that these liberties [including, they argued, the right to "labour freely"] are the gift of God—that they are not to be violated but with his wrath?"[52] Another editorial, concerned as well with the strength of the republic, purported than an "economy of free than slave labour" promoted "public enterprise, general intelligence, and virtuous habits."[53] It was their unwavering faith in the possibility of liberty and equality that led blacks to invest, however critically, in the idea of free labor. "The experiment of our government," wrote J.W. Lathroop of the Abolition Society of Stark County, Ohio, "on the subject of equal rights, ought to have put every idea of this nature [that slavery is morally or financially advantageous] to shame." It was "freedom," he argued, that was "the property, the greatest possible wealth, of the individual himself."[54] For a people long considered property themselves, African Americans understood that lasting freedom and equality would require economic independence in addition to social acceptance and political citizenship.

Throughout its more than two-year run, *Freedom's Journal* was filled with commentary on every imaginable topic of importance to black people living in the United States. Because the uneven history of American slavery—its gradual abolition in the North, its rapid consolidation in the South, as well as the dramatic debates over its expansion into the western territories—had produced great variations in the African American experience, *Freedom's Journal* was an important medium of exchange for a disparate black community during a time of great upheaval and transition. Although every issue contained articles written by its editors, the paper also brought together the opinions and analysis of a broad spectrum of the black community: religious and community leaders, poets and educators, businessmen and common laborers, housewives and former slaves. In its broad representation of ideas and experiences, *Freedom's Journal* helped to generate a more cohesive political consciousness among African Americans who were struggling to make sense of a rapidly changing world. But it also sought to emphasize the importance of public discourse and debate, representing, as well, the internal disagreements blacks had with each other on the most pressing issues of the day. Differences of opinion were rarely glossed over or silenced; instead, diversity was celebrated as a potential source of strength for the African American community—and for American democracy generally. After all, slavery and racial prejudice were daunting obstacles to overcome, and the supporters of *Freedom's Journal* understood that if blacks were to achieve both freedom and equality, they would need to marshal every reserve of talent and initiative in their community. In doing so, they also reached out to whites, hoping that *Freedom's Journal*—the very fact of its existence as well as the quality and substance of its content—would have an influence on them as well. Each issue reprinted text from white newspapers (particularly antislavery ones like Baltimore's *Genius of Universal Emancipation*) as well as editorials and essays written by whites. This had two important effects: first, it demonstrated to white readers that African Americans took their ideas and opinions seriously (an editorial maneuver that carried with it a certain irony, given the lack of respect that had been afforded to blacks in most white periodicals over the years); and second, by printing these articles alongside one another, the editors of *Freedom's Journal* were creating a kind of textual equality, suggesting that black literary and intellectual achievement was on a par with whites. The paper thus offered the first glimpses of an emerging interracialism, strengthening the black community by giving it "a single voice," while attempting to forge alliances between blacks and whites who were willing to work together on terms of equality—quite literally, side by side—in the cause of abolitionism.

Although scholars can only speculate about the number of people who subscribed to or regularly read *Freedom's Journal*, its circulation clearly increased as time went by. Robert Levine has made persuasive claims about the paper's enlarged regional scope based on the growing number of "Authorized Agents" listed in each issue.[55] Taking into account letters to the editor and article submissions as well, we can be certain that its readership included far more than just Northern free blacks. Along with items labeled "Domestic News" and "Foreign News," a good deal of attention was given to the historical influence of ancient African civilizations on modern Western culture, to the triumph of black revolt in the Haitian revolution, and to the recent settlement of free blacks in Canada, indicating that African Americans embraced a diasporic black identity, one that incorporated a sense of being "American" without being limited by it. Still, throughout its run, *Freedom's Journal* maintained an aggressive opposition to colonization, denouncing the "schemes" of the American Colonization Society, and imploring blacks (and whites) not to support its activities. Despite its genuine interest in international issues and its regular attempts to engage white readers, *Freedom's Journal* was first and foremost an African American enterprise, principally devoted to improving the condition and ensuring the future of blacks in the United States.

It is therefore both tragic and ironic that the life of *Freedom's Journal* was cut short by a dispute over colonization. Since the publication of its first issue, editors Cornish and Russwurm were in general agreement on the major issues affecting black people. Bad health and other professional duties as a Presbyterian minister forced Cornish to relinquish his editorial duties in September 1827, after which Russwurm assumed sole proprietorship of the paper. Ever since its founding, *Freedom's Journal* had expressed a clear opposition to colonization, reflecting a majority consensus within the African American community at the time. Free blacks were especially skeptical of the American Colonization Society, suspecting that its members' interest in colonization stemmed from their desire to remove "troublesome" free blacks from the United States, rather than their commitment to placing slavery on a course to extinction. Despite its sympathy for blacks who wanted to leave the country rather than be subjected to continuing racial prejudice and discrimination, *Freedom's Journal* consistently advocated a different solution: Stay in America and fight.

This is why black readers were so angry with Russwurm when he published an editorial endorsing colonization—and even worse, the ACS itself—in the February 1829 issue. Entitled "A Candid Acknowledgment of Error," Russwurm's article was his own personal public recant on the issue of colonization, stating that he was now "a decided supporter of the American Colonization Society."[56] This came as an enormous shock and disappointment to his readership, who remembered his previous assertions that because members of the ACS "represent us disadvantageously," it was wise that blacks "would not ask the aid of the American Colonization Society to carry us to their land 'flowing with milk and honey.'"[57] In reality, Russwurm's very public about-face on colonization was not nearly as abrupt as it seemed. The young editor was never a purist on the issue, and certainly he did not share Cornish's fierce and vocal opposition to the activities and motivations of the ACS. In fact, shortly after Cornish resigned as co-editor, Russwurm took the opportunity to publish a series of pro and con articles on colonization—something Cornish would never have countenanced— that immediately generated deep concern among the readership that the paper was softening its stance on what they perceived to be the greatest threat currently facing free blacks.

For his part, Russwurm did not publicly disclose his feelings on the matter until February 1829, probably because he rightly feared retaliation from his peers. Still, Russwurm had flirted with the idea of colonization for some time. This was likely the result of his own unique background, which had inspired in him a rare cosmopolitan perspective that surely must have tempered any singular or exclusive identification with being "American."

The son of a slave woman and white Virginian planter, Russwurm was born in Jamaica and subsequently raised and educated in predominantly white communities in Quebec and Maine. Extremely well traveled and keenly interested in international affairs (he delivered a commencement address at Bowdoin on the recent success of the Haitian revolution), Russwurm developed a certain fascination with Liberia, and was even offered a position there as an agent for the American Colonization Society in early 1827. Dissuaded from accepting the offer by prominent free blacks who were discussing the idea of launching a black newspaper in New York City later that year, Russwurm decided to devote his considerable talent and energy to domestic affairs. It's hard to know how much of Russwurm's personal history was known to the readers of *Freedom's Journal*, but we do know that his public embrace of colonization in February 1829 was widely denounced as a betrayal of the paper's principles and of the interests of African Americans. Vocal protests led to Russwurm's resignation from the paper, after which he complained privately to several members of the ACS about the "violent persecution" to which he was subjected by fellow blacks. Dispirited and ever more convinced that African Americans would never achieve dignity or equality in the United States, Russwurm soon emigrated to Liberia, where he became a leader in the colony's early development. The last issue of *Freedom's Journal* was published on March 28, 1829, a little more than two years after its founding.[58]

Black print culture thus experienced a spectacular—if challenging—birth in the late 1820s. As was the case with most newspapers in the early republic, *Freedom's Journal* struggled to keep a financial and organizational infrastructure in place. It was hard enough to generate resources to launch and sustain *any* newspaper in the early republic, but this was made even more difficult by the small size and relative poverty of the Northern free black community. Still, *Freedom's Journal* was without question one of the most successful and reliable black newspapers of the seventeen to appear before the Civil War.[59] After it ceased publication, Samuel Cornish resumed his post as the principal architect of early black print culture, launching and editing *Rights of All*, the monthly successor to *Freedom's Journal* that ran from May to October 1829. Its concerns were largely the same as its predecessor, waging a print war on slavery and racism, and taking a particularly sharp stand against colonization. After more than a year without a black newspaper—during which William Lloyd Garrison launched his *Liberator* to the great delight of African Americans throughout the country—the black abolitionist John G. Stewart attempted to continue the tradition of black journalism when he launched *The African Sentinel and Journal of Liberty* in Albany, New York. This paper, too, had a very short run (just several issues, none of which have survived), but Stewart's primary motivation—that "there should be at least one public JOURNAL, conducted by a coloured man, and devoted to the interests of the coloured population throughout the country"—was in keeping with previous efforts to provide African Americans with their own independent forum to express their interests and concerns.[60]

Perhaps better than anyone of his generation, David Walker understood the power of an autonomous black print culture in a democracy still very much crippled by slavery and racism. Born in the late eighteenth century to a free mother and slave father, Walker spent his youth and early adult years, respectively, in Wilmington, North Carolina, and Charleston, South Carolina, before moving to Boston in the mid-1820s. The Southern communities in which Walker grew up boasted small but relatively sovereign black populations with significant levels of trade craftsmanship and literacy. These were communities where free blacks and slaves lived and worked side by side, where a new form of African American Methodism was flourishing, and where black resistance was widespread, reaching a fever pitch in 1822, when Denmark Vesey, a former slave who became a leader in the African Methodist Church, organized an extraordinary insurrection among slaves and free blacks in Charleston. All in all, these were dynamic settings for African Americans seeking to forge a common purpose in their struggle for freedom and equality, and an increasingly troublesome one for whites who wanted to keep slaves and free blacks separated for the purposes of perpetuating a slave society.[61]

As a product of this setting, David Walker well understood the power inherent in this "divide and conquer" system of racial subordination. Indeed, as a free man who lived most of his life in the South, Walker had an especially keen perspective on how white supremacist justifications for slavery had corrupted black and white Americans alike, thus undermining any potential success for peaceful co-existence based on the shared value of racial equality. As a highly literate black Christian, Walker's political consciousness was forged through an examination of the relationship between the secular and sacred aspects of American society—a connection that would form the basis of his famous 1829 pamphlet, *An Appeal to the Coloured Citizens of the World*.[62] Modeled formally after the U.S. Constitution, invoking the ideals of the Declaration of Independence, and written in language that reflected his own deep historical knowledge and Christian faith, Walker's *Appeal* was the most enduring achievement of his intensely political and tragically truncated life (he died mysteriously in 1830 at the age of thirty-four). It was also the most radical and far-reaching challenge yet posed by a black American writer to his brethren and fellow countrymen.

Walker was part of an impressive new generation of black activists—among whom Cornish, Russwurm, and Paul numbered—who had come of age in the nurturing context of black churches and benevolent organizations formed during the early republic. Keenly aware of the special plight of Northern free blacks, but still deeply concerned with the continuing abuses of slavery, this generation was in many respects better organized and more cohesive that its predecessor. Having benefited from the struggles against slavery and racism that were waged during and after the Revolution, this was the first generation of African Americans to enjoy genuine freedom and independence, relative professional success, and access to formal education. They were, in short, well positioned to continue the fight begun by their own "founding" generation, which included, among others, Phillis Wheatley, Benjamin Banneker, Absalom Jones, Richard Allen, James Forten, and John Gloucester, as well as the many slaves whose petitions for freedom during the era of the American Revolution constituted the first recorded black political voices of the new nation.[63] By further connecting established African American traditions and institutions with impressive new experiments in print culture, Walker and his cohort worked hard to deepen and extend the black networks of communication and affiliation that would form the essential infrastructure of the emerging abolitionist movement.

Although the precise date and route of his migration are unknown, David Walker moved to Boston from Charleston sometime between the aftermath of the 1822 Vesey conspiracy, when blacks were fleeing Charleston in droves to avoid violent and legal persecution, and 1825, when his name first appears in the Boston directory.[64] As Peter Hinks has described in great detail, Walker arrived in Boston in his late twenties with impressive talents and lofty ambitions. He lived in Beacon Hill, in the midst of Boston's small but close-knit black community, and he supported himself as the owner of a small used clothing shop on Brattle Street, near the wharves.[65] As a self-sustaining businessman and passionate antislavery activist, Walker quickly emerged as a prominent and respected leader in the African American community. After joining a local black Methodist congregation and becoming secretary of the African Lodge, in 1826 Walker became one of the founding members of the Massachusetts General Colored Association (MGCA), a black political organization committed to what Benjamin Quarles characterized as "racial betterment and slave abolition."[66] Although the MGCA was hardly the first or only group of its kind, its vision was somewhat broader in scope. Outspoken in its opposition to slavery, racial discrimination, and colonization, the MGCA was among the first black-led organizations whose mission was the improvement of conditions for all blacks, slave and free. With intentions that were more explicitly *national* than other groups at the time, the MGCA was an important precedent for the Colored Convention Movement that began in 1830, and both were catalysts for the formation of an increasingly self-conscious *American* identity within the black community in the United States.[67] Speaking at its "first semi-annual meeting" in December 1828, Walker heralded the formation of the MGCA and laid out its mission:

> [T]he primary object of this institution, is, to unite the colored population, so far, through the United States of America, as may be practicable and expedient; forming societies, opening, extending, and keeping up correspondences, and not withholding any thing which may have the least tendency to meliorate our miserable condition—with the restrictions, however, of not infringing on the articles of its constitution, or that of the United States of America. Now, that we are disunited, is a fact, that no one of common sense will deny; and, that the cause of which, is a powerful auxiliary in keeping us from rising to the scale of reasonable and thinking beings, none but those who delight in our degradation will attempt to contradict.

In effect, Walker was calling on black people to build on the bonds of identification that had already been developed in churches and benevolent societies throughout the United States, particularly in Northern cities, during the early republic. Invoking the liberating spirit of Christianity—"in the name of God, and of Jesus Christ"—and the revolutionary spirit of the age—"while almost every other people under Heaven, are making such mighty efforts to better their condition"—Walker exhorted his brethren to resist "slumbering on" as the "neutral spectators" of white anti-slavery work. In doing so, he acknowledged the "mighty efforts" of "our white brethren and friends" (American and British antislavery advocates), as well as the need to "co-operate with them," but Walker's primary objective was to challenge his own people to rise up in a united front "to hasten our emancipation." Structured around a series of rhetorical questions designed to disrupt political complacency and spiritual degradation among African Americans, Walker's speech was essentially a political call to arms delivered in the preacherly style that would have been quite familiar to his predominantly black and Christian audience. That the full text of Walker's speech was reprinted in the December 19, 1828, issue of *Freedom's Journal* was hardly surprising, as its spirit and content so closely reflected the newspaper's own political mission. Walker himself was closely associated with *Freedom's Journal*, having organized early support for the venture at a meeting in his Boston home four months before the first issue was published, and subsequently having served as one of its two Boston agents. For more than two years, Walker was one of the paper's most consistent and outspoken advocates, submitting occasional articles, running regular advertisements for his store, and working tirelessly to secure continuing moral and financial support for the paper. In many respects, Walker saw the MGCA and *Freedom's Journal* as two indispensable components of his larger vision to "unite the colored population."[68]

If newspapers like *Freedom's Journal* and organizations like the MGCA galvanized African Americans in the late 1820s, David Walker's *Appeal* radicalized them. First published in September 1829—and reprinted twice in the nine months before Walker's untimely death—it was a stirring declaration of independence for black Americans. The full title of Walker's self-published pamphlet—"An Appeal to the Coloured Citizens of the World, *but in particular, and very expressly, to those of the United States of America*" (emphasis mine)—reflects the scope and purpose of his vision. Although Walker's text abounds with favorable references to the history of African civilization and to the recent Haitian revolution, and despite being addressed to the "Coloured Citizens of the World," it, like *Freedom's Journal,* was designed "in particular, and very expressly," for black *Americans.* Its quasi-diasporist inflection was essential to the success of Walker's polemic, but its principal charge was to assert that "Coloured" people are "Citizens" of "the United States of America." From the title page, then, Walker's choice of words—how he characterizes and constructs his black audience—is deliberate, framing his central argument about the moral corruption of the American democratic experiment in language that was simultaneously racial, national, and political.

The formal elements of the *Appeal* make clear Walker's intention to incorporate blacks into the language and structure of American nationalism. Borrowing from the U.S. Constitution, Walker begins his pamphlet with a Preamble, followed by four discrete yet dialogic Articles: Article I ("Our Wretchedness in Consequence of Slavery"); Article II ("Our Wretchedness in Consequence of Ignorance"); Article III ("Our Wretchedness in Consequence of the Preachers of the Religion of Jesus Christ"); and Article IV ("Our Wretchedness in Consequence of the Colonizing Plan"). Hardly coincidental, Walker's careful and familiar structuring of his text allows him to launch his moral and political appeal to black solidarity and resistance by giving it the appearance and discursive legitimacy of American constitutionalism. In this sense, Walker's style is an example of what Henry Louis Gates Jr., has called "signifying": the "double-voiced" act of repetition, revision, and often parody designed to refashion dominant white discourses.[69] Here was Walker's attempt to "write [blacks] out" of slavery and racial degradation—"to awaken in my afflicted, degraded and slumbering brethren, a spirit of inquiry and investigation"—through a refashioning of the formal innovations of American written law.[70] This becomes apparent in Walker's reference to the complicated history of black literacy just opposite the first page of his Preamble:

> It is expected that all coloured men, women, and children (who are not too deceitful, abject, and servile to resist the cruelties and murders inflicted upon us by the white slave holders, our enemies by nature), of every nation, language and tongue under heaven, will try to procure a copy of this Appeal and read it, or get some one to read it to them, for it is designed more particularly for them.[71]

Thus, Walker calls upon his fellow blacks—many of whom, he understands, are not literate—to embark upon a new venture, one that necessarily requires them to engage in the act of reading. He knows full well that this might involve actually breaking the law—especially in the slave states, where laws prohibiting black literacy were an increasingly common response to the activities of free blacks and the resistance of slaves—and in this, he invokes a higher power ("I appeal to Heaven for my motive in writing") to inspire his brethren to "open your hearts to understand and believe the truth."[72] His appeal to literacy as a prerequisite for resistance has a twofold effect: first, to call "all coloured men, women, and children" into the written tradition of American laws and letters, formally established in the writing of the Declaration of Independence and U.S. Constitution, and second, to expose the hypocrisy of this tradition, the incorporation of slavery and the exclusion of black rights in the founding documents of "this *Republican Land of Liberty*."[73] Walker was well aware of the irony. Indeed, that was his point: if the Founding Fathers would not include his "coloured brethren" as "citizens," then Walker would do it for them.

The power of Walker's *Appeal* rests in its radical challenge to the deceptions of American nationalism. In this, Walker was responding directly to the ideological anxieties and evasions of the Founding Fathers in creating the political language and institutional framework for the new nation. Like other African Americans, Walker understood the principal tension of America's early history: the traditions of liberty, independence, and equal rights that had emerged alongside the realities of slavery, subordination, and inequality. Starting with the proposition that "the inhuman system of slavery"—what he called "that *curse of nations*"—was "the source from which most of our miseries proceed," Walker sought to expose the ideology of "race" for what it was: as a means of supporting the creation of laws "to hinder us from obtaining our freedom."[74] Indeed, ever since the founding of the republic, racial ideology allowed whites to make sense of both American slavery and African colonization simultaneously. According to this way of seeing the world, if blacks were inferior to whites, it was both necessary and just for them to be subjected to either slavery (while they remained in the United States) or removal. Freedom and equal citizenship were out of the question because they were direct violations of nature and God. Walker's brutally honest assessment of the legacy of white supremacy allowed him to name the elephant in the republic—racism—in his examination of the root causes of "our wretchedness" as "the *most wretched, degraded,* and *abject* set of beings that *ever lived* since the world began."[75] In so doing, he places "race" at the center stage of his critique of American nationalism.

Although Walker regularly excoriates white slaveholders as "an unjust, jealous, unmerciful, avaricious and blood-thirsty set of beings," he launches his sharpest attack on political leaders like Thomas Jefferson and Henry Clay.[76] Because both men were slaveholders and colonizationists, Walker's decision to single out these individuals was deliberate, one that allowed him to reject both slavery and colonization as interrelated aspects of the same white supremacist project. Walker devotes a considerable amount of space in both Articles I and II to a critique of Jefferson's infamous assertions about black inferiority in his *Notes on the State of Virginia.* Responding to Jefferson's claim that a difference in skin color has stamped blacks as inferior, Walker writes, "It is indeed surprising, that a man of such great learning, combined with such excellent natural parts, should speak so of a set of men in chains."[77] Walker's treatment of Jefferson is instructive. He neither dismisses him nor lets him off the hook. Instead he engages him directly, at times speaking as much *to* Jefferson as *about* him. "Here let me ask Mr. Jefferson," Walker writes, "(but he is gone to answer at the bar of God, for deeds done in his body while living,) I therefore ask the whole American people, had I not rather die, or be put to death, than be a slave to any tyrant."[78] It is interesting to note that Jefferson had just recently passed away—on July 4, 1826—and thus the memory of his legacy was fresh in the minds of Americans, black and white. Based on what we now know of the two men, a real debate with Walker would have been disastrous for Jefferson, whose notorious shyness and mediocre public speaking skills would have paled in comparison to Walker's well-documented oratorical brilliance. In the *Appeal,* Walker compensates for this loss of a live encounter with Jefferson through an interrogation of his most racist views.

Still, Walker respected the author of the Declaration of Independence, despite his obvious disdain for Jefferson's inability to live up to it. Referring favorably to Jefferson's "learned and penetrating" intellect as "one of as great characters as ever lived among the whites," Walker acknowledges Jefferson's "writings for the world, and public labours for the United States."[79] This has the important effect of underscoring the seriousness of

Jefferson's ideas, while demonstrating how deeply the racial prejudices inherent in them had influenced the thinking of white Americans generally. "Do you believe that this assertion is swallowed by millions of whites?" Walker asks rhetorically. "Do you believe that the assertions of such a man, will pass away into oblivion unobserved by this people and the world?"[80] Later on, Walker tempers his respect for Jefferson with a more sober assessment of his legacy. Citing Jefferson's "suspicion" that "blacks . . . are *inferior* to the whites in the endowments both of body and mind," Walker asserts that this passage from *Notes on the State of Virginia* "has in truth injured us more, and has been as great a barrier to our emancipation as any thing that has ever been advanced against us."[81] As a result, Walker encourages "each of my brethren, who has the spirit of a man, to buy a copy of Mr. Jefferson's 'Notes on Virginia,' and put it in the hand of his son."[82] Walker continues:

> For let no one of us suppose that the refutations which have been written by our white friends are enough—they are *whites*—we are *blacks*. We, and the world wish to see the charges of Mr. Jefferson refuted by the blacks *themselves*, according to their chance; for we must remember that what the whites have written respecting this subject, is other men's labours, and did not emanate from the blacks. I know well, that there are some talents and learning among the coloured people of this country, which we have not a chance to develop [sic], in consequence of oppression; but our oppression ought not to hinder us from acquiring all we can. For we will have a chance to develop them by and by. God will not suffer us, always be oppressed. Our sufferings will come to an *end*, in spite of all the Americans this side of *eternity*. Then we will want all the learnings and talents among ourselves, and perhaps more, to govern ourselves.[83]

Here, Walker betrays his agenda: to expose and then discredit the racist views of prominent white leaders; to promote literacy and intellectual achievement among African Americans; to encourage the publication of black refutations of white racism (much like his own pamphlet); and to use these advances in print culture to hasten the end of "our sufferings" such that one day blacks would "govern ourselves." In other words, Walker articulates a direct relationship between black literacy and print culture, and the goals of abolition and racial equality. For Walker, the key to emancipation was self-reliance: blacks themselves were responsible for throwing off the shackles of "ignorance" in order to create a new political consciousness. The stakes were too high, and Walker had no patience for blacks who were either complacent about or complicit in their own oppression. "Unless we try to refute Mr. Jefferson's arguments respecting us," he concluded, "we will only establish them."[84] Building on the tradition established in 1773 by the black poet Phillis Wheatley—who had been a catalyst, ironically, for Jefferson's thoughts on "race" that were recorded in *Notes*—African Americans still had to assert their equality through print.[85] Half a century after the American Revolution, the burden of proof still rested squarely on their shoulders.

For Walker's challenge to have its desired effect, blacks would also have to claim their rightful place as citizens of the United States. This is why Walker devotes so much space in the *Appeal*—some thirty pages in Article IV—to the issue of colonization, which, he argued, was as much a threat to African Americans as slavery itself. For their part, whites generally believed that free blacks were a threat to the security of the republic, especially in areas were slavery flourished. With characteristic bluntness, Walker gets to the heart of the issue: "For if the free are allowed to stay among the slaves, they will have intercourse together, and, of course, the free will learn the slaves *bad habits,* by teaching them that they are MEN, as well as other people, and certainly *ought* and *must* be FREE."[86] Here, Walker exposes the "colonizing scheme" as a deeply racist project motivated by a desire to keep slavery in tact and prevent African Americans from ever enjoying the privileges of American citizenship.

In rejecting colonization, Walker quotes at length several speeches and letters by Henry Clay, the Kentucky slaveholder who was also one of the original founders of the American Colonization Society. As a member of Congress, Clay was also the principal architect of the 1820 Missouri Compromise, which led to the admission of Missouri as a slave state and Maine as a free state, while prohibiting slavery north of the latitude 36°30' in the lands acquired through the Louisiana Purchase. The legislation was designed to dissolve bitter Congressional tensions over the westward expansion of slavery, begun in 1819 when Missouri petitioned for statehood, by preserving the sectional (and legislative) balance between the number of slave and free states in the Union. Nevertheless, the Missouri Compromise—which Jefferson described as his "fire-bell in the night"—had the effect of hardening sectional differences over slavery, and was later seen as one of the principal, if unintended, catalysts in the long road to Civil War. Although Clay was well respected by his white peers—over the course of his forty-year career as a politician, he earned a stellar reputation as "The Great Compromiser" because of his ability to delicately negotiate between Northern and Southern interests—Walker considered his political bargains over slavery, as well as his energetic advocacy of colonization, to be deleterious to African-American interests. Of Clay, he writes:

Now I appeal and ask every citizen of these United States and the world, both *white* and *black,* who has any knowledge of Mr. Clay's public labor for these States—I want you candidly to answer the Lord, who sees the secrets of our hearts.—Do you believe that Mr. Henry Clay, late Secretary of State, and now of Kentucky, is a friend to the blacks, further, than his personal interest extends? It is not his greatest object and glory upon earth, to sick us into miseries and wretchedness by making slaves of us, to work his plantation to enrich him and his family? Does he care a pinch of snuff about Africa—whether it remains a land of Pagans and of blood, or of Christians, so long as he gets enough of her sons and daughters to dig up gold and silver for him?[87]

When it came to slavery and colonization, Walker urged, whites could hardly be trusted. This position had much to recommend it in 1829, by the fact that no white American had come out publicly in opposition to colonization or in favor of the immediate abolition of slavery, and by the fact that many members of the ACS were themselves slaveholders. Regardless of their stated public intentions regarding the future of slavery or the condition of free blacks in the United States, proponents of colonization were regarded with deep suspicion among blacks. In criticizing Clay and other members of the ACS, Walker was simply giving a new public voice to long-standing private thoughts within the African-American community.

As he makes clear throughout the *Appeal,* Walker believed that the future of blacks in the United States would be determined by their willingness to demand freedom and equality on their own terms. Buoyed by a deeper understanding of their own oppression—the function, Walker describes, of a combination of slavery, racial prejudice, and widespread ignorance within the black community—African Americans would eventually rise up and say to whites: "Throw away your fears and prejudices then, and enlighten us and treat us like men, and we will like you more than we do now hate you . . . and tell us now no more about colonization, for America is as much our country, as it is yours.—Treat us like men, and there is no danger but we will all live in peace and happiness together."[88] Throughout his pamphlet, Walker writes with great urgency, and millennialist sentiments are everywhere evident in his prose. Walker considered himself a prophet and a preacher, consistently invoking God—"I appeal to Heaven"—to make his case. The *Appeal* itself is styled on the black sermon, each Article beginning with a salutation to "my brethren," and punctuated with questions designed to elicit an active response—not just a confirming "Amen"—from his reading audience (the print version of a congregation).

Although Walker fully intends for his pamphlet to be read by whites, he imagines his primary audience to be African Americans. Throughout, Walker not only moves back and forth between "I" and "you," but far more frequently invokes "we"—as well as "us" and "them"—to make clear that he identifies with his black "brethren." Walker's rhetorical choices regarding the first person—both singular and plural—suggest that he is deeply invested in the integrity of distinct racial identities for the sake of political protest. Within the context of American society, Walker places a premium on racial consciousness as a means by which African Americans can most effectively combat the various forms of white racism that have produced the pervasive "degradation" and "slumber" he has witnessed in the black community. Building on the longstanding African American tradition of merging sacred and secular discourses and imagery, Walker addresses his *Appeal* to "My dearly Beloved Brethren and Fellow Citizens," suggesting that blacks have a racial and religious bond ("brethren") and also a political identity ("citizens").

Walker's intention to merge racial, religious, and political identities is on full display in Articles III and IV, where he castigates the "American minister," who, "with the Bible in his hand, holds us and our children in the most abject slavery."[89] He notes that "pure and undefiled religion, such as was preached by Jesus Christ and his apostles, is hard to be found in all the earth."[90] Indeed, like so many of his fellow abolitionists, Walker articulates a harsh critique of Christians who use the teachings of the Bible to sanction or tolerate slavery. Invoking the word "devil" to characterize those who identify themselves as Christians and yet "keep us and our children sunk at their feet in the most abject ignorance and wretchedness," Walker launches a fierce attack that exposes the corruption of Jesus's legacy by white slaveholders and reclaims it in the image of black Christianity. To these white ministers, Walker poses a provocative alternative: Richard Allen, founder and bishop of the African Methodist Episcopal Church in the United States. In Article IV, Walker includes "an exact verbatim" letter by Allen denouncing colonization that was published in *Freedom's Journal* (intertextuality—the incorporation of other printed texts within the pamphlet itself—was another important technique used in Walker's pamphlet). Referring to Allen as "that godly man," Walker pays lengthy tribute to the black minister's work and legacy, writing: "When the Lord shall raise up coloured historians in succeeding generations, to present the crimes of this nation, to the then gazing world, the Holy Ghost will make them do justice to the name of Richard Allen. . . . he has done more in a spiritual sense for his ignorant and wretched brethren than any other man of colour has, since the world began."[91] It is no coincidence that Walker reserves such lofty superlatives for someone like Allen, who was at once black, Christian, and an early abolitionist. Drawn to his likeness, Walker's tribute to Allen functions as an example of how religious faith can be used by blacks to challenge white supremacy and cultivate new forms of African American consciousness. Using language as positive as his critiques of Jefferson and Clay are negative, Walker hopes to inspire "coloured historians" to one day restore Allen's name to the "pages of history." It is important, too, that Walker selected a member of the "founding" generation of African American history, someone who could stand with and against the likes of Thomas Jefferson as a hero of black liberation in the face of white supremacy. By incorporating Allen's words and tribute into his pamphlet—especially within the context of a critique of colonization—Walker creates an alternative "founding" myth, one that simultaneously, and conspicuously, validates the political courage and religious faith of African Americans.

The effect of this is underscored by the way in which Walker concludes his *Appeal*. In its final section, he asks for "the attention of the world of mankind to the declaration of these very American people, of the United States." He then quotes most of the first two paragraphs of the Declaration of Independence, and follows them with the question, addressed to white Americans, "Do you understand your own language?"[92] Walker continues: "Compare your own language above . . . with your cruelties and murders inflicted by your cruel and unmerciful fathers and yourselves on our fathers and on us—men who have never given your fathers or you the least provocation!"[93] In the end, then, Walker returns to the beginning, and challenges his white "brethren" to finally live up to the ideals of equality upon which the country was founded. In a text that invokes the formal structure of the Constitution—the written symbol of the Founding Fathers' bargains with slavery—this conclusion has enormous power, not merely as a declaration of independence for African Americans, but as a demand for inclusion as well. Walker poses a political challenge—in this sense, the *Appeal* functions as a kind of re-Constitution of the United States—and also as a religious one. "I call God," he writes in an earlier passage, "I call angels—I call men, to witness, that your DESTRUCTION *is at hand*, and will be speedily consummated unless you REPENT."[94] One of the most common mistakes made by the pamphlet's readers—both at the time and ever since—is to interpret it as a call for violent insurrection by blacks against whites. Nowhere does Walker actually advocate violence. But he does suggest that the millennium will come if slavery and racism are not eliminated from American society. Challenging whites to "understand your own language," Walker makes it clear that they can avoid "destruction" if they commit themselves to the practice of equality, given to man in the example of Jesus Christ. He concludes: "The Americans may be as vigi-

lant as they please, but they cannot be vigilant enough for the Lord, neither can they hide themselves, where he will not find and bring them
out."[95] Violence was inevitable only if whites continued to enslave and oppress blacks. The choice was theirs—and they had better hurry.

The response to Walker's *Appeal* was in many ways predictable. Walker
himself had developed ingenious networks for distributing his pamphlet,
relying on black and white seamen to circulate it among free blacks and
slaves during their frequent stops in southern ports. Southern whites denounced the pamphlet as "insurrectionary" and worse. Upon discovering
its circulation in his state, South Carolina's governor wrote to his counterpart, Harrison Gray Otis, in Massachusetts, demanding that Walker be put
in jail. Otis responded by saying that although he had no sympathy for the
Appeal, Walker had done nothing worthy of imprisonment. Rumors
quickly spread about various bounties being placed on Walker's head—
dead or alive—by men of "property and standing" across the South. Even
sympathetic antislavery reformers balked at Walker's radical assertions.
Benjamin Lundy, then the editor of Baltimore's *Genius of Universal Emancipation,* called the *Appeal* "the most incendiary tract ever written," and
William Lloyd Garrison, Lundy's fiery young apprentice, although more
sympathetic to Walker's "impassioned and determined spirit," considered
it "a most injudicious publication, yet warranted by the creed of an independent people."[96] African Americans were markedly less hostile to the
publication, though some had reservations about its militancy, and many
saw it as beckoning a more militant strain of abolitionism within the northern free black community. But Walker's writing would prove important in
many ways, not least of which was a catalyst for immediate abolitionism. In
this, it marked a clear turning point in the early history of abolition in the
United States. As the culmination of an impressive experiment in black
print culture, the *Appeal* did indeed manage to "awaken" Walker's "afflicted brethren." But it did something else, too. As Garrison's reaction
suggests, Walker's radicalism—in conjunction with the persistent and increasingly aggressive demands of *Freedom's Journal*—had attracted the attention of a small yet sympathetic white audience whose attitudes toward
race, slavery, and colonization were beginning to change. In the humble
yet heroic efforts of free blacks, then, we see the origins of radical abolitionism. And in their appeal to the moral and political conscience of white
people, we see the stirrings of America's first interracial struggle for social
change. It wouldn't be long before they had the whole nation's attention.

PART THREE

Revolutions

8

"Willing to Die for the Cause of Freedom in Kansas": Free State Emigration, John Brown, and the Rise of Militant Abolitionism in the Kansas Territory

Karl Gridley

We must conquer, we must slaughter;
We are God's rod, and His ire
Wills their blood shall flow like water;
in Jehovah's dread name—Fire!
—Anonymous, *"John Brown's Address to His Men"*
Osawatomie, Kansas, August 30, 1856[1]

On December 2, 1859, a trap door fell and John Brown's body swung in the midst of his marshaled mortal enemies, hanging "between heaven and earth" from a rickety gallows in Charlestown, Virginia. Some 900 miles to the west—at Miller's Hall on snowy Massachusetts Street in Lawrence, Kansas—a large antislavery meeting was taking place. Among the eleven resolutions proclaimed by the men and women assembled there was one praising John Brown's raid at Harpers Ferry, asserting that he had "given his life for the Liberty of Man," and that, during his Kansas days, John Brown was "among the first to teach the Border-Ruffian invaders of our soil the wholesome lesson, that oppressors might be made to 'bite the dust,' and flee from our soil, at a time when they imagined that their foulest deeds were on the eve of being realized."[2]

The gathering was well attended by Brown's old Kansas Free State comrades in arms, many of whom fought alongside the "Old Puritan Hero" in the early "Bleeding Kansas" skirmishes between antislavery and proslavery militias that preceded the Civil War. Reports of massacres and battles with exotic western frontier names like Pottawatomie, Black Jack, and Osawatomie often made the front pages of the eastern papers throughout 1856.[3] December 2, 1859, however, in many ways brought a symbolic closure to these territorial Kansas Wars. The sensational Virginia military hanging of "Old Osawatomie Brown"—the armed abolitionist who had figured so prominently in the affairs of Kansas a few years earlier—closed an era, and Kansas Territory was by then already destined to enter the Union as a free state.[4] His execution, however, also marked a beginning. The sectional conflict John Brown helped to spark in Kansas through word and deed now dramatically ignited the rest of the nation. There would be no turning back from the "meteor-like" events—as writer Henry David Thoreau described them—of Harpers Ferry and Charlestown.[5]

For better or worse, John Brown's role and influence in what was then known as the "Kansas Question" will likely be debated forever. But, at that meeting, on that day, there was a bitter and widespread sentiment in the cold winter air of Kansas, and throughout much of the North as well. The Lawrence *Republican* later stated: "It is safe to say, that the death of no other man in America has ever produced so profound a sensation . . . a feeling of deep and sorrowful indignation seems to possess the masses."[6]

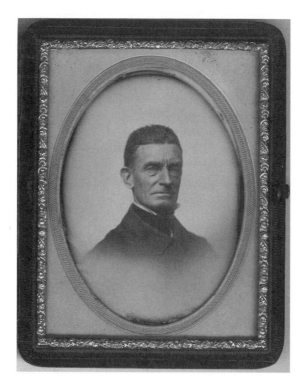

Daguerreotype of John Brown, who sat for it at the request of Amos Adams Lawrence, in Boston in 1855. Taken by Josiah Johnson Hawes. (Source: Massachusetts Historical Society)

Why was this the case? John Brown is often viewed by historians as mercurial and fanatical, a man whose militancy and radicalism essentially isolated him from the broader antislavery and abolitionist movement. Yet, in Kansas—a frontier territory where one's very survival often depended on the interconnections of families and friends—Brown could hardly have operated within a vacuum, either of sympathy or conduct. Had he been simply a lone psychopath and horse thief roaming the prairies as a renegade bit player, impoverished of any broader motivation for his actions, his legacy would be of negligible interest to historians. Instead, as extensive surviving correspondence by and about him reminds us, Brown was actively engaged, both personally and politically, with the people of the territory; he was a devoutly committed and unrepentant abolitionist, and while the irregular and often violent methods he used earned him a legion of detractors, so too did those methods garner him a fixed cadre of devoted followers among the free-state population. By 1855–56, Kansas had become the first protracted test of a nascent and organized militant abolitionist movement in the United States. Over the course of three and a half years—from October 1855 to February 1859—Brown would emerge as its unequivocal champion, its most effective and brutal practitioner, and, ultimately, its quintessential national pariah and martyr. Despite the fact that Brown's raid on Harpers Ferry ended as a military failure, within sixteen months of his hanging for treason, Union troops were singing "John Brown's Body" as they marched rank and file deep into the South to do battle with the "slave power." John Brown may well have been marginalized, but he was hardly marginal.

The Kansas-Nebraska Act, itself a direct, if aberrant, outgrowth of the national debate over slavery, became, by the very nature of its construction, a primary cause of the factional difficulties in the territory. Kansas territorial governor Andrew Reeder, after being dismissed from his position by President Franklin Pierce in 1856, spoke in September at a "Great Gathering" of New Jersey Republicans, stating:

> I start then, with the proposition that, from the year 1854 to the present time, *there has been in operation upon the plains of the West, a preconcerted, a premeditated, a well-digested and deliberate plan to force Slavery upon the people of Kansas in despite of the law, in despite of their will and in despite of all their Constitutional rights.* . . . There is no outrage which ever took place upon the soil of the Territory of Kansas that could not be traced directly to this plan.[7]

The ultimate effect of the Kansas-Nebraska Act was to set the proponents of two irreconcilable philosophies at one another's throats. The abolition-

ist editor of the *Kansas Tribune,* John Speer, wrote in his biography of
Kansas demagogue and political firebrand James H. Lane: "[L]et us remember, that in the civilizations of the world, no two such conflicting
forces ever met—certainly no two in a republican form of government like
ours—as met on the plains of Kansas. To us, 'slavery was the sum of all vil-
lainies'—to them, it was more the apple of their eye, property proportion-
ately more sacred than their flocks and herds as it was more valuable."[8]

When President Pierce signed the Kansas-Nebraska Act into law on May
30, 1854, the pressing issue of whether chattel slavery as an institution
would expand into those vast, newly opened western territories, thereby securing a Southern, proslavery advantage in Congress, gripped a nation
that had lurched agonizingly from compromise to compromise for decades with an "irrepressible conflict" looming ominously on the horizon.
With the passage of the act—which effectively repealed the Missouri Compromise of 1820—antislavery and proslavery advocates alike realized that
the time had come to fully engage each other.[9]

Almost immediately, antislavery Emigrant Aid Societies sprang up
throughout New England, with prominent reformers putting their often
considerable financial backing into the crusade to make Kansas a free
state. In the South, however, the determination was equally strong to make
Kansas a slave state. "We will before six months rolls around have the Devil
to play in Kansas," Senator David Rice Atchison of Missouri assured the
U.S. Secretary of War Jefferson Davis with confidence on September 24,
1854. "We are organizing to meet their organization. We will be compelled
to shoot burn and hang, but the thing will soon be over."

The "virgin soil" of the Kansas Territory soon proved to be the stage for
a violent prelude, bringing into the spotlight for the first time many of the
same players who later rose to prominence in the greater national conflict.
The state motto adopted for Kansas—*ad astra per aspera* ("to the stars
through difficulties")—is not an exclusively cosmological reference. The
struggle in Kansas to become the thirty-fourth star of the Union coincided
with a churning "time of troubles" for the entire nation, and the determined role eastern abolitionists played in that struggle would ultimately
prove crucial to the admittance of Kansas as a free state.[10] Like Thoreau,
and in keeping with celestial metaphors, Walt Whitman later aptly described John Brown as "the meteor of the War," his long white beard looking providential on the day of his hanging, trailing as a silent omen from
beneath his gallows cowl in the Virginia winter wind.

By midsummer of 1854 waves of emigrants began leaving towns large and
small in New England, singing John Greenleaf Whittier's "Song of the
Kansas Emigrant," and heading "in righteousness" for the newly opened

Kansas Territory.[11] Many families did so under the countenance and auspices of the Massachusetts (later New England) Emigrant Aid Company.[12] This was an antislavery organization sponsored by, among others, Eli Thayer of Worcester, John Carter Brown of Providence, and Thaddeus Hyatt, Thomas Webb, Edward Everett Hale, and Amos A. Lawrence of Boston.[13] By August and September of that year, the first companies arrived (via rail, steamboat, foot, horse and wagon) some forty miles west of the Missouri border, and there founded the fledgling free-state outpost of Lawrence.[14] Over the next five years, this little settlement on the Kansas River became the central focus of much of the nation's attention as the preliminary skirmishes of the Civil War, both political and military, were played out upon the vast central prairies of North America.[15]

To what extent were these settlers who came to Kansas Territory from New England truly abolitionists? What was the extent of their influence, initially and over time, within the physical and ideological struggle to make Kansas a free state? These issues have been hotly debated through the years, both by the participants themselves and by generations of historians. Muddying the debate are a number of monikers given to people during that period: free soilers, free staters, antislaveryites, jayhawkers, abolitionists, radical abolitionists, and racial egalitarianists. The extent to which these New Englanders, let alone abolitionists, constituted a majority in Kansas in the mid-1850s is also a point of contention. As census records show, a far larger population of emigrants to Kansas in 1855 came from Ohio and other states once part of the "old Northwest," although many Ohioans were only one generation removed from their New England roots. In general, Ohio (and Western Reserve) abolitionists often proved much more radical than those from New England.[16] Again, Kansas's most famous abolitionist, John Brown, is a clear example of this. A New England abolitionist by birth, he had lived and worked extensively in Ohio, Pennsylvania, and New York. As a consequence, he could not be easily categorized, geographically. Brown's wanderings were far ranging, and ultimately his agenda, like many of his contemporaries in Kansas, became both western (the prevention of slavery's further expansion) and southern (the abolition of slavery).

The fiery mix of motivations that existed under the broad canopies of the anti- and proslavery agendas of the period does not lend itself well to simplified assertions. Complicating any such assessments, the surviving written records often fall short in terms of indisputably proving polemical historical arguments; and, because many settlers did not write down their affiliations or politics, and because infinitely more letters and documents have been lost than have survived from the period, accurate reconstructions of the convictions and intentions of the majority of settlers in Kansas are precarious at best. We can learn, though, from cause and effect—and certainly, in the Kansas Territory, there were causes and there were effects.

It remains important to examine the political nature of those who defined themselves as abolitionists when they came to Kansas in the mid-1850s, because doing so helps to determine the extent to which their views and actions—specifically, the actions of those abolitionists who were armed and militant—actually had an impact on the eventual admission of Kansas into the Union as a free state. The admission altered forever the balance of free and slave states in the days leading up to the Civil War; and along with a number of other factors, it caused the conflict to flare openly. As historian Michael Fellman has noted, "general preconceptions, day-to-day friction, and battle turned vague feelings into strident sectional identities. In northern terms, Kansas brought antislavery up to the fighting point. . . . In the 1850s, a new generation of antislavery leaders responded to a broader antislavery public with a harsher and more vengeful ideology." [17]

Given this context, it is virtually impossible to think of Kansas during this period and not consider the most radical and militant of all American abolitionists: John Brown. Was Brown truly an isolated figure, going his own, rash way and doing things under his own special counsel with a vengeful, Old Testament God?[18] From Brown's arrival in the territory in October 1855, heavily armed with his biblical swords and modern Colts, to his frequent subsequent journeys to and from the territory, and ultimately to his final departure from Kansas in February 1859, Brown attracted an increasingly solid and loyal base of support within an influential part of the free-state population in Kansas.[19] To a great extent that support came from settlers who defined themselves, unapologetically and without qualification, as abolitionists. Brown himself in letters to his friends and family would always refer to himself as an abolitionist as well as a free-state man, and he apparently saw little need for making overly fine distinctions within, or between, these two terms.[20] Unlike many of his more politically motivated free-state contemporaries, however, he did see his mission as extending beyond the struggle simply to prevent slavery's westward expansion, and in so doing make Kansas "free"—a struggle that many in Kansas may have considered an end in itself. Brown intended prophetically and symbolically to go beyond Kansas and "carry the war into Africa."[21] In other words, Brown wanted to transform not only Kansas but the entire nation as well.

A recurring approach in historiography relating to the period, however, is to cast a skeptical eye upon the implied motives of all parties involved, whether abolitionist, proslavery, or anything in between. The "free white labor" concern of many of the settlers is often used to indict the entire antislavery emigration to Kansas as being one that was purely self-serving and essentially racist and hypocritical. To many historians of the period the antislavery movement, especially as it related to Kansas, had little to do with African American emancipation or equality, and everything to do with land and the inalienable rights of free whites in the West.[22] Among the most overlooked viewpoints, however, is that of those who specifically had the most to lose or gain from the outcome. As Gunja SenGupta mentions, "the invisibility of African Americans as anything other than objects of white discourse represents perhaps the most serious weakness of Bleeding Kansas historiography . . . the story of Bleeding Kansas will remain unfinished as long as historians fail to take account of the myriad ways in which African Americans helped define the debate over freedom in the territory as well as the nation at large."[23]

Revisionist historians from the 1930s through the 1960s—including James Malin, Paul Gates, and James Rawley—have tended to view the issues at play in 1850s Kansas as far more economic than social or "racial." For Gates, an "insatiable land hunger" and a corrupting desire to manipulate U.S. land patronage policy were at the core of the Kansas conflict; the moral issue of slavery, with its blustering detractors and adherents, became a mere side event that quickly faded in its intensity and relevance. Gates refers to abolitionists only once in his book *Fifty Million Acres,* and only then with the adjective "rabid." Rawley, much like Malin before him, sought to demythologize race and racial politics as the central motifs of the Kansas imbroglio. However, there were very basic, and, as Speer noted, diametrically opposed and irreconcilable belief systems at play in 1850s Kansas; once fully polarized, they would threaten the very survival of the Union. As Brown biographer Stephen B. Oates has stated, "the United States of [Brown's] day had institutionalized a monstrous moral contradiction: the existence of slavery in a Republic that claimed to be both Christian and free, a Republic founded on the enlightened ideal that everyone is entitled to life, liberty and the pursuit of happiness. Unable (or unwilling) to resolve such a contradiction, the country invited a messianic rebel like John Brown to appear with his sword."[24]

"Black abolitionists," Paul Finkelman would later write, "were more comfortable with Brown's violent legacy; the Harper's Ferry affair had given a new vitality to the movement to bear arms. Blacks not only accepted but truly venerated Brown's martyrdom. They only wanted to make sure that his death would not ultimately be in vain. Responding to the question, 'How shall American slavery be abolished?' Frederick Douglass declared, 'The John Brown way.' "[25] It is worth noting that at a gathering held at the

Tremont Temple in Boston to mark the first anniversary of Brown's execution, Douglass was forcibly evicted by a mob for making such a heretical assertion.[26]

The continuous operation in eastern Kansas throughout this period of
well-organized western branches of the Underground Railroad gives some
indication of the extent of the actual sympathies within the antislavery
population of the territory for abolition and emancipation.[27] Though
often considered primarily as an eastern network, Underground Railroad
routes proved highly effective from Texas and Indian territory to Kansas.
The Missouri border in particular was highly porous; slaves could use it to
escape west before heading north through Topeka and Nebraska City via
the Lane Trail into Iowa. When John Brown led his late raid into western
Missouri in December of 1858 to liberate eleven slaves, his subsequent
month-long journey, in the dead of winter, through Kansas to Nebraska
(and eventually to Canada) was fully sanctioned and facilitated by an extensive, committed, and well-organized network of Brown's personal
friends.[28] It is no accident that the majority of the men who later accompanied John Brown to Harpers Ferry were originally members of his tried
and tested Kansas guerrilla band. In breaking the news of the raid, the
Boston *Weekly Messenger* announced in its first sentence: "The insurrection-
ists are commanded by Capt. John Brown of Kansas notoriety."[29]

The point frequently made in studies of Kansas history during this period—that abolitionists constituted a minority in numbers—is true. However, the overall Kansas population was not large in the 1850s, and the
strong influence of key abolitionists was keenly felt within the territory.
"Westerners" like James H. Lane of Indiana may not have come to Kansas
as abolitionists, but many became so inclined once the advantage was
gained. Lane, certainly no racial egalitarian in 1855, eventually went on to
earn the respect of African Americans by organizing the first black Union
regiments in 1862—the First Regiment, Kansas Colored Volunteers—and
becoming an enthusiastic emancipator and enlister of slaves throughout
Missouri during the Civil War.[30]

As with any broad human migration, settlers came to Kansas for mixed
and often contradictory motives. A host of reasons existed to strike out for
Kansas in the 1850s, from "yeoman farming" and land speculation to railroads and lucrative government appointments.[31] In a great deal of the de-
bunking historiography that still blankets the period, a pervasive and often
hostile desire exists to downplay or reject any altruism or nobility of purpose among abolitionists in Kansas.[32] To some degree this comes from an
insistence that "racial egalitarianism" is synonymous with abolitionism; because it is not, tremendous fault is found with the purity of the motives of

white abolitionists. It certainly was not the case at the time that the two philosophies were mutual in scope, and there is no lack of period documents to indicate that Northern abolitionists, like the majority of white Americans at the time, were, in many ways, every bit as racist as their Southern counterparts. In contrast, however, they did not seem to possess the means or, apparently, the desire to manifest and enforce their racism with whips, branding irons, and chains.

With regard to pure racial egalitarianism, John Brown and his family stand out as remarkably enlightened, and perhaps even unique, among Americans of this period.[33] But Brown did not operate alone within Kansas, and the irrevocable severity and harsh consequences of many of his militant actions in the name of the antislavery cause would demand loyalty among his followers if his overall plans were to succeed. Brown's singularly most radical and violent act in Kansas, the Pottawatomie Massacre—which is often used by Civil War historians as evidence of Brown's criminal insanity and murderous psychosis—attracted more supporters than he had before the event. Brown's following and magnetic strength increased exponentially after the massacre. Had Brown been effectively shunned and marginalized within the overall abolitionist population in Kansas, the Harpers Ferry raid may never have occurred. Regardless of the cause for which it has been used, violence—and particularly guerrilla violence—has always had the ability to galvanize (and also potentially destroy) radical political and social movements in their defining moments of crisis. By July 10, 1856, Gerrit Smith stated: "There was a time when slavery could have been ended by political action. But that time has gone by—and, as I apprehend, forever. There was not virtue enough in American people to bring slavery to a bloodless termination; and all that remains for them is to bring it to a bloody one."[34]

Edmund B. Whitman and A.D. Searl's *Map of Eastern Kansas*—published in Boston in June 1856 by J.P. Jewett, the distinguished publishers of Harriet Beecher Stowe—reveals the extent to which prominent eastern elites were interested in what was otherwise a rather remote region and its politics.[35] The map is a unique and instructive window onto the conditions in Kansas at the time, showing encampments of proslavery Missourians encircling Lawrence, and, in the lower margin, engravings of the just-built, then-destroyed Free State, or Eldridge, Hotel. By showing a territory *en pleine guerre* and also depicting the resulting conditions of that ongoing warfare, the map works as a land agent's promotional device, extolling for a New England audience the potential spoils that could arise from this conflict.

Interestingly, the original name of Lawrence, Kansas, was New Boston, and its main street was symbolically named Massachusetts Street. Reams of correspondence dating from the period reveal the connections between prominent Boston Brahmin (as well as more common) families and those in Kansas Territory.[36] Edmund Burke Whitman, a close friend of Bronson Alcott, was the primary resident agent in Kansas for the Massachusetts and the National Kansas Committees.[37] By 1857, it was through Whitman that the so-called "Secret Six"—Gerrit Smith, George Luther Stearns, Samuel Gridley Howe, Theodore Parker, Franklin Sanborn, Thomas Wentworth Higginson—along with John Brown's other abolitionist supporters, sent their monetary support for his militant efforts.[38]

Today the old cemeteries of eastern Kansas remain the final resting places of many young New England abolitionists who heeded the call and died far from home. The epitaphs on many gravestones—like that of David Chase Buffum from Salem, Massachusetts, which reads: "I am willing to die for the cause of Freedom in Kansas"—are today lichen-covered testimony to a particular devotion many New England emigrants to Kansas felt toward the new land and its relation to the nation's promise and political future.[39] Though perhaps overdramatized at times, the perils of a journey to Kansas at the height of the troubles were often reported as "life-and-death struggles." John Brown himself, during his whirlwind New England speaking tour of 1857, referred to the war-torn eastern Kansas landscape of late 1856 as *a most gloomy scene; & like a visit to a vast sepulcre.*"[40]

This understanding that the Kansas Territory was to be a military as well as an economic and political battleground over slavery's expansion was hardly lost on the eastern backers of free-state emigration. The Massachusetts and National Kansas Committees, as well as people like Henry Ward Beecher and other New England supporters of the free-state cause, were far from shy about sending arms and ammunition to Kansas by wagon and crate.[41] "Beecher's Bibles" were the legendary Sharps carbines used in many of the Bleeding Kansas battles, and were shipped on steamers like the *Arabia* up the Missouri in wooden boxes marked with missionary stencils. This "contraband" abolitionist cargo became one of the primary reasons the Missouri River was blockaded by proslavery forces throughout the summer of 1856, and free-state emigrant trains had to be rerouted along the Lane Trail through Iowa and Nebraska. By mid-1856 Kansas had become a sort of catch-all for the nation's surplus mercenary weaponry. "We are of the opinion," said the Atchison *Squatter Sovereign*, "[that] if the citizens of Leavenworth . . . would hang one or two boatloads of abolitionists it would do more towards establishing peace in Kansas than all the speeches that have been delivered in Congress during the present session. Let the experiment be tried!"[42]

Despite the ready availability of arms, John Brown was often bitterly left waiting for the financial resources he wanted and needed for his western campaign.[43] He did, however, receive moral support for his militant abolitionist activities in Kansas, and for his later raid on Harpers Ferry, from New England transcendentalists such as Ralph Waldo Emerson and Henry David Thoreau, as well as other leading literary and religious figures in the east (Harriet Beecher Stowe, Julia Ward Howe, Lydia Maria Child, John Greenleaf Whittier, Henry Wadsworth Longfellow, and Herman Melville). In fact, Thoreau's famous speech, "A Plea for Captain John Brown," was perhaps the most eloquent example of the moral fervor Brown's actions aroused among the Boston literati.

One way of determining the militant abolitionist influence in Kansas is to examine the proslavery view of the region and of the hostilities. Almost without exception, when referring to an "outrage," proslavery newspapers blamed the "Abolitionists" or "D—d Abolitionists." Lawrence, Kansas, regardless of whether it was actually predominately populated by abolitionists, was usually attacked for being "a nest of abolitionism," and throughout the summer of 1856 the Missouri River remained blockaded to prevent "abolitionist immigration" to Kansas. On April 29, following an erroneous report of the murder of Samuel Jones, the proslavery sheriff of Douglas County, the ever-bellicose *Squatter Sovereign* proclaimed: "When a proslavery man gets into difficulty with an Abolitionist, let him think of the murdered Jones and Clark, and govern himself accordingly. In a fight, let our motto be, 'War to the knife and knife to the hilt;' asking no quarters from them and granting none. *Jones' Murder Must Be Revenged!*"[44]

Following the infamous "sack of Lawrence" on May 21, 1856, the *Doniphan Constitutionalist* of May 23 happily reported the destruction of "that notorious abolition hole, Lawrence." David Rice Atchison, then the acting vice president of the United States, had led the attack along with Sheriff Samuel Jones. Atchison made a speech that day on Massachusetts Street, stating:

> Boys, this day I am a Kickapoo Ranger, by God! This day we have entered Lawrence with 'Southern Rights' inscribed upon our banner, and not one damned abolitionist dared to fire a gun. Now, boys, this is the happiest day of my life. We have entered that damned town, and taught the damned abolitionists a Southern lesson that they will remember till the day they die. . . . Now do your duty to yourselves and your Southern friends. Your duty I know you will do. If one man or woman dare stand before you, blow them to hell with a cold chunk of lead.

By June 7, the *Independence* [Missouri] *Messenger* was "declaring [a] war of extermination against those abolition outlaws . . . abolition plunders . . .

An illustration of the "Bombarding of the Free State Hotel" during the sack of
Lawrence on May 21, 1856. The proslavery attack was directly responsible for John
Brown's retaliatory attack at Pottawatomie Creek on May 24–25, 1856. (Source:
Kansas State Historical Society)

[and] abolition freebooters," and by late summer great "armies of abolitionists" were said to roam the prairies, slaughtering peace-loving Southern families.

On July 15, the *Squatter Sovereign* warned:

> With them it is no mere local question of whether slavery shall exist in
> Kansas or not, but one of far wider significance; a question of whether
> it shall exist anywhere in the Union. Kansas they justly regard as the
> mere outpost in the war now being waged between the antagonistic
> civilizations of the North and South; and winning this great outpost
> and standing point they rightly think their march will be open to an
> easy conquest of the whole field. These [outrages] are not as some
> pretend, the mere extravagances of a few irresponsible individuals,
> but on the contrary, are chargeable to the Abolition party.[45]

Of course, hyperbole was a tactic of both camps, and exaggerated perceptions almost always trumped reality when it came to defining one's enemy.

It is useful—again using John Brown as a barometer—to look at the reasons abolitionism successfully attracted such a substantial and militant fol-

lowing in Kansas. In many ways Kansas was a blank slate, and those who came there in 1854 and 1855 defined its political landscape for themselves and for the rest of the country. The long, tortuous history of the abolitionist movement in the United States was finally nearing its climax, and John Brown became in many ways a representative figure of its difficult evolution. In this respect, Brown was far older (and more experienced) than most of his contemporaries in Kansas, and his experience and patriarchal nature allowed for a broad philosophical influence over men and women, many of whom were barely in their twenties.

Many Kansas settlers defined themselves as abolitionists and, to a greater or lesser degree, were sympathetic with the basic tenets of Brown's agenda. Among them were Charles Stearns (a nephew of Lydia Maria Child, who came from Boston to Lawrence with the First Emigrant Aid Party in 1854); Augustus Wattles (originally from the Lane Seminary in Cincinnati, he settled in Bloomington and later Moneka); John Speer (a newspaper editor originally from Pennsylvania who settled in Lawrence); John Ritchie (who came from Ohio to Topeka); Tauy Jones (from Ottawa); James Abbott and John Doy (who came from New York to Lawrence); James Montgomery (from Sugar Mound); Charles Lenhart and Aaron D. Stevens (from Topeka); Silas Soule (from Vinland); and Joseph Gardner.[46] There were also a number of prominent and outspoken Free State Kansas women abolitionists, including Clarina Nichols, of Quindaro, and Julia Louisa Lovejoy, from Lawrence.[47]

The letters of many of Brown's most devoted followers (whether eastern financial supporters or on-the-ground recruits in Kansas) indicate a highly developed abolitionist sensibility, or "calling," emanating in many ways from within an earlier American tradition. To fight and die like New England Puritans and patriots—as David Chase Buffum had done for "the cause of Freedom in Kansas"—was a clarion call and continual refrain in the territory. William H. Leeman, the youngest of John Brown's raiders to die at Harpers Ferry, joined Brown's Volunteer Regulars in Kansas in 1856 and wrote home regularly to his family in Maine. "I have got a big horse that I took from a pro slavery man," Leeman wrote to his brother on November 9, 1856. "I belong to Old Brown's Company. I suppose you have heard how we whipt them at Ossawatimy have you not we killed 30 and wounded 32 men they had 400 all mounted."[48] His later letters, though full of typical youthful boasts and enthusiasms, remain powerful testimonials to the cause Leeman was willing to die for in a hail of bullets. Two weeks before the Harpers Ferry raid Leeman wrote his mother:

I am now in a Southern *Slave State* and before I leave it, it will be a *free State*, Mother. . . . Yes, mother, I am waring with Slavery the greatest

Curse that ever infested America; In Explanation of my Absence from you for so long a time I would tell you that I have been Engaged in a Secret Association of as gallant fellows as ever puled a trigger with the sole purpose of the *Extermination of Slavery.*[49]

Two of Brown's most trusted lieutenants in Kansas who followed him to Harpers Ferry, John H. Kagi and Aaron D. Stevens, were in their letters similarly militant and high-minded about their commitment to abolitionism.

In Kansas, many of the precepts underlying Freethinking, as well as the reformist movements that inspired the European revolutions of 1848, were evident in the participation of men like the Jewish Austrian August Bondi, the Bavarian Charles Kaiser, and later, the Englishman Hugh Forbes.[50] It is intriguing that as a Calvinist, John Brown was deeply motivated by religious doctrine, yet he seemed relatively spare in forcing his theology on his followers, except as it pertained to discipline within his military companies.[51] His men came from diverse philosophical and religious backgrounds and were left to hold to their own beliefs. Though Brown was at war with slavery and its practitioners, freedom of thought and expression remained integral to his abolitionist doctrine. A contemporary profile of the Virginian John H. Kagi, Brown's "Secretary of War," illustrates this freedom:

He was a young man of clear and logical intellect; but, unlike old Brown, was a skeptic in moral and religious matters; and engaged in the military anti-slavery enterprise rather from a haughty sense of duty to a friendless race, than of obedience to any special command from Deity. Brown believed God spoke to him in visions of the night; Kagi neither believed in visions nor that God was the author of the drama of human history. He would have made his mark on any society. He died fighting. He fought on the soil of his native State—in obedience to his idea of the lessons of her greatest statesman.[52]

As John Brown prepared for his final battle, he symbolically "put on his old Kansas cap" as he got in the wagon to ride from the Kennedy farm to his destiny at Harpers Ferry.[53] It was the same dusty cap John Brown would wear on his wagon ride to the gallows. The majority of the men in his small "provisional army" at Harpers Ferry had, at one time or another, been active in Brown's Kansas guerilla campaigns, and the Kansas connection to the raid was heavily investigated in its sensationalized aftermath.

Initial condemnation in the North of the Harpers Ferry raid turned quickly to broadening support for Brown and his military strike at the heart of the "Slave Power." As Brown's close friend Frederick Douglass stated following Brown's raid and famous trial speech: "Like Samson, he has laid his hands upon the pillars of this great national temple of cruelty and blood, and when he falls, that temple will speedily crumble to its final doom, burying its denizens in its ruins."[54] The Reverend George B. Cheever was similarly effusive in a sermon he delivered on December 4, 1859, two days after Brown's execution: "You would not call John Brown's movement treason, you would not call it murder, you would not call it a wicked act, if white persons, your own relations, had been chained and claimed as property, tortured, and condemned as a race of chattels; you would call it justice, heroism, piety."[55]

The following week, the *New York Herald* carried the report of John Brown's funeral and William Phillip's eulogy at North Elba. As if to remind readers why Brown had gone to Kansas, the *Herald* also carried an agonizingly poignant, and not uncommon, report from the Missouri *Democrat* of the lynching and burning of a slave in July of the previous year:

> The negro was stripped to his waist, and barefooted. He looked the picture of despair; but there was no sympathy felt for him at the moment. Presently the fire began to surge up around him, and the effects were soon made visible in the futile attempts of the poor wretch to move his feet. As the flames gathered about his limbs and body he commenced the most frantic shrieks and appeals for mercy, for death, for water. He seized his chains; they were hot and burned the flesh off his hands. He would drop them and catch them again and again. Then he would repeat his cries; but all to no purpose. In a few moments he was a charred mass, bones and flesh alike burned into powder.

On January 29, 1861, Kansas entered the Union as a free state. Within a few months the Civil War began at Fort Sumter, and Kansas was soon sending regiments—both black and white—to fight for the Union. In a fitting historical turn, Kansas had the highest per capita casualty rate of any state in the Union during the war.

Seven weeks after the Battle of Gettysburg, in the summer of 1863, Lawrence, Kansas, suffered the worst civilian massacre of the war, when William Clarke Quantrill and 450 Confederate irregulars descended on the town before dawn, slaughtering 200 people.[56] The cause of the attack was multilayered, but its roots lay in the bloody turmoil of the 1850s. Most of the men who died were members of the original Emigrant Aid Companies from New England, and the reputation of Lawrence as a "nest of abolitionism" helped seal its fate on that scorchingly hot August morning.

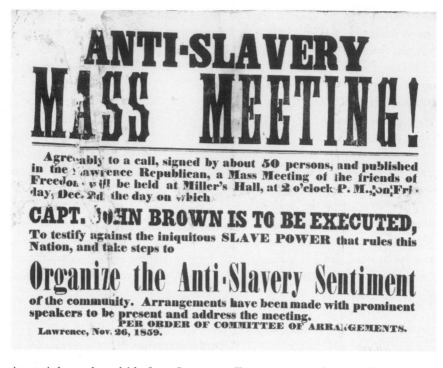

ANTI-SLAVERY MASS MEETING!

Agreeably to a call, signed by about 50 persons, and published in the Lawrence Republican, a Mass Meeting of the friends of Freedom will be held at Miller's Hall, at 2 o'clock P. M., on Friday, Dec. 2d, the day on which

CAPT. JOHN BROWN IS TO BE EXECUTED,

To testify against the iniquitous SLAVE POWER that rules this Nation, and take steps to

Organize the Anti-Slavery Sentiment

of the community. Arrangements have been made with prominent speakers to be present and address the meeting.
PER ORDER OF COMMITTEE OF ARRANGEMENTS.
Lawrence, Nov. 26, 1859.

An anti-slavery broadside from Lawrence, Kansas, announcing a gathering upon the occasion of the hanging of John Brown in Virginia, December 2, 1859. (Source: Kansas State Historical Society)

John Brown's old ally, the Jayhawker James Lane—known in Missouri as the "Grim Chieftain"—was the primary target of Quantrill, who hoped to capture Lane and take him back to Missouri to be "burned at the stake." Lane, a close friend of Abraham Lincoln, barely escaped Quantrill's dragnet.[57]

In the ensuing years Kansas became, in many respects, indistinguishable from other midwestern states through its codified racism and debilitating Jim Crow laws.[58] Still, the abolitionist legacy of John Brown inspired a variety of memorials designed to commemorate a time of nobler endeavors.[59] Among the more poignant is a large Carrara marble statue, erected in 1910 at the site of old Quindaro in Kansas City, Kansas. Funded with nickels and dimes provided by the local Colored Washerwomens' Fund, the image of John Brown gazes out over what once was an Underground Railroad settlement. The words "Erected to the Memory of John Brown by a Grateful People" are carved prominently upon the statue's base. Today, the area is blighted, poor, and broken, but one has the sense that, after all, here is where John Brown would want to be. Recently, the Underground

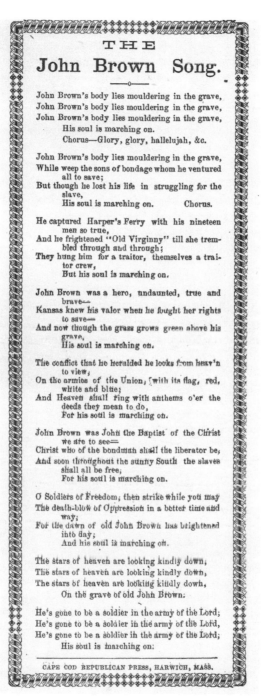

"The John Brown Song," published by the Cape Cod Republican Press, Harwich, Massachusetts, in 1861, which Julia Ward Howe would later turn into "The Battle Hymn of the Republic." (Source: Collection of the author)

Railroad safehouse ruins of Quindaro, Kansas, became a part of the National Park Service.

Some two hundred years after his birth John Brown is not a remote historical figure consigned to the ever fluctuating opinions and footnotes of his biographers. Throughout eastern Kansas today there are families, many descended from New England free-state emigrants, who have lived on the land for generations and will share stories of great-grandparents who fought alongside John Brown or sheltered him from his pursuers.

Abolitionism in the mid-1850s proved a vital, pivotal, and defining political force in helping to resolve the decades-long struggle over slavery and freedom, and the brutal sectional violence it inspired, in the Kansas Territory. The militant abolitionism of John Brown and his numerous followers, practiced on behalf of the free-state cause, quickly overtook the Garrisonian abolitionist argument of "moral suasion" and "peaceful resistance" in this region. The successes of small-scale guerrilla actions and state emancipations in Missouri and Kansas ultimately led abolitionist participants to widen their sphere of influence and attempt the attack on Harpers Ferry in the fall of 1859. In so doing they set the nation on an irreversible course to the catastrophic violence of the Civil War, and the full emancipation that followed.

9

Regional Black Involvement in John Brown's Raid on Harpers Ferry

Hannah Geffert (with Jean Libby)

More than 140 years after the famous raid on Harpers Ferry, the name John Brown still elicits an enormous emotional response. For some he was a terrorist; for others he was a madman; for still others he was a freedom fighter. Yet consistently, from the time of his death to the present day, African Americans have embraced John Brown as a hero. Perhaps this is because, unlike other white men of his time, John Brown's analysis of the situation in which slaves found themselves in mid-nineteenth-century America was similar to that of many free blacks. His conclusions about what needed to be done were in concert with the most radical black abolitionists. It is with these radicalized blacks that John Brown hoped to make common cause, and on whom he relied for assistance with the raid on Harpers Ferry.

Conventional wisdom holds that when Brown moved on Harpers Ferry in October 1859, free and enslaved Africans of the region ignored his call and did not participate in the raid—the exception being those few slaves who were thought to have been "kidnapped" by Brown's men. However, a careful examination of Brown's reasons for choosing Harpers Ferry, and of activities during and after the raid, indicate that Brown was meeting with blacks in the region, that they knew of his plans, and that some were willing to join him.

For the purposes of this essay, I define this region as the tristate area of Virginia, Maryland, and Pennsylvania, radiating from Harpers Ferry (now part of West Virginia) at the center. The region is bisected by the Potomac River; Harpers Ferry is located less than 90 miles upriver from the nation's capital. In places the river can be crossed on foot. Just a few miles north, where the Mason-Dixon Line separated slavery from freedom, the Philadelphia Wagonroad cut across the Potomac, leading farther north to Chambersburg, and then on to Philadelphia.

Travel was possible by rail, canal boat, or wagon from Baltimore to Cumberland, then to Pittsburgh and the Ohio Valley. The National Road (now

Highway 40) had been built. The railroads connected the region in 1859 far better than today, and were effectively used by Brown and his associates as a way to move his free black volunteer army from Baltimore and Philadelphia to Harpers Ferry.[1]

The Appalachian Mountains are the south-north radiant of the region. Brown came to focus his attention on the Appalachian fugitive slave route of the Shenandoah Valley, known as the Great Black Way, which was suggested to him by fellow abolitionist Harriet Tubman.[2] For many years, the mountains of Virginia had provided a comparatively safe route to freedom. Tubman, who participated in planning the raid, had used the Great Black Way in her efforts to aid escaping slaves.[3] Knowledge that the safest natural entrance to the Great Black Way was through Harpers Ferry, Jefferson County, Virginia (now West Virginia), was an important factor in Brown's choice of Harpers Ferry. It was also the site of a major federal arsenal, which, he thought, could be used to arm his black guerrilla army that would lead slaves to freedom.

Jefferson County had a high percentage of free Africans and nonslave-holding whites. It had been settled in two distinct waves of immigration—one from the tidewater region of Virginia, the other from Pennsylvania. These Virginians, who began sending overseers and slaves west of the Shenandoah River as early as 1738,[4] included a number of prominent Southern families—the Pages, Lees, and Washingtons, for example. Starting in the 1730s and 1740s, Pennsylvania Quakers began to make their way into the Shenandoah Valley.[5] Free blacks and whites from Pennsylvania crossed the Potomac into western Virginia following the old Philadelphia Wagonroad, the first settlers arriving in the county in the fall of 1731. They were Joist Hite, a German Quaker, and his family, accompanied by a free black family, the Johnsons.[6] Because both Southerners and Northerners had settled the area, political sentiment in Jefferson County reflected the full range of political alignment seen across the nation.

From 1830 to 1860, the ratio of whites to blacks in the country remained fairly constant, about two to one. There were about 540 free Africans, but slaves made up the vast majority of blacks.[7] By the 1840s the free black population of Harpers Ferry, Bolivar, and Virginius Island was equal to that of the slave population.[8] At the time of the raid the total black population there was about 200.

Most slaves were scattered across the rural sections of the county but some were in the towns, while the free African population was concentrated in small self-contained black communities or in towns. For example, free Africans congregated in Johnsontown, located five miles northwest of Charles Town in the Leetown-Bardane area, a contained community of free blacks surrounded by white Quakers and Free Will Baptists who provided a buffer between the black community and the predominately white county.[9]

In Jefferson County, the Quakers, free blacks, and slaves who operated the ferries in Harpers Ferry and in nearby Shepherdstown aided fugitive slaves along the Great Black Way.[10] Loss of slave property was so prevalent that a petition was sent to the Virginia state legislature requesting that a company be incorporated to insure against such losses, urging that Pennsylvania be encouraged to pass laws that would make it possible to recapture slaves found within its borders.[11]

There were free blacks north of the Potomac River in Maryland and along the Shenandoah River in Virginia. Free black artisans and entrepreneurs worked near the arsenal and musket factory complex of Harpers Ferry, although few slaves or free blacks worked in the factories in 1859.[12] However, the development of the iron industry to supply the arsenal had previously relied on Africans for the bulk of its labor. Since colonial times, enslaved colliers, blacksmiths, and mineworkers had formed the core of the iron industry in the South, as well as the base for the first free black populations in the region.[13] Enslaved ironworkers of the region had negotiated pay for their tasks during the 1830s and 1840s and refused to submit to the bullying of white immigrant workers. In a previously unknown primary source related to John Brown and African Americans recovered in 1978, a local minister, a former enslaved blacksmith and pastor to the Antietam Ironworks, wrote of a "young insurrection" that took place about 1835. The slaves won the argument.[14]

During the 1850s the iron industry near Harpers Ferry was in sharp economic decline; by 1859 it was in bankruptcy.[15] Many enslaved ironworkers had been sold during this period; others had bought their manumission and remained in the region, working in the lumber industry and on the railroads.[16] Since 1850 the number of people enslaved in the region had been in decline, while the number of free people of color had increased. This was a natural place for John Brown to recruit men.

In making a decision about where to strike, Brown relied extensively upon knowledge of the area by his African American associates and of his strong knowledge of fugitive slave routes. The Underground Railroad was active in this area and connected to the iron furnaces. According to Hiram Wertz of Quincy:

The route was by way of South Mountain from the Potomac River to the Pennsylvania border. The first station was near Rouzerville [perhaps Rohrersville], called Shockey's, then by the way of Wertz's father's barn at Quincy, then on to Africa near Caledonia Furnace, owned by the great champion of the slaves, Thaddeus Stevens.

Robert Black, another captain, lived there in the vicinity. From Africa the slaves were piloted through the mountains by way of Pine Grove Furnace, Mt. Holly and Boiling Springs and then they went safely over the Susquehanna.[17]

Brown had personal knowledge of the routes in western Pennsylvania, where he lived from 1825 to 1836.[18] He also learned of routes firsthand from the free black leaders in New York, Ohio, and Massachusetts during the years 1847 to 1855, when he was organizing defense and militia organizations, such as the League of Gileadites. It was during this period that Brown met and was influenced by Frederick Douglass and Willis Hodges, both editors and publishers of African American newspapers, and both knowledgeable of the fugitive slave routes of Maryland and Virginia.[19] Henry Highland Garnet, a fugitive from Baltimore, was also among Brown's activist friends. Brown's first overt act of supporting insurrection in the South was to publish the "Call to Rebellion" by Garnet (denied publication by one vote in the Colored Men's Convention in Buffalo in 1843), which Brown printed alongside David Walker's 1829 *Appeal to the Coloured Citizens of the World* in 1848.[20]

John Brown was convinced that slavery could be effectively attacked in Jefferson County. It was strategically located, had symbolic significance (counting among its founders the Washington family), and was demographically atypical of the South. Jefferson County had a relatively high percentage of free Africans, small numbers of slaves compared with Virginia counties farther south, and many nonslaveholding whites. It had several small self-contained, free black communities who worshipped in independent churches across the Potomac River in Maryland (Virginia laws forbade black ministers) and an active Underground Railroad with which John Brown was intimately familiar.[21]

To the north of Jefferson County was Washington County, Maryland, where Brown gathered his army during the summer of 1859; to the east was Frederick, Maryland, the crossroads that linked the railroads, canals, and turnpikes of Virginia and Pennsylvania on the route presently known as Highway 15. These counties in Virginia and Maryland had similar populations: dwindling numbers of slaveholders, growing free black populations, and an industrial, rather than exclusively agrarian, economic base. Brown reasoned that if slavery could be driven out of a single county in one state, the whole system would be weakened in that state and eventually in the country as a whole.[22]

Brown was convinced that the time was right to act. Following the infamous *Dred Scott* case of 1857, it became obvious to Brown and other abolitionists that slavery would not be ended or even limited by legislative or court action. Movements to re-enslave free blacks were gaining strength, particularly in Maryland, where more than half the black population was free.[23] Brown began seeking bolder ways to weaken slavery and to invigorate antislavery agitation.[24] In 1857, at the time of the *Dred Scott* decision, Brown made a list of areas in the South as potential targets. Stephen Oates has analyzed this list and found that the common denominator was the presence of arsenals.[25]

While Brown sought funding from white abolitionists for his activities, it was among the more radical elements of the free African population that Brown sought and received his most reliable political allies. Many white abolitionists, doubting that blacks would fight for liberty, relied on their preconceptions of the slave's character as being as "submissive as Uncle Tom." Brown, however, believed that it was necessary for blacks to fight for their freedom, and rejected this widespread belief in the submissiveness of blacks.[26] Moreover, he was aware that Northern free Africans, denied admission into state militia, had formed their own military organizations, including the Massasoit Guards of Massachusetts, Attucks Guards of New York, Attucks Blues of Cincinnati, Loguen Guards of Binghamton, New York, and Henry Highland Garnet Guards of Harrisburg, Pennsylvania.[27] Through information supplied by George G. Gill, Brown also knew of the existence of such organizations "among the colored people . . . through most, or nearly all, of the slave states."[28] After the Fugitive Slave Act became law in 1850, Brown had organized a self-defense group of forty-four black men known as the League of Gileadites.[29] He also had firsthand knowledge of other black self-help groups such as the League of Freedom, Liberty League, the American Mysteries, and, in Canada, the True Bands, with several hundred members each.[30] It was with these groups that Brown was building alliances. These free Africans were often members of the independent black churches, active in the Underground Railroad, and part of Prince Hall Masons. Frequently they were delegates to black conventions that petitioned on behalf of the enslaved. Brown knew that this black infrastructure existed and regularly recruited support among its members.

Before putting his plan into action, Brown had sought a "general convention or council" of free Africans to "aid and countenance" his activities. He traveled to Chatham, Canada, to meet with Martin Delany, who, Brown believed, would be able to orchestrate such an effort.[31] This attempt to win the support of black leadership culminated in the Chatham Convention, arranged by Delany. The May 1858 convention was attended by forty-six people—twelve white, the rest black. The main order of business was the adoption of Brown's "Provisional Constitution and Ordinances for the People of the United States"—a radical refashioning of American democracy along antislavery and egalitarian grounds.[32]

It was not an accident that Brown sought out Delany. He was a native of Jefferson County, born in 1812 in Charles Town, a few blocks away from where Brown would be tried for treason. In 1822, the Delany family had been forced to leave Charles Town after Martin's free mother, Pati Delany, was accused of teaching her children to read. Although the family relocated to Chambersburg, Pennsylvania, Delaney's father was still enslaved in Martinsburg, and the family raised funds to buy his freedom.[33] Young Martin became a member of the St. James African Methodist Episcopal Church, founded in Chambersburg in the 1830s, whose members assisted Brown during the summer of 1859.

The AME congregations across the river from Harpers Ferry were founded by Reverend Thomas W. Henry, a Maryland minister whose name was listed as a person to be trusted in a letter that was discovered in John Brown's carpetbag after the raid. Reverend Henry fled north with the help of George Watkins and his cousin Frances Watkins, both known to be close to John Brown. Reverend Thomas W. Henry was a minister at the St. James AME Church in Chambersburg in 1845, and again in 1858. Also in Chambersburg, staging ground for the raid, was Henry Watson's barbershop, center of the area's Underground Railroad. Watson helped in preparations for the assault on Harpers Ferry, forwarding men, mail, and freight to the Kennedy farm in Maryland. Black members of Brown's army boarded with Watson and his wife, Eliza.[34]

Henry Watson escorted Frederick Douglass to a meeting with John Brown on August 19, 1859, at which Brown made a final appeal for Douglass's support. Brown's constitution had been written at the home of Frederick Douglass, but Douglass had not attended the Chatham Convention. The meeting occurred in an abandoned stone quarry; the site was arranged by a free black man, Joseph Richard Winters. Winters was born in Leesburg in 1816 near Harpers Ferry, where his father, James Winters, made bricks for the arsenal.[35] In his youth in the 1820s, Joseph Winters worked at making sand mold at Harpers Ferry. He was called "Indian Dick" because he was raised by his grandmother, the Indian doctor woman of Chambersburg, who was part Shawnee. On his paternal side, "Indian Dick" was the great-great-grandson of Chief Okichankonaugh, who was killed after being taken prisoner by the English in 1648. "Indian Dick" migrated to Chambersburg in 1830; his grandmother followed and the two were known for good fishing and folk medicine.[36] Joseph Richard Winters was a gunsmith, sure to be of interest to John Brown. Like Martin Delany,

Thomas Henry, and Henry Watson, Winters was a member of the St. James AME Church of Chambersburg.

Brown believed that Douglass's support was key to winning the assistance of large numbers of northern blacks and would give "the venture the air of credibility."[37] If Douglass, "the first great national Negro leader," would go to Harpers Ferry with him, others would follow.[38] Brown hoped that after gaining the confidence of the black community through initial success at Harpers Ferry, more men would join him, and that the black militia and secret societies would supply additional aid and recruits.

But Douglass refused to attack the arsenal, capture weapons, and take hostages. By the summer of 1859, Brown's initial plan, to move from plantation to plantation in guerrilla fashion, had changed considerably. Back in 1847, at a meeting in Brown's home in Springfield, Massachusetts, Brown had told Douglas that he was "looking for colored men to whom he could safely reveal his secret."[39] Although Douglass agreed with Brown's objective and rationale, he "could never quite believe that John Brown's tremendous plan was humanly possible." Douglass and other black leaders also knew that if the project failed, black men would pay the cost. Perhaps the Underground Railroad methods could be enlarged and systematized, Douglass argued, but "only national force could dislodge national slavery."[40]

Also at the quarry meeting was Shields Green, known as "Emperor." Green had escaped slavery in South Carolina after his wife died but had left a son behind. Brown had asked Douglass to bring Green, having previously met him at Douglass's home. As Douglass and Brown argued the merits of Brown's plan, Green sat and listened. When the meeting was over Douglass asked Green if he was leaving with him. To Douglass's surprise, however, "Emperor" responded, "No, I guess I'll go with the old man."[41]

Four other named Africans were known to have come in with John Brown at Harpers Ferry.[42] Osborne Perry Anderson, twenty-four, was a free-born Pennsylvanian. A printer by trade, he met Brown in Canada. John A. Copeland Jr., twenty-two, was born free in Raleigh, North Carolina, reared in Oberlin, Ohio, and educated at Oberlin College. Copeland had been one of the arrested rescuers in the Oberlin-Wellington Rescue. Lewis S. Leary, Copeland's uncle, was born in the triracial free community of Fayetteville, North Carolina, as well as his first cousin, Hiram Revels, who was in Baltimore at the time of the raid.[43] Dangerfield Newby was a freeman from the Shenandoah Valley with ties to the region. Newby's wife and six children lived in slavery about thirty miles south of Harpers Ferry in Warrenton, Virginia. Harriet Newby, a seamstress, was pregnant and about to be sold to a New Orleans trader at the time of the raid.[44] Deeply familiar with the area, Newby had lived within the community until the night of the raid, supplying Brown with information.[45]

Brown was also seeking allies in Baltimore and Philadelphia, both centers of radical free black activity. AME churches and Prince Hall Masons of Philadelphia and Baltimore were historically and institutionally linked, and both were militant and dedicated participants in the Underground Railroad. Baltimore had the largest free black community in the country. Brown's allies with Baltimore connections included Frederick Douglass, Reverend William J. Watkins, and his niece, novelist and poet Frances Watkins. Among Baltimore's free black population, there existed a militant network with ties that went directly to Cleveland, where Brown was recruiting men for his army. The black conventions held in Ohio were adopting increasingly revolutionary ideas, promulgated by Baltimoreans who held many of the leadership positions.

There is evidence that a large group was forming in Philadelphia in mid-July, when Brown began his covert operations in Pennsylvania and Maryland, and that Douglass encouraged this group to be cautious at the time of the raid. William Henry Johnson, a Pennsylvania Anti-Slavery Society leader associated with William Still, met John Brown shortly after Johnson gave the July Fourth address at the Banneker Institute in Philadelphia in 1859. Brown also met with the Frank Johnson Guards, a militia company formed by a number of black men with connections to the Underground Railroad.[46] During the summer of 1859, the night before a grand parade was scheduled in Philadelphia:

> General J.J. Simons of New York, one of Brown's lieutenants . . .
> made a speech in which he commended the Negroes of Philadelphia
> for organizing a military company and stated that there was a grand
> project on foot to invade the South with an army of northern Ne-
> groes and free the slaves. He called for recruits for this invading army
> from the Negroes of Philadelphia.[47]

Later that night a meeting was held among a dozen antislavery leaders, including Thomas Dorsey, Dr. William Henry Johnson, Frederick Douglass, Fred C. Revels, and John Brown. Brown urged that a more temperate tone be used during speeches the next day, fearing that without secrecy and caution his plan would be doomed. This led most to believe that the raid was either temporarily or permanently delayed. Brown and Aaron Stephens met again with the group leaders on October 13, 1859, telling them the raid was on and would take place on the 24th. When the plans were moved up to October 17, the Philadelphians were confused, and they did not come. The leader of the Philadelphia group, according to Dr. Johnson, was

Thomas Dorsey. Dorsey was a fugitive from Frederick, Maryland, and the primary link between John Brown and the local African Americans near Burkittsville.[48] Brown was right to be concerned about the openness of the Frank Johnson Guards. On October 22, the adjutant general of the state of Pennsylvania confiscated "forty muskets which were in possession of the colored military company that paraded in this city a few months since."[49]

How much local blacks knew about the timing of the raid is uncertain. Benjamin A. Matthews, a Storer College student who lived a generation after the raid, said the local population believed the raid was to be on the 24th of October, but that the date had been changed after a "council by the raiders."[50]

During the initial phase of the raid, Brown's men armed twenty-five to fifty black men.[51] Osborne Anderson distributed pikes to slaves who came with Brown's men from the plantations, and to others who came forward without having had communication with the raiders, an action that led to early reports that the commander of the raid was a "colored man named Anderson." John Edwin Cook and Charles Tidd also armed slaves, several of whom were farmhands who had come after hearing of the raid from "underground wires."[52] Eyewitness accounts tell of considerable local black activity; of "Negroes" during the early hours of the fight being in and around "John Brown's Fort"; and of slaves with spears in their hands near the engine house.[53] One hostage said that Harpers Ferry "looked like war—Negroes armed with pikes, and sentinels with muskets all around."[54] At least fourteen black men assisted at the schoolhouse and protected the weapons; others guarded prisoners. They transported arms from the Kennedy farm to the schoolhouse. Other blacks acted as messengers between Brown's men and spread news of the raid to the local community. The result was that many Africans "gathered to the scene of action."[55]

The hillsides became congested with frightened people seeking refuge, and for a time, armed Africans were seen in some numbers. "Armed and unarmed blacks and whites" came to see what was happening.[56] The engineer of the train stopped by the raiders took particular notice of a crowd of at least 300 persons that included black men shouting that they "longed for liberty, as they had been in bondage long enough."[57] A letter, written the day after the raid, stated "that news had come from the Ferry, that about 300 armed men, with blackened faces, had taken possession of the Armory."[58] Troops fired across the Potomac to the Maryland side at black men who had been armed the day before at the Kennedy farm. Forced to retreat, the armed black men scattered, as troops crossed the bridge in pursuit. As late as 1887, Andrew Hunter, John Brown's prosecutor, asserted that the mountains and woods were full of Brown's men.

Hostages were taken, among them Lewis Washington (great-grand-nephew of George Washington) and John Allstadt. Washington's slaves—Jim, Sam, Mason, and Catesby—and Allstadt's slaves—Henry, Levi, Ben, Phil, George, and Bill—were also taken to Harpers Ferry.[59] Washington's coachman, Jim, willingly accepted a pistol and a supply of ball cartridges. Jim was said to be one of the boldest combatants, fighting "like a tiger." When the engine house fell, Jim fled. He succeeded in reaching the Shenandoah River only to drown near Hall's Rifle Works. He had "joined the rebels with a good will," reported the Virginia Committee of Claims in turning down a petition for compensation for the lost slave property.[60] Another Washington slave, Mason, loaded weapons all day. Later he convinced Virginia authorities that he and the group with him returned to their masters as soon as they could escape.[61]

Allstadt's slave, Phil Luckum, knocked holes in the engine house wall to shoot through until he was mortally wounded.[62] Phil's brother Ben helped guard the Rifle Works, but was arrested and died in jail.[63] Upon hearing of the raid, some black men immediately agreed to join, saying that they "had been long waiting for an opportunity of this kind."[64] Others, like a house slave of Washington's, firmly refused to take part, declining to accept a pike.

Black men participated in the killing and the dying at Harpers Ferry. In the early morning, William Leeman gave a double-barreled shotgun to an elderly slave. When a white townsman ignored the slave's order to halt, the elderly slave discharged his weapon's "terrible load." The townsman "fell, and expired with out a struggle." When Dangerfield Newby was shot in the head, his "death was promptly avenged by Shields Green."[65] Of the men shot on the rocks when John Henri Kagi's party retreated to the river, some were slaves. Mill workers poured "several hundred rounds of ammunition into three of Brown's men and three local slaves at the Hall's Rifle Works."[66]

There is no agreement on how many men died fighting with Brown. Reports vary from seventeen to twenty-seven, only ten of whom were with Brown at the Kennedy farm. The others, between seven and seventeen, were blacks who joined Brown later on.[67] Some raiders were able to escape with the help of local blacks, who also then helped each other escape from bondage in Jefferson and Berkeley Counties. Five of Brown's raiders managed to escape, including Osborne Anderson. William C. Goodridge, a wealthy black man from York, Pennsylvania, gave Anderson shelter during his escape, delivering him to William Still of Philadelphia. Richard Hinton, who had been waiting in Chambersburg to join the raiders, escaped with help from local blacks.[68]

Several local blacks are known to have escaped slavery at the time of the raid; local folklore has it that Harriet Tubman returned to the area to help. Reginald Ross's father escaped then, returning after the Civil War. Charles Williams, who worked at the hotel, was not seen after the raid and presumably escaped.[69] A slave, "direct from Harper's Ferry—passed through Syracuse on the Underground Railroad," and others were expected to follow.[70] An unnamed fugitive slave from Harpers Ferry passed through Auburn, New York, on his way to Canada. Reportedly, he was "the slave who guided John Brown into the arsenal."[71] Following the Chatham Convention, Mary Ellen Pleasant, masquerading as a jockey, disseminated information in the Roanoke River area and other parts of the South about Brown's approaching assault. After the raid she too was forced to flee Virginia.[72]

As news of the raid spread via the telegraph wires of the B&O railroad, fear grew as to how far Brown's conspiracy extended among slaves and free blacks. Virginia counties organized and strengthened mounted patrols. Within four weeks Baltimore arms dealers sold over 10,000 pistols to Virginia buyers. The entire South was in a state of panic, as was Charles Town. Lewis Washington was unwilling to return home for several days, fearing his slaves would stage a revolt. Several masters were reported beaten or attacked by their servants. A.R.H. Ranson, a local slaveowner, spoke of changes in his slaves' demeanor that made him uncomfortable. The value of slave property dropped, which is fully documented in the wills and sales in Jefferson County courthouse records.

Despite the massive presence of military force after the raid, black guerrilla activity persisted. A series of fires swept the region. "[T]he heavens are illuminated by the lurid glare of burning property," reported one Richmond daily newspaper.[73] Crops, stockyards, stables, hayracks, agricultural implements, and barns of slaveholders in Jefferson and Berkeley Counties were set afire. Farmers, fearing fires, threshed wheat earlier than usual.[74]

On October 31, 1859, the *Virginia Free Press* reported the burning of the barn and stable of George Fole, the "work of a Negro boy." On November 10, 1859, "three large straw ricks belonging to John LeRue," and "the granary and carriage house of Dr. Stephenson" were destroyed by fire. Wheatland, the farm of George Turner, a slaveowner killed while looking for his bondsmen who had joined the group recruited by Shields Green and Lewis Leary, was reported burning in the *New York Times* of December 3, 1859.[75] On December 2, his cows had all dropped dead in the field. His brother, William F. Turner, had horses and sheep die suddenly as if by poison.[76] Properties owned by John Burns, Walter Shirley, and George H. Tate—all of whom served on juries that convicted John Brown's men—were destroyed within the same week.[77] A January 12, 1860, petition sent to the General Assembly of Virginia from the citizens of Jefferson County asked that Walter Shirley, the foreman of the jury that convicted Brown, be compensated for losses. The petition stated that "there is not the shadow of a doubt but that the fire grew out of his connection with the trials."[78] Additional attempts were made on the premises of John Burns. Local whites believed that the fires were being set "by the Abolition confederates of Brown & Co."[79] One victim of the guerrilla warfare stated:

> [T]hree stockyards have been burnt in this county alone since their capture and since their trial—last night one of mine was burned destroying not less than $2000 worth of property . . . we can only account for it on the grounds that it is Cook's instructions to our Negroes.[80]

Colonel J. Lucius Davis wired Governor Wise on November 19 that the fires were being set by Negroes and asked for reinforcements. The governor sent 500 more troops to Charles Town but the fires continued.[81]

The presence of Northern reporters undermined Virginia's attempts to conceal African support for the raid. Southern reporters emphasized slave loyalty and described how blacks had been terrified as Brown's men approached. Virginia wanted the world to believe that the slaves refused to join the insurrection. John Cook, captured in Pennsylvania after the raid, stated in his "Confession" that local blacks had been armed. This "Confession" greatly angered John Brown, who feared reprisals against local participants and other Africans. But Brown never lost faith in the black community's ability to fight for its liberation. With typical concern for their well-being, Brown wrote to his wife Mary in New York that he "hoped the fires that were burning would not be blamed on their friends."[82]

Many of the accounts of the raid left by black men or abolitionists were ignored. Some historians felt that black remembrances of the raid could not be trusted or that white eyewitnesses were exaggerating the black presence and contribution. However, there is mounting evidence that blacks of the region were much more involved with the raid than conventional wisdom has heretofore asserted.[83]

For example, while renovating his maternal great-grandfather's home on the historic Winters Lane, Charles Cephas of Catonsville, Maryland, found five antique guns in the attic, two of which were stamped with the words Harpers Ferry. Cephas's great-grandfather was Philip Woodland, a coachman for wealthy whites in Baltimore and Catonsville. As Philip Woodland was among the founders of the Grace African Methodist Episcopal Church of Catonsville, the Woodland family had given shelter to traveling AME ministers.

A tie to the Grace AME Church has enormous significance. When John Brown was arrested, his captured trunk contained a handwritten letter stating: "Mr. Thomas Henrie, a colored man formerly of Hagerstown, was a trusted man." This is the same Thomas W. Henry who was twice pastor of St. James AME Church of Chambersburg—the same church that Martin Delany, Joe Winter, and Henry Watson attended.[84] Thomas Henry's son, Reverend John R. Henry, served as the first minister of the Grace AME congregation, founded in 1868, then called St. John's.[85] Although John Henry was suspected of conspiring with Brown, he did not have to flee Maryland as his father had. Reverend Henry escaped arrest with assistance from AME ministers in Baltimore and from a white Freemason who fronted for him at the railway, buying him a ticket to Philadelphia.[86] Most significantly, the Woodland family and Thomas Henry were originally from St. Mary's County, Maryland. The St. Mary's County connection also linked the Henry and Woodland families, many of whom were veterans of the Civil War, as well as members of the AME Church.

Other things about the Woodland family fit a pattern of African support of the raid. As stated, Brown was building alliances with free blacks who were members of the independent political network made up of black churches, the Underground Railroad, and Prince Hall Masons. Philip Woodland was a Prince Hall Mason, as were Reverend Henry and Martin Delany. So was Reverend Hiram Rhoads Revels, who had lived in Baltimore and who, in 1870, became the first United States senator of known African ancestry. Revels was the first cousin of Lewis Leary, and second cousin of John Copeland, who died fighting against slavery with John Brown.

The weapons found by Charles Cephas were authenticated by the National Rifle Association's firearms museum. This collection included two 1858-model Harpers Ferry rifles made in 1860, just months too late to have been taken from the arsenal during the raid. The two rifles had rack numbers in close sequence, indicating they had been issued to members of the same military unit. Additionally, these rifles were often issued to colored troops. The Remington pistol was a standard army issue of the same vintage.

The other two long guns were also of interest. One was an antebellum, double-barreled shotgun of foreign make and average quality. The other long gun was an unusual fowling piece (bird gun) of prewar vintage and foreign make. It was a very expensive, top-of-the-line weapon.

On the stock of the gun were carved the initials "G.W." or "J.W." Another interesting marking was a small brass plate with an elegantly engraved initial, "W," indicating the original owner. The Harpers Ferry rifles and the Remington pistol had been manufactured after the raid. They could not have been given to Africans during the raid, although there is

much documented evidence that similar weapons were distributed, especially in Maryland. However, it is very likely that these weapons were issued
to colored troops.

By searching the Soldiers and Sailors database and pension files, other
members of the Woodland family who were linked to Philip Woodland
were found. Twenty-three Woodlands served with the United States Colored Troops. Six of the Woodlands were in the 19th U.S.C.T. The 19th regiment was composed of blacks from Maryland, and had been garrisoned in
Harpers Ferry to recruit slaves in the area into army service. Three Woodlands who served in the 19th had a connection to the Philip Woodland
family; one was his brother, William, who also served in the navy. The other
two were Henry Woodland and Austin Woodland, both of whom served in
Company I. As the rack numbers appear to be in sequence, it is likely that
the guns were issued to men in the same company.[87] And it is also likely that
these men owned the Harpers Ferry rifles that were ultimately found in
Philip Woodland's home.

It is also interesting that the family lived on Orchard Street, the "black
Fifth Avenue of Baltimore." When the Fifteenth Amendment became part
of the Constitution, guaranteeing universal manhood suffrage, the largest
celebration in the nation took place in Baltimore, with more than 20,000
people participating. As part of the celebration, a grand parade marched
through the city. The route chosen included Orchard Street because so
many politically active African Americans lived there. The parade passed
the Woodland home. Among the reasons given as to why Baltimore was
chosen as the site of the celebration was that "Frederick Douglass, Martin
Delany, and Hiram Revels were all prominent blacks who had a legacy in
Baltimore." All three men were closely connected with John Brown.

Which leads us to the last gun: the fowling piece. During the raid, on the
night of October 17, 1859, Osborne Anderson and Charles Tidd were in
the party assigned to capture Lewis Washington. By the order of Brown,
Anderson, "representing the African race," received the sword that had
been presented to George Washington by Frederick the Great. The group
also confiscated a pair of pistols presented to George Washington by
Lafayette, a wagon, a carriage, and two guns—a double-barreled shotgun
and a foreign-made, top-of-the-line fowling piece. The wagon had been
taken to Maryland, then returned after the raid. Six months after the raid,
Lewis Washington told a Senate committee that his double-barreled shotgun had been buried by a slave and then recovered, but that his fowling
piece had never been recovered.[88] According to testimony during the Senate hearings, Washington's Belgian-made gun was last seen "in the hands
of a Negro" on the Maryland side of the river.

Like the missing Washington fowling piece, the gun found in Catonsville was made in Belgium. The "W" on a brass plate to indicate ownership is consistent with the practice of some of the Washingtons in Jefferson County. And it is highly unlikely that the Woodlands would have been able to afford such an expensive weapon.[89] Although the Catonsville fowling piece can never be definitively proven to be the Washington fowling piece, there is ample evidence to suggest that it is.

There is one more intriguing piece of information. When interviewed, Lucille Woodland Cephas, Charles's mother, was apologetic that she could not remember more. The old folks did not talk too much about those days and she had been one of the younger children in the family. If her older brother were alive, he could tell more. But she did remember that even though travel was expensive and difficult for African Americans when she was a child, there was one place that her parents felt was imperative for the family to visit: Harpers Ferry.

The significance of John Brown's raid should be analyzed not as an isolated event, but in the full context of the struggle for black freedom during the nineteenth century. Brown had found many black allies who were willing to stand with him at Harpers Ferry, and who were willing to continue the struggle he started after his death. They insisted that it was vital for African Americans to fight for freedom and that they had the right to do so. During the Civil War, Frederick Douglass continually urged Abraham Lincoln to use black troops, and there is perfect symmetry in his eventual decision to do so: the first field commission awarded to a black man was presented— on direct orders from President Lincoln—to a Jefferson County native, Martin Delany.[90] In fact, before the war ended, one out of every ten Union troops was black.

For many southerners, the raid on Harpers Ferry epitomized the threat posed by Northern abolitionism. Increasingly, the South believed that it had to resort to extreme measures, even retaliatory violence, in order to stop further aggression.[91] And so the war came. As Frederick Douglass said in a stirring speech given at Harpers Ferry twenty-two years after the raid: "If John Brown did not end the war that ended slavery, he did, at least, begin the war that ended slavery."[92] There is mounting evidence that Brown began this war with the active involvement of African Americans from the region, who, like Brown, came to believe that direct, violent confrontation was necessary to fully—and finally—abolish slavery in the United States.

PART FOUR

Representations

10

A Common Nature, A United Destiny: African American Responses to Racial Science from the Revolution to the Civil War

Patrick Rael

In the decades before the Civil War, modern American science was born—not out of a glorious celebration of universal human liberty, but out of the need to justify the enslavement and dehumanization of non-white peoples across the globe. Since the time of the American Revolution, European and American thinkers had sought to understand differences within the family of man using the powerful tools of reason and observation. In the antebellum period, those ideas took on a new cast, hardening into the claim that black people were not even part of humanity. During the years between the American Revolution and the Civil War, African Americans responded in a variety of ways to scientific ideas of race. Free blacks crafted a tradition of public protest that helped shape American abolitionism, and ultimately precipitated the Civil War. This protest tradition openly confronted the arguments made by blacks' detractors—that they could never become a viable part of the body politic, and were fit only for ostracism or perpetual servitude. The usefulness of black responses to racist thought remains an important though unresolved problem.

We may usefully point to three major watersheds in the history of black responses to racial science between the Revolution and the Civil War. The first was the Revolution itself, which drew heavily on the thinking of the Enlightenment. This fostered two important ideas: universalism, which argued that everyone in the human family was inherently entitled to the same natural rights; and environmentalism, which explained differences among portions of the human family as the product of differing physical conditions of life, generally in opposition to innate factors in the body. As they gradually became free, African Americans drew deeply upon these two ideas, fashioning them into their first public responses to the twin blights of slavery and prejudice.

The second important period runs from the mid-1810s through the 1830s. This period witnessed the rise of plans for African "colonization," a meretricious attempt to convince African Americans of their missionary duty to emigrate from the United States so that they might evangelize Africa. Colonization added new components to racist discourse, challenging African Americans to respond to the dual claims that black skin caused prejudice, which could therefore never be eradicated, and that once freed black people could never become useful and equal citizens. Countering the challenge of colonization placed new premiums on arguing for blacks' elevatability, as well as for their Americanness.

The third period marks the birth of what most people think of as scientific racism—the emergence of the "American school" of ethnologists, which included Samuel Morton, Louis Aggasiz, Josiah Nott, and George Gliddon. These writers lent a new credence to both polygenesis as a theory of man's origins and professional science as an arbiter of racial discourse. Though their new ideas fostered intense debate among whites, they largely confirmed rather than challenged the ultimate conclusions of popular racism, which suggested that regardless of cause blacks were irredeemably inferior to whites.

Accordingly, the general trajectory of racial thinking between the Revolution and the Civil War pointed downward. It began in a period willing in qualified ways to countenance blacks as part of the family of man, as the gradual abolition of slavery in the North attested. It moved through the retrenchment of colonization, during which American nationalism emerged as a racialized identity predicated upon whiteness. Blacks' and abolitionists' response to racial nationalism spurred antislavery thinking to radical new heights, engendering an increasingly anxious national debate over the meaning of race and slavery in national life. Antebellum racial science can be seen as the nadir of this dialogue.

By the Civil War, African American arguments against the claims of racial science had long been fully developed. In a nutshell, here's how the argument worked: people of African descent were full members of the human family, created by God different from but equal to others. Differences among the peoples of the earth, in culture and physical makeup, could be explained by reference to differing conditions of climate and geography rather than to innate differences between the races. Human variation was thus a function of nature, sanctioned by God. Those who denied the fundamental equality of all men blasphemously denied the benevolence of God's design. Slavery and prejudice did precisely this, by creating artificial and imperfect human hierarchies out of perfect nature. Worse than this, they denied man's capacity and duty to "elevate" those parts of the human character that could be developed: the mind and the morals.

They thus denied the conditions under which blacks could demonstrate the falsity of racist conclusions. The possibility of black elevation, as well as the process by which it was denied, had been obscured by the designs of blacks' enemies, who endeavored to convince the public, and even blacks themselves, of their destiny as an inferior caste designed for perpetual servitude.

The Historical Problem

This summation of black responses to racial science is meant only to suggest the broad outlines of the argument, and to serve as a foundation for understanding the important questions raised by African Americans' efforts to challenge notions about their own degradation. Black writers varied considerably in emphasis and rhetorical style, and these variations had important ramifications for understanding the significance of black challenges to racial science. Only recently have scholars begun to directly examine the relationship between black protest and the emergence of racial science in the antebellum period, and two broad schools of thought may be identified in this work. The first paints the darker picture of black responses to racial science, suggesting that in the very process of challenging their own degradation, African Americans internalized the core premises of racial science, unwittingly reinforcing its legitimacy and hence becoming complicit in fostering the very ideas they sought to combat. These studies do not deny the emancipatory intent of black protest, nor do they claim that it was wholly self-subverting, but they identify an unforeseen negative consequence in engaging so deeply with the discourse of oppressors.[1]

A second approach softens the negative consequences of the close relationship between black protest and the discourses of the antebellum public sphere.[2] Like those who lean toward the hegemony thesis, these scholars agree that in fashioning their responses to racist thought, black thinkers closely relied upon the discourses of a world dominated by whites. These scholars do not concede the inefficacy of a strategy of "appropriation"; rather, they see it as liberating. Stephen Howard Browne, for example, claims that antebellum African Americans responded to the claims of a racial hostile science not by "the repudiation of available means of persuasion but their tactical appropriation." Drawing on approaches from literary criticism, Browne stresses the capacity of the oppressed to empower themselves by borrowing and refashioning the very ideas used in their oppression. Though the strategy did involve some concession, this school of thought generally portrays a positive relationship between black protest and the discourses of the public sphere, wherein African Americans suc-

ceed through appropriation, using the premises of popular public discourses to pose their condition as mutable, and hence redeemable.[3]

What, then, was the relationship between the oppressed and the
discourses used to oppress them? How did the oppressed engage those discourses in the service of their own liberation? Of what consequence for
the freedom struggle was this engagement? Did it represent a "weapon of
the weak"[4]—an instance of "appropriation" and refashioning "dominant"
discourses in the service of emancipation? Or did it represent an instance
of ideological hegemony, in which the oppressed believed they resisted oppressive ideas, only to reinforce the fundamental terms of oppressive discourse? Should we endorse Hannah Arendt's maxim that "one can only
resist in terms of the identity that is under attack"?[5] Or do we side with
Audre Lorde's belief that "the master's tools will never dismantle the
master's house"?[6]

Understanding Black Responses to Racial Science

The reality was, as is often the case with the past, likely to be more complex
than historians' questions permit it to be. There were many sorts of relationships between black protest thought and the discourse of race, just as
there were multiple consequences to black thinkers' engagement with that
discourse. It makes sense, then, to forgo conclusions applicable to all black
thought, and focus instead on the myriad possibilities created by the shifting relationship between racial protest and racial science.[7]

Eschewal occurred when black thinkers simply failed to respond to the
arguments of racial science. Evidence for this is found in the innumerable
extant sources by African Americans that simply did not directly address
the claims of racial science. African Americans spoke and wrote about hundreds of topics; racial science was only one of them. Students of antebellum black thought should be struck first with the infrequency with which
black thinkers set out directly to refute the claims of antebellum racial science. For African Americans, the threat posed by scientific ideas of race
paled in comparison to that posed by popular forms of prejudice such as
blackface minstrelsy, proslavery arguments that were not scientific but religious or economic, the alleged indifference to racial uplift of too many of
their own people, blacks' declining status in law and constitution, racist
mob behavior, and a host of other concerns.

Of course African Americans did acknowledge the threat posed by antebellum racial science, and did not hesitate to challenge it in myriad ways.
The next highest level of engagement with the discourse of racial science
was *dismissal*. Dismissal occurred when African Americans acknowledged

the existence of scientific racism, but consciously refused to dispute its claims. A classic case of dismissal occurred in 1808, in an essay by an anonymous member of the African Society in Boston. Considering the question of "whether the Africans ought be subject to the British or Americans, because they are of a dark complexion," the author dismissed the producer of such arguments with contempt, writing: "We believe them to be so trivial, so fallacious and groundless, that we think he must have so hard a study to support it, that we think we had better postpone hearing his objection until some future period."[8]

But of course the discourse of racial science did not die of neglect. As arbiters of cultural power and legitimators of popular ideas, African Americans simply lacked the power to consign racial science into oblivion. This is a powerful counterpoint to those scholars who prize the ideological autonomy of the black working class or the enslaved. Dismissal works best when wielded by those with potent cultural authority. African Americans who practiced it, by permitting hostile speech to go unchallenged, threatened to legitimize racist thought through silence. As theories of polygenesis began gaining new credence in the 1820s, instances of dismissal declined. By the late 1830s, racist arguments that were once beyond sufferance seemed to demand pamphlet-long refutation. As early as 1827, David Walker—hardly an ideological collaborator—argued for the necessity of engaging racist discourse. Speaking of antiblack claims in Thomas Jefferson's *Notes on the State of Virginia,* Walker argued for the necessity of engagement, claiming that "unless we try to refute Mr. Jefferson's arguments respecting us, we will only establish them."[9]

As racial science gained both a new virulence and a new popular legitimacy, African Americans realized that they could ill afford the luxury of dismissal. In Gramscian terms, scientific racism, though a relatively novel form of racial thinking, was quickly becoming common sense. Blacks, aware only that they faced yet another hostile ideology, were not about to trust the outcome of the public debate over blacks' humanity to their enemies.[10]

Instead, African Americans sought *engagement* with the discourse of racial science in order to change it. Their effort to combat racist science this way was part and parcel of a larger strategy aimed at transforming public opinion on the entire range of racial matters. The centrality of this strategy to antebellum black protest thought cannot be understated. African Americans viewed it as the cornerstone of the freedom struggle. Time and again they reiterated the need to alter a "public sentiment" which had been "vitiated" by "the false doctrines, [and] base contumelies, that have been so successfully and industriously circulated" about blacks.[11] As the national convention of 1847 put it: "We struggle against opinions. Our warfare lies in the field of thought."[12] In the form of prejudice, hostile public opinion was "stalking over the land, spreading in its course its pestilential breath, blighting and withering the fair and natural hopes of our happiness."[13] The solution clearly followed: change the public mind. In a private letter to white abolitionist Gerrit Smith, James McCune Smith stated that only a complete reformation of white attitudes could compel prejudice to yield: "The heart of the whites must be changed, thoroughly, entirely, permanently changed," he wrote.[14] Throughout the period, in countless instances, African Americans sought not to dismiss claims of their inferiority, but to challenge them. Racist science was just one manifestation of these ideas.

African Americans' case against racial science has been outlined. But how effective were their rhetorical strategies? Did they emanate from an oppressive process of ideological hegemony, or from a liberating one in which blacks appropriated and refashioned ideas for their own empowerment? Complicating matters is the very range of ways black thinkers engaged racist arguments. At least five important tropes can be discerned: concession, living-proof refutation, arguments from history, the idea of racial genius, and negative environmentalism.

Concession. Frequently, the forms of protest thought directed against the conclusions of racial science appeared to result in concessions of black inferiority. It is difficult to read the words of the Northern African Americans who spearheaded the antebellum struggle for freedom without encountering such statements. Thomas Hamilton, who published New York's *Anglo-African Magazine,* claimed that "in no direction can we be said to manifest force of character equal to the whites,"[15] while Connecticut minister Amos Beman conceded that "the position which we now occupy . . . is a depressed one."[16] Others went further, claiming that blacks had been "groveling under" a humble state since their earliest existence.[17]

Concession most often sought to capitalize on the emergence of humanitarian sentiment and antislavery empathy, which required degraded subjects.[18] It posed African Americans as a group requiring redemption from injustice; through it, blacks sought to gain the moral leverage of the wronged. Since degradation offered evidence of injustice, no degradation might mean no injustice. Given the weight of proslavery claims that Africans benefited from slavery (morally through Christianization and physically through benevolent care) such arguments were far from naïve. Their critical premise was that blacks *could* be redeemed. Consider the words of a black education society in Pittsburgh, which argued that blacks' "moral depravity" arose "not from any thing in the constituent principles of their nature but wholly from their raising." Such statements appropriated the racist claim of degradation as innate only to repose degradation as imposed.[19] Blacks' natures were mutable; they could be "elevated" through the removal of oppression and the implementation of benign circumstances. Concession promised to redeem blacks' antiprogressive history by holding forth the promise of an elevation yet to come. Blacks were only temporarily degraded; it required only the removal of the undemocratic obstacles of slavery and prejudice for them to demonstrate the fact through speedy elevation. *"Free the slaves,"* challenged Peter Randolph, "give them equal opportunities with the whites, and I warrant you, they will not fall short in comparison."[20]

Black spokespersons sought to corral the non-elite into a community of the oppressed, defined by its struggle to find ways of compelling rights and liberty from whites. After complaining to black New Yorkers that "there is none learned among us," William Hamilton retreated: "I am sorry to say it," he wrote, "but I speak with the intention to quicken you."[21] Concession was double-edged. While clearly subordinated to the overwhelming need to respond to hostile arguments, black racialism nonetheless conceded much to the contemporary terms of debate. Simultaneously, spokespersons invoked claims of blacks' inherent traits to enhance black political unity. To the degree they were conceded to exist, then, inherent differences were often employed to spur black people to action.

Living-proof refutations. Another strategy of engagement involved presenting accomplished members of the race as living refutations of racial science's claims that black people were inherently and irrevocably degraded. The strategy can be traced back to at least 1791, when Benjamin Banneker, a free black astronomer from Baltimore, offered Thomas Jefferson his *Almanac* as proof that blacks could "rise" given the proper environment and inducements. Later generations of black activists enthusiastically embraced the strategy that Banneker literally sought to embody. The literature of the antebellum black protest tradition is replete with examples of such illustrious blacks. Douglass and Banneker, James McCune Smith, David Ruggles, George B. Vashon, Samuel Ringgold Ward, Charles B. Ray, Samuel Cornish, J.W.C. Pennington, Theodore S. Wright, and hosts of others were regularly invoked as examples of individual merit outdistancing the designs of slavery and prejudice.[22] Henry Highland Garnet, himself one of these "representative colored men," upheld black revolutionaries Denmark Vesey, Nat Turner, and Joseph Cinque as exemplars of black courage and elevation.[23] R.B. Lewis brought a hint of much-needed gender equity to the list by proclaiming Maria Stewart an example of modern black womanhood equal to the great women of antiquity.[24] Even black entertainers like Ira Aldridge and Frank Johnson enjoyed this treatment.[25] Exemplary blacks not only filled the present but occupied the past as well. The foundations of black history lay in the recounting of the exploits of black patriots such as Crispus Attucks,[26] while celebrations of Haitian revolutionary Toussaint L'Ouverture began to move the discussion toward national rather than individual examples.

On a broader scale, black leaders sought to make every African American a living-proof refutation of racial science's conclusions. In innumerable speeches, sermons, and addresses, black elites urged their people to live lives illustrative of the heights to which blacks as a group might ascend. "We have to act an important part, and fill an important place . . . in the work of emancipation," intoned black editor Samuel Cornish. "On *our* conduct and exertions much, very much depend."[27] Through their own actions, behavior, and comportment, African Americans could rebut the racist claims that held them back. "I think," wrote Austin Steward, "that our conduct as colored men will have a great bearing on the question that now agitates this land. . . . Let it be shown that we as a people are religious, industrious, sober, honest and intelligent, and my word for it, the accursed system of Slavery will fall, as did Satan from Heaven."[28]

Concession was inherent in living-proof refutations. The blacks offered up as exemplary were exemplary only by being atypically accomplished—a seeming paradox. Black leaders were trying to illustrate not the current state of the race, but its potential. Living-proof refutations had managed to overcome the most debilitating circumstances to rise above their oppression. But for every exemplary African American upheld before the public, the argument implied, scores lay in unelevated darkness, awaiting either the personal impetus to reform themselves, or the removal of obstacles to group elevation—a considerable concession of existing inferiority. The standards by which some were deemed debased and others elevated remained largely unexamined by these arguments; African Americans seemed to accept them rather uncritically.

The uses of the past. While modern audiences are most familiar with racial science as a set of arguments about human physiological makeup, it must be remembered that in the antebellum era the "science" of race was as much a discipline of history as it was of biology. American-school ethnologists fused methods of biological science, such as close measurement of the cranial capacities of skulls of different "races," with racial histories culled from sacred and secular sources. They argued that modern empirical method confirmed what ancient sources suggested: blacks had never been a civilized people; they had always been slaves. The terrain of debate thus covered both history and the physical sciences. For blacks, history offered a discipline with methods far more easily replicable than were those of craniology. No blacks had access to their own "golgotha" of ancient skulls such as that which Samuel Morton possessed, and only a few to the medical training and resources necessary to conduct their own research. But most had access to literary societies and other sources of books, which they mined assiduously for arguments to counter the claims of racial science.

The historical argument for black racial inferiority pointed to Africa's lack of great civilizations. Whereas Europeans could boast descent from ancient Greece and Rome, white supremacists maintained that Africans were without historical examples of advanced societies. According to American-school ethnologists, the only great historical civilization of Africa, Egypt, was ruled by white people, who kept black Africans enslaved. But blacks claimed Egyptian civilization as their own, as evidence of blacks' capacity to "rise" in the past and hence in the future. Many northern blacks produced extended arguments to claim, as did an anonymous writer for *Freedom's Journal* in 1827, that blacks descended from Egyptians, "whose learning the ancients vainly emulated, and to whose eminence in the sciences, the moderns have not attained." [29]

Once the identity between ancient Egyptians and modern-day blacks was established, the whole of Egyptian civilization could be invoked on behalf of blacks' potential for elevation. In fact, as many African American thinkers saw it, through Egypt black Africa had in fact given birth to modern civilization. They inverted accepted historical understandings, placing Africans not at the bottom of the scale of civilization as eternal children, but at its top, as first parents. Robert B. Lewis typified this approach by claiming that modern civilization was indebted to ancient Africans for rhetoric, architecture, astronomy, seafaring, navigation, the pump, the library, philosophy, mathematics, jurisprudence, medicine, magic, geometry, and fire (Prometheus was black, Lewis claimed). [30]

Antebellum black history served important rhetorical functions. That blacks had once represented the pinnacle of civilization meant that they might do so again. No achievement in civilization was beyond them, given the proper inducements. According to Samuel Cornish, the ancient record proved that black people "have all the natural requisites to make them, in science and renown, what ancient Egypt once was." [31] Through these kinds of arguments, African Americans applied the logic of environmentalism to the domain of history and nations. Just as individuals could be elevated or degraded by circumstance, so too nations and groups of people. "By the operation of favorable causes," Henry Bibb claimed, "nations may be elevated to the highest possible standard of excellence." [32]

The genius of races. Another type of engagement with racial science emanated from African Americans' responses to its historical arguments. Just as whites condemned African Americans for their incapacity to harken back to ancient models of higher civilization, they drew upon their own Anglo-Saxon past to argue for white racial superiority. White writers working in the idiom of romantic nationalism sought in history proofs that

Anglo-Saxons were, naturally, an enterprising, liberty-loving, adventure-seeking people; it was their destiny to spread their values across the globe. But, as black writers saw it, if Africans were to be castigated on the basis of the past, if history was to be fair game in the effort to oppress, then the much-vaunted Anglo-Saxon record was not free from scrutiny, either. An important strain of parody and satire ran throughout the antebellum black protest tradition, attacking whites' veneration of the Anglo-Saxon past, and calling into question the very standards by which civilizations were to be judged.

Blacks seemed to delight in appropriating whites' concern with national historical precedents, only to turn their premises against them. England, as the ancestral home of the "white" race, frequently fell under critical scrutiny. Several black authors remarked that the people of England, when first seen by the invading Romans, were hardly the epitome of civilization. According to William Craft, Julius Caesar said that the British natives "were such stupid people that they were not fit to make slaves of in Rome." [33] Britain's inglorious history continued after Rome vacated her shores. According to one black writer, "the Angles and Saxons" who replaced Rome as the dominant power on the island "were both barbaric German tribes, who stole the country of the Britons, and appropriated it to their own uses." [34] And, referring to the Norman Conquest of Anglo-Saxon England in 1066, Alexander Crummell noted that "England herself, grand and mighty empire as she is, can easily trace back the historic footprints to the time, when even she was under the yoke." [35] A writer for the *Anglo-African Magazine* suggested the significance of this ignoble history: "What is to prevent our taking rank with them, seeing that we have a common history in misfortune?" [36] As William Wells Brown put it, "Ancestry is something which the white American should not speak of unless with his lips to the dust." [37]

An important twist on this tradition of satire was a trope Mia Bay has termed, following Anna Julia Cooper, the "angry Saxon." In countless instances, African Americans portrayed whites' racial ancestors not as enterprising and liberty-loving, but as rapacious and greedy. A writer for the *Anglo-African Magazine* exemplified this trope in skewering the myth of a noble Anglo-Saxon past. While "Noah and Mrs. Noah may be ancestry enough for some folks," he joked, whites claimed that Horsa and Hengist, the two mythic Anglo-Saxons who first invaded England, "are father and mother to the great Anglo-Saxon race." White people would soon be claiming that "the ancient Egyptians themselves were Anglo-Saxons." He continued to assert that, far from imbuing them with a love of freedom, the only claim Anglo-Saxon heritage could make on the character of present-day Americans was "that it runs in the blood to steal." [38] The very foundations of

English civilization, many black writers thought, lay in a history of brutal expansion and barbaric tyranny. David Walker's study of history led him to conclude that "the whites have always been an unjust, jealous, unmerciful, avaricious and blood-thirsty set of beings, always seeking after power and authority."[39]

Satire labeled as absurd wisdom that was normally considered beyond reproach. By posing it as farcical, satire challenged the new social knowledge of scientific racism, controverting the process by which it was assimilated into "common-sense" notions of the world, and slowing its incorporation into the mainstream. As Gramsci theorized it, the authority of powerful discourses depends upon the perception of normativity; in other words, some claims seem so obviously true that they are simply beyond challenge. This was the one thing black satire would not permit. Even if they could not change white minds on racial matters, black spokespersons could at least guarantee a rhetorical space in which racist ideas would never go unchallenged. Furthermore, for African Americans satire affirmed the legitimacy of a corpus of knowledge they themselves possessed which lay outside the commonsensical knowledge authorized by public-sphere discourse. By reinforcing blacks' status as insiders in a marginal community, and by offering such a place of privilege to sympathetic listeners, satire may even have helped persuade potential allies that such knowledge was not quite as marginal as others would have it, thus buttressing a sense of community in marginality. While the title of Ralph Ellison's essay "Change the Joke and Slip the Yoke" alerts us to the emancipatory potential of appropriating and refashioning racist discourse, I would suggest similar possibilities through the use of satire by rephrasing his title "get the joke and join the folk."[40]

Negative environmentalism. A final manifestation of blacks' engagement with racial science bears discussion. It is a trope we might call negative environmentalism—a specific application of the environmentalism African Americans so often invoked. As a form of environmentalism, it conceded black degradation, only to ascribe that degradation to circumstance rather than innate nature. And like environmentalism, it posited the "mutability of human affairs," as John Brown Russwurm had put it—the idea that African Americans *could* "rise" to a level of equality with whites, if provided the proper environment. Yet while black thinkers applied "positive" environmentalism to explain why Africans lagged behind Europeans in achievements in civilization, they invoked negative environmentalism against the institution of slavery to describe its debilitating consequences. In this, negative environmentalism was a subset of the argument that slavery and prejudice subverted God's design. As that argument went, slavery had imposed conditions on black people that physically degraded them, rendering them inferior to whites. Where negative environmentalism strayed, however, was in claiming that environmentally imposed degradation could become almost permanent in blacks, inheritable from one generation to the next. In this, it seems that those African Americans who most stridently protested racial science may have come closest to internalizing its most hostile presumptions.

There was no greater prophet of negative environmentalism than Hosea Easton, the Connecticut minister who experienced firsthand the horrors of Northern prejudice. The son of a skilled ironworker who was patriarch to a family active in racial politics, Easton was raised in the creed of self-improvement. His experience in the 1830s of race riots and discrimination in his hometown of New Haven led him to reconsider the value of social-uplift ideology. The result was a pamphlet, "A Treatise on the Intellectual Character, and the Civil and Political Condition of the Colored People of the U. States," which reflected his growing disillusionment with race in America. The "Treatise," as we have seen, constituted one of the most important statements about race by a black person in nineteenth-century America, and it was significant partly because of its hopeless views of race and prejudice—factors that led directly to Easton's use of negative environmentalism. Easton reproduced an awful catalog of the "opprobrious terms" used by whites to describe inferior slaves:

> Contracted and sloped foreheads; prominent eye-balls; projecting under-jaw; certain distended muscles about the mouth, or lower parts of the face; thick lips and flat nose; hips and rump projecting; crooked shins; flat feet, with large projecting heels. . . . With regard to their mind, it is said that their intellectual brain is not fully developed; malicious disposition; no taste for high and honorable attainments; implacable enemies one to another; and that they sustain the same relation to the ourang outang, that the whites do to them.

He conceded "the truth of these remarks," but he attributed blacks' inferiority not to an original hereditary cause," but to the "lineal [i.e., causal] effects of slavery on its victims." The strategy here was a form of tactical concession: only extreme degradation could suggest the monumental injustice that had been done to the enslaved. As Easton wrote, "No language capable of being employed by mortal tongue, is sufficiently descriptive to set forth in its true character the effect of that cursed thing, slavery."[41] Only by illustrating the extraordinarily debilitating consequences of enslavement could the monumental injustice of slavery become apparent.

Others also slipped into negative environmentalism. Frederick Douglass offered a softer version of Easton's negative environmentalism in his famous speech, "The Claims of the Negro Ethnologically Considered," delivered in 1854. Douglass believed that "the *well* or *ill* condition of any part of mankind, will leave its mark on the physical as well as on the intellectual part of man." He illustrated the point by recounting the degraded state of downtrodden Irishmen he encountered on a trip across the Atlantic.[42] In the very act of directly opposing the claims of racial science, then, Douglass employed its key concept of heritability.

Negative environmentalism was concession played to its logical conclusion: since degradation offered evidence of injustice, extreme degradation might mean extreme injustice. Classic environmentalism argued that Africans lagged behind whites because they lacked the environment and geography that had propelled Europe into the global forefront, or because the light of Christianity had failed to spread to their dark continent, or even that Africans had brought this darkness upon themselves by failing to acknowledge the one true God. As such, it tended to depict black peoples' plight as the consequence of ancient or faultless causes. Negative environmentalism attributed the inferior position of blacks to slavery and the slave trade, institutions that had actively depressed the prospects of Africans and African-descended people since they came into contact with Europeans. It thus argued that Africans had been degraded in the extreme, and by fellow humans who could still admit to and atone for their sins.

Assessments

For African Americans, racial science was a tremendously important arena of ideological contestation. If blacks could not succeed in countering a set of ideas so clearly hostile to their interests, they were not likely to succeed anywhere. If they could not resist the hegemony of polygenesis, they were unlikely to resist the hegemony of any of the antebellum period's public discourses. In assessing blacks' efforts to counter racial science, it is clear that a simple judgment will not suffice. In the history of black thought we can find instances wherein African Americans appropriated elements of racial discourse only to refashion them into a force to undermine that oppressive ideology (satirical uses of history), as well as occasions in which blacks' engagement with racist thought seems to have led them to internalize elements of an oppressive discourse (negative environmentalism). In each form of engagement appear suggestions of both debilitating hegemony and empowering appropriation. What conclusions about the black response to racial science can be drawn from this analysis? What general principles about resistance to ideological oppression do such conclusions yield? Let's consider the strengths and weaknesses of each argument in turn.

The central dilemma of the appropriation thesis is that appropriation did not always equal empowerment, much less counter-hegemony. The counter-hegemonic possibilities of appropriation must be demonstrated rather than assumed. Every instance of engagement necessarily implied at least a minimal act of appropriation. Dialogue presumes latent consensus; intelligibility demands agreement on some basic terms of debate. For African Americans the mere act of responding to racist charges necessarily conceded the possibility that the original premise was credible enough to require refutation—for example, that African-descended people might have been the cursed children of Canaan, or that blacks' physical natures rendered them incapable of elevation. Furthermore, engagement tended to reify the latent assumptions built into the claims they sought to refute—in the examples just cited, the legitimacy of sacred texts for understanding race, or the fact that there were distinct races, equal or not.

Even had blacks properly understood the nature of white supremacy, it was still likely that they would have fallen into the trap of internalizing some key elements of hostile discourses; such were the intrinsic liabilities of participating in public-sphere discourse. Countering hegemony required more than mere appropriation. Appropriated values had to be refashioned and redisseminated into the public sphere, where they might counteract racist discourse in some effective fashion. Furthermore, as proponents of the hegemony thesis point out, since internalization frequently accompanied appropriation, those using this strategy had to retain sufficient self-awareness from the discourses they sought to undermine to offset the strategy's inherent liabilities. Satire often offered a means of responding effectively to racist discourse while retaining the critical distance necessary to avoid internalization, but it often strayed perilously close to—and indeed sometimes crossed over into—unwitting internalization of hostile discourse.

It was never possible to succeed entirely in appropriating and reconstructing oppressive ideas, any more than it was possible to completely internalize them. Appropriation and hegemony represent not two distinct approaches to the problem, but poles separated by a range of possibilities. Specific responses to oppressive discourse entailed both the dangers of internalization as well as the promise of countering ideological hegemony. And challenging one discourse of oppression could simultaneously lend credibility to others. How, then, do we gauge the consequences of blacks' engagement with racist discourse on the freedom struggle?

This difficulty winds up being the problem with the hegemony thesis. If blacks did internalize elements of racist discourse, how exactly did this harm the freedom struggle? In Gramsci's original formulation, overcoming hegemony required outside ideological intervention. Since the very purpose of hegemony is to uphold oppressive systems by establishing values and norms antithetical to the interests of the oppressed, effective resistance to hegemony cannot come from inside those norms. Thus, for Gramsci, the proletariat could never invoke bourgeois discourse in the service of revolution. Some movement outside the bounds of hegemonic thought was necessary.[43] This seems also to be the route touted by many radical theorists, such as Audre Lorde. For Marxists, the source of this counter-hegemonic ideology was the revolutionary party; updated versions look to the autonomous cultural formations of the oppressed themselves as sources of liberation.[44] In classical terms, then, the failure to step outside of dominant discourses constitutes an a priori incapacity to mount challenges to hegemony. As an expression of social power, the public sphere cannot constitute such a resource.

This presents a considerable problem for hegemony theorists, for quite often the oppressed were not slaves in plantation communities or peasants in closed-corporate societies, isolated from the culture of the oppressor. Often they were, like industrial workers, part of a public world the ideological parameters of which were simply inescapable. This was certainly the case with antebellum Northern blacks, who lived cheek-by-jowl with a white populace that hugely outnumbered them. For such as these, appropriating the "master's tools" was not just an ideological option, but the only conceivable source of counter-hegemonic thinking. If it was not possible to step completely outside of the discourses of the public sphere, the oppressed had to work within those discourses, and this meant landing somewhere on the slippery slope between hegemony and appropriation, complicity and empowerment.[45]

Yet if it was not possible for antebellum free blacks to craft a protest tradition from outside the dominant public discourses of the day, neither does this mean that hegemony was complete. Gramsci assumed that all internalization (appropriation) was by definition counter-revolutionary. If we concede that in responding to racial science blacks did internalize some elements of racist discourse, how exactly did it undermine their struggle for liberation? On this point scholars offer only vague evaluations, as if internalization per se, rather than its consequences, were the root problem. Bay goes farthest, suggesting that nineteenth-century black ethnology constituted an instance of "anti racist racism" of the sort Jean-Paul Sartre charged of the negritude movement of the 1940s, and points to forms of modern Afrocentrism as the least credible of its intellectual descendants. Following Sartre, she seems to uphold the vision of a "raceless proletariat" as the preferred alternative.[46]

But actually, black responses to racial science stand up quite well, far better than the hegemony thesis would have it. It is true that black thinkers imbibed elements of racist discourse. Black newspapers regularly reprinted tales of exotic Oriental peoples, and seemed willing to cite white authorities who supported the potential of black intellect at the expense of that of Native Americans.[47] Rare instances of stereotyping—one black northerner referred to Chinese people as "grotesque," people with "filthy" habits and "features totally devoid of expression"—certainly contradict the racial tolerance expected of victims of racial intolerance.[48] But the negative consequences of this internalization—the long-term undermining of the struggle to make blacks free or America better—seem nowhere near as apocalyptic as the critics sometimes seem to intimate. By every standard the hegemony thesis uses, African Americans' internalization of racist discourse did not deal crippling blows to the freedom struggle.

Whatever hegemony was at work among antebellum blacks did not seem to have blinded African Americans to their common interests or to the very fact of their oppression. The black spokespersons who engaged racist discourse clearly understood themselves as part of a group, initially defined by white supremacy, but articulating a sense of common identity built upon resistance to their shared oppression. Rather than craft their notion of blackness around a sense of organic cultural linkages, they did so around a pragmatic sense of shared oppression and historical experience. Samuel Cornish typified the thoughts of many when he wrote: "We say that our *condition* in the community is a *peculiar* one, and that we need SPECIAL EFFORTS and special organization, to meet our wants and to obtain and maintain our rights." Cornish did not "love one class of men more than another," and was as much opposed to "complexional distinctions" as anyone. "Yet we are one of an oppressed people," he wrote, "and we deem it alike our privilege and duty, to labor *especially* for that people, until *all their disabilities are removed.*"[49] At a time when many white Americans were lauding ethnic identities rooted in mythic pasts, African Americans remained remarkably committed to a sense of unity crafted only by common oppression.[50]

Ultimately, African Americans' responses to antebellum racial science suggest the power as well as the limitations of the sense of pragmatic racial identity crafted by those such as Cornish and McCune Smith. Black thinkers set forth a notion of blackness that largely avoided succumbing to the racial essentialism of their day, yet remained deeply engaged with the discourses of the American public sphere. This relationship offered tremendous benefits. It gave free blacks access to a potent set of ideas that promised to change white minds. African Americans spoke, wrote, and published in a world where powerful white enemies might be converted and powerful white allies might be enlisted. Black leaders' very proximity to power rendered their words meaningful. The men and women who forged the antebellum protest tradition engaged in what Kevin J. O'Brien has called in other contexts "rightful resistance," or the art of disputing "the legitimacy of certain political authorities and their actions while affirming (indeed relying upon) other authorities and established values to pursue their ends." Black thinkers used their proximity to power to pose a "critique within the hegemony" (to quote James C. Scott) which resulted in some of the most potent tropes in the history of black protest thought.[51]

To a critical extent they succeeded. They, even more than the radical abolitionists, spoke from the margins of American society. Yet gradually, from the 1830s onward, the fierce and fiery rhetoric of mere handfuls of radical activists began to influence the center of American politics. Slowly and painfully, the ideas of a scorned and rejected minority infiltrated public debate and polarizing public opinion, and eventually precipitating the colossal ideological battles that raged from 1848 to 1860. The antislavery ideology the Union marched to war with in April of 1861 was a hopelessly co-opted descendant of its antebellum original, yet in the maelstrom of the Civil War it was sufficient to spur the complete obliteration of the hated institution of slavery. Both that great conflict and the emancipation it demanded owed their origins to the efforts of black activists in the antebellum North.

"No Occurrence in Human History Is More Deserving of Commemoration Than This": Abolitionist Celebrations of Freedom[1]

Julie Roy Jeffrey

On July 4, 1849, Martha Barrett, a twenty-one-year-old student at a Massachusetts normal school, determined to boycott the usual festivities of the day, "for they seem a mockery, while 3 millions of slaves, are groaning in bondage in this country."[2] Like many abolitionists, Barrett refused to celebrate a holiday that applauded American freedom but ignored the ugly realities of slavery. Other abolitionists chose more public ways than did Barrett of expressing their opposition to the nation's central civic celebration. The competing July Fourth observances they organized were designed to expose the flawed nature of mainstream festivities and to contest the interpretation of the past that supported them. In sharp contrast to the usual "extravagant self-glorying" rituals of Independence Day, abolitionists in one New York community in the 1850s initiated their program at sunrise with an hourlong tolling of the church bell to mark the passing of the spirit of freedom from the nation's highest councils.[3]

Abolitionists also created new rituals centered around contemporary events that the mainstream culture either neglected or even decried. By bringing large numbers of people together to honor abolitionist interpretations of occurrences like the emancipation of slaves in the British West Indies or successful fugitive slave rescues, abolitionists intended to provide an instructive "lesson" to those who attended the events. Although much energy went into attracting people to these celebrations, their organizers, attentive to the propaganda possibilities provided by the expansion of print culture, also set their sights on another significant audience, those who would read about the event in newspaper accounts. Hoping to elicit descriptions for his paper of what had gone on at various British West Indies Emancipation Day celebrations, William Lloyd Garrison argued that "the whole country should be apprised through the medium of the press, of what is said and done today."[4]

While historians have long studied abolitionist electoral efforts, such as the creation of antislavery political parties, work in political culture suggests the value of broadening the definition of politics to include events like celebrations, parades, orations, street literature, and even festive dinners and toasts as forms of political activity. Each represented an attempt to influence those who held power and to define the public political sphere and its participants. By viewing abolitionism from this perspective, one can recognize a rich antislavery political culture ranging from the July Fourth and British West Indies Emancipation Day commemorations to the antislavery fairs organized by abolitionist women. Committed to radical change, abolitionists, many of them ordinary men and women, created occasions that may have been festive on one level but were fundamentally political in intent. They became adept at using oratory, music, banners, and displays of goods and food to publicize their ideas and goals, and to stake out their positions in the debate over slavery and the nation's future.[5]

As the struggle against slavery lengthened, these festive gatherings became ever more important and elaborate. Successful celebrations helped to recruit new members to the movement and to draw attention to abolitionist demands. For those hostile or indifferent to abolitionism, the celebrations demonstrated the power and maddening persistence of antislavery and its critique of mainstream beliefs. For avowed emancipationists, the festivities not only helped to promote a shared understanding of events, both in the distant and recent past, but also provided a sense of community and an opportunity to renew energy and commitment. Planners and organizers benefited from having a concrete goal, valuable because for many northerners, the ultimate goal of freeing the slaves must have seemed abstract and distant.

For the historian, a study of abolitionist political culture also reveals some of the dynamics of race and gender in the reform movement. This examination of the holiday commemorating the emancipation of the slaves in the British West Indies shows that, despite common understandings of the significance of that event and a common interest in bringing African Americans into the public sphere, black and white abolitionists created different rituals for the August 1 holiday. At the most basic level, the decision to honor British accomplishments challenged the American status quo. For many blacks, the August 1 celebration represented a way of claiming rights and privileges they were denied in the North and ultimately of publicizing their demands in major urban public spaces. Just as the organization of the holiday also hints at class and cultural differences

William Lloyd Garrison (1805–1879), "This is the Lord's Doing: Slavery Abolished in the British West Indies." (Source: Massachusetts Historical Society)

within the black community, the limited role allotted to black women points to concerns about black masculinity. In contrast to urban festivals planned by African Americans, predominantly white abolitionist celebrations brought people together in country settings to hear generalized antislavery messages and to have a good time. Additionally, organizers hoped to sponsor the kind of event that could attract those who knew little about abolitionism. In creating as appealing a holiday as possible, white women played a central role in the day's festivities. Their pattern of participation reflected their activism and important contributions to the antislavery cause.

Of the newly created abolitionist holidays, the commemoration of the emancipation of slaves in the British West Indies in 1834 was the most important. It eventually replaced earlier black festivities that marked the end of the American slave trade, slave emancipation at the state level, and the Haitian revolution. William Lloyd Garrison, invited to join a festive dinner in Boston after the Belknap Meeting House service in 1839, regretted the meager number of "palefaced" sisters and brothers in attendance, for August 1 was "not [merely] a colored anniversary." One of Garrison's goals was to make abolitionism an interracial movement and to enlarge the public sphere to include blacks. But despite Garrison's desire and his admonition to white abolitionists that "we must not suffer our dark-skinned friends to monopolize its pleasures," August 1 remained primarily an African American holiday in the 1830s and early 1840s. The segregated nature of these observances suggests the growing cohesion of free black communities in the North and complicated racial tensions within the abolitionist movement. White reluctance to join blacks in commemorating slave emancipation was just one factor lying behind the character of August 1 festivities. While Garrison greeted the signs of growing white interest in the holiday as a sign of declining white prejudice in 1844, he was dismayed that Boston blacks preferred to hold their own ceremonies. Although whites were invited to participate, a black speaker at the Boston celebration explained that whites "*could not,* having never been placed in the same circumstances as colored people, *feel* as they do in celebrating this great event."[6]

This felt connection with slavery quickly alerted some Northern blacks to the commemorative possibilities of slave emancipation in the British West Indies. The process of emancipation began in 1834, and within the year, the newly formed New York City Committee of Vigilance sponsored an August 1st Jubilee. In 1836, Philadelphia blacks held "quite . . . imposing" festivities including speeches and a dinner for sixty people. Despite the success of these occasions, however, the day had not yet earned an assured place in the fabric of black memory and life. In Philadelphia, a Miss Healy, after presenting a "splendid, appropriate, and chaste *Silken Banner,*" felt compelled to urge the male committee of arrangements to continue the practice of highlighting this historic event. It would be "highly gratifying" for the women, she pointed out, "were that important day publicly commemorated by our colored citizens."[7]

The fact that black women participated in the Philadelphia event and that the newspaper reported on their involvement and the gift, surely made by one of the city's black female associations, was a recognition of the important community role played by Northern black women and their female associations. The fabrication of a "splendid" banner also showed the women's understanding of the significance of visual display in creating a holiday mood and in publicizing the abolitionist message. Another banner described in some detail in the newspaper the same year testified to the awareness of the visual and symbolic potential of female handiwork. This banner was a fine white satin affair with green fringe, tassels, and an inscription printed in gold letters. "August 1st, 1834," the banner proclaimed. "Hail Birth Day / of British Emancipation / May our beloved Country continue to / fan the like flame, enkindled in / her bosom by the / LUNDY'S AND GARRISON'S / of America, / until every slave is FREE."[8]

If Healy and black women's mutual aid and improvement associations anticipated playing a major role in developing the holiday, however, they must have been disappointed. There are few signs that black women played a prominent part in planning or orchestrating Emancipation Day activities. Perhaps because black men were struggling to assert their manhood in a society that made it difficult to adhere to mainstream white gender norms, they seem to have kept control of the holiday as it became established.[9]

But it took a few years for the holiday to find its place in black urban life. Even though by 1840 New York City had more than 16,000 black residents, nine black churches, and thirty mutual aid societies, there was some question in 1839 and again in 1841, whether New Yorkers would succeed in holding a demonstration in the city. Gradually, however, the celebration of August 1 became popular in areas with substantial black communities. By 1841, the editor of the *Colored American* anticipated observances in Philadelphia, New Haven, Hartford, Albany, and Newark. Other cities that had organized festivities included Pittsburgh, Detroit, Buffalo, Rochester, Poughkeepsie, Boston, Salem, Providence, Pawtucket, and Lynn.[10]

The practice in many places of holding a public meeting to decide how to honor the day made the celebration a communal enterprise and testified to African American appropriation of American political norms of behavior. In Boston, a "respectable audience" met, voted to hold the celebration, and elected its speaker. In Newark, New Jersey, blacks gathered and adopted resolutions establishing the schedule of events. In Poughkeepsie, African Americans, pointedly described as "citizens" in the *Colored American,* held two public meetings in 1840 to agree upon a general plan which included a reading of the Declaration of Independence in the Methodist Zion Church. Usually a male committee would be appointed to take care of detailed arrangements.[11]

The first British West Indies Emancipation Day celebrations drew upon precedents established by earlier black festive commemorations. But their character was also shaped by the interpretation abolitionists gave to British West Indies emancipation, the realities of African American life, and abolitionist disapproval of the "empty pageantry" and "Bacchanalian" atmosphere of popular Fourth of July galas.[12]

Although during the first two decades of the nineteenth century, many blacks had hailed the end of the American slave trade as the harbinger of emancipation, American slavery showed few signs of disappearing. This discouraging reality increased the significance of emancipation anywhere in the New World. Thus, black and white abolitionists interpreted the end of slavery in the British West Indies not as a local but as a cosmic event. The First of August signified not just the "Birthday of 800,000 Freemen" who inhabited the islands but "the birth-day of Freedom," "the triumph of moral power, of justice and the cause of liberty." While orators might occasionally refer to the "tedious details of this history," few wanted to emphasize any problems that attended the transition of former slaves to freedom or to highlight the differences between conditions in Great Britain and the United States. They often preferred to describe emancipation in starkly dramatic and simple terms. "[With] one bolt from the moral sky," Frederick Douglass assured a Canandaigua audience, "these bloodstained irons [lay] all scattered and broken." In a flash, former slaves "were instantly clothed with all the rights, responsibilities, powers, and duties, of free men and women."

This simplified interpretation and avoidance of "tedious" details, of course, obscured the political strategies and maneuvering that lay behind emancipation and the political, social, and economic conditions that contributed to the successful passage of Parliamentary legislation. The construction of the event was intended not to illuminate the particularities of emancipation but to prove it was possible and to give the "assurance of complete victory." Even when Garrison, at the "risk of being tedious," provided a more extended narrative, he emphasized a pared-down lesson. Events leading up to emancipation "exactly resemble the features of our own conflict from the extinction of a similar, but more extended, and, if possible, more atrocious system at home."[13]

In a day devoted to thanksgiving and hope, orations, music, toasts, and visual displays refashioned the familiar national story. The mainstream narrative of the country cast Great Britain in the role of oppressor and tyrant and Americans as agents of freedom. August 1 celebrations reversed the roles and helped to create a new image of Great Britain as friend of freedom. The festivities also raised pointed questions about the meaning of American foundational documents. At a celebration held in Buffalo in 1849, toasts were made to the "greatness" of Great Britain, called a "Model for the World." While the Declaration of Independence was acknowledged as the "first promulgation of the theory" of liberty, events in the British West Indies represented "the first reduction of that theory to practice." Singers at a Deerfield, Massachusetts, celebration in 1838 hailed "Britannia, honored land" and "Freedom's holy birth," and melodiously mourned Columbia's "foul stains." Cincinnati blacks learned that the "glorious deeds" of British men and women would "be engraved on the page of history." Not surprisingly, nonabolitionists tried to dismiss this interpretation by impugning the patriotism of these August 1 gatherings, calling them *"British"* celebrations.[14]

Often lasting the entire day, August 1 observances were fashioned around a sequence of events with varied emotional styles. Like earlier celebrations of the end of the American slave trade, many British West Indies Emancipation Day exercises took place in black churches, vital centers of community life and symbols of black achievement. One Pittsburgh commemoration met in a Baptist church in the morning and in the Bethel Church in the afternoon. Poughkeepsie blacks gathered at the Methodist Zion Church. Church settings suited the theme of giving thanks for emancipation and made the obvious point that the cause of freedom was a holy one.[15]

Church observances conformed to the sedate and sacred character of the space. At the 1839 gathering at Boston's Belknap Meeting House, the service included song, anthems, "very appropriate and pointed" prayer, scripture reading, a collection, and a benediction. One reference point was obviously emancipation in the British West Indies; another was the audience itself—who they were and what rights and privileges they deserved as black Americans. Those attending the service were reminded of the complex strands of their New World identity, the now distant African heritage, the Christian faith, fruit of their forced migration, and their past, present, and future contributions to American life. Africa was recalled but with no sense that it represented a homeland. The words of one song went as follows: "On Afric's land our fathers roamed, / A free, but savage race; / No word of light their mind informed / Of God's recovering grace." According to the song, saving knowledge and new opportunities came only with emigration: "Who knows but in Americ's wild, / A Christian black may sow / The word of God—pure, undefiled, / And a rich harvest grow." In a regretfully "very short" address, one of the speakers pointed out what African Americans had already contributed to the nation. Highlighting the sacrifice of Crispus Attucks, the black man slain during the Boston Massacre, the speaker described him as the first American to shed his blood for his country. The clear message was that Northern blacks had earned the privileges and rights that Attucks had died to secure. Like August 1 celebrations elsewhere, the Bostonians also heard an ode, probably written especially for the occasion. Performed "in fine style, particularly the duett by female voice," the ode testified to the literary skills and cultivation blacks had acquired with freedom, further proof they deserved to participate fully in Northern life.[16]

Dignified and subdued as these rituals often were, the day's exercises had a place for sentiment. Most abolitionists agreed that it was important to make imaginative connections with those who suffered in slavery, whether it was through the medium of poetry, as Dickson Bruce points out in his essay in this volume, music or rhetoric. For whites, sympathetic connections bolstered abolitionist commitment; for blacks, feelings demonstrated their status as human beings. So, on August 1, speakers not only gloried in emancipation but also encouraged their listeners to feel the horrors of American slavery. Given the presence in most crowds of emancipated and fugitive slaves, it must not have been too difficult to kindle emotional sympathy. At Albany's celebration in 1838, speakers inspired the audience to "weep with those who weep." In Pittsburgh, a former slave exhibited the kind of "eloquence . . . which experience moves, and which comes from a heart which feels 'another's woes,'" and never fails to bring an audience into a similar state of feeling." The appeals to sentiment reveal that for blacks the day had a mixed emotional character, with tears mingled with rejoicing.[17]

Sunday school students, their teachers, and other children often played a prominent role in early African American festive rituals. In Troy, New York, the Yates Juvenile Anti-Slavery Society conducted exercises "with great decorum." In Cincinnati Sunday school students walked in file with "colored citizens" to the church for the services there. Scholars in Poughkeepsie and Williamsburg, New York, delivered recitations. Youthful participation ensured that children knew the wonderful facts of emancipation and encouraged them to believe in the possibility of freedom for American slaves. But the involvement of children had as much to do with African American aspirations and abolitionist hopes as it did with British West Indies emancipation. The successful acquisition of education, Christianity, and good habits came only through community effort. Education and middle-class behavior were matters of communal pride and sources of status within the black community. Additionally, the children's demeanor and ability to perform before an audience of "highly respectable" adults reflected a central abolitionist strategy. Particularly in the 1830s, black abolitionists believed that African Americans could bring about racial improvement by adopting middle-class values and habits. As the resolution presented at the Colored Methodist Episcopal Zion Church in Newburgh, New York, put it, "nothing else than a good moral character, and a proficiency in learning or literature" should be "the TEST of superiority henceforth and forever." The emphasis on education and character as a means of racial elevation would persist as one strand in black activism to the present day.[18]

Despite New York City's large celebrations in 1837 and 1838 (in the latter year, Garrison addressed more than 4,000 people, mostly African American, in the Broadway Tabernacle), most newspaper accounts suggest that early celebrations were low-key. Shane White has suggested that while

African Americans mounted flashy parades during the early decades of the century, controversy over the appropriate character of public celebrations emerged in the late 1820s and would persist as a matter of discussion within the black community long after slavery was abolished. Conservative blacks disliked the colorful parades but could not impose their tastes on others in the black community. In 1827, black New Yorkers held two commemorations of state emancipation, one with a parade, the other without.[19]

The debate over the proper way of observing holidays continued as the new celebration took hold. Expressing the viewpoint of its elite membership, the National Convention of 1834 decried public processions, as did the editor of the *Colored American*, Samuel E. Cornish. Sober, sedate, and quiet festivities demonstrated that African Americans had adopted middle-class norms of behavior, which was also a goal expressed in the pages of other early black newspapers, as Timothy Patrick McCarthy's essay in this book suggests. Yet articles in the *Colored American* also revealed that some blacks disregarded these preferences and chose to celebrate in ways the leadership considered unrefined, overly expressive, and damaging to the reputation and aspirations of responsible Northern black men and women.[20]

The concerns of black leaders about the character of public celebrations were reasonable. The realities of African American life encouraged restraint. In the 1820s, black parades in Boston, Philadelphia, and New York had generated white hostility and negative publicity. Changing racial, demographic, and class dynamics in American cities promoted violent racial confrontations in the 1830s. The *National Enquirer*'s report on Philadelphia's celebration in 1836 emphasized the respectability of the organizers and the temperance dinner. But despite the restrained character of the festivities, the *Philadelphia Gazette* had tried "to cast a slur" on the events by ridiculing the male participants as "waiters." Such a derogatory comment only hinted at simmering white hostility. Just two years earlier, a race riot had erupted in Philadelphia. It lasted for days and did considerable damage to black property. The same year an angry New York City mob wreaked its fury on both black people and their churches. Fueling racial enmity in these cities and elsewhere was a generalized opposition to abolitionism and its goal of immediate emancipation. Abolitionist speakers were threatened, and many Northern communities experienced antiabolitionist mob activity. In the 1830s, public parades of African Americans, especially if disorderly, had the real potential of triggering white violence while drunken and/or uninhibited revelers reinforced whites' negative stereotypes of blacks.[21]

Even sober celebrations could ignite violence. In 1842, a British West

Indies Emancipation Day celebration in Philadelphia included a procession of a temperance group of men and boys carrying banners. White youths interfered with the procession, and events soon escalated out of control. Rumors spread that one of the banners proclaimed "Liberty or Death" with the figure of a black man and a view of Saint Domingue engulfed in flames. The purported reference to the Haitian revolt and the imagined racial threat it implied helped to fan a riot and attacks on black property. While nonabolitionist newspapers did not approve of the riot, the *Boston Daily Times'* comment reveals what were probably widespread attitudes on the part of many Northern whites. Calling the African Americans "excitable and turbulent," the paper remarked that "the colored citizens of Philadelphia should know better than to make a public display of their anxiety to support . . . [abolitionists] and to court insults by ostentation and parade."[22]

There were thus practical reasons not to draw attention by rowdy or flamboyant behavior on public streets. The relatively small number of Northern free blacks and the prominent role children played in celebrations, suggests how vulnerable African Americans were in the midst of majority white communities. The emphasis in black newspaper accounts on the propriety and respectability of those planning the event and the public selection of a church as the meeting place were all part of an effort to attract the right sort of people to the right sort of event or to encourage the wrong sorts of people to adopt the right form of abolitionist activism. The elevated character of celebrations also reinforced the self-image of those blacks who struggled to maintain their dignity in a hostile racial environment.[23]

If showy public processions were best avoided, lavish refreshments were a feature of many celebrations. A feast suited a day of jubilation and was perhaps a special treat for those who rarely could indulge themselves. Like elite white dinners traditionally connected with mainstream holidays, the elaborate meal, especially if held in a hotel, may have also been a marker of status.[24]

While Garrison seemed to have been pleased by the array of meat, ducks, woodcocks, and pastries to which he was treated at such a dinner in 1839, the *Colored American's* editor condemned elaborate meals along with parades. He was not so much worried about white reactions as he was about limited community resources. The meal in Albany, New York, in a public house, wasted money that could better be spent on projects that would elevate blacks morally.[25] Far more praiseworthy were the one hundred plus who attended the "plain, economical, total abstinence dinner" in Cincinnati in 1838, or the all-female celebration, held probably in Philadelphia in 1836, that included only bread and water.[26]

Limited finances may well have also helped to curtail pageantry. New York's failure to hold its "usual" commemoration in 1839 and 1841 perhaps had less to do with lack of enthusiasm than money. The committee of arrangement in previous years ended up paying the lion's share of the celebration's expenses, an amount that probably few members of the black community could afford. The festivities that ultimately took place in 1841 were instead modest and cheap, with recitations from schoolchildren and addresses from a few "gentlemen."[27]

Within just a few years, however, the holiday was evolving into a more popular event in abolitionist circles. African Americans planned increasingly elaborate celebrations while white abolitionists began to hold public gatherings. Early white celebrations in Massachusetts were little more than ordinary antislavery meetings. In 1842, however, Boston abolitionists sponsored a picnic in Dedham that attracted about 3,000 people. Two years later, the Bucks County Anti-Slavery Society of Pennsylvania announced its intention to hold a mass meeting on August 1 in the woods near the Concord schoolhouse.[28]

Unlike the early festivities, these celebrations were designed to attract popular attention. Their goal was to inject "the cause of Freedom" with a "new impulse" by informing the ignorant of New World emancipation. As late as 1855, in the town of Adams in Jefferson County, New York, the day had never been observed. Those residents who did not take the papers had no idea why there should be any festivities on August 1. Frederick Douglass reported on his conversation with an old man who was impressed by all the bustle but assumed it was of interest only to the black community. " 'I hea's something was going to be, but had no idea of all this turn-out. It beats any thing I ever see—It gets ahead of the Fourth of July. Some of your great folks birthday you are going to keep I s'pose.' " When Douglass told the old man that the celebration represented the emancipation of some 800,000 former slaves, the man's jaw dropped in surprise. " *That's news to me, living away back in the country, I'd never found that out. Go it! I'll help you.* ' " A crowd of several thousand attended the festivities, most of whom were white.[29]

Predominantly white celebrations assumed their own character and purpose. Throngs of people, often arriving by train, gathered in small towns like Dedham or Hingham, Massachusetts, and processed through the streets of a friendly and tolerant white community to the grove selected for the major part of the day's activities. While the presence of black abolitionists was an important symbol of the biracial character of abolitionism, the majority of participants were white men and women. Their procession eschewed the "pomp and circumstance of military parades." At the 1844 parade in Hingham, fifty young women, dressed in white, with oak leaf wreathes in their hair, constituted the "Legion of Honor." Often organized in community delegations, marchers carried banners proudly displaying general abolitionist sentiments such as "Our fanaticism: all men are created equal," or "Immediate Emancipation, the duty of the master, and the right of the slave." The atmosphere was that of a holiday. In Hingham, bells rang out, the streets and even some stores had gay decorations.[30]

For the organizers, August 1 represented an opportunity to "muster . . . of all our antislavery forces." Divided over tactics in the 1840s, all abolitionists could agree to honor a day whose importance to the antislavery cause was becoming increasing clear "without distraction of sect or party." The gathering of abolitionists of all persuasions also offered an opportunity to display antislavery strength. Because it was important to attract large numbers to the event, both to make sure that those attending felt the movement was successful and to provide propaganda for newspaper reports, organizers encouraged abolitionists to "rally" as many to come to the event as possible. They chose easily accessible locations and sometimes were able to arrange and advertise in advance specially priced train tickets. The celebrations also offered an opportunity to recruit newcomers to the cause. A festive atmosphere and a bucolic location, as the *Liberator* explained, were vital components in luring outsiders to the antislavery event. "The novelty of the measure, and the mode of celebrating—the attractions of the blue sky, the overarching groves, 'God's first temple'—the processions, the addresses, may attract many who have held themselves aloof from the vulgar anti-slavery lecture."[31]

Every effort was made to create a sociable, colorful, and lively event. The collective procession that melded together abolitionists from various communities, the gay banners with their slogans, the march through friendly streets, set the festive and triumphant tone. Much of the day's sociability came from gathering in the grove. White women, who appear to have had a more prominent part in August 1 celebrations than their African American counterparts, played a key role in creating the convivial atmosphere. Ever "prompt and efficient," they decorated the grove and probably made most of the banners, first carried in the procession, then used to adorn the meeting place. Often the day was advertised as a "PIC NIC," so the holiday meal was important to the day's success. While those attending were often told to bring their own lunch, many celebrations also offered food for sale. Women took on the major responsibility of arranging the preparation and sale of delectables. So important was this aspect of the celebration that the handbill advertising the Liberty Party Convention to be held in the village of Arcade, New York, in 1844, highlighted the "EMANCIPATION DINNER." It was "to be served up in an adjacent Bower . . . under the supervision of the *Ladies*" who were making "preparations . . . for . . . hundreds." Beyond providing a tasty treat, the women also were raising money for the cause. As this handbill explained, Liberty Party organizers anticipated earning enough from the picnic to replace the usual collection.[32]

In his study of English political culture, James Vernon has pointed out that music helps attract crowds to a festive event and to maintain interest and attention. Music also helped popularize abolitionist themes. Along with men, women like Mary Jackman, Harriet Greene, Mary Gardner, Elizabeth Chandler, and Maria Weston Chapman wrote antislavery lyrics to popular tunes while others, like the "Misses Fuller," performed antislavery songs. And, although a majority of the speakers were men, white female orators like Lucy Stone, Abby Foster, and Nantucket's Anna Gardner addressed the crowds, as did black women like Sojourner Truth and Frances Harper. Interestingly, newspapers do not report these women, white or black, speaking at African American celebrations.[33]

The adoption of August 1 commemorations as a white abolitionist holiday suggests their recognition that British West Indies emancipation offered an increasingly powerful and realistic argument about the feasibility of emancipation. Perhaps this emphasis on practicality was connected to the rise of third parties intending to end slavery through the ballot box. Whether organizers made this connection or not, orators increasingly emphasized not just the fact of emancipation but its positive consequences. Americans had a misleading picture of postemancipation history, Frederick Douglass and others suggested, because the newspapers misinformed them. Papers announced that "The British Colonies are ruined," "The emancipated Negroes are lazy and won't work," and "Emancipation has been a failure."[34]

These characterizations, abolitionists insisted, were false. As early as 1840, some were drawing attention to the progress of schools and churches. As time passed, abolitionists accumulated more evidence to press upon "the attention of the American people." In 1852 a "pretty large" number of abolitionists, attending another picnic held outside of Philadelphia, heard about "the glorious results that have followed the breaking of the chains." Current events in the British West Indies proved "the practicality of emancipation" and undermined the passive acceptance of slavery by those who said that it just couldn't be helped. It was "folly" to try to justify American slavery, Chester Country abolitionists emphasized the following year. The process of emancipation was safe while the progress of the former slaves fulfilled all reasonable expectations. Addressing basic fears about emancipation at a Rochester celebration in 1853, white abolitionist Joseph Holley pointed out that former slaves had showed no interest in vengeance. Freedom had not resulted in a racial bloodbath in the British West Indies.[35]

Like other orators, Holley continued to remind his audience of the ironies of history. While resistance to Great Britain had prompted the Revolutionary-era leaders to proclaim that all men were created equal, Great Britain rather than the United States had acted upon this principle. Some speakers appealed to patriotism even as they praised Britain's achievements and listened to "God Save the Queen." Speaking at the Abington picnic in 1854, Thomas Higginson pointed out that Americans had had to borrow their "noblest day of freedom." But "I do not want to be an Englishman," he told the audience. "I was born in Massachusetts, and I wish to be a Massachusetts man and a freeman, at the same time. It is this that brings the tragedy home to us on days like this." Echoing this theme, a banner at the 1843 Dedham celebration posed the question: "Shall a Republic, which could not bear the bonds of a King, cradle a bondage which a King has abolished?"[36]

In the 1850s, events like the Fugitive Slave Law, the Kansas-Nebraska Act, civil war in Kansas, and the *Dred Scott* decision created new sympathy for abolitionism in general and offered compelling material for August 1 celebrations to exploit. A handbill advertising one August 1 celebration informed the public that on that day "the NEBRASKA INIQUITY" would be discussed and the "FUGITIVE SLAVE BILL" would "receive its deserts."[37] When Joseph Holley spoke of a huge cancer rotting away the nation's vital organs, Northerners could understand that the issue was no longer just slavery but attacks on northern freedoms. At the festivities in Salem, Ohio, in 1856, attended primarily by African Americans, most speeches dealt not with emancipation in the British West Indies but with current American events. Even nonabolitionist newspapers reported favorably on some of these meetings. Describing the "colored" celebration in Geneva, New York, in 1851, the Geneva Courier praised the "elaborate" speech on the Fugitive Slave law for its "learning, logical coherence, and masterly argument" and the speaker's delivery in "pure" and well-chosen English. The moving performance of a song entitled "The Appeal of the Fugitive" also met with the paper's approval. "The glistening tear in every eye, as that gentleman sang [the song] . . . showed that the bond of human brotherhood is divided by no mark of color."[38]

The new popularity of August 1 celebrations among white abolitionists did not spell the end of separate black festivities. The commitment to separation as a political strategy was and would continue to be one of the recurring strands of black protest. As Boston blacks explained in 1845, they chose not to join the country picnic because a city demonstration was necessary to remind citizens of the facts of emancipation. Their statement recognized the importance of changing attitudes in the very urban areas where most blacks lived and worked. In agreement with Boston blacks, Rochester's organizers hung banners along Main Street so that "the uninitiated" could learn "the *why* and *wherefore* of this gathering of freemen." An urban public expression of black activism also complemented the emphasis that African American abolitionists adopted in the 1840s to combat prejudice and segregation at the local and state level. In the 1850s, although the Fugitive Slave Act prompted many to flee to Canada, black abolitionists who remained in the United States adopted an increasingly aggressive stance. They planned elaborate events that signified determination to claim their place in the United States and proudly expressed an African American cultural identity.[39]

Because of the changing climate of opinion in the North, African American festivities sometimes drew biracial support. In Harrisville, Ohio, blacks called for the celebration, and a black man presided over it. The newspaper calculated that the crowd of citizens, who had come together "without regard to color," numbered about 2,000. It was the largest meeting ever held in the village. The very large New Bedford celebration of 1855 received money and assistance from white supporters, but blacks made all the arrangements, from securing the beautiful grove and erecting the stand for the chaplains, speakers, and musicians to ensuring a bountiful feast.[40]

The concern with propriety and decorum characterizing black celebrations of the 1830s persisted, but the motive was somewhat different. Now organizers wanted to attract public attention, and blacks would be on show. The "FIRST OF AUGUST will be celebrated by Colored Americans, while time shall last," *Frederick Douglass's Paper* announced. "Not with rum and rioting we trust, but in such a manner as shall shadow forth to the world and intelligent and grateful appreciation of the boon of liberty." Without direct evidence of the progress of emancipated slaves in the West Indies, the deportment and organizing skills of black Americans had to act as a proxy for the benefits and achievements of freedom there. Additionally, "the men and women and the children of every different shade and form of features, yet sufficiently sable to be identified with the [American] slave" symbolized what American slaves would become once freed.[41]

Accounts of complex and well-regulated festivities published in *Frederick Douglass's Paper* and in the *Liberator* reveal organizers' understanding of the importance of making a good impression on spectators and readers alike. Articles described orderly proceedings, well-attired crowds, and achievements of both former slaves and free persons. Arrangements to guard refreshment tables until time for the meal, a detail that strikes the modern reader as somewhat odd, demonstrated the organizing committee's determination to have a decorous feast. That some whites drew the correct conclusions from the arrangements and behavior of blacks is suggested in the *Geneva Courier*'s article about that community's 1851 celebration. The paper noted with approval "the entire good order and propriety" of the spirited events, and the "respectable" appearance of the crowd. The evening ball was just as it should be, "comfortable and quiet," and the entire event passed off in the best order. Echoing such approval was the comment of a New Bedford resident who remarked upon the "respectful procession" in that city in 1844 and praised "our colored citizens" "for their good morals and industrious and prudent habits."[42]

Colorful processions, balls, and other social events lent a distinctive character to African American celebrations. While white abolitionists favored good old-fashioned antislavery (pot luck) picnics, African Americans planned a variety of other sociable activities that strengthened communal bonds. New Bedford celebrants spent the afternoon making social calls, "a happy and profitable medium keeping bright these festivals of freedom." In Boston, African Americans met in a large hall in the evening for "a social interchange of thought and sentiments," including "some beautiful songs of Freedom . . . by a trio of juveniles . . . musical prodigies [who] excited hearty delight." Perhaps these sociable activities were particularly valued in a community in which men and women had little leisure time.[43]

At the Rochester jubilee, as the *Democrat* noted, "The evening was spent according to the various tastes of the colored folks." These tastes often included a catered meal and frequently a ball or, as in Springfield, Massachusetts, a dance on the grass. As Shane White has pointed out, dancing and music constituted the "most important forms of self-expression available to ordinary black men and women" and had been a feature of earlier black holiday celebrations. Although he suggested that dancing as a cultural form became detached from public African American rituals, dancing continued to play a part in many August 1 celebrations. Whether the dances had any relation to African traditions, African American popular culture, or class distinctions is not clear. The newspaper provided no details about the dancing on the grass in Springfield, but the outdoor frolic may have included dances popular among ordinary blacks. A mention of quadrilles and polkas performed at Boston's Colored Festival in 1859, however, and the praise white newspaper editors gave to well-managed balls hints at control, social polish, and aspiring middle-class performers.[44]

Parades now occupied a prominent and highly regarded place in African American celebrations. While white abolitionists processed through friendly streets in small towns and villages, blacks chose parade routes through city streets where in earlier times they had been attacked and insulted by hostile whites. The re-emergence of the public parade was pregnant with meaning for participants and onlookers alike. When, as in the case with parades in New Bedford, local blacks were joined by groups from elsewhere (in 1849, the visitors filled up almost two railroad cars), their presence suggested that the power and unity of northern blacks extended beyond the New Bedford's one thousand black residents. Marchers, welded into a harmonious whole, experienced a sense of camaraderie, collective racial pride, and, perhaps, relief when the crowd, often containing many white observers, signaled its approval. For the curious spectators, the good order and disciplined behavior demonstrated by the marchers conveyed (or was meant to convey) an obvious message about their social capacities as free people.[45]

The presiding marshal, as the parade's leading official, was under special scrutiny. His skill in coordinating people and groups provided evidence of the ability of black men to exercise authority. The emphasis in newspaper accounts on the marshal's manly qualities and skills suggests that at some level his performance was meant to undermine the common belief that black men were not true men and perhaps not even fully human. Perhaps it was also intended to call into question the abolitionists' sentimentalized and feminized depiction of the male slave.[46]

Black parades had a quasimilitary character that, in the early part of the century, whites and even some African Americans had ridiculed. Now the militarism was acceptable, staked out political and social claims to inclusion, and expressed growing black militance. Two private military "companies" played a prominent part in the 1855 New Bedford parade. One called itself the National Guards of Providence while the other had adopted designation of the Union Cadets of New Bedford. While neither company had any official status, their participation and chosen names highlighted their devotion to the Union and their demand for the U.S. citizenship that was the basis of military duty. Like elite white private militia companies that performed in mainstream civic parades, these smartly turned out units also were suggesting their superior fitness for the patriotic duty of defending the nation and its principles.[47]

As the decade progressed, parades and celebrations also suggested a defiant spirit within black communities. In Boston, attempts to secure state approval for a black militia grew out of the determination to defend fugitives and perhaps even to bear arms in a conflict against the South. Although the state refused to accede to African American demands, black Bostonians went ahead and formed the Massasoit guards in 1854. In the 1856 New Bedford celebration, the Independent Blues turned out with forty muskets, as did Philadelphia units a few years later. Beyond the threat of potential force, rhetoric also occasionally became fiery. In 1856, at the largely black celebration in Salem, Ohio, several speakers spoke in a spirit of violence and bloodshed and denounced the Union as meaningless to the slave.[48]

Because the participation of private military groups was loaded with symbolism, they attracted "much attention." Frederick Douglass's description of the New Bedford parade suggested the importance of the performance. Expressing a concern that seems to have been on his readers' minds, he posed the question: How did the military companies look and act? "Just like soldiers," he replied as he detailed their professional dexterity in marching, halting, wheeling, and handling their weapons.[49]

The new status of African American celebrations was evident in other ways as well. The procession in Adams, New York, that wound its way from the Presbyterian church to Jackson Hall was "escorted" by a white military company called the Northern Rangers. Douglass believed that this was the first time a white military company had overcome its "prejudice" to take part in an August 1 celebration. He could hardly contain his elation. "THE NORTHERN RANGERS, carrying with them the United States Flag, and heading the procession." Such recognition seemed to indicate the acceptance that black Americans had long been seeking. "Glory enough for one day!" commented the paper. "And our people marched as though they *felt* the glory."[50]

In communities with significant black populations, celebrations courted public attention. In Adams, a thirty-gun salute began the day. Banners flew. One New Bedford banner was "full of striking devices." "Broken fetters, riven chains," along with a freed slave reaching toward heaven in thanksgiving for his liberty, depicted a historical event that resonated with contemporary possibilities and meanings. As an account of an earlier New Bedford parade explained, "the spectators could not but perceive the significant fact, that those Americans identified by complexion with the freed men and women in the British isles were commending the glorious example to those who yet withhold the boon of liberty."[51]

Indications of the changing climate of public opinion and the aggressive stance adopted by many African American abolitionists are apparent the routes the parades took through cities and towns and the response of white residents and officials. Important civic spaces and important public thoroughfares were chosen, symbolizing the determination to have a public and political voice. In New York City, the parade marched through the "principal" streets, and, at City Hall, the mayor gave formal and official recognition of the proceedings as he reviewed the procession. Cincinnati marchers also passed through the city's most important streets as they headed for a steamer that would take them to a pleasant grove where they would spend the rest of the day. In New Bedford, the procession, made up primarily of blacks, started at City Hall. As it wound through the streets, "ladies and gentlemen" respectfully watched from windows and doors. At the grove, where the black preacher thanked God for the act of emancipation and implored his aid in bringing emancipation to American slaves, the audience, most of whom were white, included a former mayor of New Bedford (unnamed, but probably Rodney French, the city's Free Soil mayor in 1853–1854). As a New Bedford abolitionist reflected in his diary in 1856, the respectful behavior of whites offered a vivid contrast to the mobbing of the New England Abolitionist Society two decades earlier. "Here was a meeting called by colored men who alone occupied the platform, with a gratified audience of about a thousand people, a majority of whom were white and more than half women." [52]

As the case of New Bedford suggests, the study of August 1 commemorations reveals the changing status of abolitionism within Northern society. It also illustrates the ways in which abolitionists used their own history and that of emancipation in the British West Indies to create a festive culture that publicized events not known or ideas not shared by most white northerners. As Garrison had pointed out in 1838, most Americans hoped that British emancipation would prove a failure. They refused to "fire a single gun" or "hoist a single flag." Church bells remained silent. Abolitionists did all of these, and eventually some Northerners paid heed. [53]

The differences between celebrations planned by black and white abolitionists also point to variations in culture and priority between the races. For white abolitionists, the holidays offered another chance to make the general case for emancipation, to establish the biracial character of the reform, and to recruit newcomers to the cause. Emancipation in the British West Indies proved that this goal was feasible and practical, while the numbers gathered demonstrated abolitionist strength and staying power. As the Massachusetts Anti-Slavery Society bragged in its 1845 annual report, the celebration that year had drawn crowds "unsurpassed even by the gatherings of political parties." For blacks, denied many of the rights white abolitionists enjoyed, the day focused attention on what William Nell called the "oppression" of "colored citizens." [54]

Participation in the festivities allowed African Americans to become political actors and to proclaim their views on a number of pressing issues. Toasts offered in 1849 in Columbus, Ohio (and published in the local newspaper), commented on the slave trade in Washington, DC, the Mexican War, politicians, black leaders, and slave-holding Southern Christians, "legitimate heirs and faithful commissaries of Satan." During the Civil War, New Bedford residents continued to mark the day and passed resolutions declaring that it was impossible to ignore slavery as a cause of the war, that Lincoln must free the slaves, and that African Americans should enjoy the full rights of citizenship. Banners, speeches, and services served similar functions. At the same time, the rituals expressed the vigor of black cultural forms and social institutions. The move away from perhaps overdecorous commemoration to ones expressing a broader spectrum of black taste reveals a growing maturity in Northern free black communities, a more inclusive leadership, and the recognition of a culture that was African American. When Frederick Douglass described an 1859 celebration in Geneva, New York, he spoke of the "good nature and boisterous merriment of the colored people." While this behavior was not always entirely in "good taste," it was entirely in accord with a day that, like July Fourth, represented "freedom from ordinary restraints."[55]

Far from being just a holiday celebration, August 1 festivities were laden with meaning. They are a good example of the rich political culture created by abolitionists of both races who realized how the mixture of politics and pleasure could advance the cause of justice and freedom.

Print Culture and the Antislavery Community: The Poetry of Abolitionism, 1831–1860

Dickson D. Bruce Jr.

L ooking over the vast quantity of printed matter produced by the abolition movement, it is difficult not to be impressed by the enormous
amount of poetry written on behalf of the antislavery cause. Abolitionists
ranging from William Lloyd Garrison to Henry Highland Garnet wrote poetry. A few, including John Greenleaf Whittier and Frances Ellen Watkins,
contributed to the movement mainly, if not entirely, through poetry.

Poetry was everywhere. Virtually every abolitionist newspaper had its poetry corner offering original works, works borrowed from other abolitionist publications, and republications of classic pieces. Poetry was also
prominent in the gift books and annuals (such as the *Liberty Bell*) published to raise funds for the movement. Prominent poets, including Whittier and Henry Wadsworth Longfellow, created volumes of antislavery
verse, intended both to serve the cause and to raise money.[1]

Abolitionists often turned to poetry, moreover, while writing works of
prose, punctuating essays and addresses, even fugitive-slave autobiographies, with brief poetic extracts to illustrate a point. They wrote topical
poems to express their feelings about events ranging from the travails of
Anthony Burns to Daniel Webster's perfidious role in the Compromise of
1850. By their actions, many abolitionists indicated their agreement with
what Garrison wrote to introduce a topical piece published in an early
issue of the *Liberator:* "By presenting it as a poem, the story is made more
public."[2]

There is much to help account for the significance of poetry among
abolitionists. At the simplest level, the poetry that abolitionists wrote connected to a tradition of antislavery verse going back to the eighteenth century. Some of the classics of that tradition continued to appear in
abolitionist newspapers and elsewhere through the antebellum period,
helping to constitute something of an abolitionist literary canon. More im-

portant, however, there seems to have been a widely shared faith that poetry could make a difference in how people thought about slavery. Julie Roy Jeffrey has found that Eliza Earle, poet and activist, traced her abolitionist convictions to a childhood reading of William Cowper's famous late-eighteenth-century poem, "The Negro's Complaint." But many abolitionists, from Whittier in the 1830s to Charlotte Forten on the eve of the Civil War, expressed a faith in the power of poetry to attract people to the abolitionist cause.[3]

In addition, as I have argued elsewhere, the very writing of poetry was an important way in which abolitionists sought to build community. It was especially relevant to their efforts to foster an abolitionist community of gentility and "respectability"—one that, as James Brewer Stewart has discussed, would transcend a variety of socially inscribed lines, including those of color. Such an effort would have been in keeping with the way many people connected poetry and respectability, poetry and gentility. These connections significantly antedated, and endured beyond, abolitionism. Going back to the eighteenth century, at least, exchanging poetry had been an important way for men and women to express and reinforce social ties and social representations. Abolitionists, no less than others, continued the practice through the antebellum period.[4]

In the abolitionist press, poetry was given a visibility that enhanced its role in promoting and dramatizing the character of an antislavery community. When Garrison, for example, prior to an 1833 voyage to England, published a sonnet expressing his willingness to face death on behalf of his cause, Sarah Forten responded with a brief poem of her own, wishing him safety and success. Or when, a few months later, Forten herself wrote a long poem on the duties of women to abolitionism, several poets responded praising Forten, her poem, and her sentiments. Todd Gernes has documented a particularly extensive 1836 poetic conversation, conducted through the press, involving Forten, Angelina Grimké, and Eliza Earle. Similar exchanges continued to appear through the abolitionist era. Such efforts fit well within the larger framework of a genteel, respectable community in antebellum America. Publicized, they dramatized the significance of that framework for the movement as a whole, even as they reinforced the abolitionist effort, discussed in this volume by Julie Roy Jeffrey, to create a more inclusive version of the American public sphere.[5]

There was much about poetry that would have bolstered its role in creating such a refined representation of community and the public sphere. In the poetic exchanges, the answering of poem with poem created not simply a conversation, but a stylized interplay of poetic activity. However serious the ideas and concerns the poets expressed, the mutual pleasure all appear to have derived from engaging in the exchange is remarkable.

Such pleasure in poetry for poetry's sake was especially noticeable in the frequent appearance in abolitionist publications of ingenious acrostics. A form with ancient and classical roots, the acrostic had been popular in American print culture since the colonial period, but it was particularly well-suited to abolitionist purposes. In an acrostic, the first letters of each line, when read downward, form a word or, in many abolitionist examples, a name, as in this excerpt from an 1849 tribute to Frederick Douglass:

> D oubt not that the work will prosper—
> O nward with it! do not pause;
> U pward look when you are weary;
> G od will help so just a cause.
> L ook! the future smiles upon you,
> A dvancing come see freedom's band;
> S ee their number fast increasing—
> S oon they'll spread o'er all the land!

Suggesting the enjoyment to be derived from wordplay and the ingenuity required to meet the form's demands, acrostics show an interest in writing that goes beyond the simple conveying of ideas.[6]

Although it may seem odd to see playfulness in abolition, poetry inserted just that element. Again, this is not to detract from the serious intent of the movement, or even of its poetic efforts. Johan Huizinga noted long ago that the opposition of play to seriousness is false, an observation that anthropologists and psychologists have amply confirmed. But play does connote the presence of a community of people who know the rules and can use them creatively. In the case of poetry, this means assumptions made by a group of writers and readers who can understand and appreciate what poetic expression entails—who can appreciate, for example, the cleverness of an acrostic. Poetry thus would have taken on a unique role as a peculiarly self-conscious way in which abolitionists could construct what Jürgen Habermas has called a "communication community." The possibilities abolitionists saw in print for giving public shape to such a community would, again, do much to explain the prevalence of poetry corners, public poetic exchanges, and even such a print-dependent literary form as the acrostic in the abolitionist press.[7]

But an interest in poetry as such was no less important for the role it played in helping to shape the content of abolitionist verse. Abolitionists shared in what seems to have been, in antebellum America, a remarkable level of interest in poetry and the poetic process. Essays on poetics appeared in many places, from the works of literary critics to the popular magazines. The character of "the poet" was discussed, dissected, and celebrated in essays, stories, and poems. Moreover, while there were areas of debate and discussion in these antebellum writings on poetry, there was a surprising degree of consensus, as well. Poetry was to be distinguished by its moral purpose, by its role in the improvement of individuals and of society as a whole. William Ellery Channing's view that literature "is plainly among the most powerful methods of exalting the character of a nation" was widely shared, as was the view that the poet, as a man or woman of genius, should use poetic gifts for "the benefit of those who are less gifted." [8]

Guided by such thinking there was a critical consensus around the Romantic, Emersonian notion of a special connection between the poet and nature. Beauty is to be seen everywhere, critics said, and in everything; truth lies in the ability to see, feel, and to identify with nature. What makes the poet special is the ability to perceive and to communicate that beauty and truth. The task of the poet, one critic suggested, is "To draw together the most prominent beauties of nature, and show the passions of the soul in the most lively colors." Poetry, the writer continued, "heightens the pleasure, and makes what is plain appear almost enchanted." [9]

Along with this understanding of the poet's unique relationship with nature was a similar consensus emphasizing spontaneity and feeling as key sources for poetic power. A writer in the influential *Lady's Book,* John Q. Day, expressed this opinion in 1841 when he contrasted the work of poets, who "awaken in our souls those spontaneous emotions of joy, of veneration, and of love" with those whom he described as "formal moralists or philosophers" who "speculate and declaim, without much order, on man and his destiny." Julia Ward Howe, one of the most self-conscious of poets, echoed Day when she wrote, "Too little in us the Creative rules, / Wildly we war with precepts and with schools." [10]

Poetic language had a special power to convey to its reader truths that only intuition could supply. What Horace Bushnell said in 1849 of religious language—that its strength grew more from the fact that it was an "instrument of suggestion, than of absolute conveyance for thought"—was important when thinking of poetic language, as well. As one anonymous writer suggested, "We may take the dictionary in our hands and settle the definition of every word, and still know as little of the lofty conceptions of the author, as the weary traveler, who passes round in the farthest verge which is visible from the mountain, knows of the scenery which is seen from the summit." [11]

Abolitionist writers echoed such ideas in their own approaches to poetry, as when William Wells Brown, reflecting on James Whitfield's work, wrote that poetry "ennobles the sentiment, enlarges the affections, kindles the imagination," while giving enjoyment to life. They saw the connections between poetry and nature, and saw as essential to the poet's genius the

ability to see the extraordinary in the apparently ordinary. Thus, they celebrated the individual who could, as Lydia Child wrote, "rise into the infinite from the smallest earth-particle of the finite."[12]

Abolitionist writers were no less convinced than were other antebellum
critics that the power of poetry, including its moral power, lay in the feelings. Charlotte Forten said as much when, praising Elizabeth Barrett
Browning's poem "The Runaway Slave at Pilgrim's Point," she wrote, "It
seems no one could read this poem without having his sympathies roused
to the utmost on behalf of the oppressed." When an anonymous critic for
the *National Era* wrote that the language of poetry was "the language of the
soul and the affections," he summarized what most abolitionists had to say
about the power of poetry to change hearts, and minds.[13]

Such ideas about poetry had much to do with the kinds of poetry abolitionists wrote. They help to explain the key themes and motifs, and the
great variety of poetry written by abolitionists, and to give meaning to pat-
terns and juxtapositions that might otherwise appear insignificant. Finally,
they help to tie abolitionist poetry to the movement's larger purposes and
concerns.

Abolitionist poetry celebrated abolitionist leaders, the type of community abolitionists sought to create, and the movement's place in American
society and history. As they composed such celebrations, abolitionist poets
gave definition and significance to the community that poetic practice created, even as the abolitionist press helped them publicize such definitions
to a broader world. Such an effort was to be particularly visible in that body
of verse which celebrated the movement's leaders—Garrison, George
Thompson, Frederick Douglass.

John Greenleaf Whittier's 1832 poem "To William Lloyd Garrison" provides a good introduction to this work. Garrison was, Whittier wrote,
"Champion of those who groan beneath / Oppression's iron hand," standing "in the steadfast strength of truth." One could see his "spirit soar above
/ The cloud of human ill." Although acknowledging that Garrison had
been subject to the "slanderer's demon breath," Whittier encouraged him
to "Go on," though "The fate which sternly threatens there, / *Is glorious
martyrdom!*" It was only for Garrison to press on "with a *martyr's zeal*" until
he achieved his great reward: "The hour when man shall only kneel, / Before his Father—God."[14]

Similar themes and phrases recurred frequently in abolitionist poetry.
Sarah Forten's 1833 tribute to Garrison, on his way to carry the message of
abolitionism to England, celebrated him as the "Champion of the slave,"
unafraid of the perils his journey entailed, even as Garrison had described
himself as willing to face those perils for the sake of the cause. A few

months later, the popular poet Lydia Sigourney commemorated another antislavery pioneer, William Wilberforce, as "Afric's champion," one who had been "The lofty mind that never knew to swerve, / Though holy Truth should beckon it to meet / The frown of the embattled universe." In 1837, to return to Garrison, a poem in the *Colored American* praised him as "our noble champion," who "wilt go on, unbending / To Slavery's iron rod," urging him, "onward! noble martyr!" Such language was to remain current throughout abolitionism's history.[15]

The body of abolitionist poetry was constructed around a series of basic ideas framing these celebrations of heroism. These ideas defined the "martyrdom" heroes were willing to confront. They defined what it meant to be a "champion" of the slave. And they connected abolitionism to more general views and assumptions about history and morality.

When abolitionists poetically described what it meant to be a champion of the slave, they drew on several notions. One, noted by many historians, was a belief in the power of eloquence as a force in the battle against slavery. When Whittier paid tribute to Garrison, he specifically encouraged Garrison to continue speaking "As thou has ever spoken." In 1860, Frances Ellen Watkins paid tribute to Charles Sumner by declaring, "The lightning of thy lips has smote / The fetters of the slave." Speaking out against the sin of slavery was, as the poets defined it, the abolitionist's most significant role.[16]

Adapting the contemporary celebration of the poet, there was also a tendency to stress, along these lines, the poet's heroic role. James Russell Lowell, quoted in Douglass's *North Star,* once praised Whittier as one who had made "more public opinion, on the right side than any poet we can think of." Noting that no one more "deserved the title of poet," he added that Whittier had "fulfilled the truest vocation of the poet in this transition age by being in some sort the voice of one crying in the wilderness."[17]

Such words also pointed toward a common understanding of what made eloquence powerful. This understanding was captured in Lydia Sigourney's tribute to Wilberforce, emboldened by "holy Truth" to confront the "frown of the embattled universe." As images of a welcome martyrdom implied, abolitionism could draw strength and significance from its attachment to truth—often spelled, as Sigourney did it, with a capital "T". Eloquence was a weapon in the war against slavery because it was founded on truth.

This connection of abolitionism to truth was itself an important theme in abolitionist poetry. Abolitionist poets commonly linked truth to freedom and represented both as inseparable from the course of history. In 1838, Eliza Earle wrote:

> Truth shall prevail, and Freedom's light
>   Shall speed its onward course,
> Impeded by no human might,
>   Quelled by no human force.

Four years later, William W. Story, then a prominent legal scholar, contributed a sonnet to the *Liberty Bell* asserting that slavery might seem strong, "But Truth is Freedom, that all souls may own. / Falsehood shall not endure the high calm face / Of the free day—nor feel its stern rebukes."[18]

What supported the conjoining of truth, freedom, and destiny? For Frances Ellen Watkins it was the power of divine providence. She urged her colleagues on with the assurance that "in the darkest conflict / God is on the side of right." But no less crucial, as Story's sonnet was to show, was the force of nature. Freedom, he wrote, is the "birth-right nature gave." In a companion poem, Story also declared, "not surer stand / The fallen stars, that circle round the pole, / Than Truth and Justice in the immortal soul."[19]

Story—like Longfellow—was not entirely favorable toward the abolitionist movement. His poetic contributions to the *Liberty Bell* may have been a result of his friendship with Lydia Maria Child, as well as those with other prominent figures in the antislavery cause (just as Longfellow's antislavery poems owe much to his friendship with Charles Summer). But the motifs Story used appeared widely in abolitionist verse. The editor William Howard Day used them in 1856 for a short poem called "The Spirit of Liberty":

> It dwells among the mountains,
>   It lingers in the vale;
> 'Tis gurgled from the fountains,
>   It speaks in every gale.

Of liberty, he said, "All nature bears its impress," and that it spoke through "The voice of Nature's God."[20]

In terms of mid-nineteenth-century poetics, it is not difficult to see the significance of such verse. The evocations of nature, however frequent, were hardly empty, since, for many critics, the soul of poetry was the realization of nature's truths and beauty. Indeed, abolitionist poets frequently connected their cause to nature.

Abolitionist poetry further emphasized how important such connections were to people in the movement. But abolitionist poets did not confine themselves to writing about abolitionism. Many wrote the same kind of nature poems that appeared widely in nineteenth-century American magazines and newspapers. In 1848, for example, Henry Highland Garnet wrote:

> I love to hear the summer sigh,
>   When I am wandering in the dale,
> I love to see the clear blue sky,
>   When breathes the gale.

By writing such verse, Garnet and other abolitionist poets demonstrated the attraction that idealized images of "the poet" had for them, suggesting the extent to which they sought to understand themselves within the larger framework of connections involving nature, beauty, freedom, and truth.[21]

The ways in which abolitionist editors put poetry into print served much the same purpose. The "poetry corners" that appeared in abolitionist newspapers inevitably included not only poems about abolition but more generally focused verse celebrating nature, beauty, and truth. Poetry in gift books and other publications made the same kinds of juxtapositions. The result was to place abolitionist poetry, and abolitionism, within the larger context of antebellum American poetics, giving the movement profound connections with widely expressed ideals of poetic significance.

The connections forged between abolitionism and poetic ideas were far from insignificant. For one thing (in keeping with John Stauffer's discussion in this book of abolitionists' celebration of the imagination) they served to support the sense of community that the practice of poetry was meant to create. As Stauffer has shown, such abolitionists as Frederick Douglass could see the common humanity implied by the common power to imagine—a creative power that belied ordinary, arbitrary social distinctions. Both that power and its significance were tacitly asserted through black and white abolitionist poets' common evocations of nature and truth.[22]

Given the character of poetic ideals, such connections also served to emphasize and define a distinctive place for abolitionists relative to the rest of American society. The poetic appreciation for nature, in particular, resting as it did on unusual powers of perception and evocation, complemented poetic celebrations of abolitionist heroism by pointing to a community of writers and readers who could see beyond the things of this world and respond to nature's truth. Abolitionists' sense of their own distinctiveness, long noted by historians, was itself an important theme in abolitionist verse. As early as 1834, Margaretta Forten praised her co-workers as "Ye blessed few!" writing, "to ye shall still be given, / The choicest blessings of a glorious heaven."[23]

Abolitionist poets asserted the significance of distinctiveness in the many poems devoted to condemning American hypocrisy—the hypocrisy of those outside the abolitionist fold. That slavery exposed American hypocrisy and shortcomings was, of course, a theme that antedated American independence. The irony of a slaveholding republic with claims to having been founded on natural rights would, after all, have been difficult to miss. Such perceptions were particularly striking in a common—and "playful"—form of abolitionist poetry, the parody of patriotic verse. A widely reprinted 1838 example began,

> My country! 'tis of thee
> Dark land of slavery,
>   For thee I weep;
> Land where the slave has sighed;
> Land, where he toiled and died,
>   To serve a tyrant's pride—
> For thee I weep.

In 1848, the *North Star* published a "New Version of the Star Spangled Banner," by E.A. Atlee, asking, "Oh say, do ye hear, at the dawn's early light, / The shrieks of those Bondmen, whose blood is now streaming . . . ? " Should abolition not succeed, he wrote, "our Star Spangled Banner at half-mast shall wave, / O'er the death-bed of Freedom—the home of the slave." [24]

Despite the obviousness of the hypocrisy such poetry exposed, it is important to note the consistency of that poetry with more general purposes of abolitionist verse. As Wayne Booth has emphasized, a rhetoric that asserts the hypocrisy of others—as a rhetoric of irony—always privileges the perspicacity of those who use it. It is also a rhetoric of community, stressing common and distinctive knowledge and perceptions. Where that rhetoric moved over into parody and satire—as it often did—it further reinforced, by its playfulness, the kind of "poetic community" that the poetic enterprise was intended to create. [25]

The strongest poetic statement of the abolitionist community's distinctiveness was almost certainly the large body of verse devoted to racial equality. A number of historians have stressed the centrality of ideals of racial equality to abolitionism, and the movement's poetry tends to bear this out. Thus, having noted how "God gave to Afric's sons / A brow of sable dye," Lydia Sigourney wrote, " 'Tis the *complexion of the heart*" that matters. The biblical reminder that, as one poet rendered it, "of one blood / Has God created all / The nations He has spread abroad, / Upon this earthly ball" gave focus to a large amount of abolitionist verse. [26]

Such ideas also inform the many poetic tributes to great African Ameri-

can abolitionist leaders, especially Frederick Douglass. Perhaps no abolitionist was so widely celebrated, poetically, as Douglass. Evocations of his
life, career, and character captured a range of key themes in abolitionist
verse—courage, providence, eloquence, and American hypocrisy. An
1847 poem by a Philadelphian virtually summarized the case, celebrating
Douglass's courage and eloquence, while holding up Douglass as "evidence" of God's will "that men should equal rights maintain, / The rights
of freedom, brotherhood, and love." Douglass was everything an abolitionist hero should be, and compelling, living proof of the truth of racial egalitarianism, as well.[27]

In a body of verse in which celebrations of heroism loomed large, the
tributes to Douglass, or to such other figures as Henry Bibb and Charles
Lenox Remond, had a special place. As far as abolitionists were concerned,
such celebrations of African American contributions to the movement
were consistent with efforts, going back to the founding of the *Liberator,* to
create an interracial community united by common attributes and a common purpose. At the same time, for white abolitionists such poetry was also
of a piece with efforts to dramatize their own moral distinctiveness. It did
so by asserting and displaying their ability to recognize talent in men and
women across the color line, whom the rest of society viewed only in negative, stereotypical ways.[28]

But there was another aspect to these efforts that was also connected to
abolitionist ideas of truth. In one of his sonnets to freedom, William Story
not only tied truth to nature, but, using imagery drawn from nature, to the
inexorable processes of the human heart: "Nor canst thou dam that inward
sympathy," he wrote, "That tide-like swelleth ever in the breast." Whatever
else truth was connected to, its ultimate foundation, as Story's poem suggests, lay in empathy   in the ability of the soul to reach out and become
one with another.[29]

John Stauffer has emphasized the importance of empathy in understanding a range of abolitionist ideas and practices, something the works
of abolitionist poets strongly confirm. These poets portrayed empathy as,
more than anything, the attribute that could make one a champion of the
slave and a believer in racial equality. In a poem called "The Kneeling
Slave," Garrison wrote, "My heart is sad as I contemplate thee, / Thou fet-
tered victim of despotic sway; / Driven, like a senseless brute from day to
day." He concluded, "To rescue thee incessantly I'll plan, / And toil and
plead thy injuries to redress."[30]

Abolitionist poetry represented the movement's empathetic character
in a variety of ways, but the bulk of this poetry of empathy, as Garrison's
poem indicates, evoked the sorrows of the suffering slave. Among the most
significant themes in this sort of poetry was the anguish of the slave mother

as she contemplated—or experienced—the horrors slavery brought to that most basic of human ties, the relationship between mother and child. This poetry looked back to those traditions in antislavery literature that had emerged in the eighteenth century, traditions evoking the pangs of family separation, and poems telling, as Sarah Forten did in an early abolitionist piece, of a people "Torn from our home, our kindred, and our friends." During the abolitionist era, and in keeping with the period's more general celebration of motherhood and domesticity, the theme of separation came to be increasingly concentrated on the maternal anguish of a woman separated from her children.[31]

The number of such poems was large, but the themes were few. Whittier, in an 1838 poem, evoked the suffering of such a mother whose daughters were sold from Virginia "into Southern bondage":

There no mother's eye is near them,
There no mother's ear can hear them;
Never, when the torturing lash
Seams their back with many a gash,
Shall a mother's kindness bless them,
Or a mother's arms caress them.

In one of the most popular poems on this subject, Frances Ellen Watkins's "The Slave Mother," the theme of separation was portrayed through the setting of the auction block. As a boy is torn from his mother's embrace, she cries out in anguish, her "bitter shrieks" disturbing "the listening air." As Watkins wrote: "She is a mother, and her heart / Is breaking in despair." The maddening scene of the block, as even the slaveholder John Randolph of Roanoke had recognized so many years before, provided a dramatic setting in which a mother's pangs served, by themselves, to reveal slavery's brutality.[32]

Even apart from such anguished literary settings, however, maternal love could be evoked to give emotional reality to the movement's condemnation of slavery. The English abolitionist Edwin Chapman wrote his own version of "The Slave Mother," published in the *Liberty Bell,* dramatizing not the horror of separation, but, instead, a maternal despair produced by slavery itself. Speaking to her infant, "dark and drear / Appears thy future, though thou smilest now," Chapman's slave mother lamented. She asks, poignantly, "Wilt thou not curse the Slave that gave thee birth?"[33]

The gender dimensions of this poetry are certainly significant. Its images of maternal anguish relied heavily on concepts of motherhood infused with ideals of natural affection. Such ideals both shaped and were shaped by gender conventions from the first half of the nineteenth century. Abolitionists' understanding of the empathy these poems were intended to evoke had gender dimensions, as well. The suffering of slave mothers should take on special poignancy to free women who were mothers themselves, or so many abolitionists asserted. Sarah Forten made this case in a widely reprinted poem in 1836, a response to Angelina Grimké's *Appeal to the Christian Women of the South.* "Then, long as mothers' hearts are breaking / Beneath the hammer of the auctioneer," she wrote, "So long should woman's melting voice be heard, / In intercession strong and deep." Such words provided special imperatives for what Julie Roy Jeffrey, in her study of abolitionist women, has described as the unique role many believed they could play in the movement.[34]

Still, as Garrison's contemplation of the kneeling slave emphasizes, the evocation of the slave mother's anguish has to be seen as a subset of a larger body of empathetic poetry. Like Chapman's evocation of a slave mother's despair, it was also part of a larger body of verse giving voice to the despair endemic to slavery itself. An early example was Sarah Forten's much reprinted "The Grave of the Slave," first published in the *Liberator* in 1831 (and itself a gloss on George Moses Horton's "Slavery," which had appeared in *Freedom's Journal* in 1828). Forten's poem described the hardships of slave life, concluding resignedly, "The grave to the weary is welcome and blest; / And death, to the captive, is freedom and rest."[35]

Forten put her observations in the third person. Others turned to the voice of the slave to evoke similar anguish. In 1836, a poet who signed her work with the name "Josephine" had her speaker recount the joys of life in Africa before her enslavement and her desire now to go "to the climes of the blest, where my sorrows will cease, / Where my soul will find rest in the mansions of peace." Such evocations of despair would continue to find voice, putative or sympathetic, in the years to the coming of the Civil War.[36]

These poems, efforts to enter into the heart and mind of the slave, were themselves understood within the framework provided by intentions to create and express empathy. Discussing his own poems on slavery, Longfellow suggested that one of his key purposes was to counter more ridiculous representations of African Americans. He argued that, because of the prevalence of such representations, many people's "sympathies for the race are deadened." He hoped, through a fuller, more humane portrayal of the lives and, especially, of the feelings of enslaved men and women, to awaken those sympathies in his readers, "by gentle force soliciting' their hearts."[37]

At the same time, as Mark M. Smith has argued, the ability to hear and communicate the voices of slaves was often seen by abolitionists as further evidence of the moral sensibility that set the movement apart. Poetry was an important part of the process, since its language was believed to have a special power to communicate both feelings and an intuitive grasp of the other that prose could neither contain nor convey. Giving poetic voice to anguish was, thus, a way of both creating and demonstrating a degree of empathy, and an ability to listen, qualities that made the abolitionists unique.[38]

Given its main themes and purposes it is not difficult to see why abolitionists should have devoted so much time and allotted so much printed space to their poetry. What, however, can the poetry and poetics of abolitionism tell us about the movement itself? To a great extent, both seem to support the views of those historians who have seen in abolitionism one outcome of a larger search, on the part of many Americans, for a moral or spiritual anchor in the turbulent antebellum world. Although, as Paul Goodman noted, the motives behind such a quest could vary enormously among individuals—and it remains unclear why some Americans embarked on abolitionism's "spiritual journey" while others did not—the poetry, with its emphases on providence, truth, and nature, certainly supports such a perspective.[39]

Even within this framework, however, the poetry may have something more to tell us. As the common themes and purposes of the poems indicate, abolitionist poetry was not a place for carrying on debates over the movement's aims and tactics. Instead, the extent to which abolitionist poetry and poetics rapidly achieved stability and retained that stability for many years suggests that there was a widely shared set of expectations about what an abolitionist poem should be. Such conventional expectations could only have rested on no less widely shared assumptions underlying the representations of human nature and society the poetry portrayed. If so, the poetry would have represented a kind of common denominator of ideas and ideals for the movement as a whole.[40]

Such a reading supports Ronald Walter's suggestion that, despite the great divisions one can see in the history of the abolitionist movement, certain ideals and convictions were widely shared. The great amount of verse about the movement tells us that to be identified with abolitionism, to be a part of it, was important to its participants. So do the poetic techniques reflect the ideals of the abolitionist community and its distinctiveness: the poetic games (acrostics) and poetic exchanges that bound writers together and brought readers into the fold. At the same time, the poetry helps to pinpoint more specific aspects of what identifying with the movement must have meant.[41]

Abolitionist poetry, with its emphases on freedom, nature, and distinctiveness, tends to reinforce a picture of a movement that was, in essence, very "Emersonian"—and it is worth noting Lawrence Buell's suggestion that what one sees in Emerson is frequently an elaboration of widely held views. For abolitionists, as they linked their movement, and often themselves, to the ideals their poetry evoked, they signaled their ability to get beyond, as Emerson himself said, "popular standards" in order to approach "the region of absolute truth."[42]

If such a reading cannot explain why some people became abolitionists and others did not, it may at least help to explain why abolitionism had a special appeal for some—especially for those white abolitionists—who embarked on the kind of "spiritual journey" such historians as Walters, Goodman, and Robert Abzug described. For one thing, as the poetry of hypocrisy emphasized, nothing marked the gap between American professions of principle and American realities more than slavery and racial inequality. But, beyond that, in mid-nineteenth-century America, nothing marked a white American's freedom from "popular standards" more than an ability to feel deeply for those across the color line and to express that feeling openly. Where this involved sympathy for the suffering slave or the rejection of racial inequality, abolition provided a powerful way to prove, as Emerson demanded, that one could trust one's own intuitive sense of truth and virtue. Where it involved the representation of an imaginative community that acknowledged no boundaries of color, it no less clearly subordinated the superficial demands of daily life to the transcendent realities of inner selves. Hence, the centrality historians have seen in racial equality for abolitionism as a movement; and, accordingly, the ways in which a recognition of racial equality came to represent a kind of test for abolitionists, and, as they saw it, for white Americans generally. None of this is to deny the genuine empathy such people as Garrison, Whittier, Gerrit Smith, or Sarah and Angelina Grimké, felt across lines of color, nor the genuineness of the friendships black and white abolitionists made. But it is to suggest why those feelings and friendships took on the importance they did.[43]

But such a reading may also help to make more specific the significance of the abolitionists' response to the turbulent world of antebellum America. For many reasons, as Andrew Burstein, Mary Louise Kete, and others have shown, the antebellum period was marked by a heightened concern for what held society together. Issues of honesty and dishonesty in social relations, of the dangers of competitive individualism, of the fragility of social order in a democratizing society, came together in the minds of many Americans in ways that made them fear for themselves and their society. The abolitionists' poetry reveals, among other things, the extent to which they shared in the anxieties and responses to those anxieties that helped to shape the cultural and literary lives of many nineteenth-century Americans, at least outside the South. This was a response based on a vision of society held together by ties of mutual affection, community, and feeling.[44]

Poetry represented one way in which abolitionists, intentionally or not, realized that vision in themselves and made themselves an example for others. Through their poems and their poetic practices, they acted out the possibility for grounding American life in something better than the competition of individual interests or the possibilities of individual mobility within a corrupt system. In poetry abolitionists made tangible, if only on a modest scale, what that something might be.

13

Profits of Protest:
The Market Strategies of Sojourner Truth and Louisa May Alcott

Augusta Rohrbach

Striding along the Boston Common, Sojourner Truth's grandson, James Caldwell, took his place among the men that formed the famous first regiment of black troops, the Massachusetts 54th. His famous grandmother was nowhere to be seen. The day before, Louisa May Alcott had journeyed to Readville where she viewed the troops. In a journal entry for May 1863, she remarked, "saw the 54th colored Regiments . . . in town as they left for the South," concluding mildly, "enjoyed it very much."[1] Striking for its subdued tone, Alcott's comment registers the degree to which she accepted her role as spectator to this event. Having long struggled against her forced absence from the field of battle, by 1863 Alcott had found a more powerful tool than the sword. So, too, had Sojourner Truth.

Abolitionist culture, fostered by antislavery societies and their publications, gave rise to all manner of cultural production that, in turn, yielded a new and lively marketplace for ideas, goods, and services related to the cause. The careers of Truth and Alcott are two important products of the age, created out of the historical tension that was at the center of abolitionism: the need to make a living in a capitalist world without violating the evangelical morality of the mid-nineteenth century.[2] As Charles Sellers has observed, "Abolition burgeoned especially among people trying, like Garrison, to reconcile self-making egotism with ancestral altruism through the intense Christian piety of Finneyite benevolence."[3] Like Garrison, Louisa May Alcott and Sojourner Truth had an intense sense of civic duty, a goad to their productivity perhaps equal only to the pressure to earn a living.

Trading on race, gender, and class conventions, Alcott and Truth adapted themselves—and their messages—with uncanny skill to a marketplace that originated in the evangelical consumerism of the abolitionist movement.[4] Alcott and Truth used the persuasive tools of abolition—from stereotypes of plantation slavery to the genre of the slave narrative—as a means to promote their careers and, in turn, support themselves. Working a Northern, predominantly middle-class white readership through their publications, both women reached the same audience by very different methods.

In this essay, I explore the way Alcott and Truth took advantage of the confluence of forces that both advanced the cause of abolition and changed the course of literary history in the United States. Dubbed "an efficient writing machine" by literary critic Elaine Showalter, Alcott offers us one of the first models of a professional woman writer.[5] Leading what Ann Douglas has called "a double literary life," by writing popular children's literature under her own name while producing sensational potboilers under a pseudonym, Alcott's "full" career illustrates the way race, gender, and class circumscribed this white woman writer's publication choices.[6] Unlike Fanny Fern or Harriet Beecher Stowe, both of whom were enormously popular, Alcott dared to satisfy both her urge to write and her need to make a living by publishing outside the expected norms for the "children's friend" as she was advertised to readers. Her potboilers and sensational tales make way for an alternative identity—one freed from the limits imposed on her by the preconceptions that ruled the marketplace. Considered alongside the career of Sojourner Truth, Alcott's publication history can further illuminate both the limitations and the potential opportunities of race and gender as what we might call "marketing tools." Thus, though Alcott's career is a feature of my essay, it will not be my focus. Rather, I turn to Alcott only initially, training most of my attention on Sojourner Truth and her relationship to the marketplace. Alcott's publication practices provide a useful window onto the blurred boundaries between writing for money and working for reform as the nation lurched closer to civil war. Consequently, the comparison functions as a kind of lever with which we may open questions about the construction of public identity, the function of agency, and the paradoxes of capitalism as they figure across lines of race and class.

Though we can't be sure if these two dynamic figures ever met, we do know that they had much in common. In addition to their abolitionist views, both women were active in the women's rights movement, saw publication as a means to support themselves, and used their earnings to provide for themselves and their families. Yet, despite these shared interests and goals, deeply articulated race and class distinctions make a comparison between the two authors seem not only unlikely but even untenable.

Yet their experiences in the literary marketplace can function as a common denominator, offering a way to explore their identities as "authors." At the same time their use of writing as a means to make a living also raises a paradox of capitalism: How can one use the market and not be used by it?

It is precisely this question that interests me in my selection of these two figures. Alcott respected the publication conventions of her time; Truth adapted them to suit her purposes. A comparison of these two strategies will yield insight into the impact of race and class distinctions on the development of literary tastes during the Civil War era and beyond. Ultimately, I want to explore the various conventions these very unconventional women used during their lifetimes.

Louisa May Alcott's success was fueled by economic needs. Her transcendentalist father, Bronson Alcott, relied on his wife, Abba, and later his children to take care of their earthly needs while he attended to their spiritual ones. It wasn't long before Louisa May learned that her father, in her own words, "possess[ed] no gift for money making." By 1848, when Alcott was sixteen, her father's career failures had resulted in financial pressures on the entire family and all of their friends. Emerson and Hawthorne, both staunch supporters of Bronson's philosophical theories, often bailed the family out of tight financial straits.

After a series of jobs that included housekeeping, sewing, teaching, and even acting, Alcott cut her literary teeth in 1852 at age twenty with her first published poem, "Sunlight," in *Peterson's Magazine*. A few months later, she reached another important plateau by receiving payment for publication: "The Rival Painters" appeared in *The Olive Branch* alongside work by professional writers such as Fanny Fern among others. But she had yet to claim her identity as an author; these youthful works were not published under her name. Still shy and tentative, Alcott used either a sentimental pseudonym—Flora Fairfield—or simply her initials.[7] By 1854 she had published her first book, *Flower Fables,* and under her own name. The book was dedicated to Emerson's daughter, a gesture that is at once sentimental and strategic. Using her connections with the literary lights of her day could only help promote her career. So, too, did her connection to one of New England's most cherished causes: abolition.

Alcott was part of a new generation of writers who were born and bred abolitionists. So when, in 1859, for instance, she published "With a Rose that Bloomed on the Day of John Brown's Martyrdom" in Garrison's *Liberator,* her sentiments were both personal and deeply held. Her parents' house in Concord served as a refuge for the widow Brown and her young babe, a place where John Brown's portrait hung proudly in the parlor. As time went on, influential friends helped her publish in what were fast becoming the "intersecting networks of commercial and abolitionist press."[8] From then on Alcott wrote with a dual purpose: to satisfy her conscience and to make money.

But it wasn't until Alcott wrote the fictionalized memoir of her experiences in the Union Hotel Hospital in Washington, DC, that she felt the full flush of success. Called "Hospital Sketches" and first published in several issues of *The Commonwealth* in 1863, the series was praised by Henry James, among others. Through this accomplishment, Alcott attracted a publisher, an important turning point for the young author. According to an addendum to one of her 1863 diary entries, Alcott added in 1879, "Hospital Sketches" "never made much money, but showed me *'my style,'* and taking the hint I went where glory waited me."[9] The editors of *The Liberator, The Anti-Slavery Standard, The Boston Transcript, The New England Farmer,* and *The Wide World* all greeted "Hospital Sketches" with enthusiasm when it was published in book form.[10] Assured a market of evangelical abolitionist readers, Alcott knew how important it was to address topical concerns, riding the ideological wave of the times. And like her dedication of *Flower Fables* to Emerson's daughter, this book also had a sentimental link to contemporary culture indicated by the "Publisher's Announcement" printed on the fly leaf: "Besides paying the Author the usual copyright, the publisher has resolved to devote at least five cents for every copy sold to the support of orphans made fatherless or homeless by the war." While five cents may not seem like much in today's terms, it was five percent of the book's $1.25 sale price.

Using the first-person account currently in vogue with the slave narratives, Alcott signed her "letters" with the name "Tribulation Perriwinckle." And though her character declares herself an ardent abolitionist, her tales are laden with the racism typical of even the most radical abolitionists.[11] Referring to "a six years' old contraband" as "a little wooly head," modern readers recognize such details as part of a racist iconography. Focusing on what W.E.B. Du Bois later referred to as "the grosser differences of skin and hair," Alcott's characters seldom transcend the racist paradigm of the era. Rather than side with the blacks in the story, the narrator's sympathies are most poignantly expressed for the wounded soldiers. In this way, Alcott manages to preserve the customary racism while advancing the nationalist project of abolitionism. But perhaps more significantly, Alcott links her narrator with her readers. Just as they obtained the bulk of their war news from their sons, fathers, husbands and brothers at battle, Tribulation Perriwinckle learns of the war through her personal contact with the soldiers themselves. As a result, the young nurse is able, through her work on the ward, to gather accounts of battle "more graphic" than "any paid reporter could have given," thus likening her text to fact rather than fiction. Taking on a reporter-like role also implies a degree of public service and civic duty that further legitimizes this text as useful and worthy not only of publication, but of pay. Alcott declared at the age of fifteen, "I'll be rich and fa-

mous and happy before I die." She fulfilled her youthful ambition long before that.

Despite the praise she earned with her early writings, however, Alcott
longed to advance her career as well as her financial situation. Riding on
the serial success of "Hospital Sketches," she set her sights on *The Atlantic,*
and in the wake of the Emancipation Proclamation of 1863, she met her
goal with the abolitionist short story "My Contraband." Though the editors
insisted on retitling the story "The Brothers," *The Atlantic's* acceptance of
the story reflects the editors' assessment of the literary marketplace. Earlier attempts to publish in *The Atlantic* had been thwarted because her
views might, as Alcott later sniffed to a friend, "offend the South." [12] Abolition, once a local cause, had become a national crisis, one *The Atlantic*
wanted to capitalize on. Now, however, with the rush of interest prompted
by the Emancipation Proclamation, the gloves came off. Of course, the
magazine had already been caught up in the war: in 1861 it added an illustration of an American flag to its banner.

Using narrative strategies of a sentimental cast, with family and
romance at its center, the story focuses on two half brothers, one "white"
and one "black." Utilizing the device of the family torn asunder by race
that Mark Twain employed to great effect more than thirty years later in
Pudd'nhead Wilson (1894), Alcott doubles the double, depicting the black
character as divided himself. Looking at him from one side, Nurse Dane
observes that his "profile . . . possessed all the attributes of comeliness belonging to his mixed race" while the other side of his face is horribly
marred by a "ghastly wound that had laid open cheek and forehead." [13]
Clearly meant to illustrate the contrast between freedom and slavery as figured racially in white versus black features, Alcott's device, though clumsy,
would jibe completely with the prejudices held by her readership. But the
story itself takes a strong stand on the side of the freed slave and justifies his
rage against his former master and brother. By the end, the story grants
this character the peace of heaven and the promise of a spiritual reunion
with his wife.

The change in the title reflects the editor's political strategy. By calling
the story "The Brothers," *Atlantic* editor James Ticknor sought to emphasize the paradox of slavery as it played out along family lines. When asked
to reprint "Hospital Sketches," on the heels of her success with *Little
Women,* however, Alcott smuggled this controversial story into the volume
and restored its original title with a slight addendum: between the covers
of *Hospital Sketches and Camp and Fireside Stories* the story became "My Contraband; or, The Brothers." [14] Alcott's title, in contrast, calls attention to the
arbitrary and fickle nature of the law: once deemed a "slave" and now

termed "contraband," Robert is never in complete possession of himself. As the use of the possessive adjective "my" indicates, his identity is mapped and determined by those around him.

To emphasize Robert's manhood, Alcott has various characters of both sexes and races recognize his masculinity. He is the love object of a fellow slave whom he marries, a threat to the masculinity of his brother/master, and attractive to Nurse Dane herself. Appreciating his physical appearance, she admits that he is "strong-limbed and manly" with a face that "possessed all the attributes of comeliness belonging to his mixed race." But in addition to his physical demeanor, the contraband also has an air of enigma about him. Nurse Dane acknowledges that she felt "decidedly more interest in the black man than in the white" and thus helps to train her readers' attention on the "mysteries" that imbue his character.[15]

Alcott knows that Nurse Dane will astonish readers when she observes, "the captain was the gentleman in the world's eye, but the contraband was the gentleman in mine" so she has her explain, "I was a fanatic, and that accounts for such depravity of taste, I hope." Meanwhile, she clearly expects readers to share Dane's perspective as the story unfolds. Robert's past is not so mysterious and Miss Dane's judgment is not so strange. Like many slaves, he is tormented by the abuses of slavery, many of which are sexual. The child of an illicit union between master and female slave, he is now the property of his half brother. Worse than that, his half brother, who lays dying and in the care of Nurse Dane, has raped Robert's wife and ultimately caused her death through his atrocious behavior. Unable to live with the shame and fear of a possible repeat performance, Lucy, Robert's wife, killed herself. As son of his master and sibling to the dying man who violated his wife, Robert has endured all of slavery's injustices.

Rejoicing in 1868 that she had "lived in the time of this great movement, and known its heroes so well," Alcott made her affinity for the causes of the time central to her work, but not to the detriment of her popularity.[16] Stories as virulent as "My Contraband" are unusual. Typically, when Alcott did write in strident tones against social norms—in works such as "Behind a Mask" for instance—she tended to adopt a pseudonym or publish anonymously. No one delighted in her marketability as much as Alcott herself. Conspiring with editors and publishers to place as many stories as she could manage to write, she actively manipulated her work to fit various venues so as to earn as much as possible. The year that "Hospital Sketches" came out, Alcott noted in her journal that she made $600 from it and a variety of other writing projects.[17] But in order to make this kind of money, Alcott had to adapt herself to the market. As Madeline Stern observed of Alcott's post–*Hospital Sketches* success, "Between realistic hospital sketches and blood-and-thunder narratives, she alternated, glad to supply the requests of her publishers, attempting all types of stories."[18] The variety of her writing projects and publishing venues are sometimes called "conflicting literary impulses" by critics.[19] In light of her participation in several different mutually exclusive niche markets, however, we might see her choice to publish broadly—if sometimes anonymously—as a strategic way to maintain control over her productive energies and play the market against itself. What might otherwise seem as competing markets thus became complementary as long as Alcott maintained power over her identity. Her use of pseudonyms allowed Alcott to preserve a degree of agency over her writerly activities that would otherwise have been denied to her. She chose alternative identities in order to protect her lucrative market niche as "the children's friend."

And it wasn't just Alcott who was sensitive to the impact of public opinion on her literary reputation. When she had penned an especially lurid tale called "A Modern Mephistopheles," her editor found a place for it through a new marketing tool he invented to profit from celebrity while also protecting reputations. Placing it in what he called his "No Name Series"—anonymously written books by prominent authors—he capitalized doubly on her fame as a children's writer and the possibility that she could have written such an unsavory tale, offering the plausibility of her as author without fully paying the price that owner/authorship of the tale would cost.[20]

After reminding her that they spent ample funds on national advertising for her books, her publishers used royalty payments as a way to shore up Alcott's confidence when she became dismayed about her prospects. Writing to her in 1870, her publisher Thomas Niles reassured Alcott of her success: "I do not now think of any author, male or female, in these United States who can congratulate him or herself on any like experience [in their accounts]. The amount due you $6212.00 I shall pay over . . ."[21] From time to time, Niles would invoke an ever more explicit comparison with other well-known authors, providing her with confidential information on Stowe's earnings, for instance: "We do not pay Mrs. Stowe as much as we pay you, nor do we pay any other more than we pay Mrs. Stowe, and I suppose there is no living American author who can command more than Mrs. Stowe today."[22] Despite all these reassurances, however, Alcott continued to dog Niles for a higher royalty rate. He answered her firmly:

> You have had publishers who have failed to make a market for your books—you might find them still. Any publisher would undoubtedly be glad to give you more today; publishers are "grasping" as well as authors and an author of a successful book is a prize to be secured. But you, I am quite sure, without ample reason, would never desert

those who both by their brains and their money have helped you to achieve the position you hold today.[23]

In later years, he rewarded her loyalty to the firm with a 12 percent royalty instead of the usual 10 percent. Her constant pressure to raise the rate of remuneration finally paid off. However, her rising place in the market had its price.

Alcott critically—if not as openly—questioned gender norms and stereotypes in her fiction. Despite her privileged status as a white woman writer, depending on her reputation as "the children's friend" limited her ability to voice these opinions publicly. Writing from "behind a mask"—to borrow a title from one of the sensational stories she published pseudonymously—she did find a way to express her anger over the strictures of ladyhood, particularly as they cut across boundaries of class and age.

The heroine of "Behind a Mask," an aging woman who must find a means to make a living in a society that prefers young, unmarried, educated girls, masquerades as a youthful governess. A former actress, she uses her theatrical experience to dupe an unsuspecting family into taking her in and giving her a job. Blinded by their own prejudices, the characters in the story are not privy to the view of "Miss Jean Muir" that we are given. Playing the meek, young woman to each male in the family, Miss Muir manages to establish herself as a love interest with every one of them. Although she plays at being naïve and demure, readers quickly learn that she is a bitter and angry woman "worn out with weariness and pain." Alcott's use of "double vision" in this story encourages readers to see how foolish the family's expectations are and how easily norms and conventions can be perverted for other means. By the end of the story, the lowly actress-playing-governess takes over the house by marrying the heir, leaving the family in shambles. Never daring to publish this story under her own name, we know it to be hers only due to the literary detective work of Madeline Stern.

Alcott's use of anonymous and pseudonymous publication shows us how she sought to use the marketplace and yet not be limited by it. It is also suggestive of her need to protect her status as a white genteel woman. Ironically, as a result of her identity she found herself limited by her own success. For different reasons and in different ways, so would Sojourner Truth. Most people know Sojourner Truth as the African American former slave who, as Jean Fagen Yellin has observed, "proposed a redefinition of womanhood based on her own experience" as immortalized in her question: "Ar'n't I a Woman?"[24] This question "transformed the formal antislavery inquiry encircling the abolitionist—Am I a Woman and a Sister?" into a revolutionary chorus.

Born Isabella Van Wagener, in about 1797, Truth's first language was Dutch—not the Southern dialect that many have associated with her. She spent her years in slavery in upstate New York, not on a plantation as many assume. Her *Narrative,* published in 1850, tells of her experiences in slavery and of how, in 1837, she left her master and moved to New York to begin a life with nothing more than a peerless faith in pentecostal religion and her own charisma. Six years later she reinvented herself and took the name "Sojourner Truth," the moniker that became her trademark. It was as Sojourner Truth that the public came to know her as an outspoken and striking figure in abolitionist and women's rights circles.

Sojourner Truth may not have been a writer, and nor did she have the support of the publishing world of Boston as Alcott did, but she did have a keen sense of the publishing market and used it to her advantage. Inspired by Frederick Douglass's success in 1845 with his first narrative, Truth began dictating her life story to Olive Gilbert, a white woman we know little about beyond the fact that she collaborated with Truth on this project.[25] Like Douglass's narrative, Truth's enjoyed brisk sales through many editions. After its 1850 publication, Truth purchased her first house by obtaining, and later paying off, a mortgage with profits from book sales.[26]

Unlike Douglass, however, Truth chose to shoulder all the costs of publication herself so that she could control not just the copyright of her book, but also the physical plates from which the book was made. Owning the stereotype plates meant controlling how many editions were printed. Up through 1820, authors lost control of their works when they did not own the plates, because publishers could sell copies of the plates to other printers, who then made and sold additional copies of the book without compensating the author. In the period after Washington Irving and James Fenimore Cooper, authors began to purchase the plates with the profits of the first printing of their works, if they could afford to do so. By owning the plates, authors could license the right to print the book as well as negotiate for the degree of profit from the sales.[27]

In this respect, Truth departs in another way from Douglass's approach to the marketplace. Instead of pricing her book at the going rate of $.75 to $1.25, she sold the volume for a mere $.25. She believed—as did Longfellow—that in the long run a cheap book circulates more widely and does more for an author than the short-term cash income a higher price would generate. She even admonished Garrison, who was acting as a liaison between Truth and the printer Yerrington, not to send bound volumes, stating plainly, "I can't sell the bound volumes."[28] In addition to maintaining control over production costs, her ownership of the plates reduced the risk of piracy—something many writers fell victim to in the mid-nineteenth century.

Yet perhaps the most radical aspect of Sojourner Truth's career is her relation to writing itself. Though a successful "author," she remained illiterate throughout her life. Believing that literacy might somehow corrupt her own natural talent, she is known to have ridiculed Frederick Douglass for his ardent pursuit of literacy. Indeed, one might say she out-Douglassed Douglass.[29] By remaining illiterate while also being a published "author," she retained all the markers of slavery while also claiming her freedom from it.

To understand this seeming paradox, we might first turn to the *Narrative* itself. There, Olive Gilbert relates an early experience Sojourner Truth had in the world of capital and free labor. Truth was given fifty cents to hire someone to shovel snow. Rather than broker the job to someone poorer than herself as the employer intended, Truth did the job she was asked to farm out. She did not take pride in earning what Louisa May Alcott may have called "head money." Though Truth pocketed all of the money (otherwise she would have had only a percentage as a broker's fee), she felt she had to explain that she was just as poor as those around her and that she might as well do the work and keep the money for herself. Protecting her against possible criticism and using this story to describe her spiritual development, the *Narrative* explains:

> this insensibility to the claims of human brotherhood, and the wants of the destitute and wretched poor, she now saw, as she never had done before, to be unfeeling, selfish, and wicked. These reflections and convictions gave rise to a sudden revulsion of feeling in the heart of Isabella, and she began to look upon money and property with great indifference, if not contempt—*being at that time unable, probably, to discern any difference between a miserly grasping at and hoarding of money and means, and a true sense of the good things of this life for one's own comfort, and the relief of such as she might be enabled to befriend and assist.*[30] [Emphasis mine.]

It would take Sojourner Truth some time to find a way to fit capitalism into her evangelical agenda—as it was for many important figures of the day. But even she finally found a way to reconcile capitalism to suit her needs. Distinguishing between wealth ("a miserly grasping at and hoarding of money and means"), wages ("and a true sense of the good things of this life for one's own comfort") and charity ("the relief of such as she might be enabled to befriend and assist") in this passage, Truth's choice is to take the full wage, getting paid for both "head" and "body" work. This episode shows her willingness to value intellectual work as property and worthy of a wage. It is also an important act of resistance; she refuses to be defined by others. Her continued defiance can be traced through the publication (and republication) of the *Narrative.*

In her *Narrative,* Sojourner Truth resists significant features of the slave narrative form and the ideals that the form upheld, most notably, the idea of literacy as a gateway to freedom, and the categorical condemnation of all slaveholders. Truth ends her narrative with a homage to her former master for recognizing that slavery was evil; she rejoices in this as evidence of his saved soul. In a decidedly evangelical ending, Truth values her religious beliefs over the ethics that inform the slave narrative genre.[31] Her resistance to follow the literary conventions of the slave narratives bears on another one of Truth's unconventional choices: her decision to remain illiterate. Preferring religion over politics and orality over the written word, Truth's choices provide us with an understanding of a bigger issue— Truth's philosophy of language.

Sojourner Truth did not shun the written word, she simply preferred not to read or write it herself. Through the help of others, she exchanged letters with friends and associates and enjoyed listening to people read aloud. In her preference for the spoken word, Sojourner Truth shows her anxiety over the way written language accumulates meaning. Insisting that children read to her from the Bible, she routinely turned down offers to read to her made by adults, wanting to preserve the biblical passages in some idyllic and imaginary state. Her reasoning was simple: adults had a tendency to intermingle "ideas and suppositions of their own" with the sacred text as they read. These more mature readers threaten the authority of the text and risk distorting it. The *Narrative* uses this example as "one among the many proofs of her energy and independence of character," but it also works well as evidence of her philosophy of language and its attendant narrative theory.[32] Truth seems to believe that text is negotiated through the reader; the act of reading becomes a form of response that shapes the text in uncontrollable ways. A text risks misapprehension in a way that speech, for Truth, doesn't. In speech she has the power to negotiate and renegotiate with her audience to achieve her goal.

Throughout her career, she published *as a speaker,* and emphasized the spoken word over the written, what we call today in the language of deconstruction: presence over absence. Readers would encounter another of Truth's important publishing innovations as they opened her book. Prominently placed on the green paper cover of the first edition of the *Narrative* are the words, "WITH A PORTRAIT."

For several reasons, it is fitting that Truth's *Narrative* is preceded by a picture of the author. The portrait reinforces Truth's own position on the politics of the word by making herself present and visible. In addition, as Olive Gilbert writes in *The Narrative:* "The impressions made by Isabella on her

NARRATIVE

OF

SOJOURNER TRUTH,

NORTHERN SLAVE,

EMANCIPATED FROM BODILY SERVITUDE BY THE STATE OF

NEW YORK, IN 1828.

WITH A PORTRAIT.

'SWEET is the virgin honey, though the wild bee store it in a reed;
And bright the jewelled band that circleth an Ethiop's arm;
Pure are the grains of gold in the turbid stream of the Ganges;
And fair the living flowers that spring from the dull cold sod.
Wherefore, thou gentle student, bei'd thine ear to my speech,
For I also am as thou art; our hearts can commune together;
To meanest matters will I stoop, for mean is the lot of mortal;
I will rise to noblest themes, for the soul hath a heritage of glory.'

BOSTON:
PRINTED FOR THE AUTHOR:
1850.

Cover of the first edition, 1850, of the *Narrative of Sojourner Truth.* (Source: Houghton Library, Harvard University) auditors, when moved to lofty or deep feeling, can never be transmitted to paper." Words, when printed, as this passage explains nicely, cannot render Sojourner Truth's message sufficiently. Her text is more than mere language. Rather, *The Narrative* goes on to say, in order to "read" Truth, language must be transformed by some "Daguerrian art" in order "to transfer the look, the gesture, the tones of voice, in connection with the quaint, yet fit expressions used, and the spirit-stirring animation that, at such a time, pervades all she says."[33] Thus, greeting her readers through a portrait at the start of the narrative of her life, Sojourner makes her presence felt to readers.

Yet the portrait of the author—like the slave narrative itself—is also deeply part of the capitalistic culture of the book. A common feature of book publication in the mid-nineteenth century, six out of ten slave narratives published in the United States between 1845 and 1870 provided a portrait of the author in a frontispiece.[34] These portraits served two important functions. First, they offered proof that the author was real and indisputably black.[35] In that sense, the portrait of the author functions as a central textual element—one used to produce the black body with the

SOJOURNER TRUTH.

This engraving purports to come from a photograph of Truth as Isabella, though no such photograph was ever taken. This drawing, by an unknown artist, is from imagination and appears in all editions of the *Narrative of Sojourner Truth*. (Source: Houghton Library, Harvard University)

black text, as Robert Stepto has argued.[36] But, at the same time, such portraits also help heighten the effect of what I call "humanitarian realism" by
invoking the physical body of the author.[37] Locating the author as a physical body helps foster the reader's empathy with her story. In order to be
successful, such texts must identify the author as a subject whose suffering
is not just plausible (as in the fictional setting) but *real.*

The author portrait serves another important function: to identify and
mark the former slave as author. Such portraits contextualize the writer in
the tradition of writers whose images—from Byron's famous open-collared
portrait on—pressed upon the volume the seal of authorship. Thus the necessity of the portrait to verify the writer's racial status also conferred the
status of authorship that was typically reserved for more celebrated figures
such as Lowell, Longfellow, and Stowe, whose portraits were sold separately and as accompaniments to their works. With this background in
mind, let us return to the author portrait of Sojourner Truth.

Looking closely at the portrait, we see that Truth's use of iconography is
striking. The white head wrap, for instance, became such a characteristic
part of her image that almost every description of her makes mention of
it.[38] Through this article of clothing, Truth references her African past and
therefore, in the American literary context of the day, she also calls attention to her connection to slavery. And it was precisely this connection that
made the biggest difference in her market appeal. In fact, most descriptions of Truth made use of another icon of slavery: Southern dialect, an
issue I will revisit more fully later in this essay. What's important to observe
now, however, is that though Truth was aware that many who transcribed
her speech often gave her voice a Southern twang, she never sought to correct this either in her own speeches or in her publications. This is especially fascinating because Truth was not afraid to fight to correct wrongs.
Aside from her public participation in abolitionist and women's rights
movements, thrice in her life she took discrepancies to the courts—on one
occasion, in 1835, bringing suit against two white people for libel and winning $125 in damages.[39] Rather than correct inaccurate representations of
her accent, Truth promoted and preserved the association with Southern
plantation slavery, as it was in her best interest marketwise. Coded references to the South, either through apparel or diction, identified her as a
former slave and located slavery in the South. Thus, despite the fact that
she was, as her book's title page proclaims, "a Northern Slave," she, unlike
her Southern counterparts, was emancipated by the state while Southern
slaves remained in bondage. Through this kind of complex negotiation of
the markers of slavery, she avoided offending the Northern abolitionists
who were her readers.

Her republication of the 1850 *Narrative* provides another way to track

Sojourner Truth's courting of the marketplace as she sought to establish herself within the constructs of authorship. After hiring Garrison's printer to issue the book, Truth, not surprisingly, asked Garrison to write a new introduction. As she was preparing to bring out this new edition, however, she rejected Garrison's introduction in favor of one that would align her more closely with the literary world. In 1853 she traveled to Andover and got the seal of approval necessary to boost sales and link her to the literary world—an introductory note from Harriet Beecher Stowe.[40] In Stowe's description of the book as "more remarkable and interesting than many narratives of the kind which have abounded in late years," Stowe firmly situates Truth's *Narrative* as competitive within a larger marketplace.[41]

For perhaps a more a direct view of Sojourner Truth's approach to the marketplace we might look at her use of another popular trend in publicity. Though many authors utilized the *carte de visite* as a way to make money, Truth put her own mark on the form. By appending what we might call an advertising slogan, "I sell the shadow to support the substance," Truth encourages additional sales by making her need for financial support known through this textual addendum. As with so many of her actions, her adaptation of this popular form of fundraising bears her own distinct mark—indicating a level of engagement with the marketplace that has not registered with scholars.

We know of no fewer than seven separate versions of this photograph, suggesting a degree of intentional craft and artful manipulation that might be masked by what may otherwise seem a stereotypical portrait of the era. Indeed, part of Sojourner Truth's success had to do with her use of various conventions to ensure success. This photo places Truth behind the mask of evangelical white ladyhood—the Quaker cap, the shawl, the flowers, the knitting and the open book. Posing as one of "them," she uses these objects to trade on the gender norms of nineteenth-century domesticity and establishes an alliance with the white, evangelical, middle-class readers who were her targeted customers.

One of the last editions of the *Narrative* on which Truth collaborated before her death is further evidence of Truth's relationship to the market. To that 1875 edition, Truth, with the help of Frances Titus, a new partner in the project, appended a section called "Book of Life," an assembly of materials that "celebrate" Truth. Included is a piece by Harriet Beecher Stowe called "Sojourner Truth: The Libyan Sibyl," originally published in *The Atlantic* in 1863—the same year of the Emancipation Proclamation. Reams of material appeared on slaves and on Sojourner Truth in particular in 1863 in response to this piece of legislation. Of course, Stowe's article would be especially interesting to Truth for other reasons. Not only did Stowe write it, but she published it in one of the most important venues in

I Sell the Shadow to Support the Substance.

SOJOURNER TRUTH.

Sojourner Truth (c. 1797–1883) in an 1864 photograph by an unknown artist. (Source: National Portrait Gallery, Smithsonian Institution)

the U.S. at the time: *The Atlantic Monthly*. Clearly, Truth was proud of the prominence that this piece achieved upon initial publication and thus reprinted it in her own "Book of Life."

But there was something very peculiar about this piece that might have argued against its inclusion—certainly in something she was calling her "Book of Life." Stowe spoke of Sojourner Truth in the past tense, memorializing her with the remark, "though Sojourner Truth has passed away from us as a wave of sea, her memory still lives." Rather than correct this implication of death, even when the "Libyan Sibyl" piece was appended to a later edition of her narrative, Sojourner seems to be using it to capitalize on her transformation from famous to legendary—indeed, this is the Sojourner Truth we know today.

Finally, we might take a look at the 1851 speech that made Sojourner Truth famous and became a clarion call for feminism both then and now. As transcribed by Marius Robinson, the speech appeared in the *Anti-Slavery Bugle* of June 21, 1851, less than a month after it was delivered at the Woman's Rights Convention in Akron, Ohio. Three important features of the speech stand out. First and foremost, Sojourner Truth never asks "Ar'n't I a Woman?"—the question that has made her famous. Putting aside the question of authorship and treating the speech as we would any other literary document, the absence of this remark is notable. Lacking the rhetorical power provided by that resounding question, this speech proceeds with a cool reserve, beginning with Truth's somewhat demure request to speak: "May I say a few words?"

Also remarkable are Truth's biblical references. Though, as she declares to her listeners with quiet pride, "I can't read but I can hear," she goes on to discuss several biblical passages.[42] For instance, Truth turns to the story of Martha, Mary, and Lazarus, the man whom Christ raises from the dead. Her selection of biblical text demonstrates her ability to use text to fit her purposes precisely. Typically, this passage is used either as an instance of resurrection or as an example of how women can be pitted against each other. As Truth uses it here, we see why feminist theologians have claimed Truth as a forerunner. Her rendering treats Mary and Martha as united by gender, focusing not on their differences but on how Christ took them seriously and granted their request.

Finally, the language itself has a special quality. It is not quite formal—the presence of contractions, for instance, suggests the spoken rather than the written word. Yet, though the language is colloquial, it is not dialect. Linking this speech with the *carte de visite* provides us with further insight. This portrait, like the earlier version of the speech, makes use of the conventions of white ladyhood. Demurely posed with knitting and shawl, the Sojourner Truth of the 1851 speech asks permission to speak and waits without comment until it is granted. Her language, too, is polite even if it is somewhat colloquial. But her message, like her gaze, remains straightforward and direct.

A later and more popular version of this speech has less in common with the ladylike portrait and the 1851 text. This version was "transcribed" by Frances Dana Gage, a women's rights activist and chair of the Ohio meeting where Truth spoke. More than ten years after it was delivered, Gage published the speech in the *New York Independent* on April 23, 1863, in part as a response to Harriet Beecher Stowe's "Libyan Sibyl" article, which had appeared in *The Atlantic* that same month.

An important feature of Gage's version are the "stage directions" that she supplies. These editorial intrusions give Gage an important role in shaping the reader's interpretation of Truth's performance. Heightening Truth's ability to mesmerize an audience, Gage dramatically sets the stage:

> Slowly from her seat in the corner rose Sojourner Truth, who, till now, had scarcely lifted her head. "Don't let her speak!" gasped half a dozen in my ear. She moved slowly and solemnly to the front, laid her old bonnet at her feet, and turned her great, sparkling eyes to me. There was a hissing sound of disappropriation above and below. I rose and announced, "Sojourner Truth," and begged the audience to keep silent for a few moments. The tumult subsided at once, and every eye was fixed on this almost Amazon form, which stood nearly six feet high, head erect, and eye piercing the upper air, like one in a dream. At her first word, there was a profound hush.

Throughout the speech Gage continues to shape reader response with editorial comments like these and skews the text in a noticeably theatrical way.

The diction of the speech, in contrast to the earlier version, is noteworthy; this speaker uses a crude form of Southern dialect. Yet Truth was not from the South. She spent her slavery years in upstate New York and her first language was Dutch. Thus, the use of Southern dialect is meant to denote a regional affiliation that would link her with plantation slavery. And then, of course, there's the flourish of the repeated rhetorical question, "Ar'n't I a Woman?" As it turns out, the question is a complete fabrication if the first version has any credibility—and why would a reporter omit a feature that adds drama so remarkably? The question, like the dialect, seems to be an editorial flourish rather than a rhetorical one.[43] Despite its inauthenticity, however, it is difficult to part with. And we don't have to, because Sojourner Truth decided to claim it for herself.

Astonishingly, Truth reprinted this version of her speech in the section titled "The Book of Life," the 1875 appendix to her *Narrative*, in which "The Libyan Sibyl" appeared. What sorts of conclusions might we draw from this? It might mean that she recognized a certain value in this more alliterative version, which like the frontispiece trades on the racist stereotypes of the day. It also suggests that she turned to those stereotypes as one might to market conventions to help solidify her position in the literary marketplace—one largely defined by the moral consumerism of evangelical capitalism.

"I am a self-made woman," Sojourner Truth announced in the 1875 edition of the *Narrative*.[44] And in many ways she's right. That edition tells the story of not *just* that she made herself but *how* she made herself. Of course, she also had to make some sacrifices. Asked why she looked so young late in life, she explained that she had two skins—a black one covering a white one. As troubling as her attitudes on race were, her internalized racism becomes a way for us to understand her conception of the world she lived in. She knew that race mattered and that as a black woman with dark skin, she needed to find ways to make race work to her advantage. Sporting a turban in the author portrait and, later, draping herself in the trappings of white femininity in the photo on her *carte de visite* are shrewd markers of her efforts. When she says she sold the shadow to support the substance, we might understand "shadow" to mean "race," and therefore recognize in Truth's catchy slogan another way in which she engaged in the race trade that fueled the market of the period.

There were other sacrifices as well. By adapting her message to the market for slave narratives, for instance, her evangelical message was sometimes muffled by the noises of authorship. Yet in this connection we might also talk about the decidedly evangelical ending Truth/Gilbert chose for the *Narrative*. She stresses the saving of her former master's soul over the condemnation of slavery and its practitioners.[45] Eschewing generic conventions rather than kowtowing to readership expectations, Truth's narrative choice asserts her religious beliefs and banks on her canny understanding of the marketplace.

Sojourner Truth's use of the marketplace and its conventions reveals that she did not simply collapse when faced with its rules. Her grasp of the financial end of publishing and its ancillary activities reveals a multilayered agenda that led her out of the slave trade and into free trade. Her story provides an illuminating look at the complexities of agency within the context of the marketplace. We also see the struggle and inevitable sacrifice that success in the marketplace brings. Like Louisa May Alcott who wrote under pseudonyms in order to hold on to her niche in the children's literature market, Isabella Van Wagener boldly took on generic conventions in favor of Truth—the figure she constructed out of the moral imperatives that directed her life. Composed in part through a clever manipulation of the racist paradigms set for blacks who wished to use publication as a means to make a living, the works she published—as well as the speeches she gave and the images she circulated—appear under what we might call a trademark rather than a pseudonym, in the tradition of Fannie Fern.

To fully appreciate the pressure of the race and gender conventions that weighed on Sojourner Truth's choices, we might turn to the literary history of Harriet Wilson's 1859 novel *Our Nig* and consider Wilson's experience as a cautionary tale. Wilson violated convention by using the form of the novel instead of autobiography, and focused on the taboo subject of Northern slavery—elements that Sojourner Truth handled quite differently. Known to us today because of its rediscovery by Henry Louis Gates Jr., *Our Nig* had moldered in obscurity. In stark contrast, Sojourner Truth's image and words are known the world over. As her amanuensis, Olive Gilbert, later wrote to her in 1870: "I did not think you were laying the foundation of such an almost world-wide reputation when I wrote that little book for you, but I rejoice and am proud that you can make your power felt with so little book-education."[46]

Throughout the nineteenth century, American women writers not only crowded the marketplace with their work, they came to define it through their successful negotiations with it. Their engagement with abolition, women's rights, and the cult of true womanhood, among other issues, coincided with the rise of authorship as a profession, and thus places the work of women writers at the center of the burgeoning literary marketplace of their era. It was Nathaniel Hawthorne, writing to his publisher, William Ticknor, in 1855, who complained that "America is wholly given over to a damned mob of scribbling women." What we now know about the canny engagement with the marketplace of Louisa May Alcott and Sojourner Truth is that it was never a case of simple domination. As women vied for a piece of the market, they were as guided by race, class, and gender expectations as they were by the dictates of genre and other publishing conventions. Abolitionism created a set of market conditions that encouraged writers to promote its cause while protecting its prejudices. Most clearly displayed by Sojourner Truth's manipulation of dialect and image, those prejudices provided both opportunities and limitations. Opening up the possibility of authorship as a profession and a means to make a living for women writers, the spirit of abolition allowed women to take up their pens—instead of their swords—in the interest of reform. At the same time, social conventions continued to circumscribe the variety of ways in which a woman could and should express herself. What we see in the careers of Louisa May Alcott and Sojourner Truth is that although they played by the rules, they bent them to suit their needs and to meet their markets. While Alcott disguised herself by writing under the cloak of pen names, Truth invented a self conditioned, in part, by white expectations. Their approaches to the market, in other words, were as different as black and white.[47]

14

Creating an Image in Black: The Power of Abolition Pictures

John Stauffer

O ne picture is worth ten thousand words," the adman Frederick R. Barnard said in *Printer's Ink Magazine* in 1927. His quip has, of course, become a truism, though he may have only given authorship to a saying that had been around for decades. Advertisers were not the first group to champion the use of pictures as a means to sell their wares. In the nineteenth century, abolitionists were doing much the same thing. They, like advertisers, relied on images to sell ideas of the good society. But the source of their desire was much different: they sought to end slavery and racism, and transform the means of production, rather than generate demand and fuel consumption.[1]

Reformers throughout America and Europe became enraptured with the power of the picture beginning around 1830, once changes in lithography and line drawings had enabled large-scale mass production of images in newspapers and magazines.[2] Their enemies—the politicians and gatekeepers of the existing order—felt so threatened by their images that they tried to censor them.[3] When the young William Lloyd Garrison began publishing *The Liberator* in 1831, what most offended Southerners in the periodical were the images—particularly its masthead, which depicted a slave auction in front of the Capitol, the flag of liberty atop its dome, a whipping post in its plaza, and in the foreground a grieving slave family at auction and a discarded Indian treaty (Figure 1). Vice President John C. Calhoun, an ardent proslavery advocate, was so outraged by the masthead that he attempted, unsuccessfully, to ban newspapers with "pictorial representations" of slavery from the mails. Abolitionist texts were tolerable, in his mind, but not images.[4]

Black abolitionists were particularly invested in the power of images. Some of the most prominent, from Frederick Douglass and William "Ethiop" Wilson to James McCune Smith, Sojourner Truth, and Harriet Jacobs, embraced the black image as an aid in their reform work. Their rise to public prominence from the mid-1840s through the 1860s paralleled

Figure 1. *The Liberator* masthead, 1831.

the rise of visual culture, when Americans increasingly began to define themselves with images.[5] The twin rise of visual culture and black public personas is not coincidental; black abolitionists relied on images as a way to acquire a public voice, enter into the public sphere, and revise public opinion. Yet the ways in which they used, appropriated, and thought about visual images have been largely ignored.[6]

Most critics, when discussing African Americans and pictures, focus on how blacks have been objectified and how photography functions as a tool of white society. They view the black image as part of the process of exploitation. To be placed in front of the camera lens, to have one's body represented, photographed, *taken*—symbolically, if not literally—is to render that body powerless.[7] Gazing becomes a masculine, empowering (and "white") condition, while being seen is a feminine (and "black") one.[8]

Yet the process of visual representation is much more complicated. Robyn Wiegman has argued that in the twentieth century, the commodified appearance of the black body became a "representational sign for the democratizing process of U.S. culture itself."[9] Little has been said about the ways in which black abolitionists sought, in effect, to objectify themselves as a source of power in their reform work. From their perspective, the relation between subject, object, and power looks much different. They *wanted* to be objects rather than subjects—art objects, in particular— and at times wrote eloquently about the power of pictures. I want to explore the nature of this objectification.

•   •   •

Frederick Douglass relied as much on his image as on his voice and words
to create his public persona. Indeed, he created a public persona through
words and images. He was widely viewed as the "representative black man"
in the United States during his lifetime, and he liked the designation. By
representing himself, he hoped to reconstruct America's attitudes toward
slavery and race. He was one of the most perceptive writers on the uses of
pictures.[10]

Part of Douglass's fascination with images stemmed from his faith in
"true" art as a social leveler. "True" art for him meant accurate and "authentic" images of blacks, rather than caricatures such as blackface min-
strels. Through speeches, writings, and images, he sought to fashion
himself as an art object, or performer, that would confer on both his persona *and* his white perceivers the "gift of life" (to borrow from Elaine
Scarry), which would link them together and dissolve social barriers. The
slave as "thing," or the black man as object, acquired life and humanity, in
the minds of viewers, when it was represented as an art object or performer. And the perceiver acquired new life by perceiving that thing as
human.[11]

The representation of the black body as an *objet d'art* that could transform whites depended on how that body was represented. Douglass continually sought to control how he appeared in his portraits. In an 1849
review of *A Tribute for the Negro,* by the Quaker abolitionist Wilson Armistead, he praised the prose but attacked the imagery, including the engraving of himself (Figure 2). The engraver had cut the image of Douglass
from a painting (Figure 3), but had added a smile, rendering him with "a
much more kindly and amiable expression than is generally thought to
characterize the face of a fugitive slave," as Douglass accused. Although he
was no longer a fugitive slave, Douglass wanted the look of a defiant but respectable outsider. "Negroes can never have impartial portraits at the
hands of white artists," he stated:

> It seems to us next to impossible for white men to take likenesses of
> black men, without most grossly exaggerating their distinctive fea-
> tures. And the reason is obvious. Artists, like all other white persons,
> have adopted a theory respecting the distinctive features of Negro
> physiognomy.

The vast majority of whites could not create "impartial" likenesses of
African Americans (even though they might be able to write about them
impartially) because of their preconceived notions of what blacks looked
like.[12]

Figure 2. *Frederick Douglass.* An engraving reproduced in Wilson Armistead, *A Tribute for the Negro,* 1849.

Douglass's criticism of white artists helps to explain why he was so taken with photography: he thought that the veracity of the daguerreotype—the most popular form of photography in America from its invention in 1839 through the mid-1850s—prevented distortions of blacks that came from the hands of white artists. He also knew that the vast majority of daguerreotypes (over 90 percent) took the form of portraits. The photograph, and accurate renditions or sympathetic engravings drawn from the photograph, became his medium of choice for representing himself visually.[13]

Douglass was so taken with daguerreotypy that he called Louis Daguerre, the inventor of the daguerreotype, "the great discoverer of modern times, to whom coming generations will award special homage." Because of Daguerre's invention, he said, "we have pictures, true pictures, of every object which can interest us." "Men of all conditions and classes," he added, "can now *see themselves as others see them and as they will be seen by those [who] shall come after them.* What was once the special and exclusive luxury of the rich and great—is now the privilege of all. The humblest servant girl may now possess a picture of herself such as the wealth of kings could not purchase fifty years ago." For Douglass, the photograph was no respecter of persons; it represented all people accurately, reflecting their common humanity.[14]

Douglass attacked slavery and racism by championing the "truthfulness" of the photograph, and by stressing the picture-making proclivity of all humans. In his mind, all humans sought accurate representations both of material reality and of an unseen spiritual world. This affinity for pictures is what distinguished humans from animals: "Man is the only picture-making animal in the world. He alone of all the inhabitants of earth has the capacity and passion for pictures." To make and appreciate pictures required imagination, and for this reason Douglass emphasized the superiority of imagination over reason. While "dogs and elephants are said to possess" the capacity for reason, he argued, only humans sought to recreate nature and portray both the "inside soul" and the "outside world" through such "artificial means" as the photograph. The power of the "imagination," he added, was "a sublime, prophetic, and all-creative power." Imagination could be used to create a public persona in the form of a photograph or engraving. It could also be used to usher in a new world of equality, without slavery and racism. The power of the imagination linked humans to "the Eternal sources of life and creation." It allowed them to appreciate pictures as *accurate* representations of some greater reality, and it helped them to realize their sublime ideals in an imperfect world. As Douglass aptly put it: "Poets, prophets, and reformers are all picture makers—and this ability is the secret of their power and of their

Figure 3. *Frederick Douglass.* Oil on canvas, ca. 1845.

achievements. They see what ought to be by the reflection of what is, and endeavor to remove the contradiction." He considered himself all three: a poet (by which he meant "artist"), a prophet, and a reformer. He drew on divine sources to create sublime pictures of a new world of interracial equality. It was a millennial vision defined in nationalist terms.[15]

Douglass went so far as to suggest that the "moral and social influence of pictures"—and "representation" more generally—were *more* important in shaping the nation than "the making of its laws." Art, in other words, was more important than politics for changing society. It is a remarkable statement, for Douglass always defined himself as an abolitionist and reformer, and throughout the 1850s and 1860s he was deeply committed to political action. But art was the engine of social change.[16]

Douglass highlights the power an authentic black image can have on a white subject in his only work of fiction, "The Heroic Slave" (1853). The narrative opens with Mr. Listwell, a white man, chancing upon a slave, Madison Washington, talking to himself in the forest and vowing to be free. Listwell, who is aptly named because he can "listen well" to what blacks have to say, stands at the edge of the forest, gazing at Washington without the latter's knowledge. Washington is the inadvertent object of Listwell's gaze.

Listwell is utterly transformed after gazing at Washington and hearing his "soliloquy." The sight and speech of Washington rang "through the chambers of his soul, and vibrated through his entire frame." "From this hour," Listwell vows, "I am an abolitionist. I have seen enough and heard enough, and I shall go [home] resolved to atone for my past indifference to this ill-starred race." He treats Washington's performance as authentic, an accurate representation of his person.[17]

Listwell's capacity to "see well" surpasses his ability to listen well, for five years later, when he finally meets Washington, he recognizes him instantly. "Ever since that morning . . . you have seldom been absent from my mind." "From that hour, your face seemed to be daguerreotyped on my memory."[18]

Daguerreotyping a character was a common trope in abolitionist narration. (For example, Harriet Beecher Stowe "daguerreotype[s]" Uncle Tom "for [her] readers."[19]) It conveyed more than physical description or even photographic memory, for a daguerreotype was thought to penetrate the perceiver's soul as well as his mind.[20]

Americans saw God's work in the daguerreotype. Douglass and his contemporaries widely believed that daguerreotypes were "likenesses" in a religious sense—part of the individual's essence, "a matter of spiritual similarity" rather than a mere "picture."[21] A daguerreotype, it was thought, contained part of the body and soul of the subject. It was a unique, one-of-a-kind, silver-plated sheet of copper, covered with glass, whereas subsequent products of photography, such as *cartes de visite*, were made from a negative and were thus reproducible. Having Washington "daguerreo-typed" on Listwell's memory connects the two men's souls, and they become equals and friends. Both men benefit from their friendship: Listwell gains his spiritual freedom by atoning for his sin of indifference to slavery; and Washington gains his physical freedom, with help from his friend.

Daguerreotyping a character reflected a level of authenticity that went beyond representation to include the essence of the referent. Although this faith in authenticity, not to mention the notion of spiritual essence, may seem bizarre to us today, it was widespread in antebellum America. Many theatergoers treated actors on stage as the real thing, inseparable from the roles they played. Lawrence Levine describes the effects of this confusion between representation and reality. During a production of *Othello* in Albany, New York, a canal boatman interrupted the performance, and screamed at Iago, "You damned scoundrel, I would like to get hold of you after the show and wring your infernal neck."[22]

Sojourner Truth was possibly more famous for her *cartes de visite* than for her actual presence in abolition meetings. Her carefully chosen portraits made her a familiar presence to millions of viewers (see pp. 247, 250). They depicted "a respectable, middle-class matron," as Nell Painter has summarized, which subverted beliefs that blacks could never be respectable.[23] Truth's famous maxim, "I sell the shadow to support the substance," links her image (shadow) to her self (her substance), as well as to a growing consumer ethos. She wanted the image she sold to be an extension of herself. Her maxim suggests that she wanted to extend the "aura" of the daguerreotype onto other forms of photography, in order to preserve the connection between image and reality, shadow and substance, without distortion.[24]

James McCune Smith believed, with Douglass, that an authentic black persona could be extremely effective in breaking down racial barriers. In 1855 he reviewed a performance of the singer Elizabeth Greenfield, known as the "Black Swan," at the Broadway Tabernacle, and concluded that *"true* art is a social leveler, and thoroughly isocratic," or egalitarian. Greenfield's performance was so powerful that she collapsed racial barriers and created an integrated community in the Tabernacle: "Never was the Tabernacle so thoroughly speckled with mixed complexions; blind gentlemen sat side and side with dark ladies," and "colorblind" white women sat next to black men. Greenfield refused to succumb to "the requirements of American Prejudice"; instead of trying to hide her ancestry, she stood forth "simple and pure a black woman." For McCune Smith, Greenfield's stage presence reflected her true self.[25]

But McCune Smith also recognized the shortcomings of relying solely on a performative self to combat racism. "The colored man must do impracticable things before he is admitted to a place in society," he acknowledged in 1854. "He must speak like a [Frederick] Douglass, write like a[n Alexandre] Dumas, and sing like the Black Swan before he could be recognized as a human being." McCune Smith knew, too, that his own medium of choice, the essay, had limited popular appeal, especially compared with public speaking, photography, and stage performance. One reason for his comparative lack of popularity was that he rarely had his picture taken and was not a brilliant performer, and so did not stand everpresent, as it were, before people's eyes.[26]

William Wilson, a colleague of McCune Smith and the Brooklyn correspondent of *Frederick Douglass's Paper,* used ekphrasis—representing visual objects with words—to create an "Afric-American Picture Gallery." Writing under the pseudonym "Ethiop" to emphasize his black persona, Wilson wrote a series of seven "papers" in 1859, describing twenty-six images in his picture gallery that summarized the social, political, and cultural conditions of America. "I always had a penchant for pictures," Ethiop confesses at the beginning of his series. "From a chit of a boy till now, my love for beautiful, or quaint, old pictures has been unquenched." In one of his "rambles" in search of pictures, he "stumbled over the Afric-American Picture Gallery"; it since became one of his "dearest retreats."[27]

Ethiop guides his readers through the various images, characters, and settings in his picture gallery. The images are emblems of black resistance and achievement: Toussaint L'Ouverture's significance to America; a "Young Tom," who, unlike "Uncle Tom," is full of mischief and rebellion; the Underground Railroad; the head of Phillis Wheatley; and a black artist–prophet who stands erect in the "Black Forest," a setting that affirms black identity.[28]

What is significant about Wilson's Picture Gallery is his attempt to transform writing into images for greater effect. A "true" picture, he argued, had a moral dimension that writing lacks. Truth and beauty stemmed from God; they illuminated America's present condition, and pointed the way to a new age. For Wilson, Douglass, Truth, and McCune Smith, the authentic black image was a source of power: it brought new life to blacks, and transformed whites into seeing the full humanity of blacks.[29]

While a black image was a source of power, a black viewer was comparatively powerless. Harriet Jacobs describes this powerlessness in *Incidents in the Life of a Slave Girl* (1861) where she becomes a viewer behind a lens. For nearly seven years she hid from her captors in the attic of a house. The sensation she describes resembles that of being inside a camera obscura.

While daguerreotypists draped themselves behind the camera, Jacobs sat inside her box, as it were, at the lens:

> Countless were the nights that I sat late at the little loophole [the lens] scarcely large enough to give me a glimpse of one twinkling star. . . . Season after season, year after year, I peeped at my children's faces, and heard their sweet voices, with a heart yearning all the while to say, "Your mother is here."

In viewing her children, Jacobs is ineffectual. At the same time, through her narration she objectifies herself for her readers, which, she hopes, will empower her and transform them into abolitionists. She appears as both object and observer for her readers.[30]

When legal freedom came, Americans began to lose faith in the veracity and "aura" of the image and the value of authenticity. Nancy Armstrong notes that Alfred Stieglitz "sought to make photography counter its own object-dependency, and so renounce the very realism that had fostered its development as a popular medium." In his 1892 short story "The Real Thing," Henry James has his protagonist, a popular illustrator, declare that he prefers "the *represented* subject over the *real* one," because "the *defect* of the real one was so apt to be a lack of representation": "I liked things that *appeared;* then one was sure. Whether they *were* or not was a subordinate and almost always a profitless question."[31]

This loss of faith in the "truthfulness" of the picture, and in the direct link between image and material referent, was not limited to white artists. At the turn of the century, black reformers began embracing the trope of the "New Negro," which was "only a metaphor," as Henry Louis Gates Jr. has noted. It signified "a black person who lives at no place" and at no time. The New Negro was an image without a natural referent, as is suggested by the fantastic, collage figure of the "The New Negro" from the 1928 *Carolina Magazine* (Figure 4).[32]

W.E.B. Du Bois was, like Douglass, profoundly influenced by the power of the image. And like William Wilson, he thought narratives should aspire to the condition of an image. He employs the metaphor of the image to state his purpose in the opening pages of *The Souls of Black Folk:* "I have sought here to sketch, in vague, uncertain outline, the spiritual world in which ten thousand Americans live and strive." But Du Bois's spiritual world resembled the metaphor of the New Negro—it was a fragmented image, detached from its material referent. This fragmentation stemmed from a "vast veil," producing a double self and obstructing the link be-

Figure 4. Allan R. Freelon, *The New Negro*. Reproduced in *Carolina Magazine*, 1928.

tween black object and white perceiver that could give both subject and object new life.[33]

Du Bois had lost faith in the truthfulness of pictures, including photography. In a column entitled "Photography" in *The Crisis*, he argued that "the average white *photographer* does not know how to deal with colored skins, and having neither sense of their delicate beauty of tone nor will to learn, he makes a horrible botch of portraying them." It is a striking contrast from Douglass's faith in photography. While Douglass saw photography as an antidote to white artists who "grossly exaggerated" blacks' "distinctive features," Du Bois believed that photography was as biased and inauthentic as other forms of representation; for him, there was no direct link between image and referent. His solution was to call for more "colored photographers" to correct the distortions. Perhaps the endpoint of this obstruction between black image and white perceiver is Ralph Ellison's Invisible Man, who *refuses* visibility as an act of resistance.[34]

Douglass, Truth, McCune Smith, and other black abolitionists embraced visibility as an act of resistance and empowerment. They defined their spiritual selves through their material selves, and saw their images as containing, if not their essence, at least an authentic representation of it. But after Reconstruction, whites no longer treated authentic black images as the real thing, much as the laws prescribing black freedom lost their prescriptive power. It is profoundly ironic that black representation, which sought to combat slavery, was itself dependent on slavery for its proliferation and strength. In one sense, you could say that slavery was a muse that inspired the power of the black image—and black art more generally—which in turn sought to vanquish slavery.[35] As a consumer society replaced a "slave republic," the black image, lacking a natural referent, lost much of its prescriptive power.

15

Abolitionists in American Cinema:
From *The Birth of a Nation* to *Amistad*[1]

Casey King

The topic of my essay is abolitionists in film. Why bother? Historical film, like historical fiction, is often considered a sub-genre of real art, true expression's idiot man-child cousin, best left chained in the basement of the artistic hierarchy. This was not always the case. Historical fiction constitutes a good deal of the American canon.[2] The ferment of realism, however, overwhelmed Walter Scott's American legacy of historical romance, and literary critics and novelists alike began to regard historical fiction with disdain.[3] This disdain continues today. Anyone who has studied fiction writing knows three things: "Show me, don't tell me"; "Don't have your characters wake up at the end having realized it was all a dream"; and, most important, "Write what you know." What we are supposed to know is what we have lived, and it is from this interesting, varied, and hopefully war-torn personal past that we craft stories. As we cannot possibly "know" those things that existed before our ability to experience them, they cannot ring true, cannot be realistic.[4] Of course, postmodernity causes us to question even that which we have lived, reminding us that we can't even know *that* with any certitude. This may explain, in part, why, during the last decade of the twentieth century, there had been a renewed acceptance of the historical novel, attempted by several fine literary novelists, but that is a different matter altogether. The point is that realism requires experience. Historical novels are inescapably anachronistic, and therefore, to many, a lesser form of art. Now, movies, movies are never art, unless, of course, they are called films, and even if a movie is called a film there is no guarantee that it will be called art. Therefore, to the serious critic, "historical film" is just a nice way of saying "crap."[5]

Historians are equally displeased with historical films, but for different reasons. Basically, filmmakers encroach upon sacred ground, in a manner that Howard University filmmaker Abiyi Ford once called, "toddlers with automatic weapons, capable of doing great harm, but without any capacity for understanding the ramifications of their actions."[6] Historians often speak of what they do in language more often used to describe a spiritual quest, or personal pilgrimage. Historian Jonathan Spence captures this spirit when he writes that "the point of the endless and often exasperating search for knowledge about the past is . . . to throw one's whole energy into the quest for interpretation and modes of recording that are as true as one can get to the spirit and contingencies of the past. If that can be done, even to some extent, then the historian earns the right to bear a kind of witness, to speak with greater authority than others about what might have been and what could not have been."[7] Bearing witness, earning authority through careful work, these are rights one earns, and with them almost sacred responsibilities. It is no wonder that it grates when those who would venture into the historical past invoke poetic license as an excuse for a lack of intellectual rigor or attention to historical detail.[8]

Adding insult to injury is the fact that filmmakers claim that what they create is not only history, but "real" history, unlike the "fake" history passed off by scholars blinded by years of the painstaking pursuit of accuracy, wasting their time learning foreign languages and reading moldy primary documents. This strange presumption is well illustrated in the recent Steven Spielberg/Debbie Allen production based on the story of the historical slave ship *Amistad*. Before the movie was released, the film's production studio, DreamWorks, sent "educational" packets to classrooms across the country. The stated purpose of these packets was to help engender "critical thinking about the value of history in light of the long faded chapter [of the *Amistad*] restored to American history in the film." They further claimed that they "took great care to make every detail of this historical drama authentic." They then leveled a serious charge against historians: that "real history has been castrated—left out—and great historians have done it."[9] There's the rub. To Jonathan Spence, real history is the serious endeavor to achieve the closest approximation of truth. To film producers like Debbie Allen, real history is either missing a penis, or *is* a missing penis, depending on how we interpret the packet's stunningly ambiguous use of language.

Of course, that doesn't keep people from going to see these films and believing that what they see constitutes "what really happened." And that is at the very crux of the answer to the question, Why bother? Millions of people go to these films, and their view of historical events, figures, villains, heroes, and even abolitionists is profoundly shaped by these productions.

This has been true since the first moving picture shows found their way onto the American scene in the late nineteenth and early twentieth centuries. Theater critic Walter Eaton marveled at the pervasive power of the new technology:

When you reflect that in New York City alone, on a Sunday 500,000 people go to the moving picture shows, a majority of them perhaps children . . . you cannot dismiss the canned drama with a shrug of contempt. . . . Ten million people attended professional baseball games in America in 1908. Four million people attend moving picture theaters, it is said, every day.

By the end of the twentieth century there were an estimated 1.42 billion cinema admissions sold every year.[10] This number does not take into account made-for-television movies, cable productions, or the home video audience for motion pictures. We have become a nation of watchers. And while historians and artists may deplore the uses and popularity of movies, their cultural influence is irrefutable.

But there is another reason to look at filmic portrayals of abolitionists. Irrespective of accuracy, films can be seen as cultural artifacts. These artifacts provide unusually accurate and sometimes disturbing insights into our national mentality. This is true for two reasons. First, film is the most collaborative of artistic media. Producers, writers, actors, directors, sound engineers, editors, cameramen, key grips, and best boys—the list of credits goes on. Some filmmakers, such as Stanley Kubrick, are legendary in their attention to detail and desire to control every facet of their productions. But even if Kubrick could have controlled everything, he was an anachronism.

Secondly, as the most popular films are created to appeal to the largest audience, they in some way speak to a culture's "mental climate." Most producers want to make films that attract large numbers of people so that they can realize a return on their considerable investment. Therefore, film can both reflect and reinforce certain cultural notions.

All right, then, what about abolitionists in film? When I began my study, I was surprised to learn that the subject had received scant attention. On further inquiry, I learned that the reason it has been ignored by those who write on film is that abolitionists themselves have been ignored by filmmakers. If historians now recognize that the crusade against slavery is one of the most important reform movements in human history, the film industry, and American culture in the twentieth century, fail to concur. There are almost no films on abolitionists, per se. *The American Film Institute Catalog,* one of the most comprehensive filmographies, with entries on movies produced from 1893 to 1970, includes neither antislavery nor abolitionism as indexed subjects.[11] In Ken Burns's twelve-hour documentary on the Civil War, no more than five minutes are devoted to abolitionists.[12]

That is not to say they don't exist in movies. There are simply too few to merit a category of their own. With a few notable exceptions, attitudes toward abolitionists and the abolitionist movement must instead be teased

from films about the Civil War: those that address slaves and slavery or attempt to portray nineteenth-century black life or culture. This teasing is
beyond the scope of my essay; I will, instead, deal primarily with the notable exceptions, those films in which abolitionists, a particular abolitionist, or the antislavery movement play a more primary role in the movie's
narrative. That is, abolition must appear on the marquee, even if it does so
with a stage name. The films I will consider in this essay are *The Birth of a
Nation, Souls at Sea, Santa Fe Trail, Conquest of the Planet of the Apes,* and *Amistad*.[13] Examining the depictions of abolitionists in these films helps us
gauge not only changing attitudes toward race, but changing attitudes toward reform, central to which are certain questions: What is the American
attitude toward reform movements? Does this help explain the absence of
films that deal with the crusade against slavery? Do Americans distinguish
between different sorts of reform? How do larger national and international events shape these attitudes? What is the attitude of Americans toward religion, and in what ways does this affect their attitude toward
abolition? How does the need to recognize African Americans' role in
their own emancipation have an impact on the legacy of the abolitionist
movement?

The films suggest certain answers. Early attitudes toward antislavery
were neutral, if not respectful, driven by a South interested in regional reconciliation. It wasn't antislavery that troubled the South, it was the political
and social empowerment of African Americans as tools for the ambitions
of Northern white politicians who sought to rule the region. During the
mid twentieth century, after the white South's cultural victory became
more secure (the South, culturally, did rise again), historical antislavery activism was largely viewed by Hollywood as the purview of lunatics, opportunists, and people who don't shave (often a sign of moral perfidy in
Hollywood). During the 1960s, when we might have expected the elevation of the abolitionists and their movement, they are still conspicuously
absent. The need for black agency, and the very important mission of recognizing African Americans as participants in the struggle for their own
emancipation, became more important than the task of historical inclusion. Historical black abolitionists are completely neglected, though individual acts of black resistance, both actual and imagined, are showcased.
Historical white abolitionists are ignored in keeping with the tenets of
black power and good white liberalism. The fact that white reformers sacrificed and risked their lives, fortunes, and families to end slavery was no
longer relevant to the political imperatives of the 1960s. Paternalism is
often paved with good intentions. Were they alive in the 1960s, white abolitionists would have probably recognized the necessity of their absence,
and would willingly have sacrificed one more thing, small by comparison:

their cinematic historical legacy. In the 1990s Hollywood finally discovered black abolitionists, and imagined a more pluralistic pleading for equality. But a profound mistrust of religiously inspired reform has served to further denigrate the historical role of abolitionists, and the historical reality of the religious basis of all profound American reform.

Of all the historical films of the twentieth century it is David Wark Griffith's *The Birth of a Nation* that we most love to hate. And with good reason. It is so thoroughly politically and ideologically repugnant that it has become, since its first release in 1915, a sort of cottage industry of outrage. Countless reviews, numerous articles, and even political protests have been devoted to Griffith's odious film, and the nation that would give birth to *The Birth*. Those who celebrate Griffith's achievement often attempt to separate aesthetics and artistic innovation from message. But praising the aesthetics or originality of *The Birth of a Nation* is almost like saying that even though the Nazis did some terrible things, they had a wonderful fashion sense or flare for nocturnal spectacle.[14] So let me preface my discussion of *The Birth of a Nation* by reiterating its rich perniciousness.

That said, white abolitionists receive more explicit cinematic respect in *The Birth of a Nation* than they do in any other film in the twentieth century. Surprised? Me, too. Griffith does not devote a great deal of time in his film to abolitionists, just one scene early in the film. But this scene is nonetheless significant. It stands as an important foil to the Northern carpetbaggers and scalawags that later dominate his film and help convey his intention: one of regional reconciliation, a message that not all Northerners are bad, even antislavery Northerners, provided that they don't try to push equality for African Americans down white Southerners' throats.

Meaning in silent film is conveyed by three distinct components: the images themselves, title cards that preface and link scenes, and the accompanying musical score. These form distinct visual "chapters" in a silent film. Each chapter contains several shots. Scene two in *The Birth of a Nation*, devoted wholly to abolitionists, consists of six shots.

As the second scene or chapter begins, the score, composed by Louis Gottschalk, sounds with hymnal triads and high church harmonies on thirds and fifths, in 4/4 time, in a composition reminiscent of "A Mighty Fortress is Our God." As the music plays, a scene card reads, "The Abolitionists of the 19th century demanding the freeing of the slaves." The establishing shot is filmed from the back of a meetinghouse or some other public space. The viewer's vantage point creates the illusion that one is standing behind a gathering of a dozen or so men and women of a variety of ages. These disciples are well dressed, the men in coats and ties, the women with simple bonnets and shawls. They dominate the foreground of the shot as they respectfully listen to a speaker on stage. A man in the close foreground leans toward another so that he can make a comment without disrespect to the speaker.

The speaker is the focal point of the shot. He is a man with a balding head that stands in stark relief to the austerity of his long black frock. He may be a clergyman, but explicit Christian iconography, apart from the mood established by Gottschalk's pseudo-hymn, is absent. Before him, at his feet, sits a small black child. To his right sits a woman in a simple white dress listening quietly. Behind him, to the viewer's right, is a portrait of George Washington, father of the country and Virginia slaveholder. The establishing shot conveys the sense of these abolitionists not as hotheaded radicals, but as members of an orderly society, as men and women sit quietly listening to a speaker. It is a man who is speaking. A woman is on the stage, but she knows her place, not speaking but seated. Her white dress suggests a purity or chastity that is consistent with propriety. Both Washington and the black child, too, know their respective places: Washington somewhere behind and above it all, and the hopes of a black future at the white man's feet (even the Northern white man's feet). The message is clear. Those who speak out against slavery, and those who come to listen, may recognize the institution of slavery as wrong, but speaking out against slavery is not tantamount to a call for full equality. In this room, as in the country, order is possible among former slaveholders, Northern men and women, and even freed black people, provided everyone knows his or her place.

These thematic elements are reiterated in the second shot of the scene, a close-up on the speaker. He holds his hands low and open in supplication to the people, looking somewhere to the left of the camera. To the speaker's right sit two African American men, who are quietly listening. This, then, is an interracial gathering in what is supposed to be antebellum America. But here, too, the black people know better than to sit among the white people. They are cordoned off from the white crowd as exhibits, and while they may listen, they listen as subjects of the discourse, objects of attention, rather than as meaningful participants in the discourse on their status. Still, Griffith does not use blackfaced, grotesque caricatures here as he does later in the film. As a matter of fact, these men elicit a certain sympathy as the speaker leans down and clasps one on the shoulder as one would clasp a child, with paternalistic encouragement or avuncular approbation.

The scene quickly shifts to the image of a white woman in the audience watching intently. While Griffith would later exploit white anxiety of miscegenation to further his racist politics, here he makes a different choice: matronly sympathy. The shot is a close up of a plump, elderly woman in silhouette. She is clothed in a black dress with white lace. Her gray hair peeks from a black bonnet. She sits alone, looking through small wire glasses, listening expressionless, exuding a careful neutrality, or perhaps a guarded schoolmarmian disapproval. She is the Northern woman, widow/mother, spinster/listener, the embodiment of Northern maternal morality, asexual, on guard to potential impropriety.

The shot then returns to the back of the meeting house. The speech is apparently finished and the crowd is applauding in approval. A small black child is held by the shoulders and walks down the center of the meeting house, guided by a white man.

The next shot interrupts the scene with a very short, less than a second-long closeup of the African American child with the white man, presumably the abolitionist standing behind him. It is a poignant still image. While most portrayals of African Americans in Griffith's film surrender to the pull of racist stereotype, this image is decidedly different. It is a haunting, sympathetic portrayal of a small African American boy. Other than George Washington, he is the only "actor" in the scene to look directly into the camera, and as such, seems to address the viewer directly. He looks sad, and seems to be quietly beseeching the camera, as if echoing the white abolitionist, to end slavery.

The scene ends with the child returning to the foot of the speaker as a collection hat for the cause is passed around the group. The matronly woman previously described is in the foreground. She holds a hanky to her face and seems to be crying for the child.

The scene, all six shots, takes up roughly twenty-two seconds of the entire film. It is, nonetheless, unexpected that the first visual treatment of abolitionists in film history portrays them in a sympathetic light, given the virulence of Griffith's racist beliefs.

What explains this puzzling depiction was Griffith's goal in making the film. His object was not Northern alienation, but reconciliation. A more nuanced view affords a more subtle invitation, and a reinvention of an origin myth in which "we the people" becomes "we the white Southerners." It is not the "sin of slavery," but the sin of the political and cultural inclusion of "brutish" African Americans against which we should stand. As such the more damning and thorough indictment of antislavery preoccupies the rest of the film. There is an implicit criticism of ending slavery, and therefore abolitionists, in Griffith's depiction of a world turned brutish and chaotic by the liberation and empowerment of African Americans. It is this image of the damage wrought by the effects of an ill-considered, sudden ending of American slavery that would persist in American popular culture. Griffith's film enjoyed a wide popularity until the advent of sound cinema.

Some years later, two Hollywood films moved the theme of antislavery to center stage: *Souls at Sea* (1937) and *Santa Fe Trail* (1940). Given the cultural context of the Great Depression, I would argue that each film on some level engages the validity of radical reform. I use the term radical here in a very specific sense to mean operating outside the law, sometimes through violent means, to further some perceived higher goal or more noble purpose. Of the two, *Souls at Sea* is the more radical, a film that seems to condone violence, especially given the restrictive dictates of the Motion Picture Production Code. *Santa Fe Trail*, on the other hand, is very much a New Deal picture, with a recognition of societal ills, but a profound denunciation of violent or abrupt means of addressing those ills. Although ultimately a conservative film, with a strong current of racist ideology, it is not without a sincere recognition that slavery is wrong.

In Paramount Picture's 1937 *Souls at Sea*, Gary Cooper stars as radical anti-slave trade activist named Michael "Nuggin" Taylor. The film was directed by Henry Hathaway, whose sixty-six screen credits spanned thirty years and included such notable films as *Lives of a Bengal Lancer* (1935) and *True Grit* (1969). It was written by Grover Jones, who also wrote an early screen adaptation of *Huckleberry Finn* (1931). One can only speculate on Twain's influence on Jones, given the sympathetic treatment of both slaves and antislavery reform in *Souls at Sea*.

The film opens in a Philadelphia courtroom in 1854. "Nuggin" sits with stoic, silent resignation on the witness stand. The prosecutor stands before him—before us—introducing the viewer to Taylor's predicament. "Even his wise and experienced counsel," the prosecutor begins, "have been able to only weakly claim that he saved as many as he killed." Now addressing the jury and packed courtroom, the prosecutor asks that they weigh Taylor's character and his innocence or guilt by considering his profession: "A slaver." The prosecution spits out the word as if he has just tasted a piece of bad fruit. He then pauses momentarily to allow the weight of this fact and Taylor's capacity to commit murder to settle on the courtroom. He continues, "Do these facts present to you a philanthropist? A generous, warm-hearted saver of human lives? They do not. They present him for what he is—an incredibly intolerant, callous, cold-hearted mass murderer." Taylor struggles as if biting his tongue, but offers no response. The prosecution need say no more. Taylor's participation in the slave trade is proffered as self-evident proof of his capacity to commit the gravest of all sins.

But before we jump to the conclusion that slave traders are bad, and therefore antislavery activists are good, we should remember that the U.S. Constitution called for the end of the slave trade after fifty years, while explicitly protecting the right to hold slaves, and implicitly condoning if not codifying the validity of the institution itself.[15] After all, natural increases in the slave population in the South in the nineteenth century made the slave trade unnecessary to the perpetuation of slavery in the United States and the "Southern way of life." Southern slaveholders like Thomas Jefferson could detest the slave trade, but there are few historians who would consider him an abolitionist.[16] All right, then, in the late 1930s slave trading is depicted as a bad business, just as it was in the late eighteenth and early nineteenth century. This does not necessarily mean that antislavery activism is a good thing.

But *Souls* does more than vilify the slave trade while justifying racism and slavery. The rest of the film examines in flashback the events leading to Taylor's prosecution. It is in the next scene, the very first scene of our backward glance, that the film strikes out on truly original and radical grounds (for a dominantly regressive Hollywood at any rate), as it raises the plight and status of Africans and elevates their exploitation to the level of Shakespearean tragedy. A large three-masted ship gently rocks at full sail, silhouetted by the moon on a calm, night sea. The sound of a sad, repetitive African song is audible as the camera pans first to the ship's name, *4 Blackbird* (Hollywood is rarely subtle when it comes to symbolism), then to the Africans chained below deck, chanting in dignified and profound desperation. The filmmaker does not use black-faced whites, does not render bondage as pleasant (this is not the "happy darkies" enjoying a nice sea voyage scene), and does not attempt to dehumanize or bestialize the enslaved (as was commonly done to justify their enslavement).[17] The moment invokes a profound pathos, a sympathetic portrayal of the middle passage the likes of which will not be approximated again until sixty years later, in *Amistad*.

The camera then pans to the white sailor at the helm, who manages the ship without expression, seemingly impervious to the desperate sounds of his African cargo. We then cut to Taylor, lying on deck reading by lamplight, his sidekick, Powdah (George Raft), asleep beside him. "To die, to sleep," Taylor begins, reciting Hamlet's soliloquy, "To sleep no more."

"What are you reading?" Powdah asks.

"The tragedy of Hamlet."

"What's it about?"

"It's about a man who couldn't make up his mind."

"About what?"

"About whether he wanted to live or die. Kind of like those blacks down there."

This is a remarkable moment in American cinema. Thirty years before the civil rights movement, a mainstream Hollywood film starring Mr. Deeds proclaims not only the equality of Africans, but imparts a nobility to their suffering, equating them with perhaps the most articulate of all Shakespearean sufferers. It should not distract us that the specifics of the African chanting is in an African language. It is probable that Shakespearean iambic pentameter was as unintelligible to the average American viewing audience. It is certainly unintelligible to our representative American everyman, Powdah, who charges Taylor with being "too sentimental."

But the captain of the *Blackbird* is less reflective than Taylor. To quiet the chanting he appears in the next scene with a whip above the cargo hold. Our perspective—and, by implication, sympathy—is with the slaves as the shot is framed from below deck. The captain looms, his malevolent figure and intent framed by the night sky as he deliberately, repeatedly brings the lash down. The camera pans down to the Africans, seemingly helplessly chained, squirming to avoid the whip. Finally, one man grabs the whip and pulls the captain below. The enslaved quickly surround him, but the action of their just retribution is obscured from our view. This is an interesting and revealing choice. In *Amistad*, by contrast, the portrayal of the African self-liberation and retribution is the central focus of the opening sequence. The dispatch of the captain is explicit, displayed in grotesque detail (and subconsciously plays into American cultural stereotypes of violent blacks). The more profound and lasting image is not the provocation of the middle passage but the slave rebel Cinque's violent rage. In *Souls at Sea* the filmmaker allows the beating to occur off-screen. The more persistent and lasting image is the captain's provocation rather than the Africans' response to it.[18]

In addition, unlike *Amistad*, where Cinque drove a sword through the captain and groaned with uncontrollable vengeful rage after killing, the captain of the *Blackbird* is beaten almost, but not quite, to death. The captain is brought to the deck, from below. The enslaved seem to bear no grudge against the other crew members who carry the captain's body back above deck, and allow them to do so unchallenged. The viewer both through Taylor's sympathy, and through directorial choice, is led to believe that the captain's fate was justified. This is a significant moment, too, in American cinema history. It is 1937. This is a Gary Cooper picture. White men and women sit in the cinema, separated by law through most of the United States from their black fellow Americans, are there to see the new Paramount Pictures film starring one of the most popular leading men of the decade. The film opens by portraying the beating and eventual death of a white man by black men. This could, potentially, as in the case of *The Birth of a Nation*, exploit white fears of black empowerment, or alternatively, as is the case in *Amistad*, confirm white stereotypes of the black capacity for extreme violence.[19] The film avoids either response. The plight of the enslaved is nothing less than high tragedy, not primitive or visceral, but profound and poetic. The enslaved response to the captain's violence is not excessive, but measured and appropriate. To resolve any doubt of this, after the captain's death Powdah comments matter-of-factly, "Well if the blacks didn't get him, then the crew would have."[20]

The captain's last act was to assign command of the *Blackbird* to Taylor, whose first act as captain is to chart a course directly into waters patrolled by the British navy, thus seeming to deliberately engineer her capture. Once

Taylor is in the hands of the English, we begin to understand his true intentions, if not his political proclivity. The British, too, suspect that Taylor might have ulterior motives. The captain of the ship responsible for his capture, several officers, and the minister in charge of British antislavery efforts meet around a large conference table to discuss their suspicions. It is reported that Taylor is directly linked to the demise of at least two other slave ships. One "caught fire" before taking on its human cargo, the other ran aground in Africa "in broad daylight permitting over a thousand slaves to escape."

The British captain then asks, "Are you by any chance suggesting that Captain Taylor is waging a kind of private war against the slave trade?" This wonderfully clumsy bit of dialogue explicitly answers the dramatic question driving the first act of the film: How is it that Mr. Deeds is a bad guy? Well, he's not. He's actually a noble saboteur, willing to risk his life (slavers were routinely hanged) in an attempt to do violence to the slave trade.

If they are correct, the British recognize an opportunity in having a "covert operative" in Taylor. But before they can engage him, they attempt to definitively ascertain his purpose and commitment. Taylor is invited into the secret "war room" of the British antislavery efforts. It is a ponderous room, consistent with the gravity of its purpose, laden with wood and obvious world geographic tools, a large globe, an even larger map with pins and string, a heavy wooden table.

"I can assure you, Mr. Taylor," the British minister begins, "that you are the first slaver that ever set foot in this room. On that map is the location of every British patrol ship. Across this desk are reports of every slave ship picked up or sunk, every slaver hanged. Are you interested?"

"What interests me more," Taylor answers, hands in pockets, "is why you persist in regarding me as a Quaker or an abolitionist." Why does Taylor ask this question, seeming to explicitly disavow a connection to abolitionists? There is room for several interpretations, the most simple of which is that Taylor is just trying to maintain his "cover" as a slaver. There are others. It is possible that this is an attempt to explicitly draw a distinction between anti-slave trade efforts and antislavery efforts and is therefore an anti-abolitionist film. Perhaps the film hopes to "have it both ways": disavowing abolitionism, and a connection to a radical reform movement that was widely blamed for "causing" the Civil War, by showing one man personally opposed, not to slavery, but to the slave trade. It certainly is curious. But I would argue against this interpretation. Cooper's character should be judged by his actions, not his disavowal under interrogation. Certainly his compassion for the Africans and his expression of their equality, "they like Hamlet," would have placed him more closely with the Garrisonians than the anti-slave trade forces that condoned the institution itself. The opposition to the slave trade was historically (through the Revolutionary era) considered the "trojan horse," the first step to ending slavery itself. In addition, the abolition movement in the United States was marked by a wide range of expressions and strategies all categorized under the general term "abolition."[21]

Even if Taylor disavowed his connection, his actions place him in the forefront of radical reform. Let's review his "accepted lengths" thus far: lying, stealing, falsifying identity, destroying property (the ship in the case of the contrived confiscation, at the very least, and the slave property to the slavers). What is even more shocking, and decidedly radical, is that the filmmaker even seems to justify the murder of white people, some of whom are innocent, for the sake of saving black men and women.

The murders occur in the penultimate scene of the film, aboard the *William Brown* bound for Savannah. Nuggin' Taylor, recently "released" from arrest, and still posing as a slaver, carries orders for the continued smuggling of slaves for the next six months. The English have, thanks to Taylor, carefully perused the orders. Their plan is to have a patrol ship lying in wait for each slaver. But the plan is contingent upon Taylor safely reaching Savannah and maintaining his disguise.

The ship accidentally catches fire at sea and there is only one viable lifeboat. Taylor, while trying to persuade Powdah to climb on, is knocked out cold and falls into the lifeboat.[22] Once he regains consciousness, Taylor assumes command of the lifeboat, too late, of course, to return to the *William Brown* and save his friend. The problem is that it is an extremely popular lifeboat, being the only one that floats. It soon becomes overburdened and dangerously close to sinking. Despite Taylor's many efforts to impose order on the inevitable chaotic clawing for survival, the lifeboat takes on water quickly and looks as if it will soon sink. Taylor then throws a few men overboard, urging them to "hold on to the sides of the boat." These are not the villains, but "extras," innocents fighting for survival. When they threaten to capsize the lifeboat, Taylor shouts at them and then fires his pistol three times, taking what seems to be quite deliberate aim. The boat is righted again as the men disappear beneath the surface of the black sea.

What are we to make of this? There are a number of creative options that could have been exercised by the filmmaker. He might have rendered the action off screen, in retrospect. Or perhaps he might have made one of the clinging men less sympathetic, shown a scowl or explicit disregard for others. The director might have rendered a medium shot of the ship about to capsize, cut to a child threatened or some other coded sympathetic cinematic element, and then pulled tight on Gary Cooper whose face, wracked with regret, is forced to pull the trigger. The director might have put us in the lifeboat, a camera positioned somewhere among the thick, frenzied throng, the black water threatening; as the boat tilts, we hover precariously on the precipice of our mutual demise, happy when in front of us someone has the good sense to discharge a pistol, returning the boat to a reassuring balance. Instead, the scene is jarring, disturbing, as we see the boat from a distance; the viewer is not quite in the water, but perhaps on some other lifeboat, watching Gary Cooper fire three times, presumably killing three innocent men. No classic Hollywood "warning shot" or "don't worry just-a-flesh wound." Taylor, Gary Cooper, points his pistol and "bang-dead, bang-dead (slight pause) bang-dead" the hot, white smoke from the pistol discharge billows around him, as flailing arms disappear beneath the water's surface. One contemporary review described the scene as "a truly appalling shipwreck which only the strongest nerves could accept as entertainment." [23]

Even for a twenty-first-century audience, dulled by the surfeit of fictional violence, this scene is profoundly disturbing. Unlike most modern Hollywood narratives there is no hyperviolence precipitated by a just and vengeful rage, or highly stylized, senseless if choreographed violence. This moment feels "real" as we watch a character for whom we have tremendous sympathy kill innocent men in order to further a higher cause. This scene is even more striking when seen within a historical context. In 1930, in response to criticism from American religious leaders, guidelines were published for films, later supported by the creation in 1934 of the Production Code Administration (PCA). *Souls at Sea* seems to at least push the limits of the code, which remained in force until explicitly challenged by Otto Preminger in the 1950s. The Code states that "Crimes against the law . . . shall never be represented in such a way as to throw sympathy with the crime as against the law and justice"; that "the sympathy of the audience should never be thrown on the side of crime, wrong doing evil or sin." [24]

Taylor commits three murders on screen. These are murders of white men, committed in order to save the lives of black men and women who would otherwise be enslaved if Taylor fails in his mission.

The scene then returns to the courtroom. The English minister asks permission to speak to the court. He faces the judge, but the camera then cuts to a close-up as he looks directly into the camera—at us—and makes explicit what the film would like us to conclude:

> With a determination that nothing could weaken he brought that frail craft to safety. Then he went on to Savannah to finish his appointed task. When he decided to save his own life it was to further a great cause. Later, in this same room, and faced with the danger of losing more than life, he made not the slightest move to save himself. I humbly crave the court's forgiveness for withholding my statement until now but the very nature of our endeavor made secrecy until the last moment imperative.

Nuggin' Taylor is granted a new trial and the viewer is left with the impression that he will be found not guilty. At a time when the nation struggled with the need for reform, *Souls at Sea* was a radical proclamation of not only the necessity, but also the righteousness, of violent means to achieve more noble purposes. Not surprisingly, it was not a great box office success for Paramount.

A much more popular film that deals with similar themes was *Santa Fe Trail*. But other than general thematic content, these two films bear few similarities, imparting profoundly different attitudes toward radical reform, African Americans, and antislavery. In many ways, *Santa Fe Trail* is much more like *The Birth of a Nation* than *Souls at Sea*. *Birth* and *Trail*, both written by Southerners, call for national unity and decry regional strife. Both films regard calls for equality as mad, naive, or insincere. Both fictions predicate their idealized America on the exclusion of African Americans, bemoaning the loss of "those happy, carefree days" in bondage, ended when freedom, which they neither wanted nor could manage properly, was rudely foisted upon them. If *The Birth of a Nation* is the film we most love to hate, I propose that *Santa Fe Trail* is equally, if not more, worthy of our disdain. *Santa Fe Trail* is the single most virulent filmic denunciation of abolitionists and abolitionism in the twentieth century.

The film opens with one of the Hollywood signposts of historical films, perhaps left over from silent pictures: the prefatory, superimposed written proclamation of setting, an explicit signal to the audience that we are entering a different time and place. In this case, 1854, the tiny garrison of West Point, under the command of the "brilliant commandant Robert E. Lee." These large-font words fade as soldiers on horseback drill under the vigilant stillness of Lee and his historically accurate beard. But while historical facial hair is observed, we soon learn that actual historical events are less important.[25] As Hollywood would have it, West Point in 1854 is a sort of "who's who" of future Civil War generals, played by some of Hollywood's top leading men, including George Custer (Ronald Reagan) and Jeb Stuart (Errol Flynn). George Pickett, James Longstreet, John B. Hood, and Philip Sheridan are all here, too, representing what one contemporary reviewer described as an "exceedingly annoying" disregard for both the spirit and facts of American history.[26]

After the cavalry drill, as the men groom their steeds, the good-natured banter is disrupted by the high-hoofed bray and whinny of an intractable horse pulling with desperate discontent at its lead. The horse is restrained by its rider, the Northerner Carl Rader (Van Heflin), who with a snarl and sneer chides the animal, "You devil. If you weren't so hard headed, you wouldn't hurt your mouth."

Jeb Stuart looks on disapprovingly and responds, placing blame not on the horse, but on the cruelty of its master. "I told you before we started that you had that curb chain on too tight. It isn't the first time you cut his tongue."

"I suppose it takes one of you Southerners to handle a horse," Rader counters, laying the trap.

"Well at least we know how to harness them," Stuart answers innocently.

"You know how to harness Negroes down South, too, I hear. With a strap across their back." Rader quickly departs with his unhappy mount.

Well, sometimes a horse is just a horse, but this is not one of those times. Rader makes the connection between the horse and Southern slaves explicit. But, significantly, it is the Northerner who treats the animal without proper regard, abusing his position of master of the steed. Jeb Stuart, by contrast, gently strokes the buttocks of his horse with clean hay, in a symbolic reciprocity, a happy interdependence, the horse working for the man, the man for the horse, the horse loving the man, the man loving the horse. They "scratch each other's backs" quite literally in this scene. If you treat an animal with kindness, if you are a good master, both the harnessed and the harnesser benefit.

The virtues of Southern paternalism are contrasted with the evils of Northern paternalism as the film, here and in later scenes, attempts to undercut notions of Northern masculinity as traditionally defined. The Northerner cannot understand slavery because he fails to understand the responsibilities incumbent upon paternal power, as evidenced by Rader's mistreatment of his horse. In this way, the Northerner falls short of the conventional idealized standard of American masculinity, which is based on, and extended from ancient English theories of kingship.[27] As a man's home is his castle, he reigns over his subjects with a firm but just hand, never abusing his power or absolute authority. Paternal power, in this idealized masculinity, is a solemn duty. This brief introductory scene serves to justify slavery at the hands of a good master, contrasting the bad paternalism of the North with the good paternalism of the South.[28]

But this theme of "bad father"—that is, malicious or irresponsible paternalism—is reiterated later in the film when the cavalry, led by Stuart and Custer, discover the secret hideout of John Brown and gallop at it in force. Brown learns of their approach and decides to evade them, recognizing the need to "travel light" and "move fast." One of his men asks, "What about the Negroes? We can't take all of them." In the background we hear "the Negroes" singing a spiritual. These are theoretical, distant "Negroes." Discussions of their freedom and the principle of liberty for them are easy as long as they remain theoretical. Their actual physical reality proves a more difficult issue, much like a parent who likes the idea of children, but can't stand changing diapers.

"We're not taking any of them," Brown answers definitively. He turns from his men toward the singing, his black rounded hat and thigh-length coat silhouetted by the bright light from a barn. There is a radiant semicircle splashed before Brown, illuminating his path and purpose.

It is here we find the African Americans whom he has liberated from bondage. It is curious seeing them in a kind of bizarre barn ghetto, a segregated housing unit, in the camp of the most radical of abolitionists. They don't wander around the camp or interact with the whites. They don't carry weapons or display any visible participation in the struggle for their freedom. They know their place, packed in the separate-but-equal barn, like some purgatory between the hell of slavery and the heaven of liberation, waiting to be lifted by some agent of the divine. John Brown is happy to oblige.

"My children," he begins. "The hour of deliverance I promised you has come. I am leaving Kansas now to continue God's holy way."

Again, notice the self-conscious evocation of paternal prerogative. Not "my brothers," "my friends," or "my fellow Americans," but "my children."

"For Gideon took ten men of his servants and did as God had said unto him. And it was so that he did it by night. And when the men of the wicked city arose early in the morning . . ."

"Please Captain Brown," one African American man asks, "What does that mean? Whatcha gonna do with us?"

"It means that you are free. The first of many millions to whom I shall give freedom from slavery."

"Does just saying so just make us free? How we gonna live, get food and shelter?" Even this "simple" man grasped the distinction between platitudes and the logistics of the quotidian. He was not seduced by the rhetoric, fearing the impending "reality."

Brown is unmoved. "There are many good people in Kansas who will give you work and protection. From now on you must fend for yourselves as other free men do." He then turns from the questioner and, looking very self-satisfied, proclaims, "My work here is done."

The "nation" (read "white people") is presented with a choice on behalf of African Americans, as even among the abolitionists blacks are viewed as children. They may be given a nice Southern father who will care for them, feed them, clothe them, and protect them (and who knows what's best for them), or a Northern father who will treat them badly (as with Rader), or who loves them in theory (like Brown), but will abnegate his parental responsibilities when caring for them proves inconvenient.

It is safe to conclude, then, that *Santa Fe Trail* is decidedly critical of John Brown. But, as mentioned earlier, the abolition movement in the United States was characterized by a diversity of expressions, methods, and objectives. A condemnation of John Brown is not necessarily tantamount to a re-nunciation of abolition or abolitionists.[29] Many people quite sympathetic to the cause of antislavery, both yesterday and today, have denounced John Brown (though obviously in different terms than *Santa Fe Trail*).[30]

But in *Santa Fe Trail* John Brown is presented as the equivalent, or "best example," of historical abolition. The terms *John Brown* and *abolition* are used interchangeably throughout the movie, or grouped as "John Brown and the abolitionists." For example, once Stuart and Custer graduate from West Point they are sent, by rail, along with some other green cavalry cadets, to their first posting at Fort Leavenworth, Kansas Territory. As the train jostles along, one cadet turns to Cyrus K. Holliday, a Kansas businessman and railroad magnate, and asks him to explain the "true situation" in Kansas.

"Well, Kansas is a territory not a state," Holliday explains. "We're ready to join the union but the big question is whether we're to go in as slave state or a free state. On the one side you have the pro-slavers, people who came from the South. The other side is the abolitionists led by John Brown and his sons. And we know too well they've made Kansas a boiling pot." Consider the dichotomy created by the "true" situation in Kansas. Representing the slave power are "people from the South." Representing "freedom" is John Brown and the abolitionists. It is as if there is no larger political struggle in the American Congress, or in the nation over the issue in which Kansas is a pawn in the struggle for power and national identity. It is a struggle between pro-slavery people, nice people like Jeb Stuart, and thugs and subversives, John Brown and the abolitionists.

While the equating of John Brown and abolition runs throughout the film, it is made most explicitly when John Brown travels "at great personal risk" to Boston, apparently the well-heeled hub, and not-so-secret head-quarters, of all coordinated abolition activity in America. Brown seeks support for his planned attack on Harpers Ferry.[31] When he proposes his plan, one Boston abolitionist gentleman protests, "Captain Brown, this plan of yours is mad, worse than mad, it's high treason."

"Such a brazen attack would lead to civil war," another protests.

"Exactly," Brown shouts, "That is exactly what I want."

"Is it your wish, then, to destroy the Union?"

"My answer to that is, yes, to the devil with the Union"

After a brief private discussion, the Boston gentlemen agree to give Brown the support he requests. It is they who deserve the blame for the American Civil War through their "madness," "high treason," and desire to destroy the Union. They themselves recognize Brown and their own "madness." His plan is mad and they willingly support it.

Antislavery, then, is damned not only by its being equated with the historical Brown, but more by being equated with the ahistorical, *Santa Fe*

Trail John Brown.[32] This Hollywood John Brown was described by one contemporary critic as a "crack-pot villain," one who "deserves a better classification in the minds of impressionable moviegoers than that just one peg above a marauding cattle rustler from Bloody Gulch."[33] Part of the problem is Raymond Massey's performance. He is an absolutely convincing "crack-pot villain."

Let's then recap what's going on in *Santa Fe Trail* by way of its attitude toward abolition: Antislavery was John Brown; John Brown was mad and villainous; therefore, antislavery was mad and villainous. It is a clever argument, convincing to the uninformed, and absolutely damning to the notion of both radical reform and historical antislavery.

It also had a very profound contemporary resonance. Earlier, I referred to this as a "New Deal film." What I mean by this is a film that reflects President Franklin Roosevelt's emphasis on unity and balance, against the swelling tide of fascism, communism, false utopian visions, demagoguery, and more violent and extreme solutions to the social ills of American culture in the 1930s. The decade was marked by the proliferation of such extreme ideologies, organizations, and individuals as the Silver Shirts, American Nationalists, Father Coughlin, National Watchmen, Crusaders, Khaki Shirts—the list is longer than can be detailed here.[34]

Roosevelt's stated objective was "balance . . . balance between agriculture and industry, and balance between the wage earner, the employer and the consumer."[35] New Deal theorists are decidedly preoccupied with the idea of "balance," as it is the word, according to historian William E. Leuchtenburg, that appears most often in their writings.[36]

In a bizarre inversion of reality, *Santa Fe Trail* capitalizes on the anti-demagoguery by casting Brown and the abolitionists in that unfavorable light, without any recognition whatsoever of the fascist implications of American racism. This implication was recognized by the black press as early as 1933, and, reluctantly, by the United States government during the cold war. Even German observers during the 1930s referred to the connections between Nazi racial policies and the attitudes common in the Southern United States, decrying the double standard of a country that could protest the race theory of Nazi Germany while accepting Southern lynching justice.[37]

But not so in *Santa Fe Trail.* It is not the South, but John Brown who embodies fascistic tendencies, the character played with what film scholar Thomas Cripps called "Hitlerian bombast."[38] Brown is portrayed as the destructive representative of radical reform, as a force of demagoguery, threatening an otherwise happy, balanced Union. It is the South that espouses the ideology of the New Deal. A particularly poignant illumination of this historical irony is the 1854 West Point graduation speech depicted in the film: "We are a new nation among the powers of the world," the speaker begins.

Just eighty years ago we were fighting desperately for our freedom
and we're still fighting to keep it. We are not yet a wealthy nation, except in the spirit and that unity of spirit is our greatest strength. You
men have but one duty, one alone: America. With your unswerving
loyalty and the grace of God our nation shall have no fears for the future and your lives will have been spent in the noblest of all causes,
the defense of the rights of man.

Who is this speaker, this defender of the Union and the Rights of Man? Why
it's none other than Jefferson Davis, future president of the Confederate
States of America. His message, however, is clear: as long as we are joined in
our commitment to oppression, to the disenfranchisement and brutal exploitation of African Americans, we can continue to fight for the "rights of
man." *Santa Fe Trail* reads historical antislavery through early 1940s anti-
demagoguery, and in so doing re-invents the mid-nineteenth century for
"impressionable moviegoers" to the detriment of the rights of man.

It is shocking to a modern audience that this speech could appear in a
mainstream American film without a hint of irony. It reflected, however, the
diminishing legacy of abolitionists in both the American academy and
American cultural memory. But with Roosevelt, during the antifascist World
War and subsequent anti-Communist cold war, the United States was increasingly under international and self-scrutiny for the same sort of profound contradictions conveyed by Jefferson Davis's speech in *Santa Fe Trail.*

After the legal victories for African Americans in the 1950s, and during
the civil rights movement, there was a concomitant cultural elevation of
the historical role of abolitionists in American history.[39] The abolitionists
became what one scholar would call "the new left hero class"; as civil rights
activists they would celebrate their lineal descent. "To the New Left the
label 'New Abolitionists' for modern civil rights militants is more than a
metaphor." [40]

But this cultural restoration would never reach Hollywood. The *Souls at
Sea* of the 1960s would never be made. Why?

Fear? In part. It might be dangerous to celebrate radical reform in a
predominantly conservative Hollywood, recently "purged" of alleged radicals by blacklists and Communist-hunters, surrounded by a nation radically transforming, and intimidated by the "clear and present danger" of
the Soviet Union and its minions overseas. But it was also, and perhaps
more importantly, that those most sympathetic to the struggles of African
American men and women turned their attention instead to the very real
need to detail black life and culture; to assail dominant stereotypes, discover black history and black resistance, not as objects of white endeavor,
but as protagonists in their own struggle. White people had no place in this

new narrative of emancipation. Charges of paternalism and the need for empowerment often came at the expense of cultural outsiders, both historic and contemporary.

The call for black empowerment and leadership in the struggle for equality was hardly new. As early as 1827 in *Freedom's Journal* it was expressed as the "wish to plead our own cause. Too long have others spoken for us."[41] But this desire to "plead one's own cause" was translated as the need to exclude any white voices from those pleadings. This was best represented, perhaps, in 1966 when the Student Nonviolent Coordinating Committee (SNCC), a multiracial activist organization, voted to expel all white members.[42] Stokely Carmichael explicitly identified white participation in SNCC as "the biggest obstacle" in "Black folks getting liberation."[43] For Carmichael and others like Bill Ware of SNCC's Atlanta Project, white participation signified the "perpetuation of the missionary mentality, of the so-called good white men that had us looking toward them for our solution rather than looking toward ourselves."[44] For many African Americans it was "humiliating" to look to white people for fundamental rights and guarantees, as if "begging to be let in."[45]

What could "good" white people do to help?" Frederick Douglass had part of the answer over one hundred years earlier: "Listen well."[46] But Black Power now demanded an additional concession—that "good" whites recognize the need for their own subordination in, or exclusion from, the movement. "Sensitive white people," Carmichael argued, would recognize the problematic nature of their presence in SNCC and resign. "Those that don't understand that ought to be expelled."[47]

Hollywood seemed to have figured out and I think correctly so, that neither good white liberals nor good black activists were interested in a historically accurate film that portrayed white people giving black people anything. Historical films that dealt with slavery dealt primarily with the horrors of the institution, focusing on stories about good black families shattered by very bad Southern white people. The South became, during this period, synonymous with racism and oppression. The individual African Americans who endured and triumphed, whether through resistance or simply survival, were the New Left heroes of this period in American cinema. Northern abolitionists were simply absent, as this was not their story; they were minor actors in the struggle for individual, as opposed to institutional, freedom.

Yet in these depictions there was the unconscious and unintentional perpetuation of the myth that all black folks before the Civil War were slaves, as if this represented the "authentic black experience." Black abolitionists struggled both separately and alongside their white counterparts, but it took time for scholars and Hollywood to discover them.

While it is generally assumed that Hollywood's first depiction of a black abolitionist was rendered in *Amistad* in the character of Joadson (Morgan Freeman), this is not the case. Strangely, Hollywood's first depiction of a black abolitionist was not set in the past, but in the "future"—in that frighteningly futuristic sounding year, 1991—in a science-fiction movie released in 1972. The movie is titled *Conquest of the Planet of the Apes,* and it is the fourth in the five-film saga. While race is a subtext throughout the series, it is in *Conquest of the Planet of the Apes* that the issue of slavery and abolition is made most explicit.[48]

I realize that the inclusion of *Conquest* is outside the realm of the discussion of historical fiction, but it is certainly firmly in the realm of filmic treatments of antislavery. Science fiction, like satire, often critiques culture from a distance, by creating otherworldly representations of this world's society. *Gulliver's Travels* is not called science fiction, but had it been written today the talking horses, giants, and tiny men would have required Gulliver to travel in a spaceship rather than a sea ship. I don't mean to imply that we should regard the *Apes* series as in any way a profound artistic expression. Only that *Apes,* like Swift, self-consciously comments on contemporary society, as satire requires a self-consciousness not shared by other literary productions inevitably influenced by their times. The original film was based on the sophisticated French satiric novel *Le Planète des Singes* written by Pierre Boulle, perhaps best known in America for the screen adaptation of his novel, *The Bridge on the River Kwai.* But *Conquest,* an original screenplay, had a different resonance, a different satiric object, as producer Frank Capra Jr. explains: "The imagery of the Watts riots had been played on television night after night after night . . . [these images] were certainly in [director] J. Lee [Thompson's] mind."[49]

What is troubling about these veiled depictions of the Watt's Riots is that in the movie the riots occur as the first act, and seemingly natural result, of emancipation from slavery. Freedom is defined not as the right to self-determination and equal rights before the law, but as the right to violently invert the hierarchy, with apes on top and humans on the bottom. In this way *Conquest of the Planet of the Apes* bears an uncomfortable likeness to *The Birth of a Nation,* though produced fifty-seven years later and in the wake of the civil rights movement. Both portray the historical fallacy of the destructive effects of an ill-considered, "premature" emancipation, and the empowerment of "subhumans" emotionally and intellectually "ill-equipped" to manage the awesome responsibilities of personal liberty. It is essentially a pessimistic, or perhaps realistic, depiction of power and its effects on humans and apes, consistent with the cynicism of the early 1970s. Power corrupts. Those that would work to empower the disenfranchised and oppressed are, in fact, working not for justice, but for their own disempowerment. Whoever is on top should work to stay there.

Conquest begins at a time when Earth was still a planet run by humans. A strange virus from outer space has wiped out all the traditional pet choices available to mankind. Imagine a world with no dogs, no cats, no cat ladies. Humans tried to use simians to fill the void in their nihilistic, petless lives. They quickly learned that simians could do far more than just fetch the morning paper. They were capable of performing more complex tasks. Apes who started as beloved pets quickly became slaves. *Conquest of the Planet of the Apes* is full of images of apes performing slave labor. While industrial and agricultural labor is noticeably absent in this vision of the future, pouring water, mopping, and fetching things from across town are portrayed with great accuracy. There is unquestionable degradation. The apes are treated with great impatience when they fail to pour properly or make hospital corners on beds; the masters never say thank you, the apes look hurt; clearly all they want is what we all want, a kind word and a smile. It's not slavery that's bad in *Conquest,* but the way that having that sort of power leads to a society without proper courtesy. Like *The Birth of a Nation* and all other film portrayals of benign slavery, the slavery in *Conquest* is really no worse than most menial jobs in Los Angeles or New York City. Some people have the power to compel labor, others are too in debt to resist.

The society is kept orderly by a governor with a bad, fake Southern accent, and his black-clad storm trooper police force that looks suspiciously Third Reich in their fashion choice. Into this world a talking chimp arrives, a better sort of monkey, who, raised far from the degradation and humiliation of slavery, was allowed to achieve his full potential. He is clever, sensitive, rational and, of course, an enormous threat to the slave power. Given the opportunity to name himself by pointing at a book, he chooses Caesar. This is not only a reference to the general-then-emperor, but also has resonance with the practice in historical American slavery of choosing names from antiquity for slaves.

There are two sympathetic humans in the movie. The first is Caesar's handler, Señor Armando, the white, Spanish circus impresario played by Ricardo Montalban. Señor Armando and Caesar arrive by helicopter to promote the circus. Armando loathes the brutal treatment of the apes, but as a circus impresario it is implied that he feels that minstrel shows are all right. He warns Caesar to act more like a primitive, to be less conspicuous. "After 20 years you've picked up evolved habits from me. That could be dangerous, even fatal." The evolved habits are habits aped from the human, not inherent in Caesar's nature.

Armando is never explicitly critical of the institution of slavery, but we might think of him as at least sympathetic to antislavery thought, as he looks truly pained at the various manifestations of ape degradation, and as he does do his best to protect Caesar. But after irresponsibly bringing him in close proximity to extremely powerful and dangerous humans for the sake of his circus, he deserts him when he can no longer defend him. In a moment similar to the John Brown, bad paternalism scene in *Santa Fe Trail,* Armando abandons Caesar. But unlike *Santa Fe Trail,* in which the good white people of Kansas will take over for other "good white people" who are burdened by their responsibility, Armando urges Caesar "to go to your people." Apes (blacks) must no longer look to humans (whites), no matter how seemingly sympathetic, as ultimately there is no place for cultural outsiders in minority cultural liberation movements. After he abandons Caesar, Armando is tortured, betrays his trust to Caesar, and ends up accidentally plunging to his death. There is a veiled message here, too, for the well-meaning cultural outsider.

The other "good human" is the governor's assistant, played by an African American. He is clearly not only critical of the institution of slavery, but argues for humane treatment of the apes, and actively helps Caesar escape. He is, perhaps, a comment on the black middle class: neither of the white mainstream dominant culture, nor of the black masses, caught between, benefiting from class affinity, but feeling the pull of race responsibility. This modern black abolitionist hopes that Caesar's rise to power will end a society based on oppression, but this does not happen. Instead, Caesar apes his human counterparts and promises to be as bad, if not worse. *Conquest,* exploiting black anger, and reflecting the 1970's liberal retreat, conveys revolution without reform, a stillborn millenial vista—all the violence of rebirth and none of the utopian aftermath. The governor's assistant, our first black film abolitionist, while his life is spared, is simply lumped in with the other humans and has effectively undermined his own place within the status hierarchy. After the 1960's fête of reform, *Conquest of the Planet of the Apes* captures the spirit of a nation hung over.

If *Conquest of the Planet of the Apes* implies presence of the first black abolitionist in an imagined American future, it is *Amistad* that first explicitly recognizes the historical presence of black abolitionists. It is somewhat beside the point, for the purposes of this essay, that *Amistad*'s black abolitionist, the character of Joadson, is not based on an actual historical figure. He is, rather, a composite based in part on the Connecticut African American abolitionist James W.C. Pennington, imagined through the requirements of what one cultural critic called, "the sensibilities of the multicultural nineties audience."[50]

But why fabricate this Joadson? The filmmakers are perfectly eager to inaccurately imagine Roger Baldwin, Cinque, Grabeau, Louis Tappan, John Quincy Adams, Martin Van Buren, John C. Calhoun, among others. Why they would choose to invent an imaginary black abolitionist rather than to dramatize Pennington (who did, in fact, play a role in defending the *Amistad* captives) is beyond me. It seems a bit odd here to all of a sudden have some high standard of historical accuracy, but only in the case of the African American abolitionist, and to answer the demands of this new standard with the creation of an entirely fictional character that is easily dismissed as such. It is more likely that they never heard of Pennington, or if they did, they forgot. I am sure, in their defense, that if they had known anything about him, they would have been perfectly happy to inaccurately imagine him as well.

But as I mentioned, this is really beside the point here. *Amistad* has already been taken to task for its historical inaccuracies in scholarly books and articles, national periodicals, and at conferences organized to minimize the historical damage. Rather than reiterate these objections or further bemoan or deconstruct the ways in which *Amistad* missed its chance to serve history, I would rather look at the work it does. For the purposes of this discussion the question "How does *Amistad* wrong history?" is of less interest than "How does *Amistad* imagine reform and, more specifically, historical antislavery?"—and do so as a late-twentieth-century cultural artifact.[51]

As a nation, we are constantly reinventing the past to serve the requirements of our present national senses of self. As slavery became sin, Jamestown ceded its place to Plymouth Rock as the "birthplace of America." Never mind that New Englanders held slaves. This cultural amnesia was as much a result of regional as national requirements.[52] I speak not of the historical record, but the ways in which the nation imagined itself. Historian Jon Butler convincingly argues that the Puritans played a rather small role in the historical record in "making America."[53] I would argue that the function that they served, however inaccurately, to reinvent an acceptable American origin myth, makes them essential to American history.[54]

Amistad functions in ways that do a disservice to the historical record, but a service to the needs of our present sense of self. This is accomplished not only in the creation of a composite black abolitionist, but in the attempt to ahistorically secularize the abolition movement.[55] In so doing, like *Santa Fe Trail*, it is aggressively dismissive of the religious basis of reform, black or white. *Amistad* conveys a profound disdain for those who would invoke Christ, the cross, or any other explicit religious symbol or dogma. This sentiment is mingled with a dismissive portrayal of an impotence born of naïveté, as reformers pray to God, sing hymns, and get in the way (both literally and figuratively), while trying to save the captives' souls. Meanwhile, those who live "in the world," not steeped in religion, do the actual work of trying to save the captives' lives.

Illustrative of this distinction is a scene early in the film, set in a New Haven restaurant, when Louis Tappan (Stellan Skarsgård) and Joadson, disappointed by their inability to engage the services of John Quincy

Adams (Anthony Hopkins) in the defense of African captives, turn instead to Roger Baldwin (Matthew McConaughey). Baldwin is eating. He is a sloppy, unseemly fellow who consumes his meal with the relish of a man who does not often eat well. He is flanked by Tappan and Joadson.

Joadson summarizes for Baldwin the possible dire consequences of "losing" the case. He speaks in terms of what will likely happen to the *Amistad* captives if they are not successful in their efforts to free them. "If the captain prevails, he is most likely to sell them to Spain, and they'll be executed."

"I'm a little confused by something," Baldwin interrupts, mouth still full of food, "What are they worth to you?"

"We are discussing the case, not its expense," Tappan intercedes.

"Oh, the case, of course. Well the case is much simpler than you think, Mr. Tappan. It's like anything, isn't it? Land, livestock, heirlooms, what have you."

"Livestock," Tappan repeats, looking at Joadson, disgusted by the association.

"Yes, consider," Baldwin continues, seemingly oblivious to his ideological faux pas. "The only way one can purchase or sell slaves is if they are born slaves. . . . Forget mutiny, forget piracy, forget murder and all the rest. Those are subsequent irrelevant currencies. Ignore everything but the pre-eminent issue at hand—the wrongful transfer of stolen goods. Either way, we win."

Tappan rears up in his chair. "Sir," he begins, using the word as if intended ironically, "this war must be waged on the battlefield of righteousness."

"The what?"

"It would be against everything I stand for to let this deteriorate into an exercise on the vagaries of legal minutiae."

"Well, I don't know what you're talking about, Mr. Tappan, but I'm talking about the heart of the matter."

"As am I. It is our destiny as abolitionists and as Christians to save these people. These are people, Mr. Baldwin, not livestock. Did Christ hire a lawyer to get him off on technicalities? He went to the cross, nobly. You know why? To make a statement as must we."

"But Christ lost. You at least . . ."

"No, he did not, sir."

"Or at least you," Baldwin continues turning now to Joadson, "want to win, don't you?

"Yes." Joadson answers, nodding his head. Joadson, the composite black abolitionist, while he may be troubled by the association of the Africans to livestock, is willing to put aside his principles to free these African men. Tappan, steeped in religion and principle, objectifies the captives as completely as Baldwin. While they may not be "livestock" they are still not people, but ideas.

This is followed by a scene of abolitionists who solemnly march to the gate of the jail. The Africans see them coming and are puzzled by their presence and intentions.

"Who are they, do you think?" Grabeau asks his fellow slave rebel Cinque, as the abolitionists kneel to pray.

"Looks like they're going to be sick," Cinque answers. The shot is framed from inside the jail. The abolitionists are distant, incomprehensible, framed through the bars, as they are framed through a modern incomprehension of religion, and religiously inspired reform. We, too, are prisoners of our present cultural context, one that mistrusts religious inspiration, or associates it with televangelists, or the Dalai Lama, Jimmy Carter, holy men better off in the desert than the real world, too removed from the requirements of a world driven by power to protect their interests, or the interests of the people whom they represent. We once prayed to God. Now we pray to science.[56]

Then they begin to sing "Amazing Grace" (and not terribly well).

"They are entertainers," Cinque concludes. "But why do they look so miserable?" he asks before uttering a dismissive click and walking away. Even to those they endeavor to save, the abolitionists are dismissed, not only as religious zealots, but as something far worse—"bad entertainers." For Hollywood there can be no greater crime.

Bad entertainers, irresponsible parents, condescending patriarchs, zealots, rogues, and opportunists—abolitionists have not fared well in twentieth-century American cinema. Joadson offers some hope, but, again, the balanced, sensitive treatment of an abolitionist seems possible only if written as black, or detached from the larger movement, with individuals acting independently, as do Souls at Sea's Taylor or Amistad's John Quincy Adams. It seems unlikely, for now, that this trend will abate. At the birth of the twenty-first century we watch people die and kill for what they believe in, religiously inspired "reformers," whose actions anger and perplex us. It is interesting to speculate on what influence they may have on further treatments of abolitionists in history and film. But one thing is certain—now when we view historical acts of reform, even when perpetuated for reasons in which we believe, we will to a greater extent condemn violent expressions of reform, especially when they are couched in terms of martyrdom.

Afterword

Martin Duberman

Some forty years ago, when the seventeen essays that comprise *The Anti-slavery Vanguard* were finally in hand and the time had come to do an introduction to the volume, I wrote that "our aim will have been accomplished if it offers enough new data and new insights to demonstrate that a re-evaluation [of the abolitionist movement] is both possible and necessary."

When I wrote those words in 1964 (*Vanguard* was published the following year), a shift in perspective on the abolitionists had already begun and the negative view of them that had long dominated both public consciousness and the historical profession itself had begun to fray at the edges. That view, which had reigned since the end of Reconstruction, held that those "immediatists" who fought to end slavery were misguided, neurotic fanatics responsible for the Civil War *and* the worsening conditions for the slaves themselves in the decades that preceded the war.

In the climate of the mid-1960s, when social justice issues were on the front burner and anti-authoritarianism happily rampant among the young, the views propounded in *The Antislavery Vanguard* took hold fairly rapidly. But as historians well know, any re-evaluation is itself soon destined for scrutiny. Our understanding of the past constantly evolves as additional source material is uncovered and as shifting cultural imperatives cue a new generation to search for aspects of historical experience to which we were previously blind.

Since the mid-1960s, for example, white racism has notably reoriented its basic strategy, shifting from a genetic to a cultural set of "explanations" for black "inferiority." Where the earlier emphasis centered on the claim that African Americans are *intrinsically* (biologically) handicapped, born lazy and irresponsible, with no rational capacity for analysis or logic, more recent forms of racist expression stress instead that black deprivations basically derive from the subculture's disdain for education and intellectual accomplishment, and its refusal to acquire the negotiable skills and "appropriate" (read "white middle-class") behavioral attitudes that would make further assimilation possible. This realignment in racist discourse has in turn generated new lines of counter-argument that reveal areas of black achievement and new evidence of black accomplishment previously minimized or ignored.

One of the great strengths and unique contributions of *Prophets of Protest* lies precisely in the ingenious way many of its contributors have uncovered source materials and mounted arguments that attest to the accomplishments and contributions of African Americans in the pre–Civil War period. Drawing (as Dickson Bruce and Augusta Rohrbach have) from nineteenth-century poetry and fiction, or studying (as John Stauffer has) previously overlooked photographic representations, or (as Timothy Patrick McCarthy and Patrick Rael have) unknown or unstudied early newspapers, periodicals, "scientific" treatises, and histories, the contributors to *Prophets of Protest* have greatly widened the lens through which we view the origins and formations of abolitionism. In a related area, Casey King has, by turning to film, illuminated the overwhelmingly negative depiction of those who became abolitionists, uncovering a profound bias that had managed simultaneously to distort the historical record and to imprint on several generations a version of the past that, by implication, discredits *in general* all those who struggle for social reform.

The two editors of *Prophets of Protest*, Timothy Patrick McCarthy and John Stauffer, greatly help to redress the balance by emphasizing in their introduction how Northern free blacks who became involved in the abolitionist movement utilized "a range of institutions and media—including African American churches, annual freedom celebrations, political pamphlets, and serial newspapers—to assert their opposition to slavery . . ." And we now know (thanks to the essays by Robert Forbes, Julie Winch, and Manisha Sinha) that they did so in far greater numbers than we were previously aware, even though a number of black scholars—including Martin Delany, William Wells Brown, Carter Woodson, and Dorothy Porter—had tried to tell us long ago that the abolitionist movement from its very inception relied heavily on the activities of the black community itself.

Until the publication of *Prophets of Protest*, historians have continued to de-emphasize both pre–Civil War black activism *and* the early-twentieth-century black historians who tried to call attention to it. The dominant older narrative mostly credited privileged white men for creating and carrying forth the struggle to win freedom for black slaves. That narrative has been losing credibility for some time now, thanks to the work of a number of feminist and black historians (and even some white male ones). To name only a few: Benjamin Quarles (*Black Abolitionists*), Shirley Yee (*Black Women Abolitionists*), Jean Fagan Yellin (*The Abolitionist Sisterhood*), Julie Roy Jeffrey (*The Great Silent Army of Abolitionism*), and Patrick Rael (*Black Identity and Protest in the Antebellum North*).

Thanks to those previous books and to this volume, we now know that the older narrative is in need of sharp revision, one that would for the first time give proper due to the significant, and perhaps paramount, contributions of women and African Americans who (as the editors put it) represented "every class, color, circumstance, and creed" in the country.

If I can be allowed a personal note, it's deeply satisfying to me, as the editor of *The Antislavery Vanguard* way back in 1965, to witness, after some forty years of additional scholarship and changing social values, the field of antislavery studies taking, with *Prophets of Protest,* yet another giant leap forward in expanding our understanding of this central experience in our national history. *Prophets of Protest* has, successfully I believe, recentered the abolitionist movement as an interracial struggle.

The new findings and interpretations presented here, revealing so many little-known truths, will, of course, run up against the entrenched determination of those who favor (and profit from) the status quo to maintain the hegemonic narrative that long excluded or minimized the voices and contributions to abolitionism made by an interracial rank and file. But so rich is the material in *Prophets of Protest,* and so well reasoned its arguments, that I believe it will overcome the resistance to its message. The great achievement of this volume is that we are finally able to hear many more of the voices, and to appreciate far more profoundly the significance of their contributions to the ongoing struggle for a decent society.

Acknowledgments

This book was inspired by all the excellent scholarship on abolitionism that has been published during the last two generations. With this is mind, we'd like to start by thanking the senior scholars in the field who continue to challenge us, as well as those who have passed on whose work first blazed the trails that now, thankfully, seem well-worn and familiar. We have dedicated this book to the late Benjamin Quarles and the late Herbert Aptheker. Dr. Quarles and Dr. Aptheker were to African American history what Frederick Douglass and John Brown were to the abolitionist movement, and we are honored and humbled to have the opportunity to labor in their vineyard. Rest in peace.

We are pleased to acknowledge all the contributors to this volume: Dave, Rob, Hannah, Karl, Casey, Thea, Julie, Rich, Patrick, Augusta, Manisha, Julie, and Sandi. As the book goes to press, we would like to thank each and every one of them for their kind friendship, heroic patience, and judicious criticism. From start to finish, this was a truly collective, and collegial, effort. The abolitionists would be proud.

We are also extremely grateful to Martin Duberman and Michael Fellman, who have generously supported this project from its inception. Marty and Michael are model scholars, teachers, and citizens, and we are honored to have them on board for this project—especially since they have long since "had their say" with respect to the abolitionists. Michael's thorough and astute comments on the initial drafts of these essays enhanced the book beyond measure.

It is safe to say that we would not be where we are without the guidance we've received, and the inspiration we've taken, from Eric Foner and David Brion Davis, our graduate advisors at Columbia and Yale. Their scholarly influence should be obvious to anyone who reads this book, but it is their personal influence—their rare example of how to combine research and teaching with moral and political engagement—that is their greatest gift to us. We were lucky to study with them in graduate school; we are even luckier, now, to be able to call them colleagues and friends.

We would like to thank the following friends and colleagues who have prodded us over the years to think about the abolitionists (and a lot of other things, too) in new ways: Bob Abzug, Erica Armstrong, Iver Bernstein, Steve Biel, Richard Blackett, David Blight, Al Brophy, Vincent Brown, Larry Buell, Richard Bushman, Jon Butler, Eliza Byard, Chris Cappozzola, Catherine Clinton, Cathy Corman, Neal Dolan, David Herbert

Donald, Ann Douglas, Jim Downs, Jonathan Earle, David Ekbladh, Stanley Engerman, Ann Fabian, Devin Fergus, Robert Ferguson, Johanna Fernandez, Bill Ferris, Karen Flood, Mike Foley, Thelma Foote, Jonathan Fortescue, John Hope Franklin, William Freehling, Henry Louis Gates Jr., David Gellman, Paul Goodman, Farah Jasmine Griffin, Jacquelyn Dowd Hall, Bob Hanning, Phillip Brian Harper, Evelyn Brooks Higginbotham, Hua Hsu, John Jackson, Mark Jerng, Martha Jones, Steve Kantrowitz, Robin D.G. Kelley, Gary Kornblith, Nadine Knight, Carol Lasser, Ian Lekus, Bob Levine, Jean Libby, David Luis-Brown, Manning Marable, Waldo Martin, Jack McKivigan, Rebecca McLennan, John McMillian, Joanne Pope Melish, Louis Menand, Josh Miller, Steven Mintz, Sharon Musher, Martha Nadell, Megan Nelson, Sam Otter, Colin Palmer, Bob Paquette, Lewis Perry, David Quigley, Jeanne Follansbee Quinn, Matt Raffety, Harry Reed, Adam Rothman, Maggie Sale, Roger Scotland, Werner Sollors, James Brewer Stewart, Patricia Sullivan, Durahn Taylor, Joe Thompson, Alan Trachtenberg, Zoe Trodd, Jeremy Varon, Priscilla Wald, Harry Watson, Cornel West, Conrad Wright, Joe Wood, Dag Woubshet, Don Yacovone, and Howard Zinn.

Over the years, our Harvard students have demonstrated heroic patience and good humor as we've tried to convince them that the abolitionists are: (1) important; and (2) nothing like what they saw in *Amistad*. In the Departments of English and Afro-American Studies, in the Committee on Degrees in History and Literature, and in the graduate program in American Civilization, we have been fortunate to teach some of the best undergraduates and young scholars in the world. We would especially like to thank our students from "American Protest Literature," for engaging the abolitionists with such enthusiasm, despite their obvious desire to get on to more "modern" stuff like feminism, civil rights, and Hip Hop. We've had a blast—all the way from Tom Paine to Tupac.

For research assistance, we are indebted to the librarians and archivists at Yale University, Columbia University, New York University, the University of North Carolina at Chapel Hill, the Oberlin College Archives and Special Collections, the Boston Public Library, the Massachusetts Historical Society, Houghton Library and Widener Library at Harvard University, the American Antiquarian Society, and the Boston Anthenaeum. Special thanks, too, to C. Peter Ripley and the editors of the Black Abolitionist Papers, an invaluable resource, and to the kind people at Sir Speedy copiers (1001 Massachusetts Avenue), without whom we couldn't have finished this book.

The New Press supported this project when it was still just an idea. We are grateful to André Schiffrin for bringing us on board, and for creating a progressive space in the publishing world. Our editor Marc Favreau is as patient and kind as he is smart and gifted (for Tim, it's been a special treat to work with Marc again). Melissa Richards has responded to what seems like a million phone calls—and nearly twice that many emails—with unwavering good cheer and efficiency (even when we didn't deserve it). John Morrone copyedited the manuscript with brilliant precision and a keen eye for literary gaffes, historical inaccuracies, and footnote absurdity. And Maury Botton carefully shepherded the whole thing into print as managing editor. We couldn't have asked for a more talented and hardworking editorial team.

A very special note of thanks to our parents—Tom and Michelle McCarthy and Bill and Jean Stauffer—and to our siblings and their families: Malcolm and Tiffanie Green, Dian Jones, Rachel and Jim Lawson, and Mark, Becky, and Connor LeFavre. Although we don't say it enough, we love you.

Recently, each of us has finally found a life partner. To Kenneth Wilson and Deborah Cunningham, we thank you for your support, inspiration, humor, and intellect—and also for helping us find the one thing that always eluded us: true love.

Finally, we'd like to thank each other. For almost a decade now, we have read each other's work, traveled together to conferences, developed and co-taught a course, helped each other through personal trials, celebrated each other's triumphs, and spent many hours breaking bread, drinking strong coffee, and talking about everything that inspires and angers us as humanists living in a world that is not always humane. So in addition to its scholarly merits, *Prophets of Protest* is also a testament to friendship—a very good one that we hope will last until our assessment of American abolitionism needs its own reconsideration.

Timothy Patrick McCarthy and John Stauffer
Cambridge, MA, November 2005

Contributors

Dickson D. Bruce Jr., is professor of history at the University of California at Irvine. He specializes in nineteenth-century American cultural and intellectual history, and his work has focused on African American literature and thought as well as on the history of the antebellum South. His books include *And They All Sang Hallelujah: Plain-Folk Camp-Meeting Religion, 1800–1845* (University of Tennessee Press, 1974), winner of the Southern Anthropological Society's James Mooney Award; *Violence and Culture in the American South* (University of Texas Press, 1979); *Black American Writing from the Nadir* (Louisiana State University Press, 1989); and *The Origins of African-American Literature, 1680–1865* (University Press of Virginia, 2001).

Martin Duberman is Distinguished Professor of History *Emeritus* at Lehman College and the Graduate School of the City University of New York. He is the founder and first director (1986–1996) of the Center for Lesbian and Gay Studies at the CUNY Graduate School, the country's first such research center. Duberman is the author and editor of more than twenty books and plays, including *Haymarket: A Novel* (Seven Stories, 2003); *Left Out: The Politics of Exclusion/Essays, 1964–1999* (Basic Books, 1999); *Stonewall* (Dutton, 1993); *Cures: A Gay Man's Odyssey* (Dutton, 1991); *Paul Robeson* (Knopf, 1989); *Hidden from History: Reclaiming the Gay and Lesbian Past* (New American History, 1989); *Black Mountain: An Exploration in Community* (Dutton, 1972); and *In White America* (Houghton Mifflin, 1964). He also edited *The Antislavery Vanguard: New Essays on the Abolitionists* (Princeton University Press, 1965). Duberman has received many prestigious awards, including the Bancroft Prize and a citation from the American Academy of Arts and Letters for his "contributions to literature." He lives in New York City.

Michael Fellman is professor of history at Simon Fraser University. He is the author of numerous books, including *Citizen Sherman: A Life of William Tecumsah Sherman* (Random House, 1995); *Inside War: The Guerilla Conflict in Missouri During the American Civil War* (Oxford University Press, 1989); *The Unbounded Frame: Freedom and Community in Nineteenth-Century American Utopianism* (Greenwood Press, 1973); and *The Making of Robert E. Lee* (Random House, 2000). He also co-edited, with Lewis Perry, *Antislavery Recon-*

sidered: New Essays on the Abolitionists (Louisiana State University Press, 1979). He lives in Vancouver, British Columbia.

Robert P. Forbes received his Ph.D. from Yale University in 1994 and has helped to direct Yale's Gilder Lehrman Center for the Study of Slavery, Resistance, and Abolition since its inception in 1998. He is the co-author of several books and numerous articles and encyclopedia entries. His most recent study, *Slavery and the Meaning of America: The Missouri Compromise and its Aftermath,* is forthcoming from the University of North Carolina Press. He is active in educational outreach and public history, where his current research is focused on the role of New England and the Long Island Sound in the triangle trade with the West Indies and Africa.

Hannah Geffert is a member of the faculty in the political science department at Shepherd College in Shepherdstown, West Virginia. Some of her publications include *An Annotated Narrative of the African-American Community in Jefferson County, West Virginia; Voices from the Fields: An Oral History of Migrant Farmworkers; An Oral History of Shepherd College;* and *West Virginia Union Widows and the Military Pensions System.* She received both her undergraduate and graduate degrees from Temple University.

Karl Gridley, a graduate of the University of Kansas, is an independent scholar whose work focuses on the regional history of Kansas and the Great Plains.

T.K. Hunter is an historian of colonial America and the British Atlantic world. She has graduate degrees in both art history and history and was awarded her Ph.D. from Columbia University in May 2004. Her dissertation, entitled "Publishing Freedom, Winning Arguments: *Somerset,* Natural Rights, and Massachusetts Freedom Cases, 1772–1836," examines through newspapers the social and legal role of the *Somerset* case in the proliferation of natural rights ideology among enslaved African Americans as they sued for freedom in court. She served as an off-camera consultant on Episode 2 ("Revolution") for Boston's WGBH-TV history production *Africans in America,* and is credited as writer and researcher for Simon Schama's *Liberty and Slavery in the Early British Empire,* a BBC/Fathom online seminar complementing the BBC documentary on the history of Britain. Dr. Hunter is the recipient of Columbia University's President's Fellowship, a University of Glasgow Fellowship, and an Andrew W. Mellon Fellowship. She has been a visiting scholar at Columbia University for two years, and is currently an assistant professor of history at Western Connecticut State University.

Julie Roy Jeffrey is professor of history at Goucher College. She is the author of *The Great Silent Army of Abolitionism: Ordinary Women in the Abolitionist Movement* (University of North Carolina Press, 1998); *Converting the West: A Biography of Narcissa Whitman* (University of Oklahoma Press, 1992); *Frontier Women: The Trans-Mississippi West, 1840–1880* (Hill and Wang, 1979); and with Gary Nash et al., *The American People: The History of a Nation and a Society* (HarperCollins, 1986). She is currently working on a study of abolitionist memoirs.

Casey King studied abolitionism at Yale University with David Brion Davis, and film and video at Howard University with Abiyi Ford and with the late Marlon Riggs, formerly of the University of California at Berkeley. King wrote, produced, and directed a documentary on the nineteenth- and twentieth-century African American painter Henry Osawa Tanner. The video—funded in part by grants from the National Endowment for the Humanities and the Ford Motor Company—was co-produced with the Philadelphia Museum of Art, toured the country with an exhibition of Tanner's work, and appeared on local PBS stations. King has served as a panelist on the Metropolitan Museum of Art's "Program for Art on Film," and as a guest speaker at the American Museum of Art, Smithsonian Institution. In addition to his work on Tanner, he is also the author of a nonfiction book for young adults on the civil rights movement, *Oh, Freedom!* (Knopf, 1997), based on a seven-year oral history project.

Co-editor of *Prophets of Protest*, **Timothy Patrick McCarthy** is lecturer on history and literature at Harvard University, where he has received numerous awards for outstanding teaching and advising. McCarthy is co-editor, with John McMillian, of *The Radical Reader: A Documentary Anthology of the American Radical Tradition* (New Press, 2003), which has been adapted for staged readings in New York City and Providence. Educated at Harvard and Columbia, McCarthy is currently working on two books—the first, based on his doctoral dissertation, about abolitionist print culture and changing conceptions of equality in nineteenth-century America; the second, entitled *The Fires This Time*, about black church burnings in the post–civil rights South. An activist as well, McCarthy is an outspoken advocate for civil rights, economic justice, educational equity, youth empowerment, and peace.

Richard S. Newman teaches at Rochester Institute of Technology and is an educational advisor to Strong Museum in Rochester, New York. He is author of *The Transformation of American Abolitionism: Fighting Slavery in the Early Republic* (University of North Carolina Press, 2002), and co-editor, with Patrick Rael and Philip Lapsansky, of *Pamphlets of Protest: An Anthology of Early African American Protest Writing, 1790–1860* (Routledge, 2001). He is completing a biography of Bishop Richard Allen entitled *Black Founder: Richard Allen, African Americans, and the Early Republic.*

Patrick Rael is associate professor of history at Bowdoin College. He is co-editor, with Richard S. Newman and Philip Lapsansky, of *Pamphlets of Protest* (Routledge, 2001), and the author of *Black Identity and Black Protest in the Antebellum North* (University of North Carolina Press, 2002), which won honorable mention for the 2003 Frederick Douglass Book Prize from the Gilder Lehrman Center for Slavery, Resistance, and Abolition. He has held fellowships from Princeton's Center for the Study of Religion, the Smithsonian Institution, the American Historical Association, the Library of Congress, and the Library Company of Philadelphia. He earned his Ph.D. from the University of California at Berkeley in 1995.

Augusta Rohrbach is assistant professor of English at Washington State University. During the 2004–05 academic year, she was the Watts Visiting Professor of Book History at Brown University. She is author of *Truth Stranger than Fiction: Race, Realism, and the U.S. Literary Marketplace* (Palgrave, 2002), and is currently working on *Ar'n't I a Writer?: Trading on Race and Gender in the Literary Marketplace,* the book-length project from which her essay in this collection is drawn.

Manisha Sinha is associate professor of African-American Studies and History at the University of Massachusetts at Amherst. She is the author of *The Counterrevolution of Slavery* (University of North Carolina Press, 2000), and co-editor, with John H. Bracey Jr., of the two-volume *African-American Mosaic: A Documentary History of African Americans from the Slave Trade to the Twenty-First Century* (Prentice Hall, 2004). At present, she is working on a book about African Americans in the movement to abolish slavery from 1775 to 1865. She is the recipient of several fellowships, including grants from the American Philosophical Society and the American Council of Learned Societies.

Co-editor of *Prophets of Protest,* **John Stauffer** is professor of English and American Civilization at Harvard University. Stauffer received his Ph.D. in American Studies from Yale University in 1999, and won the Ralph Henry Gabriel Prize for the best dissertation from the American Studies Association. His first book, *The Black Hearts of Men: Radical Abolitionists and the Transformation of Race* (Harvard University Press, 2002), was the co-winner of the 2002 Frederick Douglass Prize from the Gilder Lehrman Institute;

winner of the Avery Craven Book Prize from the Organization of American Historians; and runner-up for the Lincoln Prize. He is editor of Frederick Doug-lass's *My Bondage and My Freedom* (Modern Library, 2003), and co-editor, with Zoe Trodd, of *Meteor of War: The John Brown Story* (Brandywine Press, 2004). He is currently at work on a new book project, *By Love of Comrades: Interracial Friendships and Dreams of Democracy,* forthcoming from Yale University Press.

Julie Winch is professor of history at the University of Massachusetts at Boston, where she has taught since 1985. She has published four books and numerous scholarly articles on the lives of free people of color in antebellum America. Her most recent book, *A Gentleman of Color: The Life of James Forten* (Oxford University Press, 2002), won the Wesley-Hogan Prize, awarded each year by the American Historical Association for the best book on a topic in African American history.

Sandra Sandiford Young is a lecturer at Boston College and program assistant for the Boston College Black Studies Program.

Notes

Introduction

1. Eugene Debs, "Address to the Jury," in Timothy Patrick McCarthy and John McMillian, eds., *The Radical Reader: A Documentary Anthology of the American Radical Tradition* (New Press, 2003), 311–12.

2. William Lloyd Garrison, "To the Public," *The Liberator,* January 1, 1831, in William E. Cain, ed., *William Lloyd Garrison and the Fight Against Slavery: Selections from* The Liberator (Boston: Bedford Books, 1995), 72.

3. By the time he issued his Emancipation Proclamation on January 1, 1863, Lincoln had considerably revised his earlier disdain for the abolitionists. See William S. McFeely, *Frederick Douglass* (New York: Simon and Schuster, 1991); James M. McPherson, *The Negro's Civil War: How American Negroes Felt and Acted during the War for the Union* (New York: Pantheon, 1965); and Benjamin Quarles, *The Negro in the Civil War* (Boston: Little, Brown, 1953).

4. Quoted in David Herbert Donald, *Lincoln* (New York: Simon and Schuster, 1995), 64.

5. Abraham Lincoln, "Second Inaugural Address," March 4, 1865, in Don E. Fehrenbacher, ed., *Abraham Lincoln: A Documentary Portrait through His Speeches and Writings* (Stanford, CA: Stanford University Press, 1964), 278.

6. Martin Duberman, ed., *The Antislavery Vanguard: New Essays on the Abolitionists* (Princeton: Princeton University Press, 1965), vii–viii. Contributors to this volume included: David Brion Davis, Larry Gara, Fawn M. Brodie, Donald G. Matthews, Irving H. Bartlett, Benjamin Quarles, Leon Litwack, James M. McPherson, Willie Lee Rose, Staughton Lynd, John L. Thomas, Silvan Tomkins, Robin W. Winks, Howard R. Temperley, Robert F. Durden, Howard Zinn, and Martin Duberman.

7. Lewis Perry and Michael Fellman, eds., *Antislavery Reconsidered: New Perspectives on the Abolitionists* (Baton Rouge: Louisiana State University Press, 1979), vii–viii. Contributors to this volume included: Ronald G. Walters, C. Duncan Rice, Donald M. Scott, Carol V. R. George, Leonard L. Richards, Alan M. Kraut, Douglas C. Riach, James B. Stewart, Jonathan A. Glickstein, William M. Wiecek, Ellen Du Bois, Blanche Glassman Hersh, Bertram Wyatt-Brown, Lewis Perry, and Michael Fellman.

8. Ronald G. Walters, "The Boundaries of Abolitionism," in Perry and Fellman, *Antislavery Reconsidered,* 3.

9. Gilbert Hobbs Barnes, *The Antislavery Impulse, 1830–1844* (New York: Appleton-Century, 1933).

10. Walter Hugins, ed., *The Reform Impulse, 1825–1850* (Columbia, SC: University of South Carolina Press, 1972), 1.

11. The best survey of these shifts, emphasizing the connection between reform and religion, is Robert Abzug, *Cosmos Crumbling: American Reform and the Religious Imagination* (New York: Oxford University Press, 1994).

12. See Thomas Bender, ed., *The Antislavery Debate: Capitalism and Abolitionism as a*

Problem of Historical Interpretation (Berkeley: University of California Press, 1992); and James L. Huston, "Abolitionists, Political Economists, and Capitalism," *Journal of the Early Republic,* 20:3 (Fall 2000): 487–521. For more on the relationship between slavery, abolitionism, and capitalism in the U.S., see Eric Foner, *Free Soil, Free Labor, Free Men: The Ideology of the Republican Party* (New York: Oxford University Press, 1974); and in the British West Indies, see Eric Williams, *Capitalism and Slavery* (Chapel Hill: University of North Carolina Press, 1944).

13. David Brion Davis, *The Problem of Slavery in Western Culture* (New York: Oxford University Press, 1966); and *The Problem of Slavery in the Age of Revolution, 1770–1823* (Ithaca: Cornell University Press, 1975). In the latter study, Davis argues that the abolitionists achieved "ideological hegemony" in England, but not in America, during the Age of Revolution. In his debate with Thomas Haskell, Davis elaborates on the point that "Anglo-American Quakers [whom Davis considers the first American abolitionists] cannot be said to have enjoyed 'hegemony.' " Davis continues: "In the United States it was only after the Civil War and after slave emancipation, that antislavery ideology succeeded in validating the view that a voluntary contract exemplified 'equivalence,' the polar opposite of the slave-master relation." See Davis in Bender, ed., *The Antislavery Debate,* 304.

14. See Ira Berlin, *Many Thousands Gone: The First Two Centuries of American Slavery in North America* (Cambridge, MA: Harvard University Press, 1998); Joanne Pope Melish, *Disowning Slavery: Gradual Emancipation and "Race" in New England, 1780–1860* (Ithaca and London: Cornell University Press, 1998); Arthur Zilversmit, *The First Emancipation: The Abolition of Slavery in the North* (Chicago: University of Chicago Press, 1967); and Leon Litwack, *North of Slavery: The Negro in the Free States, 1790–1860* (Chicago: University of Chicago Press, 1961).

15. See James Oliver Horton and Lois Horton, *In Hope of Liberty: Culture, Community and Protest among Northern Free Blacks, 1700–1860* (New York: Oxford University Press, 1997); and Floyd J. Miller, *The Search for a Black Nationality* (Urbana: University of Illinois Press, 1975).

16. For an extensive discussion of the American Colonization Society, see P. J. Staudenraus, *The African Colonization Society, 1816–1865* (New York: Columbia University Press, 1961). Three earlier studies by distinguished historians argued this point: Benjamin Quarles, *Black Abolitionists* (New York: Oxford University Press, 1969); Herbert Aptheker, *Abolitionism: A Revolutionary Movement* (Boston: Twayne, 1989); and Paul Goodman, *Of One Blood: Abolitionism and the Origins of Racial Equality* (Berkeley: University of California Press, 1997). Aptheker actually made this point—about the black protest origins of American abolitionism—long ago in his pamphlet, *The Negro in the Abolitionist Movement* (New York: International Publishers, 1941).

17. These distinctions are used in the two most popular syntheses of abolitionism published in the last generation: James Brewer Stewart, *Holy Warriors: The Abolitionists and American Slavery* (New York: Hill and Wang, 1976); and Ronald G. Walters, *The Antislavery Appeal: American Abolitionism after 1830* (New York: W. W. Norton, 1978); John Stauffer also uses them in *The Black Hearts of Men: Radical Abolitionists and the Transformation of Race* (Cambridge: Harvard University Press, 2002) but he also points out the overlap that sometimes existed between radical and political abolition.

18. Aileen S. Kraditor, *Means and Ends in American Abolitionism: Garrison and His Critics on Strategy and Tactics, 1834–1850* (New York: Vintage, 1969), 276.

19. Michael Warner, *Letters of the Republic: Publication and the Public Sphere in Eighteenth-Century America* (Cambridge, MA: Harvard University Press, 1990); and Cathy N. Davidson, *Revolution and the Word: The Rise of the Novel in America* (New York: Oxford University Press, 1986).

20. Jane Tompkins makes this point forcefully in her introduction to *Sensational Designs: The Cultural Work of American Fiction, 1790–1860* (New York: Oxford University Press, 1985).

21. Louis Menand, "The Historical Romance," *The New Yorker*, March 24, 2003, 80.

22. As Forbes points out, many Americans have created new stories to show that thousands of blacks fought as Confederate soldiers. It is a popular history that reflects modern trends, for it redeems the South without ignoring the agency and humanity of blacks.

23. See Davis, *The Problem of Slavery in the Age of Revolution*, 262; and Davis, *Challenging the Boundaries of Slavery* (Cambridge, MA: Cambridge University Press, 2003), 33. See also Richard S. Newman, *The Transformation of American Abolitionism: Fighting Slavery in the Early Republic* (Chapel Hill: University of North Carolina Press, 2002).

24. For a provocative intervention into the debate over "race" and the Enlightenment, see Charles W. Mills, *The Racial Contract* (Ithaca: Cornell University Press, 1997).

25. Phillis Wheatley, "To His Excellency General Washington," in *The Collected Works of Phillis Wheatley*, John Shields, ed. (New York: Oxford University Press, 1988), 145–146. Jones and Allen, Hall, and Forten quoted in Richard S. Newman, Patrick Rael, and Phillip Lapsansky, eds., *Pamphlets of Protest: An Anthology of Early African American Protest Literature, 1790–1860* (New York: Routledge, 2001), 42, 47, 67.

26. See Davis, *The Problem of Slavery in Western Culture;* and Davis, *Slavery and Human Progress* (New York: Oxford University Press, 1984), 5–8. See also Eugene D. Genovese, *From Rebellion to Revolution: Afro-American Slave revolts in the Making of the Modern World* (Baton Rouge: Louisiana State University Press, 1979).

   During the Spartacus Revolt of 73 BCE, Spartacus and his soldiers enslaved many of their former masters. The Zanj rebels of 869 CE, the largest servile war before the Haitian Revolution, held numerous slaves. And most maroon slave communities exploited people as slaves. See Junius P. Rodriguez, ed., *The Historical Encyclopedia of World Slavery, Volume II* (Santa Barbara: ABC-CLIO, 1997), 608, 713.

27. See Davis, *The Problem of Slavery in Western Culture*, part III; Davis, *The Problem of Slavery in the Age of Revolution*, 113–163, 184–196; C.L.R. James, *The Black Jacobins: Toussaint L'Ouverture and the San Domingo Revolution* (1963; revised, New York: Vintage, 1989); Laurent Dubois, *Avengers of the New World: The Story of the Haitian Revolution* (Cambridge, MA: Harvard University Press, 2004); and Jack P. Greene, "'A plain and natural Right to Life and Liberty': An Early Natural Rights Attack on the Excesses of the Slave System in colonial British America," *William and Mary Quarterly*, 57:4 (October 2000): 793–808.

   One might conclude that Vermont's 1777 state constitution, the first constitution in history to prohibit slavery outright, was also an example of immediatism. But Vermont's antislavery constitution was possible only because there were few blacks in the state. The first instance of gradual abolition is usually seen as the famous 1688 Germantown Friends antislavery petition. Another eighty-six years would elapse before the Philadelphia Yearly Meeting of the Society of Friends, in 1774, adopted rules forbidding Quakers from buying or selling slaves. St. Domingue's constitution in 1801, which prohibited slavery forever, is especially remarkable given that ten years earlier, when the rebellion began, most of the island's occupants were slaves.

28. See David Brion Davis, "The Emergence of Immediatism in British and American Antislavery Thought," in *From Homicide to Slavery: Studies in American Culture* (New York: Oxford University Press, 1986), 238–257.

29. There are examples of lower-class whites and blacks commingling and fraternizing in the colonial period, but there is very little evidence to analyze whether they befriended one another as equals, and embraced the ideal of equality, in the way the abolitionists later did. In this earlier period, blacks and whites at the bottom of the social ladder formed alliances based on shared material conditions and common purposes, but the degree of egalitarian beliefs is largely unknown. They may have come together simply as part of a shared quest for survival, for when whites rose in rank, they abandoned their formal alliances. Over time, plebian whites increasingly used "whiteness" to preserve their self-respect and distance themselves from blacks. See James Brewer Stewart, "The Emergence of Racial Modernity and the Rise of the White North, 1790–1840," *Journal of the Early Republic*, 18:2 (Summer 1998): 181–217; Stewart, "Modernizing 'Difference': The Political Meanings of Color in the Free States, 1776–1840," *Journal of the Early Republic*, 19:4 (Winter 1999): 691–712; Leslie M. Harris, *In the Shadow of Slavery: African Americans in New York City, 1626–1863* (Chicago: University of Chicago Press, 2003), 1–95; and Graham Russell Hodges, *Root and Branch: African Americans in New York and East Jersey, 1613–1863* (Chapel Hill: University of North Carolina Press, 1999), 69–138. For more on "whiteness" and its relation to working-class social relations, see David R. Roediger, *The Wages of Whiteness: Race and the Making of the American Working Class* (New York: Verso, 1991); and Noel Ignatiev, *How the Irish Became White* (New York: Routledge, 1995).

30. See Horton and Horton, *In Hope of Liberty*, pp. 177–236; Stewart, "Modernizing 'Difference,' " 692–712; and John Stauffer, "In the Shadow of a Dream: White Abolitionists and Race," *Collective Degradation: Slavery and the Construction of Race*, Gilder Lehrman Center Conference, Yale University, November 2003 (forthcoming from Yale University Press).

31. For a comprehensive analysis of this theme, see Eric Foner, *The Story of American Freedom* (New York: W. W. Norton and Company, 1998).

32. The American Colonization Society never received constitutional approval for its colony, which led a few statesmen, such as former president John Quincy Adams, to claim that it was unconstitutional. See Charles Francis Adams, ed., *The Memoirs of John Quincy Adams, Volume IV* (Philadelphia: J.B. Lippincott., 1875), 292–293, 476. See also Staudenraus, *The African Colonization Society*, 52–53.

33. "Walker's Appeal," in Cain, *William Lloyd Garrison and the Fight Against Slavery*, 77.

34. David Brion Davis notes that "slave insurrections, even with the sparing of white lives and massive turnout of thousands of rebels, were suicidal." (The St. Domingue rebellion was successful because it became embroiled in civil war.) In North America, according to William Freehling, "the surest way to free one-

self, under domestic servitude, was not to join a revolution but to betray one to the patriarch." See Davis, "Some Nineteenth-Century Slave Conspiracies and Revolts," in *In Human Bondage* (New York: Oxford University Press, 2006); and William W. Freehling, *The Road to Disunion: Secessionists at Bay, 1776–1854* (New York: Oxford University Press, 1990), 79.

35. On the relationship between a "slave republic," the alienation of white radicals like Brown, and interracial friendship and unity, see Stauffer, *The Black Hearts of Men;* Stauffer, "In the Shadow of a Dream"; and Manisha Sinha, "The Caning of Charles Sumner: Slavery, Race, and Ideology in the Age of the Civil War," *Journal of the Early Republic,* 23:2 (Summer 2003): 233–262.

36. In 1861 Frederick Douglass went so far as to suggest that "moral and social influence of pictures"—and graphic representation more generally—were more important in shaping the nation than "the making of its laws." Although he was thoroughly committed to political action, he viewed art as a principal engine for social change. See Douglass, "Pictures and Progress," in John Blassingame, ed., *The Frederick Douglass Papers, Series One, Volume Three* (New Haven: Yale University, 1985), 453.

37. Two recent volumes of poetry suggest that scholars are beginning to pay more attention to this important genre and historical source for understanding slavery and abolition. See James G. Basker, ed., *Amazing Grace: An Anthology of Poems About Slavery, 1660–1810* (New Haven: Yale University Press, 2002); and Marcus Wood, ed., *The Poetry of Slavery: An Anglo-American Anthology* (New York: Oxford University Press, 2003).

38. Eric Hobsbawm, *The Age of Extremes: A History of the World, 1914–1991* (New York: Vintage, 1994), 3.

1. "Truth Systematised": The Changing Debate Over Slavery and Abolition, 1761–1916

1. See, e.g., a recent column of Bill O'Reilly, host of the FOX News show *The O'Reilly Factor:* "[T]here is no question that the black family structure was devastated by slavery and that catastrophe continues to this day in some situations." O'Reilly, " 'Honest life' rewards black Americans, too," *New Haven Register,* June 29, 2002. Another recent column of O'Reilly's wrote off the entire continent of Africa as a worthwhile recipient of U.S. foreign aid.

2. Scott Malcomson, *One Drop of Blood: The American Misadventure of Race* (New York: Farrar, Straus, and Giroux, 2000), 174.

3. Roger Bruns, ed., *Am I Not a Man and a Brother* (New York: Chelsea House, 1977), 221.

4. Granville Sharp, *Serious Reflections on the Slave Trade and Slavery; wrote in March, 1797* (London, 1805), 16–17.

5. David Walker, *Walker's Appeal, in Four Articles; Together with a Preamble to the Coloured Citizens of the World, but in Particular, and Very Expressly, to Those of the United States of America* (Boston, 1830), 18.

6. Ibid., 23.

7. Stanley M. Elkins, *Slavery: A Problem in American Institutional and Intellectual Life,* third ed. (Chicago: University of Chicago Press, 1976), 1.

8. On black Confederates, see, Richard Rollins, ed., *Black Southerners in Gray: Essays on Afro Americans in Confederate Armies* (Murfreesboro, TN: Southern Her-

itage Press, 1994), and Charles Kelly Barrow et. al., *Forgotten Confederates: An Anthology About Black Southerners* (Atlanta: Southern Heritage Press, 1995). For the controversy over slave trade demographics, see, J.E. Inikori, "Measuring the Atlantic Slave Trade: an assessment of Curtin and Anstey," *Journal of African History* 17, (1976): 197–223. The key polemical text arguing the centrality of Jews in the slave trade is *The Secret Relationship between Blacks and Jews* (Chicago: Nation of Islam Historical Research Dept., 1991).

9. Elkins, *Slavery*, 1.

10. For an overview of works on British abolition written after 1944, see Roger Anstey, "The historical debate on the abolition of the British slave trade," in R. Anstey and P.E.H. Hair, eds., *Liverpool, the African Slave Trade, and Abolition* (Liverpool: Historic Society of Lancashire and Cheshire, 1976), 157ff. Also see David Brion Davis, "Slavery and the Post–World War II Historians," *Daedalus*, 103:2 (Spring 1974): 1–16. For a personal view of the controversy since U.B. Phillips, see Robert Fogel, *The Slavery Debates, 1952–1990: A Retrospective* (Baton Rouge: Louisiana State University Press, 2002).

11. The distinction is not as cut-and-dry as we might like, because many early writers continued to use the word "providence" as a loose substitute for "progress." See J.B. Bury, *The Idea of Progress* (New York: Dover, 1955), 219, 232–33.

12. Quoted in Bernard Semmel, *The Methodist Revolution* (New York: Basic Books, 1973), 87.

13. Perry Miller, *Jonathan Edwards* (New York: William Sloane Associates, 1949), 52, 72, 88–99.

14. The recent literature on this subject is voluminous. Three particularly useful older treatments are Robert A. Gross, *The Minutemen and Their World* (New York: Hill and Wang, 1976); Nathan O. Hatch, *The Sacred Cause of Liberty: Republican Thought and the Millennium in Revolutionary New England* (New Haven: Yale University Press, 1977); and Charles Royster, *A Revolutionary People at War* (New York: W. W. Norton & Company, 1981).

15. Mary Turner, *Slaves and Missionaries* (Urbana: University of Illinois Press, 1982), 4.

16. Semmel, *The Methodist Revolution*, 4.

17. An exception would be Ford K. Brown, *Fathers of the Victorians* (Cambridge: Cambridge University Press, 1961).

18. Winthrop D. Jordan, *White over Black* (Chapel Hill: University of North Carolina Press, 1968), xiii.

19. Wesley, *Thoughts on Slavery*, 55.

20. Averell Mackenzie-Grieve, *The Last Years of the English Slave Trade* (New York: A. M. Kelley, 1968), 192.

21. Eric Williams, *British Historians and the West Indies* (New York: Africana Publishing Corporation, 1972), 23.

22. James D. Richardson, ed., *A Compilation of the Messages and Papers of the Presidents, 1789–1897* (Washington: Government Printing Office, 1903), 1:52.

23. Alexander Pope, *Essay on Man*, I:10.

24. "[O]n n'a jamais prétendu eclairer les cordonniers et les servants." Cited in Bury, 182–183.

25. Leon Poliakov, "Racism from the Enlightenment to the Age of Imperialism," in D. van Arkel and R. Ross, ed., *Racism and Colonialism: Essays on Ideology and So-*

cial Structure (The Hague: Martinus Nijhoff Publishers, 1982), 55. The anti-clerical motivation in later theories of polygenesis remains a dominant theme through the first half of the nineteenth century, I believe.

26. Quoted in Bury, *Progress,* 173.

27. Ibid., 174–175. Bury also makes the point (p. 176) that "By liberty the Economists meant economic liberty. Neither they nor the philosophers nor Rousseau, the father of modern democracy, had any just conception of what political liberty means."

28. Quoted in ibid., 94–95.

29. Merrill D. Peterson, ed., *Thomas Jefferson: Writings* (New York: Library of America, 1984), 266.

30. Ibid., 265. Jefferson here appears to be following the lead of the Scottish *philosophe* Lord Monbodo; see his *Of the Origin and Progress of Language* (Edinburgh, 1774), chap. IV.

31. Peterson, *Thomas Jefferson: Writings,* 455.

32. Davis, *Problem of Slavery in the Era of Revolution,* 148–149, 168, 195.

33. Both sides in the American Civil War were to quote Jefferson in their defense; and the Southerners appear to have held the trump card: Jefferson owned slaves.

34. James Walvin, "The Propaganda of Anti-Slavery," in Walvin, ed., *Slavery and British Society, 1776–1846* (Baton Rouge: Louisiana State University Press, 1932), 60.

35. Drescher, "Public Opinion and the Destruction of Slavery," in Walvin, ed., *Slavery and British Society,* 26, 29.

36. For interesting explorations of this theme, see James Walvin, "The Rise of British Popular Sentiment for Abolition, 1878–1832," in Bolt and Drescher, eds., *Anti-Slavery, Religion, and Reform: Essays in Memory of Roger Anstey* (Folkestone: Wm Dawson & Sons Ltd, 1980), 149–162; and Brian Harrison, "A Genealogy of Reform in Modern Britain," in ibid., 119–148.

37. This neglect has been partially remediated by Richard S. Newman, *The Transformation of American Abolitionism: Fighting Slavery in the Early Republic* (Chapel Hill: University of North Carolina Press, 2002).

38. "Literary Sources and the Revolution in British Attitudes to Slavery," in Bolt and Drescher, eds., *Anti-Slavery, Religion, and Reform,* 329.

39. Mackenzie-Grieve, *English Slave Trade,* 295; Frank J. Klingberg, *The Anti-Slavery Movement in England* (New Haven: Yale University Press, 1926), 202–203.

40. Alfred A. Cave, *An American Conservative in the Age of Jackson: The Political and Social Thought of Calvin Colton* (Fort Worth: Texas Christian University Press, 1969); Perry Miller, *The Life of the Mind in America from the Revolution to the Civil War* (New York: Harvest Books, 1970).

41. The effect on the reform movement in Britain of the economic failure (from the exporters' point of view) of emancipation is traced in Seymour Drescher, *The Mighty Experiment: Free Labor versus Slavery in British Emancipation* (New York: Oxford University Press, 2002), 158–230.

42. See William Wilberforce, Papers of William Wilberforce, 1780–1933.

43. John Pollock, *Wilberforce* (New York: St., Martin's Press, 1977), xiv.

44. Robert Anstey, "Pattern," 32–33. See also David Eltis, *Economic Growth and the Ending of the Transatlantic Slave Trade* (New York: Oxford University Press, 1987), 111–112, 207–22.

45. David Brion Davis, "Slavery and 'Progress,' " in Bolt and Drescher, eds., *Anti-Slavery, Religion, and Reform*, 363–364.

46. Walvin, *Slavery and British Society*, 18.

47. *Congressional Globe*, 25 Cong., 2d Sess., 127.

48. The term first appeared in [John O'Sullivan,] "The Great Nation of Futurity," *The United States Democratic Review*, 6 (November 1839), 426–430.

49. *The Works of Thomas Carlyle* (New York: Charles Scribner's Sons, 1898), vol. 29, 1.

50. Julian Symons, ed., *Carlyle: Selected Works, Reminiscences and Letters* (Cambridge: Harvard University Press, 1970), 271.

51. Reginald Horsman, *Josiah Nott of Mobile: Southerner, Physician and Racial Theorist* (Baton Rouge: Louisiana State University Press, 1987), 101, 95. In their influential *Types of Mankind* (1854), Nott and Gliddon wrote that in ancient Egypt, " 'de same ole Nigger' of Southern plantations could spend his Nilotic sabbaths in saltatory recreations and 'Turn about, and wheel about, and *Jump Jim Crow.' " Quoted in Richard B. Erno, "Dominant Images of the Negro in the Ante-Bellum South: A Study in the Development of Southern Attitudes Toward the Negro as Reflected in Ante-Bellum Diaries" (Ph.D. dissertation, University of Minnesota, 1961), 222.

52. Darwin, *Origin of Species*, 373. Herbert Spencer has been effectively discredited by historians and sociologists for generations (see especially Richard Hofstader, *Social Darwinism in American Thought* [Boston: Beacon Press, 1955]), while Darwin has been, for the most part, a subject of reverent hagiography. William Irvine's excellent *Apes, Angels and Victorians* (New York: McGraw-Hill, 1955) is still useful, but badly out of date. Mary Midgley's *Evolution as a Religion* (New York: Methuen, 1985) continues the tradition of exculpating Darwin while excoriating his disciples. A critical examination of *The Origin of Species* in the context of nineteenth-century natural history and philosophy is long overdue; biologists have been left to carry out the task of revising Darwinism with very little assistance from historians.

53. *Origin of Species* 373.

54. A striking example of this attitude may be found in Darwin's comments on the differences between the sexes: "It is generally admitted that with woman the powers of intuition, of rapid perception, and perhaps of imitation, are more strongly marked than in man; but some, at least, of these faculties are characteristic of the lower races, and therefore of a past and lower state of civilization." (*The Descent of Man*, 873.)

55. Kenneth L. Little, *Negroes in Britain: A Study of Racial Relations in English Society* (London: Kegan Paul, Trench, Truebner & Co., 1947), 214.

56. Allan Chase has passionately exposed these concepts and their modern intellectual descendants in *The Legacy of Malthus: The Social Costs of the New Scientific Racism* (New York: Knopf, 1977), 30

57. B.L. Putnam Weale [Bertram Lewis Simpson], *The Conflict of Colour: The Threatened Upheaval Throughout the World* (New York: The Macmillan Co., 1910), 15. Emphasis in the original.

58. Basil Davidson, *The African Slave Trade* (Boston: Atlantic–Little, Brown, 1961), 120.

59. E. F. Schumacher, *A Guide for the Perplexed* (New York: Harper & Row, 1977), 61.

60. Davis, "Slavery and the Post–World War II Historians," 13.

61. Tom Stoppard, *Jumpers: A Play* (New York: Grove Press, 1972), 46.

62. Malcomson, *One Drop of Blood*, 250.

2. Coming of Age: The Historiography of Black Abolitionism

1. Betty Fladeland, "Revisionists vs. Abolitionists: The Historiographical Cold War of the 1930s and 1940s," *Journal of the Early Republic* 6 (Spring 1986): 1–21; Merton L. Dillon, "The Abolitionists: A Decade of Historiography, 1959–1969," *Journal of Southern History* 35 (November 1969): 500–522.

2. For this view see Martin Duberman, ed., *The Antislavery Vanguard: New Essays on the Abolitionists* (Princeton, 1965); Aileen S. Kraditor, "The Abolitionists Rehabilitated," *Studies on the Left* 5 (Spring 1965): 103–106; Herbert Aptheker, *Abolitionism: A Revolutionary Movement* (Boston, 1989).

3. Lawrence J. Friedman, " 'Historical Topics Sometimes Run Dry': The State of Abolitionist Studies," *The Historian* 43 (1981): 177–194. For the social control model of antebellum reform, including abolition, that highlights its conservative nature see Clifford Griffin, *Their Brothers' Keepers: Moral Stewardship in the United States, 1800–1865* (New Brunswick, 1960); Paul S. Boyer, *Urban Masses and Moral Order in America, 1820–1920* (Cambridge, MA., 1978); Paul Johnson, *A Shopkeepers' Millenium: Society and Revivals in Rochester, New York, 1815–1837* (New York, 1978); Alan Dawley, *Class and Community: The Industrial Revolution in Lynn* (Cambridge, Mass., 1979).

4. Benjamin Quarles, "Black History's Antebellum Origins," *Proceedings of the American Antiquarian Society* 89 (April 18, 1979): 89–122. Also see John Ernest, *Liberation Historiography: African American Writers and the Challenge of History, 1794–1861* (Chapel Hill, 2004).

5. William C. Nell, *The Colored Patriots of the American Revolution* (New York, 1968; reprint of the original Boston edition of 1855), 369, 374–375.

6. William Wells Brown, *The Black Man, His Antecedents, His Genius, and His Achievements* (Boston, 1863). See also William Edward Farrison, *William Wells Brown: Author and Reformer* (Chicago, 1969); R.J.M. Blackett, *Beating Against the Barriers: The Lives of Six Nineteenth-Century Afro-Americans* (Baton Rouge, 1986).

7. Martin R. Delany, *The Condition, Elevation, Emigration, and Destiny of the Colored People of the United States Politically Considered* (New York, 1861).

8. George R. Price and James Brewer Stewart, eds., *To Heal the Scourge of Prejudice: The Life and Writings of Hosea Easton* (Amherst, 1999): 111–112; Bruce Dain, *A Hideous Monster of the Mind: American Race Theory in the Early Republic* (Cambridge, MA, 2002). Dain adopts a catholic position to his discussion of what he calls the "science" of race, refusing to term it pseudoscientific by accepting it as the knowledge of the day. Mia Bay, *The White Image in the Black Mind: African American Ideas About White People, 1830–1925* (New York, 2000); Stephen Jay Gould, *The Mismeasure of Man* (New York, 1981). For Patrick Rael, see chapter ten of this volume.

9. James W.C. Pennington, *A Text Book of the Origin and History, &c. &c. of the Colored People* (Hartford, 1841): 56, 74–90. Interestingly, neither Dain, Bay, nor Rael include Pennington in their analyses. On Pennington see Blackett, *Beating Against the Barriers,* chapter 1.

10. Henry Highland Garnet, *The Past and Present Condition and the Destiny of the Colored Race* (Troy, NY, 1848): 6, 25–29.

11. Martin R. Delany, *Principia of Ethnology: The Origins of Races and Color, with an Archeological Compendium of Ethiopian and Egyptian Civilization, from Years of Careful Examination and Enquiry* (Philadelphia, 1879); Frederick Douglass, *The Claims of the Negro Ethnologically Considered: An Address Before the Literary Societies*

of Western Reserve College, At Commencement, July 12, 1854 (Rochester, 1854), 5, 7–9, 13–16, 28–31, 34. The quotation is from p. 10.

12. Dickson D. Bruce, *Archibald Grimke: Portriat of a Black Independent* (Baton Rouge, 1993); George Washington Williams, *History of the Negro Race in America, From 1619 to 1880.* (New York, 1883): Vol. II, Chapters V and VI. W.E.B. Du Bois, *John Brown* (Philadelphia, 1909); and *Black Reconstruction in America, 1860–1880* (New York, 1935).

13. See Carter G. Woodson, ed., *The Mind of the Negro as Reflected in Letters Written During the Crisis, 1800–1860* (New York, 1926), and *Negro Orators and Their Orations* (New York, 1925); Benjamin Brawley, ed., *Early Negro American Writers* (Chapel Hill, 1935); Charles H. Wesley, *Prince Hall: Life and Legacy* (Washington, D.C., 1977) and *Richard Allen: Apostle of Freedom* (Washington, D.C., 1935).

14. Herbert Aptheker, *The Negro in the Abolitionist Movement* (New York, 1941) Howard Holman Bell, ed., *Minutes of the Proceedings of the National Negro Conventions, 1830–1864* (New York, 1969); Dorothy Sterling, ed., *Speak Out in Thunder Tones: Letters and Other Writings by Black Northerners, 1787–1865* (New York, 1973), and *We Are Your Sisters: Black Women in the Nineteenth Century* (New York, 1984); Philip S. Foner, ed., *The Life and Writings of Frederick Douglass* (New York, 1950–1975); Philip S. Foner and George E. Walker, eds., *Proceedings of the Black State Conventions, 1840–1865* (Philadelphia, 1979, 1980); Louis Filler, *The Crusade Against Slavery, 1830–1860* (New York, 1960); Dwight Lowell Dumond, *Antislavery: The Crusade for Freedom in America* (Ann Arbor, 1961).

15. For contemporary collections see Stanley and Emma Nogrady Kaplan, eds., *The Black Presence in the Era of the American Revolution* (Amherst, 1989); C. Peter Ripley, ed., *The Black Abolitionist Papers* (Chapel Hill, 1985–1992); John W. Blassingame, ed., *The Frederick Douglass Papers* (New Haven, 1979–1992); Marilyn Richardson, ed., *Maria W. Stewart, America's First Black Woman Political Writer: Essays and Speeches* (Bloomington, 1987); Brenda Stevenson, ed., *The Journals of Charlotte Forten Grimke* (New York, 1988); Richard S. Newman, Patrick Rael, Phillip Lapansky, eds., *Pamphlets of Protest: An Anthology of Early African American Protest Literature* (New York, 2001); Robert S. Levine, ed., *Martin R. Delany: A Documentary Reader* (Chapel Hill, 2003).

16. Gilbert Hobbes Barnes, *The Antislavery Impulse, 1830–1844* (1933—Reprinted in New York, 1964); Dwight Lowell Dumond, *Antislavery Origins of the Civil War in the United States,* Merton L. Dillon, "In Retrospect: Gilbert H. Barnes and Dwight L. Dumond: An Appraisal," *Reviews in American History* 21 (1993) 539–552; Stanley M. Elkins, *Slavery: A Problem in American Institutional and Intellectual Life* (Chicago, 1959), Part II; John L. Thomas, *The Liberator: A Biography of William Lloyd Garrison* (New York, 1963); David Donald, "Toward a Reconsideration of Abolitionists," in *Lincoln Reconsidered: Essays on the Civil War Era* (New York, 1947): 19–36, *Charles Sumner and the Coming of the Civil War* (New York, 1960), and *Charles Sumner and the Rights of Man* (New York, 1970); Aileen S. Kraditor, *Means and Ends in American Abolitionism: Garrison and His Critics on Strategy and Tactics, 1834–1850* (New York, 1967); Benjamin Quarles, "The Breach between Douglass and Garrison," *The Journal of Negro History* 23:2 (April 1938): 144–154.

17. Benjamin Quarles, *Black Abolitionists* (New York, 1969), ix; "Letters from Negro Leaders to Gerrit Smith," *The Journal of Negro History* 27 (October 1942): 432–453.

18. Benjamin Quarles, *Black Mosaic: Essays in Afro-American History and Historiography* (Amherst, 1988).

19. See especially Duberman, ed., *The Antislavery Vanguard;* Merton L. Dillon, *The Abolitionists: The Growth of a Dissenting Minority* (DeKalb, 1974); John H. Bracey Jr., August Meier, and Elliot Rudwick, eds., *Blacks in the Abolitionist Movement* (Belmont, CA, 1971).

20. Jane H. and William H. Pease, *They Who Would be Free: Blacks' Search for Freedom, 1830–1861* (New York, 1974). Leon F. Litwack, *North of Slavery: The Negro in the Free States, 1790–1860* (Chicago, 1961), Chapter 7, and "The Emancipation of the Negro Abolitionist," reprinted in Duberman, ed., *The Antislavery Vanguard.*

21. See Lewis Perry, *Radical Abolitionism: Anarchy and the Government of God in Antislavery Thought* (Ithaca, 1973); Lawrence J. Friedman, *Gregarious Saints: Self and Community in American Abolitionism, 1830–1870* (Cambridge, UK, 1982); Louis S. Gerteis, *Morality and Utility in American Antislavery Reform* (Chapel Hill, 1987).

22. George M. Fredrickson, *The Black Image in the White Mind: The Debate on Afro-American Character and Destiny, 1817–1914* (New York, 1971), Chapter 4; Joanne Pope Melish, *Disowning Slavery: Gradual Emancipation and "Race" in New England, 1780–1860* (Ithaca, 1998), and "The 'Condition' Debate and Racial Discourse in the Antebellum North," *Journal of the Early Republic* 19 (Winter 1999). For a critique of the tendency to obfuscate racism with "race" and "racial identity," see Barbara J. Fields, "Of Rogues and Geldings," *American Historical Review* 108 (December 2003): 1397–1405.

23. Wilson Jeremiah Moses, *The Golden Age of Black Nationalism, 1850–1925* (Hamden, CT, 1978); Tunde Adeleke, *Unafrican Americans: Nineteenth-Century Black Nationalists and the Civilizing Mission* (Lexington, KY, 1998). For a more charitable though largely uncritical view see Lamin Sanneh, *Abolitionists Abroad: American Blacks and the Making of Modern West Africa* (Cambridge, MA, 1999).

24. For a criticism of the "assimilationist petite bourgeoisie" strain of pre–Civil War black activism see Ernest Allen Jr. "Afro-American Identity: Reflections on the pre–Civil War Era," *Contributions in Black Studies* 7 (1985–6): 45–93. On slave fugitives see William Still, *The Underground Railroad* (Philadelphia, 1872); Wilbur H. Siebert, *The Underground Railroad from Slavery to Freedom* (New York, 1898); Stanley W. Campbell, *The Slave Catchers: Enforcement of the Fugitive Slave Law, 1850–1860* (Chapel Hill, 1968); Larry Gara, *The Liberty Line: The Legend of the Underground Railroad* (Lexington, KY, 1961); Carol Wilson, *Freedom at Risk: The Kidnapping of Free Blacks in America, 1780–1865* (Lexington, KY, 1994); Kathryn Grover, *The Fugitive's Gibraltar: Escaping Slaves and Abolitionism in New Bedford, Massachusetts* (Amherst, 2001); Albert J. Von Frank, *The Trials of Anthony Burns: Freedom and Slavery in Emerson's Boston* (Cambridge, MA, 1998); Gary Collison, *Shadrach Minkins: From Fugitive Slave to Citizen* (Cambridge, MA, 1997); Thomas P. Slaughter, *Bloody Dawn: The Christiana Riot and Racial Violence in the Antebellum North* (New York, 1991); Jonathan Katz, *Resistance at Christiana, The Fugitive Slave Rebellion, Christiana, Penn., Sept. 11, 1851: A Documentary Account* (New York, 1974). Ira Berlin, unpublished paper (2002), in author's possession.

25. See Shane White, *Somewhat More Independent: The End of Slavery in New York City, 1770–1810* (Athens, GA, 1991); Gary B. Nash and Jean R. Soderlund, *Freedom By Degrees: Emancipation in Pennsylvania and Its Aftermath* (New York, 1991); Gra-

ham Russell Hodges, *Slavery and Freedom in the Rural North: African Americans in Monmouth County, New Jersey, 1665–1865* (Madison, 1997); Arthur Zilversmit, *The First Emancipation: The Abolition of Slavery in the North* (Chicago, 1967); Leon F. Litwack, *North of Slavery: The Negro in the Free States, 1790–1860* (Chicago, 1961); Leonard P. Curry, *The Free Black in Urban America, 1800–1850: The Shadow of a Dream* (Chicago, 1981); Harry Reed, *Platform for Change: The Foundations of the Northern Free Black Community, 1775–1865* (East Lansing, 1994); Elizabeth Rauh Bethel, *The Roots of African American Identity: Memory and History in Antebellum Free Communities* (New York, 1997); Gary B. Nash, *Forging Freedom: The Formation of Philadelphia's Black Community, 1720–1840* (Cambridge, MA, 1988); Graham Russell Hodges, *Root and Branch: African Americans in New York and East Jersey, 1619–1863* (Chapel Hill, 1999); Christopher Phillips, *Freedom's Port: The African American Community of Baltimore, 1790–1860* (Urbana, 1997); Letitia Woods Brown, *Free Negroes in the District of Columbia, 1790–1846* (New York, 1972); Shane White, *Stories of Freedom in Black New York* (Cambridge, Mass., 2002); Craig Steven Wilder, *A Covenant with Color: Race and Social Power in Brooklyn* (New York, 2000), and *In the Company of Black Men: The African Influence on African American Culture in New York City* (New York, 2001); James Oliver and Lois E. Horton, *Black Bostonians: Family Life and Community Struggle in an Antebellum City* (New York, 1979); James Oliver Horton, *Free People of Color: Inside the African American Community* (Washington, D.C., 1993); James Oliver and Lois E. Horton, *In Hope of Liberty: Culture, Community, and Protest Among Northern Free Blacks, 1700–1860* (New York, 1997). Leslie M. Harris, *In the Shadow of Slavery: African Americans in New York City, 1626–1863* (Chicago, 2003).

26. Blackett, *Beating Against the Barriers*, xiii; William Cheek and Aimee Lee Cheek, *John Mercer Langston and the Fight for Black Freedom, 1829–1865* (Urbana, 1989); Carol M. Hunter, *To Set the Captives Free: Reverend Jermain Wesley Loguen and the Struggle for Freedom in Central New York, 1853–1872* (New York, 1993); Carol V.R. George, *Segregated Sabbaths: Richard Allen and the Emergence of Independent Black Churches, 1760–1840* (New York, 1973); Lamont D. Thomas, *Paul Cuffee: Black Entrepreneur and Pan-Africanist* (Urbana, 1988); Julie Winch, *A Gentleman of Color: The Life of James Forten* (New York, 2002).

27. Frederick Cooper, "Elevating the Race: The Social Thought of Black Leaders, 1827–50," *American Quarterly* 24 (December 1972): 604–625. Also see Julie Winch, *Philadelphia's Black Elite: Activism, Accommodation and the Struggle for Autonomy, 1787–1848* (Philadelphia, 1988); David W. Blight, "In Search of Learning, Liberty, and Self-Definition: James McCune Smith and the Ordeal of the Antebellum Black Intellectual," *Afro-Americans in New York Life and History* 9 (July 1985): 7–25; Waldo Martin, *The Mind of Frederick Douglass* (Chapel Hill, 1984); David W. Blight, *Frederick Douglass' Civil War: Keeping Faith in Jubilee* (Baton Rouge, 1989); Robert S. Levine, *Martin Delany, Frederick Douglass, and the Politics of Representative Identity* (Chapel Hill, 1997); John Saillant, *Black Puritan, Black Republican: The Life and Thought of Lemuel Haynes, 1753–1833* (New York, 2003).

28. Richard J.M. Blackett, *Building an Antislavery Wall: Black Americans in the Atlantic Abolitionist Movement, 1830–1860* (Baton Rouge, 1983). Also see Benjamin Quarles, "Ministers Without Portfolio," *Journal of Negro History* 39

(January 1954): 27–43; Patrick Rael, *Black Identity and Black Protest in the Ante-bellum North* (Chapel Hill, 2002); Eddie S. Glaude Jr., *Exodus! Religion, Race and Nation in Early Nineteenth-Century Black America* (Chicago, 2000).

29. See Alma Lutz, *Crusade for Freedom: Women of the Antislavery Movement* (Boston, 1968); Blanche Glassman Hersh, *The Slavery of Sex: Feminist Abolitionists in America* (Urbana, 1978); Ellen C. Du Bois, *Feminism and Suffrage: The Emergence of an Independent Women's Movement in America, 1848–1869* (Ithaca, 1978); Keith E. Melder, *Beginnings of Sisterhood: The American Women's Rights Movement, 1800–1850* (New York, 1977); Lori D. Ginzberg, *Women and the Work of Benevolence: Morality, Politics and Class in the 19th Century United States* (New Haven, 1990); Susan Zaeske, *Signatures of Citizenship: Petitioning, Antislavery and Women's Political Identity* (Chapel Hill, 2003). For some important exceptions see Jean Fagan Yellin, *Women and Sisters: The Antislavery Feminists in American Culture* (New Haven, 1989); Karen Sanchez-Eppler, *Touching Liberty: Abolition, Feminism and the Politics of the Body* (Berkeley, 1993); Jean Fagan Yellin and John C. Van Horne, eds., *The Abolitionist Sisterhood: Women's Political Culture in Ante-bellum America* (Ithaca, 1994); Julie Roy Jeffrey, *The Great Silent Army of Abolitionism: Ordinary Women in the Antislavery Movement* (Chapel Hill, 1998); Anne M. Boylan, *The Origins of Women's Activism: New York and Boston, 1797–1840* (Chapel Hill, 2002); Debra Gold Hansen, *Strained Sisterhood: Gender and Class in the Boston Female Anti-Slavery Society* (Amherst, 1993); Wendy Hamand Venet, *Neither Ballots nor Bullets: Women Abolitionists and the Civil War* (Charlottesville, 1991). Black women abolitionists rarely command equal space with their white counterparts.

30. Nell Irvin Painter, *Sojourner Truth: A Life, A Symbol* (New York, 1996); Melba Joyce Boyd, *Discarded Legacy: Politics and Poetics in the Life of Frances E.W. Harper, 1825–1911* (Detroit, 1994); Jane Rhodes, *Mary Ann Shadd Cary: The Black Press and Protest in the Nineteenth Century* (Bloomington, 1998); Carleton Mabee with Susan Mabee Newhouse, *Sojourner Truth: Slave, Prophet, Legend* (New York, 1993); Jennifer Fleischner, *Mrs. Lincoln and Mrs. Keckley: The Remarkable Story of the Friendship Between a First Lady and a Former Slave* (New York, 2003); Sibyl Ventress Brownlee, "Out of the Abundance of the Heart: Sarah Ann Parker Remond's Quest for Freedom," (Ph.D. dissertation, University of Massachusetts, 1997); Brenda Stevenson, ed., *The Journals of Charlotte Forten Grimke* (New York, 1989); Jean Fagan Yellin, ed., *Incidents in the Life of a Slave Girl Written By Herself* (Cambridge, MA, 1987); Marilyn Richardson, ed., *Maria W. Stewart* (Bloomington, 1987); Emma Jones Lapansky, "Feminism, Freedom and Community: Charlotte Forten and Women Activists in Nineteenth-Century Philadelphia," *The Pennsylvania Magazine of History and Biography* 113 (January 1989): 3–19; Carla L. Peterson, *"Doers of the Word": African American Women Speakers and Writers in the North, 1830–1880* (New York, 1995). Also see Jacqueline Bacon, *The Humblest May Stand Forth: Rhetoric, Empowerment, and Abolition* (Columbia, SC, 2002); Francis Foster Smith, *Written By Herself: Literary Production by African American Women, 1746–1892* (Bloomington, 1993); Rosalyn Terborg-Penn, *African American Women in the Struggle for the Vote, 1850–1920* (Bloomington, 1998); Gayle Tate, *Unknown Tongues: Black Women's Political Activism in the Antebellum Era, 1830–1860* (East Lansing, MI, 2003); Shirley J. Yee, *Black Women Abolitionists: A Study in Activism, 1828–1860* (Knoxville, 1992).

3. Geographies of Liberty: A Brief Look at Two Cases

1. There were numerous court cases in the intervening years between James Somerset and Med. Following William Wiecek's suggestion that the English court case *Chamberlain v. Harvey* (1697) is the direct legal precursor to the *Somerset* case (1771–72), I argue that *Somerset* is the predecessor of the *Commonwealth v. Aves* case (1836). See William Wiecek, "Somerset: Lord Mansfield and the Legitimacy of Slavery in the Anglo-American World," *University of Chicago Law Review* 42 (1974), 91.

2. Over the course of the history of British North American colonies, slaves absconded to various Native American populations, as well as to portions of Canada and Florida, and other territories held by France and Spain. When the colonies became states with sectional differences, many slaves in the South risked their lives to make their way north. Still, even after they identified certain geographical locales as being more conducive to liberty, slaves understood that escape or relocation might not guarantee their freedom.

   Geographers such as Nicholas Blomley and David Delaney have just begun to explore the intersection of law, place, and power. Philosophers like Edward Casey are also interested in the place as an ideological, as well as geographical, concept. See Nicholas Blomley, David Delaney, and Richard T. Ford, eds., *The Legal Geographies Reader* (Oxford: Blackwell, 2001); and Edward S. Casey, *The Fate of Place: A Philosophical History* (Berkeley: University of California Press, 1997). See also David Delaney, *Race, Place and the Law: 1836–1948* (Austin: University of Texas Press, 1998). Eliga H. Gould considers geography as a useful tool, although his work tends to extend Jack P. Greene's center/periphery model of Britain's imperial relationship with its New World plantation colonies. See Gould, "Zones of Law, Zones of Violence: The Legal Geography of the British Atlantic, circa 1772," *William and Mary Quarterly*, vol. 60, no. 3.

3. For a discussion of the ideology of liberty among the lower and working classes, see John Lax and William Pencack, "The Knowles Riot and the Crisis of the 1740s in Massachusetts," *Perspectives in American History* 10 (1976), 163ff. Peter Linebaugh and Marcus Rediker devote several pages to the 1747 Knowles riot in *The Many-Headed Hydra* (Boston: Beacon Press, 2000), 215–217.

4. Limitations of space make it impossible to recount the history of the British slave trade and the development of plantation slavery in the Caribbean; there is no dearth of literature on this subject. Suffice it to say that white indentured servitude, the main form of labor initially employed by the British, declined over the course of the seventeenth century, as Africans increasingly comprised the labor force.

5. Nicholas Blomley uses the phrase "geographies of law" to describe the intersection of both human geography—the space occupied by people in their daily lives—and law—a topic, he notes, "that has historically been both poorly documented and inadequately theorized. Not only have geographers and legal theorists shied away from an encounter, but there seem powerful barriers—institutional and theoretical—to such a meeting. . . . Legal geographies . . . bear directly and powerfully upon social and political life." See Blomley, *Law, Space, and the Geographies of Power* (New York: Guilford Press, 1994), vii.

6. On the African presence in Britain, see James Walvin, *Making of the Black Atlantic,* 5; Seymour Drescher, "Manumission in a Society without Slave Law:

Eighteenth Century England," *Slavery and Abolition* 10; 3 (December 1989), 86. For the absolute rights of individuals, see Sir William Blackstone, *Commentaries on the Laws of England*, A Facsimile of the First Edition of 1765–1769, *Of the Rights of Persons* (1765), Volume 1, with an introduction by Stanley N. Katz (Chicago: University of Chicago Press, 1979), 117–140.

7. See *Black's Law Dictionary* for definitions of "common law" and "statutory law." Daniel Boorstin provides an accessible and useful discussion of the wonders of the law, with particular reference to the production of William Blackstone's *Commentaries*, the preeminent codification of English common law written in the mid-eighteenth century. See Boorstin, *The Mysterious Science of the Law: An Essay on Blackstone's Commentaries* (Chicago: University of Chicago Press, 1969).

8. Thomas Jones Howell, *A Complete Collection of State Trials*, Vol. 20, 1771–1777. "The Case of James Sommersett [sic], a Negro, on a Habeas Corpus, King's Bench: 12 George III. A.D. 1771–72. This is a report consisting largely of Francis Hargrave's arguments on behalf of Somerset. There is another reporting of the trial done earlier by Capel Lofft. His report of *Somerset v. Stewart* [sic] provides less detail than Howell's version. See 1 Lofft 1/98 Eng. Rept. 499.

9. See Blackstone, *Commentaries*, 123.

Edward Chamberlayne, in his *Angliae Notitia or the Present State of England* (1669), was conversant with the idea of the seemingly innate powers of English soil (514). In 1580, William Harrison, in his *Description of England* (which was contained in Raphael Holinshed's *Chronicles of England*) included the statement regarding the lack of slaves and bondsmen in England.

10. See Jack P. Greene, *Peripheries and Center: Constitutional Development in the Extended Polities of the British Empire and the United States 1607–1788* (Athens, GA: University of Georgia Press, 1986).

11. There were several things at stake in these cases, not the least of which were ideological and legal consistency. Justices trod carefully as careless declaration could easily undermine English authority in the colonies. In that instance, Chief Justice John Holt presided. *Chamberline* [sic] *v. Harvey*, 5 Mod. 182/87 Eng. Rept. 596, continuing at 5 Mod. 186/87 Eng. Rept. 598.

12. There are a number of accounts of the *Somerset* case, which I have addressed at length in "Entitled to the benefits of liberty," the first chapter of "Publishing Freedom, Winning Arguments: Somerset, Natural Rights and Massachusetts Freedom Cases, 1772–1836" (Unpublished Ph.D. dissertation, Columbia University, 2004). See also F.O. Shyllon, *Black Slaves in Britain* (London: Oxford University Press, 1974).

13. Howell, *State Trials*.

14. Ibid., 65, 66.

15. Ibid., 56–64. Villeins were forced to take oaths that they would not leave the manor to which they were bound and experienced a variety of corrective measures should they break the oath. Serfdom, villeinage, and servant are often discussed at length in English history with an indiscriminate exchange of terms.

16. *The London Chronicle*, 466. Lord Mansfield was a particularly complex justice whose many sides cannot be addressed here. In calling Mansfield's view of the law "literalist," I do not mean to imply a pejorative; indeed the tendency is not to be thought of as being in opposition to the spirit of the law. Rather, Mansfield's tendency toward the literal speaks to his intense belief in and trust of the law. Though the law is created and enforced by people—and thus is dynamic—

Mansfield sometimes leaned in the direction of preferring the law over the people who, he thought, attempted to manipulate it.

17. Howell, *State Trials,* 82.

18. Mansfield could have looked to Blackstone's *Commentaries,* wherein the latter asserted the firmness with which the spirit of liberty was embedded in the constitution and soil of England. Blackstone actively invoked the protective power of English law and the transformative power of English soil to restore natural rights and render the beneficiary *eo instanti* a freeman. See Blackstone, *Commentaries,* p. 123. Mansfield's complex personal, political, and judicial history—along with the significance and difficulties of being Scottish in the mid-eighteenth century—are discussed at length in my dissertation (see note 12).

19. Howell, *State Trials,* 82.

20. The Boston Female Anti-Slavery Society, *Annual Report of the Boston Female Anti-Slavery Society: Being the Concise History of the Cases of the Slave Child, Med, and of the Women Demanded as Slaves of the Supreme Judicial Court of Massachusetts with all the Other Proceedings of the Society* (Boston: Published by the Society, 1836), p. 66.

21. Paul Finkelman, *The Law of Freedom and Bondage: A Casebook* (New York: Oceana Publications, Inc., 1986), 78–79.

22. In the end, the Missouri Compromise forestalled the crisis over slavery in America only a little. In the years that followed, frontal attacks against slavery (such as David Walker's militant *Appeal* in 1829, and Nat Turner's violent slave uprising in 1831) helped to inspire a more radical abolitionist movement, led by people like Frederick Douglass and William Lloyd Garrison. The abolitionists regularly cited the defects and moderation of legislation dealing with slavery to justify their crusade.

23. Thomas Aves was the father of Mary Slater and the father-in-law of Samuel Slater, Mary's husband and owner of Med. Thomas Aves was charged for several reasons: he was resident in the Commonwealth of Massachusetts (his daughter wasn't), and Med was found in his house. Mary Slater was away in the countryside at the time. Concerning the writ of habeas corpus obtained by Captain Levin Harris, and Thomas Aves's Return to the Writ, see pamphlet "Case of the Slave-Child, Med Arguments of Counsel, and the Opinion of the Court in the Case of Commonwealth vs. Aves Tried and Determined in the Supreme Judicial Court of Massachusetts" (Boston: Isaac Knapp, 1836).

24. Leonard Levin, *The Law of the Commonwealth and Chief Justice Shaw,* 63; Finkelman, *The Law of Freedom and Bondage: A Casebook* (New York: Oceana Publications, 1986), 70–71.

25. *The Liberator,* September 3, 1836, 143. See also Wiecek, *Sources of Antislavery Constitutionalism,* 194; and Levy, *Law of the Commonwealth,* 63.

26. Concerning Curtis's arguments, see *The Liberator,* September 3, 1836, 143.

27. Ibid., 143.

28. *The Liberator,* September 24, 1836, 154. Again, legally speaking, "foreign law" was law from outside of the jurisdiction in which a case was being heard. Loring's five points were as follows: (1) Comity should not be exercised where there was doubt; courts were meant to prefer their local law over foreign law; (2) Comity was founded upon mutual consent and reciprocity; in the current case no consent of nations prevailed on the matter of slavery; (3) Comity had no place where specific regulations on a subject existed; specific regulations on slavery did exist; (4) If comity could not be applicable where specific regulations existed it was even less applicable where contestation and dispute sur-

rounded the subject; and (5) The law of foreign domicile is generally confined to situations of simple contracts; there is no contract involved in slavery.

29. For a discussion of this conflict, see Robert Cover, *Justice Accused: Antislavery and the Judicial Process* (New Haven: Yale University Press, 1975), chapter 5, especially 87ff. It is interesting to note that while Francis Hargrave had largely avoided arguing against James Somerset's status as a slave on primarily moral grounds, Med's counsel, by contrast, argued by underscoring the immorality of slavery. One possible explanation for the change of emphasis would be the maturity of the antislavery movement by the mid-1830s.

30. "Free soil" would later become a political issue in America as the country expanded and the question of slavery likewise expanded. A "Free Soil" party developed in the mid-1840s, although the party was more concerned with the ways in which free white workers were disadvantaged by the introduction of slavery into newly acquired territories than with the ills of slavery itself. Many free-soilers were antislavery (opposed to the extension of slavery) but not abolitionist (in favor of the abolition of slavery). See Eric Foner, *Free Soil, Free Labor, Free Men: The Ideology of the Republican Party* (New York: Oxford University Press, 1975). Concerning *Forbes v. Cochrane*, 1824, see 2 Barn. & Cres. 448/107 Eng. Rep. 450. Briefly, a group of enslaved men, women, and children escaped from a plantation in East Florida and sought refuge on board an English warship. They were effectively considered by the court to be on free English soil. This is an evocative example of what is meant by my phrase "geographies of liberty," for it illustrates the enduring power of such ideologically constituted geographies. In this case, one need not have been on actual soil—terra firma—to experience the force and the substantiality of the imagined geography.

31. *The Liberator*, October 8, 1836, 161.

32. The full text of the quote reads: "no bond slavery, villanage [sic], or captivity amongst us, with the exception of lawful captives taken in just wars, or those judicially sentenced to servitude, as a punishment for crime."

33. *The Liberator*, October 22, 1836, 169.

34. See Hall, Wiecek, and Finkelman, eds., *American Legal History: Cases and Materials*, 200ff.

4. "A Chosen Generation": Black Founders and Early America

1. Allen's and Jones's pamphlet is reprinted most recently in Richard Newman, Patrick Rael, Philip Lapsansky, eds., *Pamphlets of Protest: An Anthology of Early African American Protest Literature, 1790–1860* (New York, 2000), 33–42.

2. Charles Wesley, *Richard Allen: Apostle of Freedom* (Washington, 1935).

3. Tom Brokaw, *The Greatest Generation* (New York, 2004); John Fierling, *Setting the World Ablaze* (New York, 2002); Richard Brookhiser, *Alexander Hamilton* (New York, 2000); Saul Cornell, *The Other Founders* (Chapel Hill, 1996).

4. John Bracey, August Meier, Elliot Rudwick, eds., *Blacks in the Abolition Movement* (Belmont, CA., 1971). Ray Allen Billington was the only author to consider a black abolitionist (James Forten) in that collection. See also Benjamin Quarles, *Black Abolitionists* (New York, 1968). Martin Duberman's *The Antislavery Vanguard* (Princeton, 1964), impressively had two essays (out of seventeen) on black reformers: Benjamin Quarles's "Abolition's Different Drummer: Frederick Douglass" and Leon Litwack's "The Emancipation of the Negro Abolitionist."

5. The best books on race and slavery in the early republic include: Mia Bay, *The White Image in the Black Mind: African-American Ideas About White People, 1830–1925* (New York, 2000); Bruce Dain, *A Hideous Monster of the Mind: American Race Theory in the Early Republic* (Cambridge, MA, 2002); Douglas Egerton, *He Shall Go Out Free: The Lives of Denmark Vesey* (Madison, 2000); Graham Russell Hodges, *Slavery and Freedom in the Rural North: African Americans in Monmouth County, New Jersey, 1665–1865* (Madison, 1997); Mitch Kachun, *Festivals of Freedom: Memory and Meaning in African American Emancipation Celebrations, 1808–1915* (Amherst, 2003); Elizabeth McHenry, *Forgotten Readers: Recovering the Lost History of African American Literary Societies* (Duke, 2002); Joanne Pope Melish, *Disowning Slavery: Gradual Emancipation and "Race" in New England, 1780–1860*. See also James Brewer Stewart, "The Emergence of Racial Modernity and the Rise of the White North 1790–1840," *Journal of the Early Republic* 18 (Summer 1998): 181–217; and Richard S. Newman, "Not the Only Story in *Amistad:* The Fictional Joadson and the Real James Forten," *Pennsylvania History* (Spring 2002): 218–239.

6. See Julie Winch, *A Gentleman of Color: The Life of James Forten* (New York, 2002); and John Saillant, *Black Puritan, Black Republican, The Life and Thought of Lemuel Haynes, 1753–1833* (New York, 2002).

7. Weekly *Anglo-African* (October, 1859).

8. On emancipation and free black life, see Gary Nash, *Forging Freedom: The Formation of Philadelphia's Black Community, 1720–1840* (Cambridge, MA, 1988); Shane White, *Somewhat More Independent: The End of Slavery in New York City, 1770–1810* (Athens, GA, 1991); Julie Winch, *Philadelphia's Black Elite* (Philadelphia, 1993).

9. On the growth of free black society in the North, see especially James Horton and Lois Horton, *In Hope of Liberty* (Oxford, 1997); and Patrick Rael, *Black Identity and Black Protest in the Antebellum North* (Chapel Hill, 2002).

10. See Douglas Egerton, *Gabriel's Rebellion* (Chapel Hill, 1996).

11. See Richard S. Newman, *The Transformation of American Abolitionism: Fighting Slavery in the Early Republic* (Chapel Hill, 2002).

12. See Papers of the Pennsylvania Society for the Abolition of Slavery . . . [Pennsylvania Abolition Society, Microfilm Edition, Reel 7, Report of Committee for Improving the Condition of the Free People of Color].

13. George Price, James Brewer Stewart, eds., *To Heal the Scourage of Prejudice* (Amherst, 1999).

14. James Oliver Horton, *Free People of Color: Inside the African American Community* (Washington, 1993), 43–46.

15. See Kevin Gaines's admirable and important work, *Uplifting the Race* (Chapel Hill, 2001), for a challenge to Allen's leadership vision.

16. "Summary" of Committee of Guardians activity, Papers of the Pennsylvania Society for the Abolition of Slavery . . . [Pennsylvania Abolition Society, Microfilm Edition], Reel 7, Report of Committee for Improving the Condition of the Free People of Color, 67, 69, 73.

17. For more on runaways to Philadelphia, see Newman, *The Transformation of American Abolitionism,* Chapter 3.

18. Stephen Hahn, *A Nation Under Our Feet* (Cambridge, 2003).

19. *New York Gazette of the United States* (May 1790).

20. See William S. McFeeley, *Frederick Douglass* (New York, 1991).

21. Allen's essay is reprinted in Peter Hinks, ed., *David Walker's Appeal to the Coloured Citizens of the World* (University Park, PA, 2000), 62.

22. Albert J. Raboteau, *Canaan Land: A Religious History of African Americans* (New York, 1999), 27.

23. Ibid., 26–27.

24. Allen's eulogy is reprinted in Philip S. Foner, Robert James Barnham, eds., *Lift Every Voice: African American Oratory, 1787–1900* (Tuscaloosa, AL, 1998), 67–69.

25. See Daniel Coker, "A Dialogue Between a Virginian and an African Minister" (1810), in Newman et al., eds., *Pamphlets of Protest*, 52–65.

26. Shane White, *Stories of Freedom in Black New York* (Cambridge, 2002), 40–41.

27. See Hinks, *David Walker's Appeal*, xx–xxii, 59–61.

28. Dorothy Porter, ed., *Negro Protest Pamphlets* (New York, 1969), i–iii.

29. See Joseph Ellis's insightful and thoughtful book *Founding Brothers* (New York, 1999), especially Chapter 17.

30. Forten's pamphlet is reprinted in Newman et al., eds., *Pamphlets of Protest*, 66–72.

31. See Saillant, *Black Puritan, Black Republican*, 73.

32. Hamilton, "An Address to the New York African Society for Mutual Relief" (New York, 1809); reprinted in Dorothy Porter, ed., *Early Negro Writing, 1760–1837* (Boston, 1971), 33–41.

33. In particular, see Elizabeth McHenry, "Dreaded Eloquence: The Origins and Rise of African American Literary Societies and Libraries," *Harvard Library Bulletin* II:2 (Spring 1995): 32–56. See also Newman et al., eds., *Pamphlets of Protest*, Introduction.

34. Thomas and John Fleet published Hall's 1792 pamphlet; Benjamin Edes published the 1797 edition.

35. Williams's tale is reprinted in David Brion Davis, ed., *Antebellum American Culture* (Lexington, MA, 1979), 295–98.

36. On Revolutionary-era deference politics in general, see Gordon S. Wood's provocative article, "Interests and Disinterestedness in the Making of the Constitution," in Richard Beeman, Stephen Botein, Edward C. Carter II, eds., *Beyond Confederation: Origins of the Constitution and American National Identity* (Chapel Hill, 1987), 69–112.

37. William Hamilton, "Address Before the African Society," 1809.

38. The full text of Allen's and Jones' address is reprinted in Porter, *Negro Protest Pamphlets* (New York, 1969), 21–23.

39. For a reprint of Philadelphia blacks' anticolonization address, see Lawrence B. Goodheart, Hugh Hawkins, eds., *The Abolitionists: Means, Ends, and Motivations* (Lexington, MA, 1995), 37–38.

40. "Minutes and Reports of the State Convention of Colored Citizens of Pennsylvania . . . Dec. 13 and 14, 1848" (Philadelphia, 1849), 1–24.

41. *Frederick Douglass' Paper* (March 1855).

5. "Onward, Onward, Is Indeed the Watchword": James Forten's Reflections on Revolution and Liberty

1. For a detailed discussion of Forten's business activities, see Julie Winch, *A Gentleman of Color: The Life of James Forten* (New York: Oxford University Press, 2002), Chapter 4.

2. See, for instance, *National Antislavery Standard,* March 10, 1842.
3. S.H. Cowles to Leonard Bacon, February 9, 1825; Bacon Family Papers, Sterling Library, Yale University.
4. Winch, *Gentleman of Color,* 8. For evidence that at least one member of the Forten family took a degree of pride in being a British subject, see Philadelphia County Wills, Book O, 258, no. 196 (1768), Philadelphia City Archives.
5. Winch, *Gentleman of Color,* 26.
6. *Liberator,* March 11, 1842; *North Star,* March 10, 1848; James Forten, *Letters from a Man of Colour on a Late Bill Before the Senate of Pennsylvania* (Philadelphia, 1813), 1.
7. Winch, *Gentleman of Color,* 24–25. For the full text of Pennsylvania's Gradual Abolition Law, see Roger Bruns, ed., *Am I Not a Man and a Brother: The Antislavery Crusade of Revolutionary America, 1688–1788* (New York: Chelsea House, 1977), 446–450.
8. Winch, *Gentleman of Color,* 37–43.
9. Stephen H. Gloucester, *A Discourse Delivered on the Occasion of the Death of Mr. James Forten, Sr., in the Second Presbyterian Church of Colour in the City of Philadelphia, April 17, 1842* (Philadelphia: I. Ashmead, 1843) 21–22; Robert Purvis, *Remarks on the Life and Character of James Forten, Delivered at Bethel Church, March 30, 1842* (Philadelphia: Merrihew and Thompson, 1842), 6
10. Purvis, *Remarks,* 6. On the relationship between Brewton and Forten, see Winch, *Gentleman of Color,* 49, 301, 327.
11. On Forten's fondness for Addison, and especially his drama *Cato,* see Winch, *Gentleman of Color,* 170.
12. Forten, *Letters from a Man of Colour,* 3.
13. Ibid.
14. Ibid., 8.
15. Haytien Emigration Society of Philadelphia, *Information for the Free People of Colour, Who Are Inclined to Emigrate to Hayti* (Philadelphia: J. H. Cunningham, 1825), 5–6. On Forten's lifelong admiration for Lafayette, see *Minutes and Proceedings of the Third Annual Convention, for the Improvement of the Free People of Colour in These United States, Held by Adjournments in the City of Philadelphia, from the 3rd to the 13th of June Inclusive, 1833* (New York: By Order of the Convention, 1833), 26, 30–31.
16. Forten, *Letters from a Man of Colour,* 4.
17. For the text of the petition, see John Parrish, *Remarks on the Slavery of the Black People: Addressed to the Citizens of the United States, Particularly to Those Who Are in Legislative or Executive Stations in the General or State Governments: and also to Such Individuals as Hold Them in Bondage* (Philadelphia: Kimber, Conrad, 1806), 49–50.
18. "James Forten to Hon. George Thatcher [sic], 1800," Cox, Parrish, Wharton Papers, Box 11, Historical Society of Pennsylvania.
19. Ibid.
20. In the debate over whether Congress should consider the Philadelphians' petition, South Carolina's John Rutledge Jr. had declared, "Already had too much of this new-fangled French philosophy of liberty and equality found its way . . . among these *gentlemen* in the Southern States." Peter M. Bergman and Jean McCarroll, comps., *The Negro in the Congressional Record, 1789–1801* (New York: Bergman, 1969), 241.
21. On Servance, see Winch, *Gentleman of Color,* 126, 134, 185.

22. Isaac V. Brown, *Biography of the Rev. Robert Finley*, 2nd ed. (Philadelphia: John W. Moore, 1857), 123; S.H. Cowles to Leonard Bacon, February 9, 1825.

23. Haytien Emigration Society, *Information*, 6.

24. Brenda Stevenson, ed., *The Journals of Charlotte Forten Grimké* (New York: Oxford University Press, 1988), 218.

25. Purvis, *Remarks*, 11–12.

26. "Magawisca" in *Liberator*, March 26, 1831; "Ada" in ibid., January 4, 1834. On Sarah Forten's literary career, see Winch, *Gentleman of Color*, 264–271.

27. *Liberator*, March 19, 1831.

28. James Forten to William Lloyd Garrison, December 31, 1830; Antislavery Manuscripts, Boston Public Library.

29. Forten to Garrison, January 13, 1831; Antislavery Manuscripts, BPL.

30. *Liberator*, February 12, 1831.

31. Forten to Garrison, October 20, 1831; Antislavery Manuscripts, BPL.

32. *Liberator*, March 12, 1831.

33. Ibid., August 20, 1831. On the authorship of the letter, see Winch, *Gentleman of Color*, 244–45.

34. James Forten, Robert Purvis, and William Whipper, *To the Honourable the Senate and House of Representatives of the Commonwealth of Pennsylvania* (Philadelphia, 1832), 1, 2, 3, 7.

35. *Liberator*, March 19, 1831.

36. Forten to Garrison, February 23, 1832; Antislavery Manuscripts, BPL.

37. Forten to Garrison, October 20, 1831; Antislavery Manuscripts, BPL.

6. John Brown Russwurm's Dilemma: Citizenship or Emigration?

1. William M. Brewer, "John Brown Russwurm," *Journal of Negro History*, Vol. XIII, 417. See editorial published in *Freedom's Journal*, March 21, 1829.

2. Mavis C. Campbell, *The Dynamics of Change in a Slave Society* (Rutherford, NJ, 1976), 52–63.

3. Beryl M. Brown, "The Development of Port Antonio, 1723–1921." Eighth Conference of Caribbean Historians, Martinique, April 5–9, 1976, 9–10. A petition to the Jamaican Assembly in 1784 by the white settlers of the Port Antonio region in which they requested the government's support for establishing a school at Titchfield stated, "a means of having the succeeding generations properly educated without putting parents to the enormous expense of sending their children off the island." From the *Journal of the Assembly of Jamaica*, Vol. VIII, November 24, 1784.

4. James T. Hall, "Walks in Eastern Cemetery No. 3," Maine Genealogical Society, Portland, Maine. John Brown Russwurm Papers, Bowdoin College Manuscript Collection.

5. Elizabeth F. Chittenden, "Bowdoin's First Black Graduate John Brown Russwurm 1799–1851," Bowdoin College Manuscript Collection.

6. John Brown Russwurm to John Sumner Russwurm, North Yarmouth, July 19, 1819, John Sumner Russwurm Collection, Tennessee State Archives.

7. JBR to John Otis, North Yarmouth Academy, June 22, 1819. Owned by R.E.M. Smith, held in the Rowland Bailey Howard Papers, Bowdoin College Manuscript Collection.

8. JBR to JSR, July 19, 1819, Tennessee State Archives.
9. Robert C. Hayden, *The African Meeting House: A Celebration of History,* Museum of Afro American History (Boston, 1987), 12.
10. James Oliver and Lois E. Horton, *Black Bostonians: Family Life and Community Struggle in the Antebellum North* (New York, 1979), viii.
11. Wilson Jeremiah Moses, *Golden Age of Black Nationalism, 1850–1925* (New York, 1978), 7.
12. Ibid., 8–9.
13. P.J. Staudenraus, *The African Colonization Movement, 1816–1865* (New York, 1961), 9.
14. Ibid., 13.
15. Ibid., 19.
16. Ibid., 5.
17. Imanuel Geiss, *The Pan-African Movement: A History of Pan-Africanism in America, Europe and Africa;* translated by Ann Keep (New York, 1969), 80.
18. Julie Winch, *Philadelphia's Black Elite: Activism, Accommodation, and the Struggle for Autonomy, 1787–1848* (Philadelphia, 1988), 42.
19. Hayden, *The African Meeting House,* 15–17.
20. Horatio Bridge, *Personal Recollections of Nathaniel Hawthorne* (New York, 1968; reprint of 1893 ed.), 27.
21. JBR to John Otis, North Yarmouth Academy, June 22, 1819. Owned by R.E.M. Smith, held in Rowland Bailey Howard Papers, Bowdoin College Manuscript Collection.
22. JBR to JSR, January 9, 1826, Tennessee State Archives.
23. "Letters to the American Colonization Society, written in New York, February 26, 1827," *Journal of Negro History,* Vol. 10, 156.
24. John Brown Russwurm, "The Conditions and Prospects of Hayti," Bowdoin College Manuscript Collection, 1.
25. Wilson Jeremiah Moses, *Alexander Crummell: A Study of Civilization and Discontent* (New York, 1988), 11–13. See also Timothy Patrick McCarthy's essay in this volume (Chapter 7).
26. Staudenraus, *The African Colonization Movement,* 15–16.
27. Ibid., 19.
28. Early Lee Fox, *The American Colonization Society, 1817–1840* (Baltimore, 1919), 17.
29. Ibid., 17.
30. Staudenraus, *The African Colonization Movement,* 19.
31. Sheldon H. Harris, *Paul Cuffe: Black America and the African Return* (New York, 1972), 231–239.
32. Staudenraus, *The African Colonization Movement,* 20.
33. Harris, *Paul Cuffe,* 244
34. Leon F. Litwack, *North of Slavery: The Negro in the Free States, 1790–1860* (Chicago, 1961), 24–25.
35. Staudenraus, *The African Colonization Movement,* 32.
36. Harris, *Paul Cuffe,* 244
37. *Freedom's Journal,* March 14, 1828.
38. Ibid., March 14, 1828.
39. Ibid., July 18, 1828.
40. Ibid., August 15, 1828.
41. Ibid.

42. Ibid., May 18, 1827.
43. Ibid., February 29, 1828.
44. Ibid., January 25, 1828.
45. Ibid., July 11, 1828.
46. Nehemiah Cleaveland and Alpheus S. Packard, ed., *History of Bowdoin College* (Boston, 1882), 353.
47. Maryland State Colonization Society Manuscripts, *Letters;* Vol. XIV, Russwurm to Latrobe, Cape Palmas, December 23, 1843; Vol. XV, Russwurm to Latrobe, Cape Palmas, January 12, 1844.
48. On matters of colony business, see Maryland State Colonization Society Manuscripts, *Letters:* Vol. XV, Russwurm to Latrobe, Cape Palmas, February 13, 1844; Russwurm to Latrobe, Cape Palmas, August 24, 1844; Vol. XVIII, Russwurm to Latrobe, Cape Palmas, May 13, 1846; *Latrobe Letter Books,* Vol. III, Latrobe to Russwurm, Baltimore, June 12, 1844; Vol. III, Latrobe to Russwurm, Baltimore, November 12, 1844; Vol. III, Latrobe to Russwurm, Baltimore, April 24, 1846; Vol. III, Latrobe to Russwurm, Baltimore, November 30, 1846. On matters of citizen behavior, see MSCS, Mss. *Letters:* Vol. VIII, Russwurm to Latrobe, Harper, April 26, 1838; Vol. XVI, Russwurm to Hall, Cape Palmas, October 27, 1844; Vol. XVIII, Russwurm to Latrobe, Cape Palmas, January 23, 1847.
49. MSCS *Letters:* Vol. XIX, Russwurm to Latrobe, Cape Palmas, March 1, 1851; *Latrobe Letter Books,* Vol. III, Latrobe to Russwurm, Baltimore, July 17, 1851.
50. Cleaveland and Packard, *History of Bowdoin College,* 353.
51. John H. Latrobe, *Latrobe Letter Books,* 73–74n.

7. "To Plead Our Own Cause": Black Print Culture and the Origins of American Abolitionism

1. Nathaniel Paul, "An Address on the Celebration of the Abolition of Slavery in New York State," in Philip S. Foner, ed., *The Voice of Black America: Major Speeches by Negroes in the United States, 1797–1971* (New York: Simon and Schuster, 1969), 38–42.
2. Jane H. Pease and William H. Pease, *They Who Would Be Free: Blacks' Search for Freedom, 1830–1861* (New York: Atheneum, 1974), 23.
3. Genevieve Fabre, "African-American Commemorative Celebrations in the Nineteenth Century," in Fabre and Robert O'Meally, eds., *History and Memory in African-American Culture* (New York: Oxford University Press, 1994), 72.
4. Arthur Zilversmit, *The First Emancipation: The Abolition of Slavery in the North* (Chicago: University of Chicago Press, 1967). For more on the process of abolition in New York and throughout the North, see Shane White, *Somewhat More Independent: The End of Slavery in New York City, 1770–1810* (Athens: University of Georgia Press, 1991); Joanne Pope Melish, *Disowning Slavery: Gradual Emancipation in New England, 1780–1860* (Ithaca: Cornell University Press, 1998); Leon Litwack, *North of Slavery: The Negro in the Free States, 1790–1860* (Chicago: University of Chicago Press, 1961); and Ira Berlin, *Many Thousands Gone: The First Two Centuries of Slavery in North America* (Cambridge: Harvard University Press, 1998).
5. For the most extensive discussion of the transformation of the abolitionist movement from a moderate white movement advocating gradualism (and African colonization) to a more radical interracial movement advocating immediatism (and rejecting colonization), see Richard S. Newman, *The Transfor-*

mation of American Abolitionism: Fighting Slavery in the Early Republic (Chapel Hill: University of North Carolina Press, 2002). For additional studies that empha-size the central role that blacks played in this transformation, see Benjamin Quarles, *Black Abolitionists* (New York: Oxford University Press, 1969); Herbert Aptheker, *The Negro in the Abolitionist Movement* (New York: International Pub-lishers, 1941); and Paul Goodman, *Of One Blood: Abolitionism and the Origins of Racial Equality* (Berkeley: University of California Press, 1998).

6. *Freedom's Journal,* March 16, 1827.

7. A great deal of black writing—from Phillis Wheatley's poems and Benjamin Banneker's scientific writings to pamphlets and slave petitions—predated *Freedom's Journal.* The importance of this early literature in establishing an African American literary tradition can hardly be overstated. In calling particular at-tention to *Freedom's Journal,* I want to emphasize that the formal beginning of black journalism in 1827 represented a new form of black political expression that helped to initiate radical abolitionism, and to create a broader, more in-terracial public sphere. Moreover, abolitionist newspapers played a crucial role in the creation and dissemination of literary culture—from poems and short stories to slave autobiographies and serialized fiction. See Dickson D. Bruce, Jr., *The Origins of African American Literature, 1680–1865* (Charlottesville: Uni-versity Press of Virginia, 2001); William L. Andrews, *To Tell a Free Story: The First Century of Afro-American Autobiography* (Chicago: University of Illinois Press, 1986); and Blyden Jackson, Jr., ed., *A History of Afro-American Literature* (Baton Rouge: Louisiana State University Press, 1989).

8. For discussions of the simultaneous rise of black slavery and white freedom—and the ideologies of "race" that developed as a result—see Edmund S. Mor-gan, *American Slavery, American Freedom: The Ordeal of Colonial Virginia* (New York: W.W. Norton, 1975); John Hope Franklin, *From Slavery to Freedom: A His-tory of Negro Americans* (New York: Knopf, 1967); Winthrop Jordan, *White Over Black: American Attitudes Toward the Negro, 1550–1812* (Baltimore: Penguin, 1969); David Brion Davis, *The Problem of Slavery in the Age of Revolution, 1770–1823* (Ithaca: Cornell University Press, 1975); Ira Berlin, *Many Thou-sands Gone;* and Barbara Jeanne Fields, "Slavery, Race, and Ideology in the United States of America," *New Left Review* 81 (May-June 1986), 95–118.

9. See Fabre, "African-American Commemorative Celebrations in the Nine-teenth Century," 72-91; William B. Gravely, "The Dialectic of Double-Consciousness in Black American Freedom Celebrations, 1808–1863," *Journal of Negro History* 67 (1982), 302–317; Benjamin Quarles, "Antebellum Free Blacks and the Spirit of '76," *Journal of Negro History* Vol. LXI, No. 3 (July, 1976), 229–242; Leonard L. Sweet, "The Fourth of July and Black Americans in the Nineteenth Century: Northern Leadership Opinion within the Context of the Black Experience," *Journal of Negro History* Vol. LXI, No. 3 (July 1976), 256–275; William H. Wiggins, " 'Lift Every Voice': A Study of Afro-American Emancipation Celebrations," in Roger D. Abrahams and John F. Szwed, eds., *Discovering Afro-America* (New York: Leiden, 1975), 46–57.

10. William Hamilton, "An Oration Delivered in the African Zion Church, on the Fourth of July, 1827, in Commemoration of the Abolition of Domestic Slavery in This State," quoted in Gravely, 310. See also Quarles, *The Negro in the American Revolution* (Chapel Hill: University of North Carolina Press, 1961); and William Cooper Nell, *The Colored Patriots of the American Revolution* (Boston, 1855).

11. For more on the American Colonization Society and the free black commu-

nity's protest of its activities, see P.J. Staudenraus, *The African Colonization Movement, 1816–1865* (New York: Columbia University Press, 1961); Douglas R. Egerton, " 'Its Origins Is Not a Little Curious': A New Look at the American Colonization Society," *Journal of the Early Republic* 5 (Fall 1985), 463–480; Lawrence J. Friedman, "Purifying the White Man's Country: The American Colonization Society Reconsidered, 1816–40," *Societas* 6 (Winter 1976), 1–245; David M. Streifford, "The American Colonization Society: An Application of Republican Ideology to Early Antebellum Reform," *Journal of Southern History* 45 (May 1979), 201–220; and Goodman, *Of One Blood*, 1–64.

12. I do not want to suggest that all African Americans were abolitionists, in the strict sense of being part of the movement, any more than I would argue that all slaves tried to resist or overthrow slavery. However, I do assert that African Americans—by virtue of their status either as property (slaves) or as quasi-citizens (free blacks)—had a different and more pragmatic (one might say *immediate*) interest in the outcome of abolitionism; for blacks, these were matters of life and death. See Quarles, *Black Abolitionists*, viii, 249.

13. Benedict Anderson, *Imagined Communities: Reflections on the Origin and Spread of Nationalism*, 2nd ed. (New York: Verso, 1991), 36.

14. For discussions of political ideology and dissent literature in the era of the American Revolution, see Bernard Bailyn, *The Ideological Origins of the American Revolution* (Cambridge: Harvard University Press, 1967); Eric Foner, *Tom Paine and Revolutionary America* (New York: Oxford University Press, 1976); Michael Warner, *Letters of the Republic: Publication and the Public Sphere in Eighteenth-Century America* (Cambridge: Harvard University Press, 1990); and Robert A. Ferguson, "The Commonalities of *Common Sense*," *William and Mary Quarterly* vol. LVII, no. 3 (July 2000), 465–506.

15. For the best work on cultural theories of "racial" difference and inferiority during this period, see George M. Fredrickson, *The Black Image in the White Mind: The Debate on Afro-American Character and Destiny, 1817–1914* (Middletown: Wesleyan University Press, 1971); Mia Bay, *The White Image in the Black Mind: African-American Ideas about White People, 1830–1925* (New York: Oxford University Press, 2000); and Jordan, *White Over Black*.

16. *Freedom's Journal,* March 16, 1827; Hamilton quoted in Foner, *The Voice of Black America,* 26.

17. Genevieve Fabre argues that freedom celebrations "should be analyzed as a political gestus which contributed to the development of a collective memory—not just memory of past events but the memory of the future, in anticipation of action to come—and of the historical consciousness of a people who are often perceived as victims rather than as historical agents." Moreover, she sees the sermons that occupied a central place at these commemorations as being part of a cultural continuum, as interacting dynamically, with the written word. She writes: "Celebrations gave rise to an impressive production of speeches which belong to an oral tradition of harangues and rhetoric. Delivered in a culture where the spoken word prevailed, they reached out beyond their immediate contemporary audiences and eventually found their way into written forms. . . . The ability to put into words was also very much part of their own culture. . . . Freedom celebrations were freedom performed . . . [but] African-Americans were not simply performing culture, they were performing crucial social and political acts." See Fabre, "African-American Commemorative Celebrations in the Nineteenth Century," 73–75.

18. The editors reported that soon after its inception, "The Office of the 'Freedom's Journal' is removed to No. 152 Church-street." See *Freedom's Journal,* May 4, 1827.

19. See Robert S. Levine, "Circulating the Nation: David Walker, the Missouri Compromise, and the Rise of the Black Press," in Todd Vogel, ed., *The Black Press: New Literary and Historical Essays* (New Brunswick: Rutgers University Press, 2001), 23.

20. *Freedom's Journal,* March 16, 1827.

21. Donald M. Jacobs, ed., *Antebellum Black Newspapers* (Westport: Greenwood Press, 1976), 3–4.

22. *Freedom's Journal* (March 16, 1827).

23. Ibid., October 12, 1827.

24. Ibid., June 8, 1827.

25. Ibid., March 23, 1827.

26. Ibid., July 13, 1827.

27. Ibid., July 13, 1827.

28. Ibid., March 16, 1827.

29. Ibid., March 16, 1827. The same advertisement appeared in every issue during its two-and-a-half-year run.

30. Phyllis F. Field, *The Politics of Race in New York: The Struggle for Black Suffrage in the Civil War Era* (Ithaca: Cornell University Press, 1982), 34. Field notes that in 1841, the New York State legislature authorized any school district that so desired to establish segregated schools for black children. By 1847, fifteen out of fifty-nine counties had done so, a number that increased throughout the antebellum era. As late as 1868, twenty-two counties—containing 75.9 percent of New York's black population—had established segregated schools.

31. *Freedom's Journal,* May 13, 1827.

32. Ibid., June 1, 1827. While it has often been the assumption that schools were established where the largest numbers of blacks resided, it was also the case that cities attracted large black populations because they offered greater educational and economic opportunities.

33. Ibid., April 20, 1827.

34. Ibid., March 30, 1827.

35. Ibid., May 13, 1827.

36. Ibid., August 31, 1827.

37. Ibid., December 21, 1827.

38. Field, *The Politics of Race in New York,* 30.

39. See Iver Bernstein, *The New York City Draft Riots: Their Significance for American Society and Politics in the Age of the Civil War* (New York: Oxford University Press, 1990).

40. Philip S. Foner, ed., *Life and Writings of Frederick Douglass, Volume 2* (New York: International Publishers, 1950), 249–50. For more on the tensions that existed between antebellum white and black workers, and on the racism of recently arrived immigrants in the mid-nineteenth century as they struggled to "become white," see David Roediger, *The Wages of Whiteness: Race and the Making of the American Working Class* (New York: Verso, 1991); and Noel Ignatiev, *How the Irish Became White* (New York: Routledge, 1995).

41. Litwack, *North of Slavery,* 159.

42. There seems to be evidence that wealth was distributed more unevenly in New York City than in other, more rural, regions in the state. However, because

blacks were disproportionately confined to urban areas, the impact of economic inequality was more burdensome for them relative to rural (or urban) whites. See Edward Pessen, "Political Democracy and the Distribution of Power in Antebellum New York City," in Irwin Yellowitz, ed., *Essays in the History of New York City: A Memorial to Sidney Pomerantz* (London: National University Publications, 1978), 21–42.

43. *Freedom's Journal*, July 27, 1827.

44. Ibid., March 30, 1827.

45. See Eric Foner, *Free Soil, Free Labor, Free Men: The Ideology of the Republican Party before the Civil War* (New York: Oxford University Press, 1995), ix; and Sean Wilentz, *Chants Democratic: New York City and the Rise of the American Working Class, 1788–1850* (New York: Oxford University Press, 1984), 14–15.

46. Foner, *Free Soil, Free Labor, Free Men*, xi.

47. See Ibid., xvii. As Foner notes, the rise of wage labor, and "its institutionalization in the law, posed a profound challenge for the ethos that defined economic dependence as incompatible with freedom." Furthermore, despite the fact that the market revolution ostensibly sought to promote individual freedom to determine one's future, the expansion of capitalism resulted in the opposite for many Americans, especially blacks.

48. Ibid., xi, xvi–xvii.

49. *Freedom's Journal* (June 15, 1827).

50. Ibid., June 15, 1827.

51. All quotes from *Freedom's Journal*, August 10, 1827. It should be noted that in an editorial published on June 8, 1827, the Benevolent Society of Alexandria offered a slightly different argument than the previous writer. It read: "It seems then, that a slave-labourer costs as much as a free labourer, and if he does three-fourths as much work, his employer loses by him about $15 or $20 per annum; or, in other words, the work done by him would cost this much less, if it had been performed by a freeman." While they, too, account for the many additional costs of maintaining a slave labor force—costs that would either be redistributed or negated under a free labor system—they calculated that the annual cost of a slave is equal to that of a wage laborer; the difference in annual profit/loss (in this case, loss) derives from the lower productivity of the slave to the free laborer. Conversely, the first editorial argues that slaves are both more costly and less productive. In either case, the superiority of free to slave labor, and the need to abolish slavery, is acknowledged. See *Freedom's Journal*, June 8, 1827.

52. Ibid., June 15, 1827.

53. Ibid., June 1, 1827.

54. Ibid., December 7, 1827.

55. Levine, "Circulating the Nation," 22–26.

56. Russwurm quoted in Bruce, *The Origins of African American Literature*, 174. See also John Russwurm, "A Candid Acknowledgment of Error," in *Freedom's Journal*, February 1829; subsequently reprinted in *African Repository* 4 (1829).

57. *Freedom's Journal*, March 16, 1827.

58. For more on Cornish, Russwurm, and *Freedom's Journal*, see Bruce, *The Origins of African American Literature*, 163–174; Goodman, *Of One Blood*, 24–28; and James Oliver Horton and Lois E. Horton, *In Hope of Liberty: Culture, Community, and Protest Among Northern Free Blacks, 1700–1860* (New York and Oxford: Oxford University Press, 1997), 196–202.

59. See Quarles, *Black Abolitionists*, 85, 88.

60. For more on this see C. Peter Ripley et al., eds., *The Black Abolitionist Papers, Volume III: The United States, 1830–1846* (Chapel Hill: University of North Carolina Press, 1990), 3–69, 71–91; Herbert Aptheker, ed., *A Documentary History of the Negro People in the United States, Volume I* (New York: Citadel Press, 1951), 82–85, 108–111; and Bruce, *The Origins of African American Literature*, 175–176.

61. For detailed discussions of the regions of North and South Carolina where David Walker spent most of his life, see Peter P. Hinks, *"To Awaken My Afflicted Brethren": David Walker and the Problem of Antebellum Slave Resistance* (University Park, PA: Penn State University Press, 1997), especially Chapters 1–2; Marina Wikramanayake, *A World in Shadow: The Free Black in Antebellum South Carolina* (Columbia, SC: University of South Carolina Press, 1973); Leonard P. Curry, *The Free Black in Urban America, 1800–1850: The Shadow of Dreams* (Chicago: University of Chicago Press, 1981), Chapter 2; and Ira Berlin, *Slaves Without Masters: The Free Negro in the Antebellum South* (New York: Pantheon, 1974). For more on the Vesey conspiracy in the context of the history of slave resistance, see Herbert Aptheker, *American Negro Slave Revolts* (New York: International Publishers, 1993); Eugene Genovese, *From Rebellion to Revolution: Afro-American Slave Revolts in the Making of the Modern World* (Baton Rouge: Louisiana State University Press, 1979); John Oliver Killens, ed., *The Trial Record of Denmark Vesey* (Boston: Beacon Press, 1970); and John Lofton, *Denmark Vesey's Revolt: The Slave Plot that Lit a Fuse to Fort Sumter* (Kent, OH: Kent State Press, 1983). For two different, though equally important, studies of the black church, with special attention to black Methodism, see Carol V.R. George, *Segregated Sabbaths: Richard Allen and the Rise of Independent Black Churches, 1760–1840* (New York: Oxford University Press, 1973); and Carter G. Woodson, *The History of the Negro Church* (Washington, DC: Associated Publishers, 1921).

62. Peter Hinks has done the most extensive research on Walker and his *Appeal.* See Hinks, *To Awaken My Afflicted Brethren,* especially Chapters 6–7. See also the long introduction to Herbert Aptheker, *"One Continual Cry": David Walker's Appeal to the Colored Citizens of the World (1829–1830)—Its Setting and Its Meaning* (New York: Humanities Press for AIMS, 1965). My own reading of Walker's *Appeal* has been deeply informed by Hinks's and Aptheker's excellent research and exegesis.

63. This point about two distinct "generations" within the African American community from the time of the Revolution to the 1830s has been articulated most explicitly in Horton and Horton, *In Hope of Liberty;* Quarles, *Black Abolitionists;* Gary Nash, *Forging Freedom: The Formation of Philadelphia's Black Community, 1720–1840* (Cambridge: Harvard University Press, 1988); and in Richard Newman's and Julie Winch's essays in this volume.

64. See Hinks, *To Awaken My Afflicted Brethren,* 63–67.

65. In 1825, black Bostonians made up just over 3 percent of the city's total population.

66. Quarles, *Black Abolitionists,* 16. For a more detailed discussion of David Walker's activities in Boston after his arrival in the mid-1820s, see Hinks, *To Awaken My Afflicted Brethren,* Chapters 3–4; Donald M. Jacobs, "David Walker: Boston Race Leader, 1825–1830," *Essex Institute Historical Collections* 107 (1977), 94–107; and also the Introduction to Sean Wilentz, ed., *David Walker's Appeal to the Coloured Citizens of the World* (New York: Hill and Wang, 1995), vii–xxiii.

67. Lois and James Horton make this point explicitly: "After considerable debate, an 1835 national convention of blacks unanimously adopted a resolution calling for the removal of 'the title of African from [black] institutions, the marbles of churches, and etc.' The periodic black national meetings that followed were termed 'Colored Conventions,' and in the minutes of those conventions blacks referred to themselves as 'people of color.' When blacks referred to themselves as colored Americans, they were not denying or rejecting their African heritage. They were, however, asserting their rights as Americans and vehemently rejecting any public or private efforts to force them to emigrate against their wills." See Horton and Horton, *In Hope of Liberty*, 201–202. The minutes and proceedings of these annual "Colored Conventions" have been reprinted in Howard H. Bell, ed., *Minutes of the Proceedings of the National Negro Conventions, 1830–1864* (New York: Arno Press, 1969).

68. All quotes from "Address, Delivered before the General Colored Association at Boston, by David Walker," in Wilentz, ed. *David Walker's Appeal*, 79–83. Robert Levine discusses the relationship between the MGCA speech, *Freedom's Journal*, and Walker's "Appeal" by calling attention to Walker's "emphasis on written communication . . . to achieve black nationalist goals of united community. For Walker, literacy remained a key to such goals." See Levine, "Circulating the Nation," 25. See also Hinks, *To Awaken My Afflicted Brethren*, 92–93.

69. See Henry Louis Gates Jr., *The Signifying Monkey: A Theory of African-American Literary Criticism* (New York: Oxford University Press, 1988); and Gates, *Figures in Black: Words, Signs, and the "Racial" Self* (New York: Oxford University Press, 1987).

70. *Walker's Appeal*, 2. All subsequent references to Walker's *Appeal* are from the third and final edition, reprinted in Wilentz.

71. Ibid., inside front cover.

72. Ibid., 1–2.

73. Ibid., 2.

74. Ibid., 3, 16.

75. Ibid., 7.

76. Ibid., 16.

77. Ibid., 10.

78. Ibid., 14.

79. Ibid., 12, 15.

80. Ibid., 15.

81. Thomas Jefferson, *Notes on the State of Virginia*, reprinted in Merrill D. Peterson, ed., *The Portable Thomas Jefferson* (New York: Viking, 1975), 192–193; *Walker's Appeal*, 27.

82. *Walker's Appeal*, 14.

83. Ibid., 14–15.

84. Ibid., 15.

85. For Jefferson's thoughts on Phillis Wheatley and other black writers of his time, see *Notes* in Peterson, ed., *The Portable Thomas Jefferson*, 188–189. For a discussion of Jefferson and Wheatley, see Henry Louis Gates Jr., *The Trials of Phillis Wheatley: America's First Black Poet and her Encounters with the Founding Fathers* (New York: Basic/*Civitas* Books, 2003).

86. *Walker's Appeal*, 47.

87. Ibid., 50.

88. Ibid., 70.

89. Ibid., 38.
90. Ibid., 35.
91. Ibid., 58–59.
92. Ibid., 74–75.
93. Ibid., 75.
94. Ibid., 42.
95. Ibid., 76.
96. Garrison and Lundy quoted in Goodman, *Of One Blood,* 30–31.

8. "Willing to Die for the Cause of Freedom in Kansas": Free State Emigration, John Brown, and the Rise of Militant Abolitionism in the Kansas Territory

1. James Redpath, *The Public Life of Captain John Brown* (Boston: Thayer and Eldridge, 1860), 155–156.
2. "Anti-Slavery Mass Meeting—Eleven Resolutions." *The* (Lawrence, Kansas) *Republican,* December 8, 1859. Coincidentally, Abraham Lincoln was in Kansas at the time, at Troy and at Leavenworth, giving campaign speeches and speaking of Brown's execution. Condemning the raid itself, Lincoln, perhaps mindful of some members of his Kansas audience, still praised John Brown for exhibiting "great courage [and] rare unselfishness."
3. John Brown's own accounts of the Battles of Black Jack and Osawatomie appeared in the *New-York Tribune* of July 11, 1856, and the *New York Daily Times* of September 20, 1856.
4. The Wyandotte Convention of July 1859, with many of John Brown's personal friends and supporters in attendance (e.g., John Ritchie, J. J. Ingalls, Solon O. Thacher), negated the proslavery Lecompton Constitution of 1857, and would secure the admittance of Kansas into the Union as a free state on January 29, 1861.
5. See Henry David Thoreau, *The Last Days of John Brown* (Boston, 1859).
6. *The Republican* (December 22, 1859).
7. "Great Speech of Ex-Governor Reeder," *New-York Daily Times* (September 20, 1856).
8. John Speer, *Life of Gen. James H. Lane: "The Liberator of Kansas"* (Garden City, KS: John Speer, 1896), 75.
9. "Popular Sovereignty," wherein settlers were to determine for themselves the issue of the free- or slave-state status of Kansas, was an integral part of the Kansas-Nebraska Act, the principal architect of which was Senator Stephen A. Douglas of Illinois.
10. See Michael Fellman, "Rehearsal for the Civil War: Antislavery and Proslavery at the Fighting Point in Kansas," in Lewis Perry and Michael Fellman, eds., *Antislavery Reconsidered: New Perspectives on the Abolitionists* (Baton Rouge: Louisiana State University Press, 1979), 287–307. There is an extensive critical literature on the "Bleeding Kansas" period and its pivotal place in American history. In particular, see Gunja SenGupta, "Bleeding Kansas," *Kansas History* (Winter 2001–2002): 318–341; and Nicole Etcheson, *Bleeding Kansas: Contested Liberty in the Civil War Era* (Lawrence: University Press of Kansas, 2004).
11. See James A. Rawley, *Race and Politics, "Bleeding Kansas" and the Coming of the Civil War* (Philadelphia: Lippincott, 1969), 81. Class and cultural tensions sur-

faced immediately in Kansas between western Missourians and New Englanders. For a detailed analysis, see Michael Fellman, *Inside War: The Guerrilla Conflict in Missouri During the American Civil War* (New York: Oxford University Press, 1989), 11–20.

12. See *Report of the Committee of the Massachusetts Emigrant Aid Society with the Act of Incorporation and Other Documents* (Boston: Published for the Massachusetts Emigrant Aid Company, 1854).

13. For complete rosters see Louise Barry, "The Emigrant Aid Company Parties of 1854" and "The New England Emigrant Aid Company Parties of 1855," *Kansas State Historical Quarterly*, Volume XII (Topeka: Kansas State Historical Society, 1943), 115–54; 227–268. The majority of the emigrant trains departed from Boston for Kansas Territory between July 17, 1854, and July 24, 1855. Nearly all the emigrants came from the New England region. For analysis of the companies see Samuel A. Johnson, "The Emigrant Aid Company in Kansas," *Kansas Historical Quarterly* 1 (November 1932), 429–441. Edward Everett Hale's *Kanzas and Nebraska* (New York: Phillips, Sampson and Company, 1854) provided much of the political impetus and promotional momentum for New England emigration to Kansas. John Brown migrated to Kansas Territory in October 1855 under his own auspices, although his brother-in-law and half sister, Samuel and Florella Adair, had arrived exactly at Osawatomie one year prior with the Third Emigrant Aid Party of 1854. Five of John Brown's sons had preceded him to Kansas, from their homes in Ohio, in the spring of 1855.

14. The town was named for Amos A. Lawrence, though two other names—Wakarusa and New Boston—were considered.

15. The *New-York Tribune, New-York Daily Times, Boston Traveller, Washington National Intelligencer,* etc., all had Kansas correspondents in the field and carried daily dispatches from the "Kansas War" as front-page news throughout the summer and fall of 1856.

16. The first "martyr" of the free-state and abolitionist cause was Ohioan Thomas W. Barber, who was shot and killed by proslavery men from Lecompton, west of Lawrence, during the "Wakarusa War" of early December 1855. John Greenleaf Whittier wrote the poem "Burial of Barbour," published in the March 1856 issue of the *National Era*, a journal for which John H. Kagi was the Kansas correspondent. John Brown viewed Barber's body as it lay in state at the Free State Hotel, and Brown wrote home to his wife Mary in North Elba, New York, that Barber's death was "one of the sure results of Civil War." John Brown Papers, Kansas State Historical Society. John Brown letter of December 16, 1855.

17. Fellman, *Antislavery Reconsidered*, 289.

18. For a well-documented analysis of Brown's religious convictions see Louis A. De Caro, *"Fire from the Midst of You," A Religious Life of John Brown* (New York: New York University Press, 2002).

19. Brown arrived at his sons' claims, Brown's Station, Kansas Territory, with a wagonload of weaponry. He had attended the Syracuse Convention of the Radical Political Abolitionists on June 28, 1855, and attempted, with only moderate success, to raise money for arms for Kansas. See Stephen B. Oates, *To Purge this Land With Blood* (Amherst: University of Massachusetts Press, 1984), 90–91; John Stauffer, *The Black Hearts of Men: Radical Abolitionists and the Transformation of Race* (Cambridge: Harvard University Press, 2002), 13–14. Brown ended up, however, receiving the majority of the weapons he brought to Kansas from Lucius V. Bierce in Akron, Ohio. See Richard O. Boyer, *The Legend of John Brown*

(New York: Knopf, 1973), 560. It was with these weapons that Brown first arrived in Lawrence on December 7, 1855, during the height of the Wakarusa War. Brown first received the title of "Captain" here. Original muster rolls for this company are in the William I. R. Blackman Collection at the Kansas State Historical Society, and in the Ferdinand Julius Dreer Manuscript Collection at the Historical Society of Pennsylvania.

20. Brown considered himself to be an "a most *determined Abolitionist*" from the early days of his childhood, stating so in a letter he wrote on July 15, 1857, from Red Rock, Iowa, to a young Henry L. Stearns. See James Redpath, *The Public Life of Captain John Brown,* 29. In numerous letters he wrote from Kansas, Brown often referred to his being an "Abolitionist" and a "Free State man."

21. See letter to John Brown regarding the Battle of Osawatomie in Oswald Garrison Villard, *John Brown* (Boston: Houghton Mifflin, 1910), 248.

22. For an insightful view of the role of the "Westerners" in the antislavery struggle in Kansas, see Bill Cecil-Fronsman, " 'Advocate the Freedom of White Men, as Well as That of Negroes': The *Kansas Free State* and Antislavery Westerners in Territorial Kansas," *Kansas History* (Summer, 1997), 102–115. See also Eric Foner, *Free Soil, Free Labor, Free Men: The Ideology of the Republican Party Before the Civil War* (New York: Oxford University Press, 1970).

23. SenGupta, "Bleeding Kansas," 340.

24. Oates, *To Purge This Land With Blood,* x.

25. Paul Finkelman, "Manufacturing Martyrdom," in *His Soul Goes Marching On: Responses to John Brown and the Harpers Ferry Raid* (Virginia: University of Virginia Press, 1995), 60.

26. Benjamin Quarles, *Allies for Freedom: Blacks and John Brown* (New York: Oxford University Press, 1974), 156.

27. Richard Sheridan, *Freedom's Crucible* (Lawrence: University of Kansas Continuing Education Press, 1999).

28. The back of the original handwritten *Old Browns Parallels,* at the Kansas State Historical Society—a letter that Brown wrote initially to the *Lawrence Republican* on January 13, 1859, and later to Horace Greeley's *New-York Tribune* of January 22, 1859—has a list of friendly farms to stop at in eastern Kansas during the December and January 1859 journey. See William Elsey Connelly, *John Brown* (Topeka: Crane and Company, 1900), 325–326, 332.

29. "The Harper's Ferry Riot," *Boston Weekly Messenger,* (October 17, 1859). See also "The Virginia Rebellion. The Insurrection Originated in Kansas," *New-York Times* (November 5, 1859). The interrogation of Brown by Valladingham, Mason, and numerous reporters following Brown's capture often centered on the "Kansas" nexus of the Harpers Ferry operation. At his sentencing on November 2, 1859, Brown stated: "In the first place, I deny everything but what I have all along admitted: of a design on my part to free the slaves. I intended certainly to have made a clean thing of the matter, as I did last winter, when I went into Missouri and there took slaves without the snapping of a gun on either side, moving them through the country, and finally leaving them in Canada. I designed to have done the same thing again on a larger scale. That was all I intended." See *New-York Herald* (November 3, 1859).

30. See Fellman, *Inside War,* 170. Opinions on James Lane are nearly as divided along ideological lines as those on John Brown. See Speer, *Life of Gen. James H. Lane;* and Wendell H. Stephenson, *The Political Career of General James H. Lane* (Topeka: Kansas State Historical Society, 1930). See also Dudley Taylor Cor-

nish, "Kansas Negro Regiments in the Civil War," *Kansas Historical Quarterly* (May 1953), 417–429.

31. See Paul W. Gates, *Fifty Million Acres: Conflicts over Kansas Land Policy, 1854–1890* (Ithaca: Cornell University Press, 1954).

32. See James C. Malin, *John Brown and the Legend of Fifty-Six* (Philadelphia: American Philosophical Society, 1942). Malin's excoriating view of John Brown, and of eastern abolitionists in Kansas in general, came to dominate much Civil War scholarship before Stephen B. Oates wrote his even-handed biography of John Brown, *To Purge This Land With Blood* (New York: Harper and Row, 1970). See also Allan Nevins, *Ordeal of the Union: A House Dividing 1852–1857* (New York: Charles Scribner's Sons, 1947); and Rawley, *Race & Politics*.

33. In this regard see, for example, the account of Richard Henry Dana Jr. (author of *Two Years Before the Mast*) of his chance encounter with John Brown and his family at North Elba (*Journal*, June 23 and 29, 1849, Massachusetts Historical Society). Also reprinted in Villard, *John Brown*, 74. Dana's account was first published in the *Atlantic Monthly*, July 1871.

34. Herbert Aptheker, *Abolitionism: A Revolutionary Movement* (Boston: Twayne, 1989), 127.

35. In 1852 Boston's John P. Jewett published Harriet Beecher Stowe's *Uncle Tom's Cabin* and Lydia Maria Child's *Isaac T. Hopper—a true Life*. In addition to the Whitman and Searl *Township Map of Eastern Kansas*, Jewett published *Six Months in Kansas By a Lady* by Hannah Anderson Ropes in 1856, as well as Benjamin Drew's *The Refugee: or, the Narratives of fugitive slaves in Canada*. In 1856 eastern interest in the explosive situation in Kansas was exploited by other publishers, mainly in Cincinnati, Philadelphia, Boston, and New York. Crosby, Nichols and Company published, and republished, Bostonian Sara Tappan Doolittle Robinson's hugely popular *Kansas; Its Exterior and Interior Life;* Phillips and Sampson Company published William Phillips's *The Conquest of Kansas by Missouri and Her Allies;* and Derby & Jackson published Douglas G. Brewerton's *The War in Kansas, A Rough Trip to the Border, Among New Homes and a Strange People.* Thomas H. Gladstone's 1856 letters from Kansas to the *London Times* were edited with an introduction by the abolitionist Frederick Law Olmsted (who had just published his own *A Journey in the Seaboard Slave States*), and published as part of *The Englishman in Kansas: Or Squatter Life and Border Warfare* (New York: Miller & Company, 1857). Also in 1857, John H. Gihon, the secretary of Kansas territorial governor John W. Geary, published his account of the events of 1856 in *Geary and Kansas* (Philadelphia: Chas. C. Rhodes, 1857). The *Howard Report, or Kansas Affairs: Report of the Special Committee Appointed to Investigate the Troubles in Kansas with the Views of the Minority of Said Committee* (Washington: Cornelius Wendell, 1856), was a widely distributed government document, numbering over 1,200 pages. It included several affidavits of victims' relatives fully implicating John Brown in the Pottawatomie Massacre.

36. There are a vast number of collected editions of correspondence related to the 1850s New England–Kansas Territory story. For example, see Julia Louisa Lovejoy's letters to the *Independent Democrat* of Concord, New Hampshire (Kansas State Historical Society); John and Sarah Everett letters; Edward and Sarah Fitch letters (KSHS); New England Emigrant Aid Company correspondence, Massachusetts and National Kansas Committee correspondence (Boston Public Library, Massachusetts Historical Society, Kansas State Historical Society), and Thomas Webb Scrapbooks (KSHS).

37. Edmund B. Whitman's son, Alfred, was a close friend of the Alcott children, and the character of Laurie in Louisa May Alcott's *Little Women* was based on him.

38. See Jeffrey Rossbach, *Ambivalent Conspirators: John Brown, the Secret Six, and a Theory of Slave Violence* (Philadelphia: University of Pennsylvania Press, 1983); and Charles E. Heller, *Portrait of an Abolitionist: A Biography of George Luther Stearns, 1809–1867* (Westport, CT: Greenwood Press, 1996), 69–121. Following his New England fund-raising tour, and prior to the financial Panic of 1857, John Brown received modest financial support from the likes of Eli Thayer and Amos A. Lawrence. See Eli Thayer, *A History of The Kansas Crusade: Its Friends and Foes* (New York: Harper & Brothers, 1889), 190–200; and William Lawrence, *Life of Amos A. Lawrence* (Boston: Houghton, Mifflin, 1889), 122–138.

39. Old Oread Cemetery, above Lawrence, is the burial ground for many free-state casualties of Bleeding Kansas, including Thomas W. Barber and David C. Buffum. Buffum was shot and killed by Kickapoo Rangers on September 15, 1856. Barber's large monument remains in situ. Buffum's tombstone is now in the collection of the Kansas State Historical Society.

40. See *An Idea of Things in Kansas,* John Brown's manuscript for his speech given in Hartford, Connecticut, March, 1857. John Brown Papers, Kansas State Historical Society.

41. In the early autumn of 1856, members of the National Kansas Committee (NKC) sent fifty 1851 Colt Navies to Lawrence via the Lane Trail, ostensibly to John Brown, who later had difficulty obtaining them from the local National Kansas Committee agents. By the following autumn Brown had accumulated an impressive arsenal of his own donated New England weaponry. Though initially transported west to Tabor, Iowa, for possible use in Kansas in 1857, the majority of these weapons would eventually find their way to the Kennedy farm in Maryland for use in the raid on Harpers Ferry. See Franklin B. Sanborn, *The Life and Letters of John Brown* (Boston: Roberts Bros., 1885), 399.

42. Leverett Wilson Spring, *Kansas: The Prelude to the War for the Union* (Boston: Houghton, Mifflin, 1887), 167–169.

43. See "Old Browns *Farewell,* " April 1857. John Brown Papers, KSHS. Redpath, 195.

44. Villard, *John Brown,* 141.

45. Malin, *John Brown and the Legend of Fifty-six,* 120.

46. For a contemporary profile of James Montgomery, see William P. Tomlinson, *Kansas in Eighteen Fifty-Eight: Being a Brief History of the Recent Troubles in the Territory* (New York: H. Dayton, 1858).

47. See Nicole Etcheson, " 'Labouring for the Freedom of this Territory': Free-State Kansas Women in the 1850s," *Kansas History* (Summer 1998), 68–87.

48. Letter of William H. Leeman to his brother, dated "Nebraska T. Nov. 9th, 1856." Richard Josiah Hinton Papers, Kansas State Historical Society.

49. William H. Leeman to his mother, dated Harpers Ferry, October 2, 1859, in Villard, *John Brown,* 408. See William H. Leeman letters (1856–59), and also John H. Kagi letters and Aaron D. Stevens letters in the Richard Josiah Hinton Papers at the Kansas State Historical Society.

50. For broad analysis of the events of 1848, see Priscilla Robertson, *Revolutions of 1848: A Social History* (Princeton: Princeton University Press, 1952). "The Duty of the Soldier," a tract written by John Brown's drillmaster Hugh Forbes and

used by Brown in his Tabor, Iowa, training camp in 1857, employs rhetoric echoing the narrative of the European struggles over class and nationalism that erupted in 1848.

51. *By-laws of the Free State regular Volunteers of Kansas enlisted under the command of John Brown, 1856,* John Brown Memorandum, Book II, Boston Public Library; *Articles of Agreement for Shubel Morgans Company,* 1858, John Brown Papers, Kansas State Historical Society.

52. *The Life, Trial and Execution of Captain John Brown* (New York: Robert M. De Witt, 1859), 27.

53. See Osborne P. Anderson, *A Voice from Harper's Ferry* (Boston: Printed for the Author, 1861), 31.

54. Susan Ratcliffe, *The Oxford Dictionary of Biographical Quotes* (Oxford: Oxford University Press, 2001), 51.

55. Richard D. Webb, *Life and Letters of Captain John Brown* (London: Smith, Elder and Co., 1861), ii.

56. See "The Invasion of Kansas: Particulars of the Destruction of Lawrence by Quantrell: Dreadful Scenes of Pillage and Murder," *New-York Times* (August 23, 1863). "The Lawrence Massacre: One Hundred and Ninety Victims Found in Lawrence," *New-York Tribune* (August 27, 1863).

57. In June 1864, Senator James Lane of Kansas, with his usual oratorical flourish, helped sway the Republican National Convention in Baltimore to nominate Abraham Lincoln for a second term as president.

58. After statehood, segregation became institutionalized in Kansas as it had throughout the rest of the Midwest; however, this was not the result solely of hypocrisy, or dereliction of duty, among the state's abolitionists. Many among the old guard tried their best to ensure basic civil rights for blacks and women, but had the deck stacked against them from the start by a political majority that had always harbored other agendas. It would take another hundred years, and another Kansas case, *Brown v. Board of Education* (1954), for civil rights to begin to systematically advance at the state and federal levels.

59. Victor Hugo and the French republicans commissioned Belgian sculptor Jean Wurden to strike a gold medal in memory of John Brown. It was presented to Mary Brown in 1874, and later donated by the Brown family to the Kansas State Historical Society. See Hermann von Holst, *John Brown* (Boston: Cupples and Hurd, 1888), 189-196; and also Seymour Drescher, "Servile Insurrection and John Brown's Body in Europe," in Finkelman, ed., *His Soul Goes Marching On,* 283–284. A bronze statue of John Brown by Paul W. Bartlett stands in Paris, and another, cast at the same foundry in Paris as the Statue of Liberty, stands in the John Brown Memorial Park in Osawatomie, Kansas. For historical analysis of the John Brown image in art and literature, see Louis Ruchames, *A John Brown Reader* (London: Abelard-Schuman, 1959); and Merrill D. Peterson, *The Legend Revisited: John Brown* (Charlottesville: University of Virginia Press, 2002).

9. Regional Black Involvement in John Brown's Raid on Harpers Ferry

1. John Brown's use of the railroads deserves thorough study. His change of training ground and weapons storage from western to eastern Iowa in 1857 and 1858 was because he wanted to use the railroads and canals more effectively for the southern movement of his liberation invasion. The authors would like to

acknowledge the ideas of Thomas Meisenholder of San Jose, California, in this essay which he proposed after reading "Two Trains" in Jean Libby and Hannah N. Geffert, eds., *John Brown Mysteries by Allies for Freedom* (Missoula, MT: Pictorial Histories Publishing, 1999), 36–41. Meisenholder's question: "John Brown was waiting for somebody when he stopped the trains, and then let them go. If it was not for the local slaves, then who was it?"

2. W.E.B. Du Bois, "The Great Black Way," in David Roediger, ed., *John Brown* (New York: Random House, 2001), 163–183. Among historians of John Brown, only Du Bois developed the concept of the "Great Black Way." Du Bois conducted his research for his biography of John Brown in Harpers Ferry in 1906, at the second convocation of the Niagara Movement. Local African Americans were active in this session, both in meetings and in hosting the delegates at Storer College. It is likely that Du Bois asked local people to give their recollections of the raid.

3. Richard J. Hinton, *John Brown and His Men* (New York: Arno Press, 1968), 34, 172; Franklin Benjamin Sanborn, *The Life and Letters of John Brown, Liberator of Kansas, and Martyr of Virginia* (1885), 468; Wilbur H. Siebert, *The Underground Railroad from Slavery to Freedom* (New York: Arno Press, 1968), 118.

4. Vernon F. Alers, *History of Martinsburg and Berkeley County West Virginia* (Hagerstown, MD: Mail Publishing Company, 1888), 200.

5. Joint Committee of Hopewell Friends, *Hopewell Friends History, 1734–1934, Frederick County, Virginia* (Strasburg, VA: Shenandoah Publishing House, 1936), 12–98; Rufus M. Jones, *The Later Periods of Quakerism*, Volume 1 (London: MacMillan and Co. 1921), 388 [as cited in Larry D. Gragg, *Migration in Early America: The Virginia Quaker Experience* (Ann Arbor: University Microfilms International Research Press, 1980), 4].

6. Jerry M. Johnson III, *Johnsontown, West Virginia Heritage Year Book* (1987), 3.

7. In 1850, Jefferson County's population was 15,357 (10,476 white, 4341 slaves, and 540 free Negroes). The county had four main towns; Harpers Ferry was the largest, followed by Shepherdstown, Charles Town, and Bolivar.

8. In the Harpers Ferry–Bolivar area, whites outnumbered blacks nine to one with approximately 200 people of color in the two towns. U.S. Census, 1860.

9. James Fisher, Shepherd College Oral History Project, 91-93.

10. Thomas Hahn, "Towpath Guide to the C&O Canal," 5 [as cited in Jean Libby, *Black Voices from Harpers Ferry* (Menlo Park, CA: Inkling Books, 2002), 93].

11. *The Shepherdstown Register,* Vol. 1, no. 41 (September 3, 1850). On March 10, 1835, the General Assembly incorporated the Virginia Slave Insurance Company at Charles Town (Legislative Petition B 308/10819). When the Fugitive Slave Bill was being debated in Congress a faithful synopsis was printed in the *Shepherdstown Register* because it was considered to be a matter of peculiar importance in this section of the state.

12. Merrit Roe Smith, *Harpers Ferry Armory and the Challenge of Change* (Ithaca, NY: Cornell University Press, 1977).

13. Ronald Lewis, *Coal, Iron and Slaves: Industrial Slavery in Maryland and Virginia, 1715–1865* (Westport, CT: Greenwood Press, 1979); Jean Libby, "African Ironmaking Culture Among African American Ironworkers in Western Maryland, 1760–1850" (M.A. thesis in Ethnic Studies, San Francisco State University, 1991).

14. Jean Libby, ed., *From Slavery to Salvation: The Autobiography of Rev. Thomas W.*

Henry of the A.M.E. Church (Jackson: University Press of Mississippi, 1994), 26–27.

15. Michael Thompson, *The Iron Industry in Western Maryland* (Hagerstown, MD: Washington County Historical Society, 1976).

16. The demographic breakdown of the black population of Frederick County, Maryland, is developed in Chris Haugh, producer, *From the Meadows, A History of Black Americans in Frederick County, Maryland* (Frederick Cablevision/Cable 10, 1997); of Washington County, in Marguerite Doleman, *We, the Blacks of Washington County* (Washington County Historical Commission, 1976); and Libby, *Black Voices From Harpers Ferry.* Oral histories obtained by Libby in 1979 at the Mt. Moriah Baptist Church in Pleasant Hill, Maryland, trace the work history of ironworkers to railroads among congregation members.

17. Stella Fries et al., eds., "The Underground Rail Road," vol. VII, Kittochtinny Papers, 100–105, in *Some Chambersburg Roots: A Black Perspective* (Chambersburg, PA: Kittochtinny Historical Society, 1980), 12.

18. Eric Ledell Smith, "John Brown in Crawford County: The Making of a Radical Abolitionist," *Journal of Erie Studies,* Vol. 30, no. 2 (Fall 2001): 41–53.

19. I. Garland Penn, *The African American Press and Its Editors* (New York: Arno Press, 1969).

20. John Brown's financing of this publication in 1848 is remarked upon in James McCune Smith's 1865 publication, *A Memorial Discourse, by Rev. Henry Highland Garnet, Delivered in the Hall of the House of Representatives, Washington City, D.C. on Sabbath, February 12, 1865* (Philadelphia: Joseph M. Wilson, 1865).

21. W.E.B. Du Bois, *John Brown* (New York: International Publishers, 1962), 97.

22. Richard J. Hinton, *John Brown and His Men* (New York: Arno Press, 1968), 26, 31.

23. Christopher Phillips, *Freedom's Port: The African-American Community of Baltimore, 1790–1860* (Urbana: University of Illinois Press, 1997).

24. Frederick Douglass, "John Brown and West Virginia," *West Virginia State College Bulletin* (November 1953), series 40, no. 6, 20.

25. Stephen B. Oates, *To Purge This Land with Blood: A Biography of John Brown* (Amherst: University of Massachusetts Press, 1984), 213–214.

26. Benjamin Quarles, *Allies for Freedom: Blacks and John Brown* (New York: Oxford University Press, 1974), 13.

27. Ibid., 69.

28. George G. Gill's statement is reprinted in Hinton, *John Brown and His Men,* 710. Gill was a white emigrant to Kansas in 1856 who became part of John Brown's guerrilla militia, traveling with him to Iowa and Chatham, Canada, to initiate the war on slavery in 1858.

29. Du Bois, *John Brown,* 114.

30. Ibid., 243–244; see also Hinton, *John Brown and His Men,* 171–172.

31. Frank A. Rollins [Frances Rollin Whipper], *Life and Public Services of Martin R. Delany,* 85–90.

32. See Du Bois, *John Brown,* 205; Hinton, *John Brown and His Men,* 178, 180.

33. James Surkamp, *Delany: To Be More Than Equal* (Teaching Kit, 1989), 6, 12, 13. The Delany family was also in jeopardy because the eldest Delany son, Samuel Jr., was in the habit of forging passes for other family members.

34. Hinton, *John Brown and His Men,* 249.

35. Libby, *Black Voices from Harpers Ferry,* 75.

36. Edna Christian Knapper, "Outstanding Colored Citizens of Chambersburg—

Past and Present: Joe Winters," *Chambersburg Public Opinion,* January 17, 1954. Published with photographs of Winters in Stella Fries et al., eds., *Some Chambersburg Roots,* 239.

37. Quarles, *Allies for Freedom,* 76.

38. Du Bois, *John Brown,* 295.

39. Frederick Douglass, *Life and Times of Frederick Douglass* (rev. ed. of 1892; London: Crowell-Collier, 1962), 273–274, 317–21.

40. Du Bois, *John Brown,* 109–110, 344.

41. Hinton, *John Brown and His Men,* 507–508.

42. Du Bois, *John Brown,* 282; and Hinton, *John Brown and His Men,* 267–268. Six men of color were recruited by Lewis Hayden in Boston, but only one, John Anderson, a free man, reached Harpers Ferry. Whether he took part in the fight and was killed at Harpers Ferry or returned to Boston is unclear. The local Colored Elks suggest that John Anderson was killed at the rifle works battle. His name, however, is listed on the memorial to John Brown's men at the family farm in North Elba, as a Negro raider who escaped.

43. Quarles, *Allies for Freedom,* 87–88. See also Libby, "Hiram and Willis Revels, Lewis Leary and John Copeland" in *John Brown Mysteries,* 72–74.

44. Hinton, *John Brown and His Men,* 266, 310. Dangerfield Newby had attempted to buy her from her owner, Jesse Jennings. Jennings had promised to sell her and one child for $1,000 but then refused. Immediately after the raid, Harriet was sold and sent to Louisiana.

45. Du Bois, *John Brown,* 281.

46. Frank Johnson was an internationally noted musician from Philadelphia. See Charles Blockson, *African Americans in Pennsylvania Above Ground and Underground, An Illustrated Guide* (Harrisburg, PA: RB Books, 2001), 90.

47. William H. Johnson, *Autobiography of Dr. William Henry Johnson* (Albany: Argus Company, 1900), 194–195.

48. Chris Haugh, *Up From The Meadows* (1997), tells the story of the escape of Thomas Joshua Dorsey from Frederick to Philadelphia, and his subsequent success as a businessman and community leader.

49. *Chambersburg Valley Spirit,* October 1859.

50. Benjamin A. Matthews, "Harper's Ferry and John Brown," *Storer Sentinel* (1909).

51. Du Bois, *John Brown,* 314.

52. Hinton, *John Brown and His Men,* 294–295. John E. Cook's statement is reprinted in Hinton, 713–714.

53. Elijah Avey, *The Capture and Execution of John Brown* [as cited in Libby, *Black Voices from Harpers Ferry,* 102]. Interview with Mr. Graham by Dr. Featherstonehaugh, 1892, cited in Hinton, *John Brown and His Men,* 305. John E. Cook's quoted in Hinton, *John Brown and His Men,* 713.

54. John E.R. Dangerfield, "John Brown at Harper's Ferry," in Hinton, *John Brown and His Men,* 300.

55. Anderson, *A Voice from Harper's Ferry* [as reprinted in Libby, *Black Voices from Harpers Ferry,* 34].

56. Hinton, *John Brown and His Men,* 298.

57. Thomas Drew, comp. *The John Brown Invasion* (Freeport, New York: Books for Library Press, 1972), 6 [as cited in Libby, *Black Voices from Harpers Ferry,* 104–105].

58. Letter from George L. Douglass to Kearsely Carter, October 1859, in Hannah

N. Geffert, "When The Raiders Came" *Columbiad*, Vol. 4, no. 1 (Spring 2000), 111.

59. *Baltimore Weekly Sun,* October 22, 1859 [as cited in Millard Kessler Bushong, *Historic Jefferson County* (Boyce, VA: Carr Publishing Company, 1972), 187].

60. Quarles, *Allies for Freedom,* 100–101; and Hinton, *John Brown and His Men,* 295, 511, 530.

61. Letter from D.E. Henderson cited in Libby, *Black Voices from Harpers Ferry,* 138. See also Thomas Higginson, *Cheerful Yesterday* (New York: Arno, 1968), 229.

62. Jennie Chambers, "What a School-Girl Saw of John Brown's Raid," *Harper's Monthly Magazine,* Vol. 104 (January 1902); "Phil Lucker," Reminiscence of Thomas Allstadt, *Springfield Sunday Republican,* Boyd Stutler Collection [as cited in Libby, *Black Voices from Harpers Ferry,* 121–122].

63. Anderson, *A Voice from Harper's Ferry* [as reprinted in Libby, *Black Voices from Harpers Ferry,* 60].

64. Ibid., 34.

65. Hinton, *John Brown and His Men,* 298.

66. Hu Maxwell and Thomas Miller, *West Virginia and Its People,* 307 [as cited in Libby, *Black Voices from Harpers Ferry,* 94].

67. Anderson, *A Voice from Harper's Ferry,* reprinted in Libby, *Black Voices from Harpers Ferry,* 61. See also Hinton, *John Brown and His Men,* 388.

68. Libby, *Black Voices from Harpers Ferry,* 177.

69. Ibid., 140–141.

70. *The Virginia Free Press,* January 19, 1860 [as cited in Libby, *Black Voices from Harpers Ferry,* 141].

71. *The Shepherdstown Register,* January 28, 1860, reprinted from *Auburn* [New York] *Advance,* January 18, 1860 [as cited in Libby, *Black Voices from Harpers Ferry,* 141].

72. Mary Ellen Pleasant, statement to newspaper editor (1901) [as cited in Libby, *Black Voices from Harpers Ferry,* 102]. Manuscript, West Virginia University Archives [as cited in Frederick Douglass, "John Brown and West Virginia" *West Virginia State College Bulletin* (November 1953), series 40, no. 6, ii].

73. Quarles, *Allies for Freedom,* 108.

74. Ibid., 108.

75. Correspondence of the *Baltimore American* [as cited in Libby, *Black Voices from Harpers Ferry,* 176]; Villard, *John Brown,* 520 [as cited in Robert L. Bates, *The Story of Smithfield (Middleway), Jefferson County, West Virginia* (Lexington, VA: 1958), 135–136].

76. Quarles, *Allies for Freedom,* 108.

77. Correspondence of the *Baltimore American* [as cited in Libby, *Black Voices from Harpers Ferry,* 176]; Villard, *John Brown,* 520 [as cited in Bates, *The Story of Smithfield,* 135–136].

78. Archives of Virginia, Legislative Petitions, B 468/19846, Jefferson County, January 12, 1860.

79. Correspondence of the *Baltimore American,* printed in the *Dollar Pennsylvanian* [Philadelphia], November 26, 1859 [as cited in Libby, *Black Voices from Harpers Ferry,* 176].

80. Letter from I.W. [?] Ulare to Governor Wise, November 1859. Boyd Stutler Collection [as cited in Libby, *Black Voices from Harpers Ferry,* 175–176].

81. Millard Kessler Bushong, *Historic Jefferson County* (Boyce, VA: 1972), 197.

82. Herbert Aptheker, *Abolitionism: A Revolutionary Movement* (Boston: Twayne, 1992).

83. See Geffert, "The Guns of October," in *John Brown Mysteries*, 56–64.

84. Rev. Thomas Henry had also been pastor of the antecedent congregation of Grace AME, Mt. Gilboa (which is located on the historic property of Benjamin Banneker). See Libby, ed., *From Slavery to Salvation*, 116–117.

85. "Reverend John Henry held services in a small school house until the church was built and called St. Johns AME from 1868 to 1879," the only living charter member of the congregation, Mrs. Mary Frances Williams, told WPA interviewer Frank Rothbarth in 1939.

86. Libby, ed., *From Slavery to Salvation*, 53.

87. Interview with Douglas Wicklund, curator of the National Rifle Association Museum, in Fairfax, Virginia, by the authors, January 1999.

88. Osborne Anderson and Charles Tidd escaped, separately, meeting with great surprise at James H. Harris's Cleveland home. Might one of them still be holding the Washington gun? It was Tidd who armed the enslaved and free blacks in Maryland. Still carrying out John Brown's plan, Tidd enlisted, using his middle name Plummer as a pseudonym, in 1862, in the 21st Massachusetts Infantry. He died just as the regiment was loading to attack Roanoke Island, whose commander of rebel forces was the former Governor Wise of Virginia, the man who hanged John Brown and his companions in 1859. See Hinton, *John Brown and His Men*, 566–567.

89. Among the Woodlands researched was John C. Woodland (1839–1917), recruited into the army in St. Mary's County. Although John Woodland's relationship to Philip Woodland is unclear, he lived with Philip in Catonsville for a time, and in Baltimore, where he was the head of a branch of the Grand Army of the Republic. He was also associated with an entrepreneurial Christian lodge-based organization, the United Galilean League of Fishermen. One of the few other locations of the Galileans was Charles Town, West Virginia. John C. Woodland's signature, which appears twice in his pension documents, was compared with the initials carved on the stock of the fowling gun. Both the "J" and the "W" are similar. The Woodlands of Maryland were researched in the Civil War records of the National Archives by Julie DeMatteis of the Catonsville Library. See Geffert, *John Brown Mysteries*, 65–68.

90. James Surkamp, *Delany: To Be More Than Equal*, 9.

91. Du Bois, *John Brown*, 355.

92. Frederick Douglass, "Speech at Storer College at Harper's Ferry," May 30, 1882 [as cited in Du Bois, *John Brown*, 353]. Douglass's speech was given outside of Lincoln Hall as part of the festivities celebrating the fourteenth anniversary of Storer College.

10. A Common Nature, A United Destiny: African American Responses to Racial Science from the Revolution to the Civil War

1. Joanne Pope Melish, "The 'Condition' Debate and Racial Discourse in the Antebellum North," *Journal of the Early Republic* 19:4 (Winter 1999), 665, 666. I would be remiss if I did not add that I have also argued a weak version of the hegemony thesis. It speaks of "a creep toward essentialist premises" and "the in-

filtration of white supremacy's basic premises into black thought." *Black Identity and Black Protest in the Antebellum North* (Chapel Hill: University of North Carolina Press, 2002), 249, 252.

2. Jürgen Habermas, *The Structural Transformation of the Public Sphere: An Inquiry into a Category of Bourgeois Society,* Thomas Burger, trans. (Cambridge, MA: MIT Press, 1989); Geoff Eley, "Politics, Culture, and the Public Sphere," *Positions: East Asia Cultures Critique* 10:1 (Spring 2002), 219–236.

3. Stephen Howard Browne, "Counter-Science: African American Historians and the Critique of Ethnology in Nineteenth-Century America," *Western Journal of Communication* 64:3 (Summer 2000), 269, 281–282. For the general phenomenon of appropriation, see Kathleen Ashley and Véronique Plesch, "The Cultural Process of 'Appropriation,' " *Journal of Medieval and Early Modern Studies* 32:1 (2002), 1–15.

4. James C. Scott, *Weapons of the Weak: Everyday Forms of Peasant Resistance* (New Haven: Yale University Press, 1985).

5. Quoted in Grant Farred, "Endgame Identity? Mapping the New Left Roots of Identity Politics," *New Literary History* 31:4 (Autumn 2000), 637.

6. Audre Lorde, "The Master's Tools Will Never Dismantle the Master's House," in *Sister Outsider: Essays and Speeches* (Trumansburg, NY: Crossing Press, 1984), and Cherríe Moraga, Gloria Anzaldúa, eds., *This Bridge Called My Back: Writings by Radical Women of Color* (Watertown, MA: Persephone Press, 1981). Homi Bhabha's concepts of hybridity and liminality collapse this tension. See "Of Mimicry and Man: The Ambivalence of Colonial Discourse," in *The Location of Culture* (London: Routledge, 1995), 85–92. More closely related, see Mikko Tuhkanen's survey of and argument about this tension in the "lore cycle" of blackface minstrelsy. "Of Blackface and Paranoid Knowledge: Richard Wright, Jacques Lacan, and the Ambivalence of Black Minstrelsy," *Diacritics* 31:2 (2001), 9–34.

7. Stepan and Gilman make tentative steps toward such a typology in Nancy Leys Stepan and Sander L. Gilman, "Appropriating the Idioms of Science: The Rejection of Scientific Racism," in *The Bounds of Race: Perspectives on Hegemony and Resistance,* Dominick LaCapra, ed. (Ithaca: Cornell University Press, 1991), 72–103. Though my typology differs considerably from theirs, I am indebted to their example.

8. A member of the African Society in Boston, *The Sons of Africa. An Essay on Freedom* (Boston, 1808), reprinted in Dorothy Porter, ed., *Early Negro Writing, 1760–1837* (Baltimore: Black Classic Press, 1995), 17

9. David Walker, *David Walker's Appeal to the Coloured Citizens of the World,* Peter P. Hinks, ed. (University Park, PA: Pennsylvania State University Press, 2000), 18.

10. William Whipper, a black moral reformer from Philadelphia, knew of "no earthly tribunal of sufficient competency and impartiality to decide on a question involving the natural superiority of individuals and nations," and had no intention of submitting "so grave a decision" to blacks' "enemies." William Whipper, "To the American People," *Minutes and Proceedings of the First Annual Meeting of the American Moral Reform Society* (Philadelphia: Merrihew and Gunn, 1837), in Porter, ed., *Early Negro Writing,* 209.

11. J. Holland Townsend, "The Policy that We Should Pursue," *Anglo-African Magazine* 1:10 (October 1859), 324–325.

12. *Proceedings of the National Convention of Colored People, and Their Friends, Held in Troy, N.Y., on the 6th, 7th, 8th and 9th October, 1847* (Troy: J.C Kneeland and Co., 1847), 18–19.

13. *Minutes and Proceedings of the Third Annual Convention, for the Improvement of the Free People of Colour in These United States, Held by Adjournments in the City of Philadelphia, from the 3rd to the 13th of June Inclusive, 1833* (New York: By Order of the Convention, 1833), 32–33.

14. James McCune Smith to Gerrit Smith, December 28, 1846, in BAP, III, 480.

15. "A Word to Our People," *Anglo-African Magazine* 1:9 (September 1859), 295.

16. Amos Gerry Beman, "The Education of the Colored People," *Anglo-African Magazine* 1:11 (November 1859), 338.

17. Elizabeth Wicks, *Address Before the African Female Benevolent Society of Troy, on Wednesday, February 12, 1834* (Troy, NY, 1834), 4.

18. Howard Temperly, "Capitalism, Slavery and Ideology," *Past and Present* 75 (May 1977), 94–118; Thomas L. Haskell, "Capitalism and the Origins of the Humanitarian Sensibility, Part 1," *American Historical Review* 90:2 (April 1985), 339-61, and "Capitalism and the Origins of the Humanitarian Sensibility, Part 2," *American Historical Review* 90:3 (June 1985), 547–566; Elizabeth B. Clark, " 'The Sacred Rights of the Weak': Pain, Sympathy, and the Culture of Individual Rights in Antebellum America," *Journal of American History* 82:2 (September 1995), 463–493.

19. Board of Managers of the Africa Education Society of Pittsburgh, "To the Citizens of Pittsburgh and the Public Generally," *Liberator* (January 22, 1833).

20. Peter Randolph, *Sketches of Slave Life: Or, Illustrations of the "Peculiar Institution,"* 2nd ed. (Boston, 1855), 79.

21. Hamilton, *An Oration Delivered in the African Zion Church*, in Porter, ed., *Early Negro Writing*, 103.

22. See, for example, J. W. Lewis, "Essay on the Character and Condition of the African Race," 227–68, in John W. Lewis, *The Life, Labors, and Travels of Elder Charles Bowles, of the Free Will Baptist Denomination* (Watertown, CT: Ingalls and Stowell's Steam Press, 1852), 259–261; Randolph, *Sketches of Slave Life*, 78.

23. Henry Highland Garnet, "Address to the Slaves of the United States" (1848), in Richard Newman, Patrick Rael, and Phillip Lapsansky, eds., *Pamphlets of Protest: An Anthology of Early African American Protest Literature, 1790–1860* (New York: Routledge, 2001), 163–164.

24. R.B. Lewis, *Light and Truth; Collected from the Bible and Ancient and Modern History, Containing the Universal History of the Colored and Indian Race, from the Creation of the World to the Present Time* (Boston: A Committee of Colored Gentlemen, 1844), 334.

25. "The First Colored Convention," *Anglo-African Magazine* 1:10 (October 1859), 308; John H. Johnson, Untitled Lecture to the Banneker Institute, Banneker Institute Papers, Gardiner Collection, Historical Society of Pennsylvania, box 5Ga, folder 1, 1.

26. William C. Nell, "Colored American Patriots," *The Anglo-African Magazine* 1:2 (February 1859), 30.

27. *Colored American* (March 4, 1837).

28. *Colored American* (June 2, 1838).

29. "S.," "For the Freedom's Journal," *Freedom's Journal* (August 17, 1827).

30. R.B. Lewis, *Light and Truth*, 280–312.

31. *Colored American* (May 6, 1837). J.W.C. Pennington similarly recounted tales

of Aesop and Terence to demonstrate the literary capacity of ancient—and thus contemporary—African peoples. See J.W.C. Pennington, "A Review of Slavery and the Slave Trade," *Anglo-African Magazine* 1:4 (April 1859), 124.

32. *Voice of the Fugitive* (February 26, 1851).

33. Exchange by William Craft and Dr. James Hunt, August 27, 1863, in C. Peter Ripley et al., eds., *The Black Abolitionist Papers,* Volume I (Chapel Hill: University of North Carolina Press, 1985), 541

34. S.S.N., "Anglo-Saxons, and Anglo-Africans," *Anglo-African Magazine* 1:8 (August 1859), 247.

35. Alexander Crummell, *The Man; The Hero; The Christian!: A Eulogy on the Life and Character of Thomas Clarkson* (New York, 1847), 33.

36. S.S.N., "Anglo-Saxons, and Anglo-Africans," 248.

37. William Wells Brown, *The Black Man, His Antecedents, His Genius, and His Achievements* (Boston, 1863), 34.

38. S.S.N., "Anglo-Saxons, and Anglo-Africans," 247, 249.

39. Walker, *David Walker's Appeal,* 19.

40. Ralph Ellison, "Change the Joke and Slip the Yoke," in *Shadow and Act* (New York: Random House, 1964), 45–59 (also in *Partisan Review* 25:2 [(Spring 1958], 212–222). See also Miele Steele, "Metatheory and the Subject of Democracy in the Work of Ralph Ellison," *New Literary History* 27:3 (Summer 1996), 485. I am aware of no work that analyzes the role of satire in black protest in the manner I have suggested here. My understanding of the relationship between common sense and ideological hegemony here is from Gramsci. See "Introduction to the Study of Philosophy and Culture, Some Preliminary Points of Reference," in Antonio Gramsci, *Selections from the Prison Notebooks of Antonio Gramsci,* Quintin Hoare and Geoffrey Nowell Smith, eds. and trans. (New York: International Publishers, 1971), 323–343.

41. Easton, *A Treatise on the . . . Colored People of the U. States,* 85–86.

42. Douglass, "The Claims of the Negro Ethnologically Considered," 514–521.

43. See Joseph Femia, "Hegemony and Consciousness in the Thought of Antonio Gramsci," *Political Studies* 23:1 (March 1975), 35.

44. See also James Scott, "Hegemony and the Peasantry," *Politics and Society* 7:3 (1977), 289–296.

45. Lester C. Olsen, "The Personal, the Political, and Others: Audre Lorde Denouncing 'The Second Sex Conference,' " *Philosophy and Rhetoric* 33:3 (2000), 278–229.

46. Mia Bay, *The White Image in the Black Mind: African-American Ideas About White People, 1830–1925* (New York: Oxford University Press, 2000), 224–225, 228–229.

47. *Colored American* (October 19, 1839); *Freedom's Journal* (January 24, 1829). " 'The African, says Sir James Yeo, who has for a considerable time been stationed upon the coast of Africa, 'is very superior in intellect and capacity to the generality of Indians in North America. They are more sociable and friendly to strangers, and except in the vicinity of European settlements, are a fine and noble race of men.' " (Sir James Lucas Yeo's letter to John Wilson Croker, Esq. published in the New York *Spectator* for Nov. 7th, 1817.)" *Freedom's Journal,* May 18, 1827.

48. *Frederick Douglass' Paper* (September 22, 1854).

49. *Colored American* (March 29, 1838).

50. See also Eddie S. Glaude Jr., *Exodus!: Religion, Race, and Nation in Early Nine-

teenth-century Black America (Chicago: University of Chicago Press, 2000), 134–142.

51. Kevin J. O'Brien, "Rightful Resistance," *World Politics* 49:1 (1996), 34–35.

11. "No Occurrence in Human History Is More Deserving of Commemoration Than This": Abolitionist Celebrations of Freedom

1. *Liberator* (July 23, 1852).
2. Martha Barrett diary, July 4, 1849. The following year, when she was teaching and responsible for preparing her students for the procession planned to mark the holiday, she remarked, "I do not like to celebrate Independence Day in such a manner," when so many of her "country men" suffered "a bondage so servile." July 5, 1850. Essex-Peabody Library, Essex-Peabody Institute; Karen V. Hansen, *A Very Social Time: Crafting Community in Antebellum New England* (Berkeley: University of California Press, 1994), 39.
3. Frederick Douglass declared that July Fourth was the "blackest day in all the year." *Frederick Douglass's Paper* (June 23, July 21, 1854); *Pennsylvania Freeman* (August 7, 1851).
4. *Pennsylvania Freeman* (August 1, 1844); Simon P. Newman in *Parades and the Politics of the Street: Festive Culture in the Early American Republic* (Philadelphia: University of Pennsylvania Press, 1997), p. 3, suggests the popular culture and festive rites were linked together. Indeed, newspapers were critical to the success of festive rites because they could bring the message to those who did not (and perhaps would not) attend the event. *Liberator,* July 25, 1845.
5. Newman, *Festive Culture,* 6–8, 29–30, 93; James Vernon, *Politics and People: A Study in English Political Culture, c. 1815–1867* (Cambridge, U.K.: Cambridge University Press, 1993), 1, 6, 7, 207, 248; Julie Roy Jeffrey, *The Great Silent Army of Abolitionism: Ordinary Women in the Antislavery Movement* (Chapel Hill: University of North Carolina Press, 1998), Chapter 3. See also Susan G. David, *Parades and Power: Street Theatre in Nineteenth-Century Philadelphia* (Berkeley: University of California Press, 1988), and David Waldstreicher, *In the Midst of Perpetual Fetes: The Making of American Nationalism, 1776–1820* (Chapel Hill: University of North Carolina Press, 1997).
6. The emancipation of the slaves in the British West Indies was not so straightforward as the phrase suggests. In 1833, Parliament declared that slavery in the British West Indies should end on August 1, 1834, but a system of apprenticeship was to replace it until 1840. Bermuda and Antigua abolished all servitude at once while the other islands proceeded with apprenticeship arrangements. In 1838, however, those islands with a legislature abolished all servitude while the British government ended the apprenticeship system on the others. The *Colored American,* May 9, 1840, explained the changes by saying that complete abolition worked better than the gradual system of freeing the slaves, contrary to general expectations. For Garrison's references, see *Colored American* (August 31, 1839). For earlier celebrations, see Elizabeth Rauh Bethel, *The Roots of African-American Identity: Memory and History in Antebellum Free Communities* (New York: St. Martin's Press, 1997), 81–93. *Liberator* (August 9, 1844; August 11, 1843).
7. *Colored American* (July 15, 1837); C. Peter Ripley et al., eds., *The Black Abolition-*

ist Papers (Chapel Hill: University of North Caroline Press, 1991), v. 3, 168; *National Enquirer* (August 3, 17, 1836).

8. *National Enquirer* (August 17, August 31, 1836). For the importance of African American women and their associations, see Darlene Clark Hine, *Black Women in America: An Historical Encyclopedia* (Brooklyn: Carlson Publishing, 1993), 3–7 and Shirley J. Yee, *Black Women Abolitionists: A Study in Activism, 1828–1860* (Knoxville: University of Tennessee Press, 1992).

9. R.J. Young, *Antebellum Black Activists: Race, Gender, and Self* (New York: Garland Publishing, 1996), 57, 60. Young points out that manhood was a "key concept" for black activists. See also James Oliver Horton, *Free People of Color: Inside the African American Community* (Washington: Smithsonian Institution Press, 1993), 77, 94, 96, 116.

10. Ripley, *Black Abolitionist Papers*, volume 3, p. 213; *Colored American* (July 17, 1841; July 25, August 15, September 5, 1840, August 31, 1839); *Liberator* (August 10, 1838).

11. *Liberator* (July 19, 1839); *Colored American* (July 25, 1840). In New York City, it appears as if the New York Vigilance Committee organized the earliest celebrations. See *Colored American* (July 15, 29, 1837); Waldstreicher, *Perpetual Fetes*, 325, 327. Patrick Rael in *Black Identity and Black Protest in the Antebellum North* (Chapel Hill: University of North Carolina Press 2002), 69, suggests that organizing festivals was one way in which activists solidified their position as authoritative community leaders.

12. *Colored American* (July 20, 1839).

13. References for the discussion of the construction of meaning for August 1 are drawn from Bethel, *African-American Identity*, p. 87; *North Star*, July 21, 1848; *Colored American* (July 25, 1840); *Pennsylvania Freeman* (August 1, 1844); Philip S. Foner, ed., *Frederick Douglass: Selected Speeches and Writings* (Chicago, Lawrence Hill Books, 1999), pp. 359–360; *Liberator* (August 18, 1854).

14. *North Star* (August 10, 1849); Vicki L. Eaklor, *American Antislavery Songs: A Collection and Analysis* (Westport: Greenwood Press, 1988), 122–123; *Colored American* (July 25, 1840; August 25, 1838); Foner, *Frederick Douglass*, 364.

15. *Colored American* (July 25, 1840; September 5, 1840). The ideal celebration, according to WST who wrote to the *Colored American*, began at daybreak with prayers of thanksgiving. Those he visualized participating in the rituals included ministers, Sabbath school teachers and their students, scholars, and lovers of "inalienable rights," groups all at home in church (July 20, 1839).

16. "First of August. A Celebration in Commemoration of the abolition of slavery in the British West India Islands. Boston, 1839." Broadsides, 1839. American Antiquarian Society. *Colored American* (August 31, 1839); for reference to odes written for the occasion, see August 18, 1838, July 15, 1837, September 28, 1839. Bethel in *African-American Identity* discusses the importance of Attucks as a symbol of black identity and claims for inclusion. See 1–2, 10–17. Bruce Dorsey in *Reforming Men and Women: Gender in the Antebellum City* (Ithaca: Cornell University Press, 2002), p. 159, notes that because of black hostility to the scheme of African colonization, blacks began to drop the use of "African" by the 1830s.

17. Waldstreicher, *Perpetual Fetes*, 320; *Colored American* (August 18, 1838; August 15, 1840).

18. *Colored American* (September 23, 1839; July 25, 1840; July 24, 1841; August 17,

1839). Similarly, in Cincinnati in 1839, the celebrants celebrated the youth of the city for their spirit of enterprise and their desire for improvement. *Colored American* (August 25, 1839). Julie Winch, *Philadelphia's Black Elite: Activism, Accommodation, and the Struggle for Autonomy, 1778–1848* (Philadelphia: Temple University Press, 1988), 150. As Emma Lapsansky points out, the acquisition of education was no mean achievement. She suggests that as late as 1860, the majority of Philadelphia blacks were illiterate. Emma Jones Lapsansky, "Friends, Wives, and Strivings: Networks and Community Values Among Nineteenth-Century Philadelphia Afroamerican Elites," *Pennsylvania Magazine of History and Biography,* 108 (January 1984), 15.

19. Henry Mayer, *All On Fire: William Lloyd Garrison and the Abolition of Slavery* (New York: St. Martin's Press, 1998), 248–249; See *Colored American* (July 27, 1839); *National Enquirer* (August 17, August 31, 1836) for rare mentions of banners; for notice of processions, see *Colored American* (August 17, 1839; July 25, 1840). Shane White in " 'It Was a Proud Day': African Americans, Festivals, and Parades in the North, 1741–1834," *Journal of American History,* 81 (June 1994), 38–40, makes the arguments about parades, class, and culture and provides an idea of flamboyance in early parades.

20. William B. Gravely, "The Dialectic of Double-Consciousness in Black American Freedom Celebrations, 1808–1863," *Journal of Negro History,* 67 (Winter 1982), 313, n. 15; Winch, *Philadelphia's Black Elite,* 4. Young writes in *Black Activists,* 183: "The activists . . . sought to discipline and mold the mass of African Americans into a reputable following. It was an uphill struggle against both the prejudice of white society and the resistance of lower class African Americans." Rael, *Black Protest,* 56, talks of the "limited bonding" between elite and non-elite blacks.

21. Rael, *Black Protest,* 82; Waldstreicher, *Perpetual Fetes,* 334, 337, 338; *National Enquirer,* (August 3, August 17, 1836); Mayer *William Lloyd Garrison,* 189. For antiabolitionist riots of the 1830s, see Leonard L. Richards, *"Gentlemen of Property and Standing": Anti-Abolitionist Mobs in Jacksonian America* (New York: Oxford University Press, 1970).

22. *Liberator* (August 12, 1842). The paper claimed that the banner actually showed an emancipated slave, pointing to the word "Liberty" and his broken chains.

23. Rael, *Black Protest,* 56–57.

24. Newman, *Festive Culture,* 89.

25. *Colored American* (August 31, 1839; August 15, 1840).

26. *Colored American* (August 25, 1838); *National Enquirer* (August 31, 1836).

27. *Colored American* (July 27, 1839; July 17, 1841).

28. *Liberator* (August 13, 1836, August 10, 1838, July 22, August 12, 1842); *Pennsylvania Freeman* (July 27, August 1, 1844; August 14, 1845).

29. *National Era* (August 19, 1847) *Frederick Douglass' Paper* (August 10, 1855).

30. *Liberator* (July 29, 1842); *Thirteenth Annual Report Presented to the Massachusetts Anti-Slavery Society* (Boston: Andrews, Prentiss & Studley, 1845), 34; *Liberator* (August 9, 1844).

31. For a sense of these celebrations, see *Liberator* (August 19, 1842; July 14, 1843, July 18, 1844, as well as August 11, 1843, August 9, 1844, July 23, 1843; July 26, 1844, July 21, 1843). The issue of July 28, 1843, encouraged the faithful to rally support for the occasion. Bargains for tickets are described in *Pennsylvania Freeman* (August 7, 1851; July 10, 1852).

32. *Liberator* (August 12, 1842; August 11, 1843; August 19, 1842; July 12, 1844); Douglas M. Strong, *Perfectionist Politics: Abolitionism and Religious Tensions of American Democracy* (Syracuse University Press: Syracuse, 2001), 128. Terrye Baron Yizar in "Afro-American Music in North America before 1865: A Study of 'The First of August Celebration' in the United States," (unpublished Ph.D. dissertation, University of California at Berkeley, 1984), 121, notes the celebration in Concord, Massachusetts, in 1844. There was no procession and only one banner with the words "The Spirit of 76 yet lives in the Women of Concord."

33. *Liberator* (August 13, 1852; July 21, 1853; August 11, 1854; August 7, August 14, 1857). Vernon, *Politics and the People*, 71; Eaklor, *American Antislavery Songs*, 36, 43, 45, 148–149, 164. For women's important role in abolitionism, see Jeffrey, *The Great Silent Army of Abolitionism*.

34. Foner, *Frederick Douglass*, 110.

35. *Colored American* (August 1, 1840), *Pennsylvania Freeman* (August 11, 1853; July 17, August 7, 1852); *Frederick Douglass's Paper* (August 5, 1853). As one speaker in Milford, Massachusetts, pointed out, events in the British West Indies "leaves this guilty nation without excuse." *Liberator* (July 29, 1859).

36. *Frederick Douglass's Paper* (August 5, 1853); *Liberator* (August 11, 1854); for another example of appealing to patriotism while praising England, see *Liberator* (August 10, 1855; August 11, 1843).

37. *Frederick Douglass's Paper* (July 27, 1854); Jeffrey, *The Great Silent Army of Abolitionism*, p. 200; Yizar, "Afro-American Music," 147a.

38. *Frederick Douglass's Paper* (August 5, 1853; August 21, 1851; August 13, 1852) At Cincinnati in 1852, one of the speakers confined his remarks to "the wretched fugitive bill," while another chose to focus on the Whigs and Democrats.

39. *Liberator* (August 8, 1845); Rael, *Black Protest*, 61; Ripley, *Black Abolitionist Papers*, Volume 3, 19–27; Carlton Mabee, *Black Freedom: The Non-Violent Abolitionists from 1830 through the Civil War* (Toronto: Macmillan, 1970), 93–94, 112–117.

40. *Anti-Slavery Bugle* (August 10, 1850); *Frederick Douglass's Paper* (August 10, 1855).

41. *Frederick Douglass's Paper* (July 20, 1855; August 12, 1853).

42. *Frederick Douglass's Paper* (July 20, 1855; August 12, 1853; August 21, 1851); Zephania W. Pease, ed., *The Diary of Samuel Rodman: A New Bedford Chronicle of Thirty-Seven Years* (New Bedford: Reynolds Printing Co., 1927), 261, 262.

43. *Liberator* (August 15, 1851; August 6, 1847; August 25, 1854).

44. *North Star* (August 11, 1848); *Liberator* (August 14, 1857); White, "'It Was Proud Day,'" 46; *Liberator* (August 5, 1859).

45. Pease, *Samuel Rodman*, 293; Kathryn Grover, *The Fugitives' Gibraltar: Escaping Slaves and Abolitionism in New Bedford, Massachusetts* (Amherst: University of Massachusetts Press, 2001), 54, gives the census figures for 1854 as 1,008; *Frederick Douglass's Paper* (August 12, 1853). For the importance of parades, see Davis, *Parades and Power*.

46. *Frederick Douglass's Paper* (August 12, 1853; August 10, 1855).

47. *Frederick Douglass's Paper* (August 10, 1855); *Freedom's Journal* (July 18, 1828); Davis, *Parades and Power*, 67; Dorsey, *Reforming Men and Women*, 187.

48. James Oliver Horton, "Defending the Manhood of the Race: The Crisis of Citizenship in Black Boston at Midcentury," in Martin H. Blatt, Thomas J. Brown,

and Donald Yacavone, eds., *Hope and Glory: Essays on the Legacy of the Fifty-Fourth Massachusetts Regiment* (Amherst and Boston: University of Massachusetts Press and the Massachusetts Historical Society, 2001), 18; *Liberator* (August 15, August 22, 1856); communication from Jean Libby, August 2002. *Liberator* issue of August 5, 1859, mentions the Liberty Guards who marched without guns from their armory to East Cambridge, Massachusetts. This unit, the paper pointed out, owned eighteen muskets.

49. *Frederick Douglass's Paper* (August 31, 1855).

50. *Frederick Douglass's Paper* (August 10, 1855).

51. *Frederick Douglass's Paper* (July 27, August 10, 1855); *Liberator* (August 15, 1851).

52. *Frederick Douglass's Paper* (July 27, August 10, 1855); Grover, *The Fugitives' Gibraltar*, 14; Pease, *Rodman Diary*, 330.

53. *Liberator* (August 17, 1838).

54. *Thirteenth Annual Report*, 34; *Liberator* (August 8, 1845).

55. Davis, *Parades and Power*, 5; *North Star* (September 14, 1849); Newman, *Festive Culture*, 30–31, 42, 93–94, points to the importance of toasts as an expression of political views. *Frederick Douglass's Monthly* (September 1862, August 1859).

12. Print Culture and the Antislavery Community: The Poetry of Abolitionism, 1831–1860

1. See Julie Roy Jeffrey, *The Great Silent Army of Abolitionism: Ordinary Women in the Antislavery Movement* (Chapel Hill: University of North Carolina Press, 1998), 130–132; Edward Wagenecht, *Henry Wadsworth Longfellow: Portrait of an American Humanist* (New York: Oxford University Press, 1966), 56.

2. Poems on Burns appear in *Frederick Douglass' Paper* (July 6, 1854) and John Greenleaf Whittier, *Anti-Slavery Poems: Songs of Labor and Reform* (New York: Arno, 1969), 170–71; Webster poems include Whittier's "Ichabod," published in, among other places, the *Pennsylvania Freeman* (May 9, 1850), and James Whitfield's "The Arch Apostate," in *Frederick Douglass' Paper* (January 22, 1852); Garrison's comment appeared in the *Liberator* (December 17, 1831).

3. Jeffrey, *Great Silent Army*, 46. On the idea of an abolitionist canon, see Dickson D. Bruce, *The Origins of African American Literature, 1680–1865* (Charlottesville: University Press of Virginia, 2001), 237–238.

4. James Brewer Stewart, "The Emergence of Racial Modernity and the Rise of the White North," *Journal of the Early Republic* 18 (1998), 198; Bruce, *Origins*, 187. See Richard L. Bushman, *The Refinement of America: Persons, Houses, Cities* (New York: Knopf, 1992), e.g., 280; Mary Louise Kete, *Sentimental Collaborations: Mourning and Middle-Class Identity in Nineteenth-Century America* (Durham: Duke University Press, 2000), 25–26, 27; John Stauffer, *The Black Hearts of Men: Radical Abolitionists and the Transformation of Race* (Cambridge, MA: Harvard University Press, 2002), 151. Useful discussions of earlier practices appear in David S. Shields, *Civil Tongues and Polite Letters in British America* (Chapel Hill: University of North Carolina Press, 1997), Chapter 2, and Karin Wulf, *Not All Wives: Women of Colonial Philadelphia* (Ithaca: Cornell University Press, 2000), 26–27. A particularly useful nineteenth-century example may also be seen in Howard L. and Judith Rose Sacks, *Way Up North in Dixie: A Black Family's Claim*

to the Confederate Anthem (Washington: Smithsonian Institution Press, 1993), 101–115.

5. The Garrison exchange appears in *The Abolitionist* 1 (1833), 96; Forten's "Appeal to Women" appeared in the *Liberator* (February 1, 1834); a reply by James Scott appeared February 22, 1834 and one signed "Augusta" appeared March 1, 1834. The conversation with Eliza Earle is discussed in Todd S. Gernes, "Poetic Justice: Sarah Forten, Eliza Earle, and the Paradox of Intellectual Property," *New England Quarterly* 71 (1998), 229–265. See also, Bruce, *Origins*, 232–34, and Julie Roy Jeffrey's essay in this volume.

6. *North Star* (March 2, 1849); on the acrostic, see Patricia Crain, *The Story of A: The Alphabetization of America from* The New England Primer to The Scarlet Letter (Stanford: Stanford University Press, 2000), 241, n. 26; see also Patricia Demers, *Heaven upon Earth: The Form of Moral and Religious Children's Literature, to 1850* (Knoxville: University of Tennessee Press, 1993), 77–78.

7. See Johan Huizinga, *Homo Ludens: A Study of the Play-Element in Culture* (Boston: Beacon Press, 1955), 5–6, 12, 133–134; see, also, Michel Beaujour, "The Game of Poetics," in *Game, Play, Literature,* ed. Jacques Ehrmann (Boston: Beacon Press, 1971), 58–59, 62; Jonathan Culler, *Literary Theory: A Very Short Introduction* (New York: Oxford University Press, 1997), 58–59; William Gilmore, *Reading Becomes a Necessity of Life: Material and Cultural Life in Rural New England, 1780–1835* (Knoxville: University of Tennessee Press, 1989), 114; Isabelle Lehuu, *Carnival on the Page: Popular Print Media in Antebellum America* (Chapel Hill: University of North Carolina Press, 2000), 29; Jürgen Habermas, *The Theory of Communicative Action,* Volume 2, *Lifeworld and System: A Critique of Functionalist Reason,* trans. Thomas McCarthy (Boston: Beacon Press, 1989), 16–17, 97. See also Scott Romine, *The Narrative Forms of Southern Community* (Baton Rouge, Louisiana State University Press, 1999), 46–47, 60.

8. William Ellery Channing, *The Works of William Ellery Channing, D.D.* (Boston: American Unitarian Association, 1903), 126; "Talent and Conduct," *The Lady's Book* 9 (1834), 84; see Jane Tompkins, *Sensational Designs: The Cultural Work of American Fiction, 1790–1860* (New York: Oxford University Press, 1985), 157.

9. "Poetry," *Atkinson's Casket* (August 1832), 369; see also Lawrence Buell, *New England Literary Culture from Revolution through Renaissance* (Cambridge, U.K.: Cambridge University Press, 1986), 128–129; Robert D. Richardson, *Emerson: The Mind on Fire* (Berkeley: University of California Press, 1995), 538; Nancy Ruttenberg, *Democratic Personality: Popular Voice and the Trial of American Authorship* (Stanford: Stanford University Press, 1998), 338

10. John Q. Day, "The Suggestive Power of Nature," *The Lady's Book* 23 (1841), 102; Julia Ward Howe, *Passion Flowers* (Boston: Ticknor, Reed, and Fields, 1854), 137.

11. "Poetry," *Miss Leslie's Magazine* 1 (1844), 267; Horace Bushnell, *God in Christ. Three Discourses, Delivered at New Haven, Cambridge, and Andover, with a Preliminary Dissertation on Language* (New York: AMS Press, 1972), 88; see David S. Reynolds, *Beneath the American Renaissance: The Subversive Imagination in the Age of Emerson and Melville* (New York: Knopf, 1988), 444–445.

12. William Wells Brown, *Three Years in Europe: or, Places I Have Seen and People I Have Met* (London: Charles Gilpin, 1852), 205; Lydia Maria Child, *Autumnal Leaves: Tales and Sketches in Prose and Rhyme* (New York: C. S. Francis, 1857), 291.

13. Charlotte Forten Grimké, *The Journals of Charlotte Forten Grimké,* ed. Brenda

Stevenson (New York: Oxford University Press, 1988), 63; *National Era* (February 19, 1852); and see Robert Penn Warren, *John Greenleaf Whitter's Poetry: An Appraisal and a Selection* (Minneapolis: University of Minnesota Press, 1971), 19.

14. John Greenleaf Whittier, *Poems Written During the Progress of the Abolition Question in the United States, Between the Years 1830 and 1838* (Boston: Isaac Knapp, 1837 [sic]), 17–18.

15. *Liberator* (May 25, 1833, January 18, 1834); *Colored American* (September 30, 1837).

16. Whittier, *Poems Written During the Progress of the Abolition Question*, 17; *Anti-Slavery Bugle* (July 7, 1860). See, on this, Lewis Perry, " 'We Have Had a Conversation in the World': The Abolitionists and Sponteneity," *Canadian Review of American Studies* 6 (1975), 6; see also Mark M. Smith, *Listening to Nineteenth-Century America* (Chapel Hill: University of North Carolina Press, 2001), 180–81.

17. *North Star* (January 26, 1849).

18. *Emancipator* (October 11, 1838); William W. Story, "Sonnets," *Liberty Bell* (1842), 112.

19. *Liberator* (March 26, 1858); Story, "Sonnets," 112, 113.

20. On Story and Child, see Carolyn L. Karcher, *The First Woman of the Republic: A Cultural Biography of Lydia Maria Child* (Durham: Duke University Press, 1994), 325; on Longfellow, see Wagenecht, *Longfellow*, 56, and Henry Wadsworth Longfellow, *The Letters of Henry Wadsworth Longfellow*, ed. Andrew Hilen (Cambridge, MA: Harvard University Press, 1966–82), Volume II: 422. Day's poem is in the *Provincial Freeman* (January 5, 1856).

21. *North Star* (April 28, 1848).

22. See John Stauffer's essay in this volume.

23. *Emancipator* (January 14, 1834); see James Brewer Stewart, *Holy Warriors: The Abolitionists and American Slavery*, rev. ed., (New York: Hill and Wang, 1996), 57–58; Stewart, "Modernizing 'Difference': The Political Meanings of Color in the Free States, 1776–1840," *Journal of the Early Republic* 19 (1999), 707–708.

24. *Emancipator* (May 10, 1838); *North Star* (May 5, 1848).

25. Wayne C. Booth, *A Rhetoric of Irony* (Chicago: University of Chicago Press, 1974), 13–14, 29.

26. See, e.g., James McPherson, "A Brief for Equality: The Abolitionist Reply to the Racist Myth, 1860–1865," in *The Antislavery Vanguard: New Essays on the Abolitionists*, ed. Martin Duberman (Princeton: Princeton University Press, 1965), 177; Paul Goodman, *Of One Blood: Abolitionism and the Origins of Racial Equality* (Berkeley: University of California Press, 1998), 125; *Colored American* (August 11, 1838); *Emancipator* (August 18, 1836).

27. *Pennsylvania Freeman* (June 17, 1847).

28. Bruce, *Origins*, 218–220, 260.

29. Story, "Sonnets," 113.

30. Stauffer, *Black Hearts of Men*, 16; Wilson Armistead, *The Garland of Freedom: A Collection of Poems, Chiefly Anti-Slavery. Selected from Various Authors, by a Friend of the Negro* (London: W. & F. G. Cash, 1853), Part III, 90.

31. *Liberator* (January 29, 1831).

32. Whittier, *Anti-Slavery Poems*, 56; Frances Ellen Watkins Harper, *Complete Poems of Frances E. W. Harper*, ed. Maryemma Graham (New York: Oxford University Press, 1988), 5.

33. Edwin Chapman, "The Slave Mother," *Liberty Bell* (1853), 46–47, 48.

34. *Emancipator* (November 10, 1836); Jeffrey, *Great Silent Army*, 1–2, 18; see also Goodman, *Of One Blood*, 190–191.

35. *Liberator* (January 22, 1831); Joan R. Sherman, ed., *The Black Bard of North Carolina: George Moses Horton and His Poetry* (Chapel Hill: University of North Carolina Press, 1997), 56–57.

36. *Emancipator* (February 2, 1837).

37. Longfellow, *Letters*, II: 509–510.

38. Smith, *Listening*, 158–159.

39. Ronald G. Walters, *The Antislavery Appeal: American Abolition after 1830* (Baltimore: Johns Hopkins University Press, 1976), xiv, 45; Robert Abzug, *Cosmos Crumbling: American Reform and the Religious Imagination* (New York: Oxford University Press, 1994), 144, 204; Stauffer, *Black Hearts*, 17–18; Goodman, *Of One Blood*, 67–68; see also Stewart, *Holy Warriors*, 46. One important effort to explore individual motivations is Bertram Wyatt-Brown, "The New Left and the Abolitionists: Romantic Radicalism in America," *Soundings* 34 (1971), 147–163.

40. See Culler, *Literary Theory*, 58–59; Kenneth Burke, *The Philosophy of Literary Form: Studies in Symbolic Action*, 3rd ed. (Berkeley: University of California Press, 1973), 293–304.

41. Ronald G. Walters, "The Boundaries of Abolitionism," in *Antislavery Reconsidered: New Perspectives on the Abolitionists*, ed. Lewis Perry and Michael Fellman (Baton Rouge: Louisiana State University Press, 1979), 16–17.

42. Stauffer, *Black Hearts*, 16–18; Buell, *New England Literary Culture*, 78; Ralph Waldo Emerson, *The Selected Writings of Ralph Waldo Emerson*, ed. Brooks Atkinson (New York: Modern Library, 1950), 161; see Martin Klammer, *Whitman, Slavery, and the Emergence of Leaves of Grass* (University Park: Pennsylvania State University Press, 1995), 53–55.

43. Abzug, *Cosmos Crumbling*, 30; Goodman, *Of One Blood*, 125, 186; Stauffer, *Black Hearts*, 173; Bruce, *Origins*, e.g., 296.

44. See Andrew Burstein, *Sentimental Democracy: The Evolution of America's Romantic Self-Image* (New York: Hill and Wang, 1999), 266, 293; Kete, *Sentimental Collaborations*, 116; Karen Halttunen, *Confidence Men and Painted Women: A Study of Middle-Class Culture in America* (New Haven: Yale University Press, 1982), esp. Chapter 2; Walters, "Boundaries," 20–21.

13. Profits of Protest:
The Market Strategies of Sojourner Truth and Louisa May Alcott

1. *The Journals of Louisa May Alcott*, Joel Myerson and Daniel Shealy, eds. (Athens, GA: University of Georgia Press, 1997).

2. See my " 'Truth Stronger and Stranger than Fiction': Reexamining William Lloyd Garrison's *Liberator*," *American Literature* (December 2001), 73: 727–755), in which I elaborate on the ties between evangelical morality, the abolitionist reform movement, and capitalism.

3. See Charles Sellers, *The Market Revolution* (New York: Oxford University Press, 1991), 404.

4. For a full discussion of the impact of abolition on the development of mid-nineteenth-century literary culture in the United States see my *"Truth Stranger*

than Fiction": Race, Realism and the U.S. Literary Marketplace (New York: Palgrave, 2002); David Paul Nord's *Evangelical Origins of Mass Media in America (1815–1835)* (Columbia, SC: University of South Carolina Press, 1984); Karen Sanchez-Eppler, *Touching Liberty* (Berkeley: University of California Press, 1993).

5. Elaine Showalter, Introduction, in *Alternative Alcott* (New Brunswick: Rutgers, 1988), ix.

6. Ann Douglas, Introduction, in *Little Women* by Louisa May Alcott (New York: Signet, 1983), vii.

7. Madeline B. Stern, *Louisa May Alcott* (New York: Random House, 1996), 66.

8. Sarah Elbert, Introduction, in *Louisa May Alcott on Race, Sex, and Slavery* (Boston: Northeastern University Press, 1997), xxvi.

9. *The Journals of Louisa May Alcott*, 124.

10. Stern, 133.

11. For an in-depth look at the most liberal of the abolitionists and their efforts to work outside of the racist paradigms of the period, see John Stauffer, *The Black Hearts of Men: Radical Abolitionists and the Transformation of Race* (Cambridge, MA: Harvard University Press, 2002).

12. *Journals of Louisa May Alcott*, 98.

13. Louisa May Alcott, "My Contraband," in Showalter, 76.

14. Alcott never did find a place for two other important abolitionist pieces, "M.L." and "An Hour," other than in the periodical *The Commonwealth*.

15. Elizabeth Young, in "A Wound of One's Own: Louisa May Alcott's Civil War Fiction" (*American Quarterly* 48: 3 (1996) 439–474), makes a convincing argument for Alcott's use of the black figure and the wounded soldier as literary devises that invert race and gender norms. These figures provide, in her words, "a productive cultural fantasy, one that privileges female self-mastery as a metaphorical model for male development and fantasizes a reconstructed nation in which men become little women." At the close of "My Contraband" we see Young's theory played out: Robert takes Nurse Dane's name, effecting a reversal of name-changing traditions. See also Betsy Klimasmith, "Slave, Master, Mistress, Slave: Genre and Interracial Desire in Louisa May Alcott's fiction," *American Transcendentalism Quarterly* 11(2) (1997): 115–135.

16. Quoted in Martha Saxon, *Louisa May: A Modern Biography of Louisa May Alcott* (Boston: Houghton Mifflin, 1977), 296.

17. Stern, 136.

18. Stern, 133.

19. Showalter, xi.

20. This series was so successful that others in the publishing business copied it and thus sprung up a bevy of books by mystery celebrities.

21. Thomas Niles to Louisa May Alcott, June 21, 1870, Houghton Library.

22. TN to LMA, February 17, 1873, Houghton Library.

23. TN to LMA, February 14, 1870, Houghton Library.

24. Jean Fagan Yellin, *Women and Sisters: The Antislavery Feminists in American Culture* (New Haven: Yale University Press, 1989).

25. Nell Irvin Painter, *Sojourner Truth, A Life, A Symbol* (New York: Norton, 1996), 103.

26. Painter, 112.

27. William Charvat, *The Profession of Authorship in America 1800–1870* (New York: Columbia University Press 1992).

28. Letter from Sojourner Truth to William Lloyd Garrison, August 28, 1851. Department of Rare Books and Manuscripts, Boston Public Library.

29. My thanks to Tim McCarthy for this insight and formulation as provided in his editorial comments on an earlier draft to this essay.

30. *Narrative of Sojourner Truth*, 58.

31. Nell Painter, I think rightly, cites this unconventional ending as a central reason for the neglect of Truth's narrative in the scholarship on slave narratives. See Painter, 110.

32. *Narrative of Sojourner Truth*, 64.

33. Ibid., 22.

34. 58 percent to be precise. For this study I have focused on slave narratives published in the United States between 1845 and 1870 in book form. Though I have also examined many narratives published in pamphlet form, I have not concentrated on them because of their ephemeral nature. For a more detailed discussion of the use of the frontispiece in slave narratives, see my *"Truth Stranger than Fiction."*

35. Yet portraits were no guarantee of textual authenticity, as shown by the James Williams portrait that Henry Louis Gates Jr. has recently uncovered.

36. Robert Stepto, *From Behind the Veil: A Study of Afro-American Narrative* (Urbana: University of Illinois Press, 1979). For a fascinating examination of Frederick Douglass's use of the daguerreotype in the construction of a public persona, see John Stauffer's *The Black Hearts of Men*, 45–70.

37. In coining this term in *"Truth Stranger than Fiction,"* I have drawn on Thomas Laquer's "Bodies, Details, and the Humanitarian Narrative" in *The New Cultural History*, Lynn Hunt, ed. (Berkeley: University of California Press, 1989), 176–205. Laquer links the social history of eighteenth-century British humanitarianism to the proliferation and variation of narrative texts that rely on the body to prompt social action. See also Elizabeth Clark, " 'The Sacred Rights of the Weak: Pain, Sympathy, and the Culture of Individual Rights in Antebellum America," *Journal of American History* 82 (September 1995): 463–493.

38. Francis Gage's description is probably the most often cited and therefore replicated. But Harriet Beecher Stowe's description of Truth in "The Lybian Sibyl" also includes the turban as part of the description. See Stowe "The Lybian Sibyl," *Atlantic Monthly* 51 (April 1863).

39. In today's currency, that's roughly $2,500. Here I am using a rough 1:25 ratio based on John J. McCusker, "How Much is that in Real Money?" American Antiquarian Society Proceedings 101:2 (1991): 297–373.

40. Painter, 130–131.

41. Quoted in ibid., 131.

42. Beverly A. Zink-Sawyer discusses Truth's feminist relationship to biblical texts in "From Preachers to Suffragists: Enlisting the Pulpit in the Early Movement for Woman's Rights," *American Transcendentalism Quarterly* 14(3) (2000): 193–209.

43. Gage's editorial choices represent Truth in the staunchest feminist and abolitionist lights as a woman and a sister. For further discussion, see Yellin, *Women and Sisters*.

44. Quoted in ibid.

45. See Painter, 110.

46. "Extract from a Letter," in *Narrative of Sojourner Truth and the Book of Life*, Frances Titus, ed. (Boston, 1875; Battle Creek, MI, 1884), 187.

47. For a richly detailed discussion of the blurred distinction between fact and fiction as it developed in the popular press, see Ann Fabian, *The Unvarnished Truth: Personal Narratives in Nineteenth-Century America* (Berkeley: University of California Press, 2000).

14. Creating an Image in Black: The Power of Abolition Pictures

1. *Printer's Ink Magazine*, March 10, 1927, 114. Barnard was the national advertising manager of Street Railways Advertising Company.
2. On the rise of visual culture see Vicki Goldberg, *The Power of Photography: How Photographs Changed Our Lives* (New York: Abbeville Press, 1991), 1–17; Patricia Anderson, *The Printed Image and the Transformation of Popular Culture, 1790–1860* (Oxford: Clarendon Press, 1991); Alan Trachtenberg, *Reading American Photographs: Images as History, Mathew Brady to Walker Evans* (New York: Hill and Wang, 1989), 3–20; Trachtenberg, "Photography: The Emergence of a Keyword," and Barbara McCandless, "The Portrait Studio and the Celebrity: Promoting the Art," in *Photography in Nineteenth-Century America*, ed. Martha A. Sandweiss (New York: Harry N. Abrams, 1991), 16–47, 48–75; Robert Taft, *Photography and the American Scene: A Social History, 1839–1889* (1938; reprint, New York: Dover, 1964), 46–166; John Stauffer, "Daguerreotyping the National Soul: The Portraits of Southworth and Hawes," *Prospects* 22 (1977): 69–107; Beaumont Newhall, *The History of Photography, from 1839 to the Present* (New York: The Museum of Modern Art, 1988), 9–72.
3. When Louis-Philippe took the throne in France in 1830, he vowed to "free" the press from censorship. But when the "cartoon press" attacked him with caricatures, he reestablished censorship by banning images. While he tolerated political pamphlets, a caricature amounted to an "act of violence" that was deemed "too dangerous" to go unchecked. See Goldberg, *Power of Photography*, 7; Michael Melot, *The Art of Illustration* (New York: Rizzoli, 1984), 231.
4. Henry Mayer, *All On Fire: William Lloyd Garrison and the Abolition of Slavery* (New York: St. Martin's Press, 1998), 124–125. For other examples of American politicians taking offense at abolitionist imagery see Jean Fagan Yellin, *Women and Sisters: The Antislavery Feminists in American Culture* (New Haven: Yale University Press, 1989), 3–26; and William Lee Miller, *Arguing About Slavery: The Great Battle in the United States Congress* (New York: Alfred Knopf, 1996), 96–97.
5. John Stauffer, *The Black Hearts of Men: Radical Abolitionists and the Transformation of Race* (Cambridge: Harvard University Press, 2002), Chapter 2.
6. Stauffer, *Black Hearts of Men*, Chapter 2. See also Leonard Cassuto, *The Inhuman Race: The Racial Grotesque in American Literature and Culture* (New York: Columbia University Press, 1997), Chapter 3; W.J.T. Mitchell, *Picture Theory: Essays on Verbal and Visual Representation* (Chicago: University of Chicago Press, 1994), Chapters 5–6; Deborah Willis, ed., *Picturing Us: African-American Identity in Photography;* Yellin, *Women and Sisters*, 3–26.
7. Mary Niall Mitchell, " 'Rosebloom and Pure White,' Or So It Seemed," *American Quarterly*, 54:3 (September 2002): 369–410; Shawn Michelle Smith, *American Archives: Gender, Race, and Class in Visual Culture* (Princeton: Princeton University Press, 1999); Laura Wexler, *Tender Violence: Domestic Visions in an Age of U.S. Imperialism* (Chapel Hill: University of North Carolina Press, 2000), 52–93, 127–176; Shirley Samuels, "Miscegenated America: The Civil War," in

National Imaginaries, American Identities, eds. Larry J. Reynolds and Gordon Hutner (Princeton: Princeton University Press, 2000), 141–158; Marcus Wood, *Blind Memory: Visual Representations of Slavery in England and America, 1780–1865* (Manchester, England: Routledge, 2000).

There are a few exceptions to this tendency to focus on the visual exploitation of black abolitionists. See Maurice Wallace, " 'Are We Men?': Prince Hall, Martin Delany, and the Masculine Ideal in Black Freemasonry, 1775–1865," in *National Imaginaries,* pp. 182–210; Nell Irvin Painter, *Sojourner Truth: A Life, A Symbol* (New York: W.W. Norton, 1996), 185–199; Yellin, *Women and Sisters,* 3–28, 77–98; Goldberg, *Power of Photography,* 163–190.

8. The idea of the male gaze originates with Laura Mulvey, "Visual Pleasure and Narrative Cinema," *Screen* 16:3 (1975): 6–18.

9. Robyn Wiegman, "Black Bodies/American Commodities: Gender, Race and the Bourgeois Ideal in Contemporary Film," in Lester Friedman, ed., *Unspeakable Images: Ethnicity and the American Cinema* (Urbana: University of Illinois Press, 1991), 325.

10. Stauffer, *Black Hearts of Men,* Chapter 2.

11. Elaine Scarry, *On Beauty and Being Just* (Princeton: Princeton University Press, 1999), 69, 90; Stauffer, "Frederick Douglass and the Aesthetics of Freedom," in *Raritan,* 25:1 (Summer 2005): 114–136.

12. Douglass, quoted from Philip S. Foner, ed., *The Life and Writings of Frederick Douglass,* Vol. 1 (New York: International Publishers, 1950), 379–80; Stauffer, *Black Hearts of Men,* 50–51.

13. Stauffer, *Black Hearts of Men,* 51–52.

14. Douglass, "Pictures" (ca. 1864), The Frederick Douglass Papers, Library of Congress; Douglass, "Pictures and Progress," in John Blassingame, ed., *The Frederick Douglass Papers,* 1:3 (New Haven: Yale University Press, 1985), 452–473; Stauffer, *Black Hearts of Men,* 51–52.

15. Douglass, "Pictures"; Stauffer, *Black Hearts of Men,* 51–52, 54. In calling humans the only picture-making animals in the world, Douglass was paraphrasing Aristotle. See Aristotle, *Poetics,* trans. Malcolm Heath (New York: Penguin, 1996), 6–7.

16. Douglass, "Pictures"; Stauffer, *Black Hearts of Men,* 54.

17. Douglass, "Heroic Slave," in Ronald T. Takaki, ed., *Violence in the Black Imagination: Essays & Documents* (New York: Oxford University Press, 1993), 38–41.

18. Douglass, "Heroic Slave," 45.

19. Harriet Beecher Stowe, *Uncle Tom's Cabin, or, Life Among the Lowly* (1852; reprinted, New York: Penguin Books, 1986), 68.

20. Trachtenberg, *Reading American Photographs,* Chapter 2; Floyd and Marion Rinhart, *The American Daguerreotype* (Athens: University of Georgia Press, 1981), 78.

21. W.J.T. Mitchell, *Iconology: Image, Text, Ideology* (Chicago: University of Chicago Press, 1986), 31.

22. Lawrence W. Levine, *Highbrow/Lowbrow: The Emergence of Cultural Hierarchy in America* (Cambridge: Harvard University Press, 1988), 29–30.

23. Painter, *Sojourner Truth,* 187.

24. On the "aura" of an image, see Walter Benjamin, "The Work of Art in the Age of Mechanical Reproduction," in *Illuminations: Essays and Reflections* (New York: Schocken, 1968), 221–224.

25. James McCune Smith, quoted in *Frederick Douglass's Paper* (March 9, 1855).

26. McCune Smith quoted in Blassingame, ed., *The Frederick Douglass Papers*, 1:3, 74.
27. Ethiop [William Wilson], "Afric-American Picture Gallery," *The Anglo-African Magazine* (1859; reprint, New York: Arno Press, 1968), 52.
28. Ethiop, "Afric-American Picture Gallery," 53–55, 88–90, 100–103, 174–177, 216–218.
29. Ethiop, "Afric-American Picture Gallery," 87, 88, 174, 175, 176, 324.
30. Harriet A. Jacobs, *Incidents in the Life of a Slave Girl, Written by Herself*, ed. Jean Fagan Yellin (Cambridge: Harvard University Press, 1987), 148.
31. Nancy Armstrong, *Fiction in the Age of Photography: The Legacy of British Realism* (Cambridge: Harvard University Press, 1999), 248–249; Henry James, "The Real Thing," in Leon Edel, ed., *The Complete Tales of Henry James*, Vol. 8, 1891–1892 (Philadelphia: J.B. Lippincott, 1964), 237; Miles Orvell, *The Real Thing: Imitation and Authencity in American Culture, 1880–1940* (Chapel Hill: University of North Carolina Press, 1989), 122–123; Stauffer, "Daguerreotyping the National Soul," 100.
32. Henry Louis Gates, Jr., "The Trope of a New Negro and the Reconstruction of the Image of the Black," in Philip Fisher, ed., *The New American Studies*, 322, 325; Gates, "The Face and Voice of Blackness," in *Facing History: The Black Image in American Art, 1710–1940*, ed. Guy C. McElroy (Washington, D.C.: The Corcoran Gallery of Art, 1990), xxxi–xxxix.
33. W.E.B. Du Bois, *The Souls of Black Folk* (New York: Penguin, 1989), 1, 4.
34. Du Bois, "Photography," *The Crisis* 26:6 (October 1923): 247–248. See also Mitchell, *Picture Theory*, 163.
35. Gates, "Trope of a New Negro," 321. Gates notes that between 1867 and 1876, "black people published as books only two novels. Between 1895 and 1925, however, black writers published at least sixty-four novels. While the historical period known as Reconstruction seems to have been characterized by a dramatic upsurge of energy in the American body politic, the corpus of black literature and art, on the other hand, enjoyed no such apparent vitalization. . . . Once redemption had established itself as a new form of enslavement for blacks, blacks regained a public voice, louder and more strident than it had been even during slavery."

15. Abolitionists in American Cinema: From *The Birth of a Nation* to *Amistad*

1. This essay is dedicated to the memory of my friend and mentor Marlon Riggs.
2. I owe a great deal of my appreciation for the historical novel to my independent study on the subject with Robert Stepto at Yale University. John Stauffer has persuasively made the "American canon" argument to me in our conversations, as well as in his lectures on historical fiction at Harvard University. As for theories of the historical novel, the seminal text remains György Lukács, *The Historical Novel*, trans. Hannah and Stanley Mitchell (London: Merlin Press, 1962).
3. Interestingly, historical romance and the influence of Walter Scott persisted in the South much longer than in the North. The novel on which *The Birth of a Nation* is based is Thomas Dixon's *The Clansman*, subtitled "An Historical Romance of the Ku Klux Klan." For the tenaciousness of Scott on Southern litera-

ture see James Chandler, "The Historical Novel Goes to Hollywood: Scott, Griffith, and the Film Epic Today" in Robert Lang, ed., *The Birth of a Nation* (New Brunswick, NJ: Rutgers University Press, 1994), 225–249.

4. This is based, in part, on several private conversations with Robert Stone at Yale University, in the fall of 1999 and 2000.

5. For example, see the Introduction to Lang, *The Birth of a Nation,* in which he describes the film as historical melodrama that "cannot conceive of storytelling in anything other than . . . clichés." There has, however, been some fine work on historical films, much of which recognizes the problematic intersection of history and film. See *Revisioning History: Film and the Construction of a New Past,* Robert A. Rosenstone, ed. (Princeton: Princeton University Press, 1995), esp. Rosenstone's Introduction; and the chapter "Walker: The Dramatic Film as (Postmodern) History"; *Past Imperfect: History According to the Movies,* Mark C. Carnes et al., ed. (New York: Henry Holt, 1996), esp. "A Conversation Between Eric Foner and John Sayles"; Natalie Zemon Davis, *Slaves on Screen* (Cambridge, MA: Harvard University Press, 2000), esp. Chapter 5, "Telling the Truth," 121–136. General works include: Robert Sklar, *Movie Made America: A Cultural History of American Movies* (New York: Random House, 1975); *Hollywood as Historian,* Peter C. Rollins, ed. (Lexington: University of Kentucky Press, 1983); Richard Slotkin, *Gunfighter Nation: The Myth of the Frontier in Twentieth-Century America* (New York: Atheneum, 1992).

6. This was conveyed in a conversation with Professor Ford in Washington, D.C., August 1988

7. Jonathan D. Spence, "Margaret Atwood and the Edges of History," *American Historical Review,* 103 (December 1998): 1524.

8. This does not mean that all historians dislike historical fiction. Historian David Brion Davis, whose father and mother were both novelists, quoted long passages from Barry Unger's historical novel *Sacred Hunger* (New York, Doubleday, 1992) to convey to his undergraduates the horrors of the middle passage. John Demos not only proclaimed himself a 1980s "convert" to historical fiction, but has, in his work, utilized some historical novelistic techniques for the creation of his history. See John Demos, *The Unredeemed Captive: A Family Story from Early America* (New York: Knopf, 1994); and John Demos, "In Search of Reasons for Historians to Read Novels," *American Historical Review,* 103 (Dec. 1998: 1526–1529. These historians, however, are among the exceptions.

9. As cited in Robert L. Paquette, "From History to Hollywood: The Voyage of La Amistad," *New Criterion* 16, no. 7 (March 1998): 54.

10. Motion Picture Association of America, Inc., "Valenti Reports All-Time High Box Office and Highlights Importance of Rating System and Copyright Protection in Showbusiness Address," press release dated March 6, 2001. www.mpaa.org/jack/2001/2001_03_06a.

11. *The American Film Institute Catalog of Motion Pictures Produced in the United States* (Berkeley: University of California Press, 1971–1999)

12. Ken Burns, *The Civil War* (Burbank, CA: PBS Home Video: Warner Home Video, 2002).

13. In each case I refer to the VHS recordings of these films.

14. The scholarly work on *Birth* is voluminous. Even as early as 1928 the film had gained a "notorious" reputation. See Alan Reynolds Thompson, "Melodrama and Tragedy," *PMLA,* 43, 3 (September 1928), 811. An interesting treatment

of early black protest against *Birth* is Thomas Cripps, "Film," in *Split Image: African Americans in the Mass Media* (Washington, DC: Howard University Press, 1990), 125–172. Cripps places *Birth* in a larger context in *Slow Fade to Black: The Negro in American Film, 1900–1942* (New York: Oxford University Press, 1977), as does Donald Bogle, *Toms, Coons, Mulattoes, Mammies and Bucks: A New Interpretative History of Blacks in American Films* (new expanded edition) (New York: Continuum, 1989). For a good collection of articles on a variety of aspects of *Birth,* including the protests against the film and praise for Griffith's aesthetic achievement, see Lang, *The Birth of a Nation.*

15. Dixon's *The Clansman,* on which *Birth* is based, is not against antislavery, per se, but antislavery as synonymous with equal rights for African Americans. The novel advocates the ending of slavery only if accompanied by the forced expulsion of African Americans through what was called "colonization." The novel includes a scene in which Abraham Lincoln explains the validity and necessity of "colonization." *Birth* does not engage colonization directly. *The Clansman* is available as an online text at http://docsouth.unc.edu/dixonclan/dixon .html. During the nineteenth century, many Americans both black and white, including Lincoln, did advocate colonization at some point in their lives. For responses to the movement among free blacks in the nineteenth century see Louis R. Mehlinger, "The Attitude of the Free Negro Toward African Colonization," *Journal of Negro History* 1:3 (June 1916): 276–301. For Lincoln's attitude toward race colonization see George M. Fredrickson, "A Man but Not a Brother: Abraham Lincoln and Racial Equality," *Journal of Southern History,* 41:1 (February 1975): 39–58.

16. Melvin I. Urofsky and Paul Finkelman, *A March of Liberty: A Constitutional History of the United States* (New York: Oxford University Press, 2002).

17. That is not to say that Jefferson was not deeply conflicted on the subject of slavery; he most certainly was. At various times in his life, he publicly and privately expressed pro- and antislavery sentiment. For a good discussion of Jefferson's attitude toward slavery and opposition to the slave trade see William Cohen, "Thomas Jefferson and the Problem of Slavery," *Journal of American History* 56:3 (December 1969): 503–526.

18. The best single discussion of the pseudoscience of race is still Stephen Jay Gould, *Mismeasure of Man* (New York: W.W. Norton, 1981) 30–72.

19. The exploitation of "justified" black violence would not be realized until the "blaxploitation" films of the 1970s. For contemporary critiques see Rene Ward, "Black Films, White Profits," *Black Scholar* 7 (May 1976): 13–25; Alvin F. Poussaint, "Cheap Thrills That Degrade Blacks," *Psychology Today* 7 (February 1974): 26–27; Tommy L. Lott, "A No-No Theory of Contemporary Black Cinema," *Black American Literature Forum,* 25:2, "Black Film Issue" (Summer 1991): 221–236; William Lyne, "No Accident: From Black Power to Black Box Office," *African American Review,* 34:1 (Spring 2000): 39–59. *Amistad's* "Cinqué and the captain" scene can be read as historical blaxploitation.

20. Granted, this scene could also be "read" as a justification of the middle passage, as the blacks don't seem to resist all their captors, only the captain. On the other hand, their depiction, chained and packed together in the hold, and Gary Cooper's framing of them as Shakespearean tragic heroes works against this interpretation.

21. Ronald G. Walters, *The Antislavery Appeal: American Abolitionism after 1830* (Bal-

timore: Johns Hopkins University Press, 1976); David Brion Davis, "The Emergence of Immediatism in British and American Antislavery Thought," *Mississippi Valley Historical Review*, 49, 2. September, 1962), 209–230.

22. Taylor is literally "decked," knocked from one deck to the other.

23. "New Films in London: Comedy, Romance, and Murder," *The London Times*, September 6, 1937.

24. "The Production Code: Code to Govern the Making of Talking, Synchronized and Silent Motion Pictures," reprinted in *Movies and Mass Culture*, ed. John Belton (New Brunswick, NJ: Rutgers University Press, 2000), 138–149.

25. The film abandons its high standard of historically accurate facial hair when Jeb Stuart is introduced without his famous flowing red beard, but instead with the trademark pencil-thin mustache of Errol Flynn.

26. Bosley Crowther, "The Screen: 'Santa Fe Trail,' Which Is Chiefly a Picture About Something Else, Opens at the Strand," *The New York Times* (December 21, 1940).

27. Idealized kingship is a bond based on the fundamental notion of reciprocity. A king has privileges, but also has duties. The associations between king and father in the early modern period are ubiquitous, found in literature, political pamphlets, and sermons. When in *King Lear* Kent addresses Lear as "Royal Lear / Whom I have ever honour'd as my King, Lov'd as my father," he captures the essence of this fundamental relationship. This sentiment extended into the eighteenth century. During the American Revolution, Loyalist tracts and English newspapers chastised the American colonists as if they were disobedient children of a patient (but increasingly impatient) father.

28. On paternalism and slavery see Eugene Genovese, *Roll, Jordan, Roll: The World the Slaves Made* (New York: Pantheon Books, 1974).

29. For the best, most sensitive, and balanced treatment of John Brown, see John Stauffer, *The Black Hearts of Men: Radical Abolitionists and the Transformation of Race* (Cambridge, MA: Harvard University Press, 2002).

30. Ibid.

31. Brown did, in fact, receive financial aid for his Harpers Ferry raid. This was a fairly well-established fact in mainstream history by the 1930s. See Ralph Volney Harlow, "Gerrit Smith and the John Brown Raid," *American Historical Review*, 38: 1 (October 1932): 32–60.

32. Crowther writes in his *New York Times* review that "the judgment of history upon John Brown is divided. . . . Some hold that he was a great martyr to the cause of freeing the slaves, others suspect he was just a wild fanatic driven mad by a high ideal." I see more evidence from historians for the "fanatic" argument at the time. For an example of an historical characterization that closely resembles *Santa Fe Trail* see Harlow, 32–60. The writer of *Santa Fe Trail*, Robert Buckner, a Virginian, was educated at the University of Virginia and University of Edinburgh. It is remarkable how closely Harlow's *American Historical Review* article and depiction of Brown coincides with the well-educated Buckner's rendering.

33. Crowther, "The Screen," 23.

34. Martin Rubin, "The Crowd, the Collective and the Chorus: Busby Berkeley and the New Deal," in *Movies and Mass Culture*, ed. John Belton (New Brunswick, NJ: Rutgers University Press, 2000), 82.

35. Franklin Roosevelt, *The Public Papers and Addresses* (New York: Random House, 1938), 3, 125, as cited in Rubin, 81.

36. William E. Leuchtenburg, *Franklin Delano Roosevelt* (New York: Harper & Row, 1963).

37. Johnpeter Horst Grill and Robert Jenkins, "The Nazis and the American South in the 1930s: A Mirror Image?," *Journal of Southern History* 58: 4 (November 1992): 668. When this recognition was made is debatable. Some might argue that it occurred earlier in some parts of the government during World War II. Others might argue that there has never been a full acceptance of this link. For the post–World War II ties between fascism and racism with a connection to Hollywood see Steven Vaughan, "Ronald Reagan and the Struggle for Black Dignity in Cinema," *Journal of Negro History*, 77: 1 (Winter 1992): 1–16.

38. Thomas Cripps, *Making Movies Black: The Hollywood Message Movie from World War II to the Civil Rights Era* (New York: Oxford University Press, 1993), 97–98.

39. See *The Antislavery Vanguard, New Essays on Abolitionists*, ed. Martin Duberman (Princeton: Princeton University Press, 1965); Aileen Kraditor, "The Abolitionist Rehabilitated," *Studies on the Left* V (1965): 101; Irwin Unger, "The 'New Left' and American History: Some Recent Trends in United States Historiography," *American Historical Review*, 72 (July 1972): 1237–1263.

40. Unger, "The 'New Left,' " 1253.

41. *Freedom's Journal* (March 16, 1827).

42. Clayborne Carson, *In Struggle: SNCC and the Black Awakening of the 1960s* (Cambridge, MA: Harvard University Press, 1981), esp. Chapter 16.

43. As quoted in Carson, 240.

44. Ibid., 238–239.

45. "Ethel Minor Interview," Casey King and Linda Barrett Osborne, *Oh, Freedom!* (New York: Knopf, 1997), 94.

46. Robert Stepto first led me here while discussing the sympathetic white character, "Listwell," in Frederick Douglass's novel *Heroic Slave* (1854). John Stauffer addresses this aspect of Douglass in depth in his forthcoming book on interracial friendship in American history and literature.

47. Carson, 240.

48. It is, in fact, the first in the series to use the language of slavery.

49. Joe Russo and Larry Landsman, *The Planet of the Apes Revisited* (New York: St. Martin's Press, 2001), 4, 182.

50. Paquette, 54.

51. This is part of what Rosenstone means when he talks about accepting historical films on their own terms. See Rosenstone 3–4, 202–203. For more about the real contributions that historical films make in the classroom see Steven Mintz, "Spielberg's *Amistad* and the History Classroom," *The History Teacher*, 31: 3 (May 1998): 370–373.

52. John Seelye, *Memory's Nation: The Place of Plymouth Rock* (Chapel Hill: University of North Carolina Press, 1998); Joanne Pope Melish, *Disowning Slavery: Gradual Emancipation and Race in New England, 1780–1860* (Ithaca: Cornell University Press, 1998).

53. Jon Butler, *Becoming America: The Revolution before 1776* (Cambridge, MA: Harvard University Press, 2000).

54. The importance of historical memory is explored in depth in David W. Blight, *Race and Reunion: The Civil War in American Memory* (Cambridge, MA: Harvard University Press, 2001).

55. See David Brion Davis, "The Emergence of Immediatism in British and American Antislavery Thought," *Mississippi Valley Historical Review*, 49: 2 (September 1962): 209–230; Davis, *The Problem of Slavery in Western Culture* (Ithaca: Cornell University Press, 1966)

56. For the "holy men in the desert" and Carter association, I draw from an unpublished interview with Kathleen Kennedy Townsend, New York, spring, 2003. I use the term "we" loosely as, obviously, there are still plenty of people who pray to God. The parallel between God and science is ubiquitous in scholarly works, but the "Jesus vs. Darwin" bumper sticker debate captures this cultural "war" in the quotidian.

Index